PENGUIN BOOKS

WHITE TRIBE DREAMING

Marq de Villiers is an eighth-generation Afrikaner, and the son of a prominent liberal journalist. He studied International Relations at the University of Cape Town and the London School of Economics. De Villiers has been a news correspondent and journalist in Canada, the United States, Britain, Spain, the Soviet Union, and South Africa, and his work has appeared in many American and Canadian magazines. He lives in Toronto and is now editor of Toronto Life magazine.

WHITE TRIBE DREAMING

Apartheid's Bitter Roots as
Witnessed by Eight Generations
of an Afrikaner Family

Marq de Villiers

PENGUIN BOOKS

PENGUIN BOOKS
Published by the Penguin Group
Viking Penguin Inc., 40 West 23rd Street,
New York, New York 10010, U.S.A.
Penguin Books Ltd, 27 Wrights Lane,
London W8 5TZ, England
Penguin Books Australia Ltd, Ringwood,
Victoria, Australia
Penguin Books Canada Ltd, 2801 John Street,
Markham, Ontario, Canada L3R 1B4
Penguin Books (N.Z.) Ltd, 182–190 Wairau Road,
Auckland 10, New Zealand

Penguin Books Ltd, Registered Offices:
Harmondsworth, Middlesex, England

First published in Canada by Macmillan of Canada 1987
First published in the United States of America by
Viking Penguin Inc. 1988
Published in Penguin Books 1989

1 3 5 7 9 10 8 6 4 2

Passages on pages 293 and 294 are reprinted by
kind permission of Tim Keegan.
Photographs are from the author's collection.

LIBRARY OF CONGRESS CATALOGING IN PUBLICATION DATA
De Villiers, Marq.
White tribe dreaming: apartheid's bitter roots as witnessed by
eight generations of an Afrikaner family/Marq de Villiers.
p. cm.
Reprint. Originally published: New York, N.Y., U.S.A.: Viking,
1988, c1987.
Bibliography: p.
Includes index.
ISBN 0 14 01.0270 1 (pbk.)
1. Apartheid—South Africa—History. 2. Afrikaners—South Africa—
History. 3. Villiers family. 4. South Africa—History.
I. Title.
[DT763.5.D4 1989]
968—dc19   88–22587

Printed in the United States of America
Set in Goudy O.S.

To my father, an Afrikaner who has been
a peacemaker all his life, for his people
and for others.

CONTENTS

Part 1

Jacques and Abraham de Villiers:
the establishment of the Way

Part 2

Pieter Jacob de Villiers
and the Century of Wrong I:
the search for Beulah

Part 3

Jacobus Johannes Luttig de Villiers
and the Century of Wrong II:
Blood River and the consolidation of the tribe

Part 4

Jacobus Johannes de Villiers and the Century of Wrong III: the bitter defeats

Part 5

René de Villiers and the creation of the sacred history

Part 6

Marq de Villiers:
lost in Africa

LIST OF MAPS

MASTER GENEALOGY

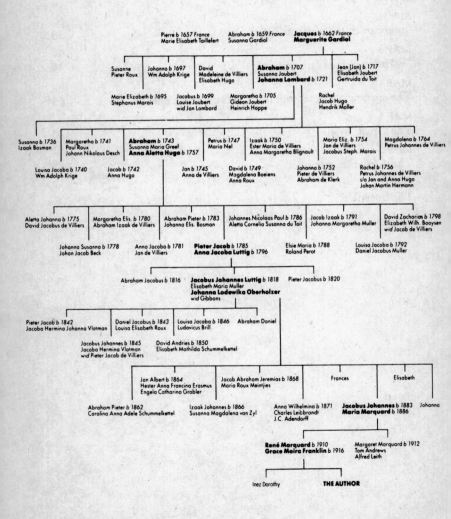

Pierre b 1657 France
Marie Elisabeth Taillefert

Abraham b 1659 France
Susanna Gardiol

Jacques b 1662 France
Marguerite Gardiol

Susanne
Pieter Roux

Johanna b 1697
Wm Adolph Krige

David
Madeleine de Villiers
Elisabeth Hugo

Abraham b 1707
Susanna Joubert
Johanna Lombard b 1721

Jean (Jan) b 1717
Elisabeth Joubert
Gertruida du Toit

Marie Elizabeth b 1695
Stephanus Marais

Jacobus b 1699
Louise Joubert
wid Jan Lombard

Margaretha b 1705
Gideon Joubert
Heinrich Hoppe

Rachel
Jacob Hugo
Hendrik Moller

Susanna b 1736
Izaak Bosman

Margaretha b 1741
Paul Roux
Johann Nikolaus Desch

Abraham b 1743
Susanna Maria Greef
Anna Aletta Hugo b 1757

Petrus b 1747
Maria Nel

Izaak b 1750
Ester Maria de Villiers
Anna Margaretha Blignault

Maria Eliz. b 1754
Jan de Villiers
Jacobus Steph. Marais

Magdalena b 1764
Petrus Johannes de Villiers

Louisa Jacoba b 1740
Wm Adolph Krige

Jacob b 1742
Anna Hugo

Jan b 1745
Anna de Villiers

David b 1749
Magdalena Boeiens
Anna Roux

Johanna b 1752
Pieter de Villiers
Abraham de Klerk

Rachel b 1756
Petrus Johannes de Villiers
s/o Jan and Anna Hugo
Johan Martin Hermann

Aletta Johanna b 1775
David Jacobus de Villiers

Margaretha Elis. b 1780
Abraham Izaak de Villiers

Abraham Pieter b 1783
Johanna Elis. Bosman

Johannes Nicolaas Paul b 1786
Aletta Cornelia Susanna du Toit

Jacob Izaak b 1791
Johanna Margaretha Muller

David Zacharias b 1798
Elizabeth Wilh. Booysen
wid Jacob de Villiers

Johanna Susanna b 1778
Johan Jacob Beck

Anna Jacoba b 1781
Jan de Villiers

Pieter Jacob b 1785
Anna Jacoba Luttig b 1796

Elsie Maria b 1788
Roland Perot

Louisa Jacoba b 1792
Daniel Jacobus Muller

Abraham Jacobus b 1816

Jacobus Johannes Luttig b 1818
Elisabeth Maria Muller
Johanna Lodewika Oberholzer
wid Gibbons

Pieter Jacobus b 1820

Pieter Jacob b 1842
Jacoba Hermina Johanna Vlotman

Daniel Jacobus b 1843
Louisa Elisabeth Roux

Louisa Jacoba b 1846
Ludovicus Brill

Abraham Daniel

Jacobus Johannes b 1845
Jacoba Hermina Vlotman
wid Pieter Jacob de Villiers

David Andries b 1850
Elisabeth Mathilda Schummelkettel

Jan Albert b 1864
Hester Anna Francina Erasmus
Engela Catharina Grobler

Jacob Abraham Jeremias b 1868
Maria Roux Meintjies

Frances

Elisabeth

Abraham Pieter b 1862
Carolina Anna Adele Schummelkettel

Izaak Johannes b 1866
Susanna Magdalena van Zyl

Anna Wilhelmina b 1871
Charles Leibbrandt
J.C. Adendorff

Jacobus Johannes b 1883
Maria Marquard b 1886

Johanna

René Marquard b 1910
Grace Moira Franklin b 1916

Margaret Marquard b 1912
Tom Andrews
Alfred Leith

Inez Dorothy

THE AUTHOR

PREFACE

AFRIKANER HISTORY WOULD have happened just the same without any de Villiers at all, of course — though it's true we bred at a prodigious rate (the de Villiers seem to have infiltrated every other settler family within a few years of their arrival at the Cape, and then they began to marry cousins and more or less distant relatives to a genetically eccentric degree). So if I use my own family as a way of dealing with the tribe, it's not because we were essential to the collective history but because longevity counts for something — we were there from the very beginning, after all, and some of us will be there until the End . . .

Along the way, we've had some good ones and some bad ones; and so we have been typical of all families, and our family typical of all communities. We started off well — my family helped set up the South African wine industry (we have a letter from the Dutch government, dated 1688, to prove it). Jacques de Villiers, my great-great-great-great-great-grandfather, began the great, grand Cape manor house called Boschendal; his brother Abraham, on the other hand, was more politician than farmer and became, in the way of many politicians, a government toady. We've had prosperous farmers and . . . some others. Jacques's nephew Jan, for instance. There was a nice guy. He was a depression landlord and wheeler-dealer: he owned most of the great houses of the Cape at one time or another, usually picking them up at fire-sale prices when the Louws or the Marais or the van der Bijls or the Jouberts went broke.

The Afrikaners were a small and close-knit community for the first 100 years or so of their existence. It's not surprising, therefore, that our family can trace (occasionally slender) connections to most of the giants of Afrikaner history. For example, Johannes Jacobus Petrus Paulus, great-nephew of my great-great-grandmother, Anna Aletta Hugo de Villiers, was at the Tugela River with the Voortrekker hero Piet Retief and was impaled on a stake alongside the great man by the Zulu king Dingaan's royal guard. Retief was himself a direct descendant of Jacques de Villiers through his mother's line. Our family had more than one genetic hook into Andries Pretorius, the hero of Blood River and the commandant general of the Transvaal republic (before he became fat and arrogant, brooding in his big house and issuing slanderous accusations against his contemporaries). We've had a chief justice in the family (my great-uncle Jaap), a captain of the South African rugby team, and the author of the national anthem, and at least one of us has been hanged by the neck until dead, for a crime we all now prefer to forget.

Any family that has stayed in place for 300 years collects its own primitive family archive, and so it is with us. The bookshelves in my father's Cape Town house and the tin trunks in storage there contain much useful and useless stuff, much of it valuable and some of it inconsequential. I have been able to draw on this material here: my grandmother's Boer War and Rebellion diaries, for instance, written carefully in ink in a school exercise book. We also have my great-grandmother's letters to her mother from the town of Winburg during the Boer War; some of these were later collected and published by my uncle Leo in a book called *Letters from a Boer Parsonage*. I have a stack of letters from Robert Sobukwe, the Pan-Africanist Congress leader, written from Robben Island jail to my great-aunt Nell.

I have relied on my father's personal reminiscences of the Afrikaners he has known, on his vivid memories of growing up in the Afrikaner heartland, and on his unwavering distinction between the Afrikaner nationalists — the architects of apartheid and of the politics of fear — and the other Afrikaners, those now lost in the clamour of the moment, who inhabited the farms and villages in the Orange Free State, where he spent his boyhood. My father's tin trunk also yielded up an old sepia photograph of himself as a baby, with his mother, grandmother, and great-grandmother, a Ziervogel who herself had known Louis Trichardt, one of the Afrikaner heroes of the Great Trek into the interior. The picture was taken in the garden of the family house on Drostdy Street in the old university town of Stellenbosch, and though much has faded the wisteria can still be made out in the background.

It should be clear, from all this, what this book is not. It is not a history of South Africa and all its peoples. It does not deal in any substantial way with the black and brown people of South Africa; nor does it devote much attention to the English-speaking white South Africans — these groups make their appearance only as they impinge on my people, the Afrikaners. I have tried to give just enough information about the other groups to make sense of the Afrikaners' actions, and no more.

Nor is this book a history, in the scholarly sense. It is an attempt to explain how the Afrikaners, the architects of apartheid, got *here* from *there*; an attempt to explain the visceral insecurities that have driven them to the perilous position they now occupy on the world stage. It is also an attempt to explain something of their tribal nature; when I call them the white tribe it is not just a facile locution — without understanding that they are a tribe in the anthropologist's definition, it is not possible to make sense of what they have done.

ACKNOWLEDGMENTS

I am grateful to the staff of the Huguenot Museum in the village of Fransch Hoek, near Cape Town, for their helpfulness in tracking down obscure members of the family. The year 1988 is the tricentennial of the arrival of the first de Villiers at the Cape, and the museum is preparing a commemorative book that will serve as the definitive history of the family. There already exists one history, by Dr. Dan de Villiers (who as a physician was responsible for overseeing my personal entry into this world). But Dan's book is eccentric; he seems to have spent much of his time attempting to prove, inconclusively, our family connection to some prominent medieval Crusaders. There is also a three-volume genealogy of the old Cape families compiled by C. C. F. de Villiers, which is reliable on the early generations and erratic on later ones (my father, for instance, is listed as his uncle's brother, so he has become a Marquard in the book instead of a de Villiers). I also want to acknowledge the South African Archives at Cape Town, where many of the de Villiers births, deaths, wills, and property transactions are recorded; I have copies now of the original land-grant deeds issued by the Dutch East India Company to the three brothers who first made their way there as refugees in 1688.

I have also drawn extensively on the many publications of the Van Riebeeck Society in Cape Town, which has issued, often in bilingual editions, hundreds of early documents, including Dutch East India Company archives and correspondence and reminiscences of early travellers to the Cape.

There are many general histories of South Africa. A few are listed in the Sources, but I would like to mention here those of George Theal (whom we studied in a truncated version at school, and who is, I now think, underestimated) and the two-volume *Oxford History of South Africa*, which remains the first and most comprehensive work that attempts to deal with *all* the peoples of South Africa, brown as well as black and white. The *Oxford*'s two general editors, Monica Wilson and Leonard Thompson, were both teachers of mine at the University of Cape Town, and though they wouldn't remember this insignificant fact, I remember them both with gratitude and affection.

Many other useful books will be found in the Sources, but I want especially to acknowledge the work of Richard Elphick, Heribert Adam, and Hermann Giliomee. Giliomee in particular seems to me to represent the best of current Afrikaner academic thinking — rooted in tradition but unafraid of intellectual heresy. I am grateful for the hours I spent with him; I am sure he will disagree with some of what I have to say, but I have nevertheless been strongly influenced by his ideas.

And a final word for my father's old friend Alan Paton, who is best known abroad for his fiction but who has written several splendid non-fiction books. His biography of the great liberal Afrikaner J. H. Hofmeyr is, I think, his best book and remains one of the most interesting explorations of Afrikaner liberalism yet produced.

AND SPECIAL THANKS
To my father, who to me exemplifies the best of the Afrikaner qualities and represents in my mind a South Africa that could have been; to Sheila Hirtle, for research among obscure family byways and in the writings of early visitors to the Cape, and for rigorous early editing; to Peter Herrndorf, the publisher of *Toronto Life* magazine, for his unwavering support and generous gift of time.

"Not knowing another fatherland,
[they] will not . . . again
depart this place."

Governor Simon van der Stel,
Cape Town,
1699

INTRODUCTION

HE WAS A SMALL MAN with leathery yellow skin and pepper-corn hair, a hat at a jaunty angle on his head. His clothes were shabby. He was walking away from the house, on the far side of the whitewashed farmstead wall and down the long avenue of bluegum trees leaning tiredly into the wind 60 feet above his head, their trunks gnarled and knotted with age. My great-great-great-great-uncle Paul planted those bluegums, and the oaks mixed in with them, 180 years ago. I guessed the little man was going home; there were smoky huts a mile or so away, down towards the highway. I was standing on the moss-stained curve of rough brick stairs at the front of the manor house of Boschendal, one of the oldest and possibly the grandest of the de Villiers family homesteads. The view from the stoop is down the long sweep of the Drakenstein Valley towards the mountains they call Wemmershoek.

This is the front-door view; the door seldom used, the view not often viewed. From the other side of the house the whitewashed buildings of the *opstal*, the homestead — the stables, the idiosyncratic hen-house, the slave quarters — frame the southern Cape's Drakenstein Mountains and the pass they call Hell's Hoogte (Hell's Heights), beyond which lie the sleepy little town of Stellenbosch and the flats at the mouth of False Bay. On most days in spring the mountains are made of soft purples and mist; the low whitewashed opstal walls, the geometric rows of vines beyond, and the gently folded purple mountains make a view of extraordinary beauty. The cars now drive in from Cape Town through the opstal. The Rhodes Fruit Farms conglomerate, which owns the farm, has made of the house a museum and has turned the stables into a restaurant. No one uses the front entrance, and no one uses the tree-lined driveway except the kitchen help, who walk in from their village a mile or two down the valley. It's a pleasant walk: the air is made of rich brown earth and crushed eucalyptus and the faint smell of lilac bound in damp mist.

In the parlour of the manor house there was a large English tourist leaning on a cane, scuffing at the polished yellow-wood floors. He was talking too loudly, using words no one uses any more in contemporary South Africa. *Kaffirs.* Kaffs — niggers. People edged away, bent to examine the furniture, wishing he would shut up. I wandered back through the front door, to the stoop. Down the driveway, the small yellow man had paused for a smoke. I caught up with him by the great iron gate close to the highway. His eyes were cautious, his grin a mix of ingratiating and sly, but the laugh lines were deeper than the frown lines. He doffed his hat. In modern South African idiom he would be called Coloured, or sometimes Cape Coloured, but his sparse tight pepper-corns — so different from the black wool of the Xhosa — signalled his Khoikhoi origins. His skin was sallow; his eyes hooded. He was slight of stature and moved with a rolling gait, as if he were a sailor. The cigarette was mangled; his teeth stained.

"Hello," I said.

"Aaai."

"Nice view," I said.

He merely waited.

"Where are you from?"

"Ag, baas, ek is maar a Hotnot."

"Ja, maar waarvandaan kom jy?"

"Die Hotnots is maar hiervandaan, baas. En baas?"

"My familie het op Boschendal geboer."

"Waar baas? Die Hotnots is hiervandaan, sommer altyd."*
The Hottentots are from here, from forever.

Six generations after the first de Villiers arrived at the Cape, and 600 miles to the north, someone asked Jacobus Johannes de Villiers, my grandfather, the same question: *Waarvandaan kom jy?* "Jim" de Villiers was then a year or two from his death; he was large and grizzled and wheezed as he drank his half-gallon a day of strong black *boerekoffie.* He was sitting on the front stoop of his farm near the village of Winburg in the Orange Free State, a long way in time and space and opulence from the manor house at Boschendal. The farmhouse was a small square structure with a corrugated iron roof, facing the endless north down a long vista of aromatic bluegums. Behind the house the lone windmill clanked; in front were thousands of acres of dry, dusty African soil. I was just a child and didn't understand the question, but the old man understood its import very well. "Ek is 'n Vrystaater," he said. "Dis tuis. Ek is hiervandaan."**

I'm from here. From always.

There is a continuity of sorrows. My grandfather, who fought the British Empire at Kimberley and Ladysmith, hardly needed to keep alive memories of the older days — the sharp struggles with the Khoikhoi, the yellow-skinned pastoralists who were the original inhabitants of the Cape; the endless wars on the eastern frontier with the Xhosa, the ancestors of Nelson Mandela — though they and the British ultimately

---

* "Oh boss, I'm just a Hotnot."
"Yes, but where are you from?"
"The Hotnots are from hereabouts, boss. And boss?"
"My family farmed at Boschendal, once."
"True, boss? The Hotnots are from hereabouts, from always."

** "I am a Free Stater. It's home. I am from here."

drove his forbears into the north. He did know a good deal about the blood oath the Voortrekkers swore after their first disastrous contact with the Zulu empire under the tyrant Dingaan — it was one of the seminal events in the history of his people. He knew of the Voortrekker triumphs and how those triumphs turned so often to ashes in defeat, withdrawal, schism, tribal squabbles, defeat again. And of course he remembered clearly the war with the British: they tried to kill his family, to conquer his place, subdue his people. Afrikaner history was bred into his bone: the sour taste of defeat, yes, but also the sense of place, of belonging, of being *hiervandaan*, from here.

Great-great-great-etc.-uncle Paul, who built the present manor house at Boschendal on the rubble of his father's more modest dwelling, left us some notes on the house itself; we will hear from him in due course. He was a man of some cultivation; he dug his roots into the Drakenstein soil while some of his brothers were already turning their gaze to the north — the immense, restless, open, unknown, endless, mysterious, irresistible north. My grandfather's father had moved with his oxen over the Swartruggens Mountains into the Great Karoo; he had stood on a hillock on the edge of the highveld and watched the mass migration of springbok, two million strong, into the distant blue haze . . . He had also put down roots and stayed: Drakenstein, Klapmuts, Fauresmith, Winburg . . . "Jim" de Villiers understood the tribe: he was its blood.

A continuity of sorrows and a fierce identification with place: the plane from America slants in over the blood red earth of Johannesburg. You can see the fires of Soweto burning and the sun glinting on the yellow of the mine tailings; and on a dump from which a billion dollars in gold has been extracted there is a huge sign that says JESUS HAS COME; and if you look back, the blue haze is settling over the Great Thirstland to the west, into which the last of the Voortrekkers vanished, searching for paradise lost and never found.

For the last two decades, Johannesburg has lived in a brittle calm. It lives in the shadow of Soweto, and in a curious way the affluent white city has become a spiritual adjunct to the black township that broods in its south-west corner. All men bend their minds to Soweto and its cauldron of passions. But Johannesburg and Soweto are not the whole place; to those of us who feel the deep stirrings of a primitive Afrikaner identification with place and spirit, the endless arid plain called the Thirstland is as emotional, because it represents a much earlier and more innocent yearning for an escape into security, a flight from defeat. Soweto represents only the Afrikaner's failure, the failure of a white tribe still trapped in a dream that soured, unable to understand how the search for Beulah turned to bitterness and how its retreat to the Land of Goshen became lost in the harsh intricacies of 20th-century cynicism: how did the longing for relief turn into the politics of privilege?

I was thinking of the Afrikaner as the plane cut through the thin highveld air. I was thinking how we — "we," the outside world — have all been given a licence to hate the Afrikaner. I read in a Canadian newspaper that Afrikaans is an "inherently ugly language"; a British journalist tells me calmly that the Afrikaners are genetically damaged. In the West, the hatred is expressed with superciliousness and in ignorance; in the Communist world, with calculation and in ignorance. The Africans no longer see clearly; through the red haze of their rage they see only racist monsters. Even to their few friends the Afrikaners are an embarrassment, a relic of their past, ridden by the demons of their history.

But how can you hate your own? How can you turn on what you are? How can you accept an outsider's judgments, especially when you know the tribe to be ridden with schism, puzzled at its destiny, locked into its dreams, troubled in its conscience as well as its politics?

What follows is not intended to be an apologia; it is only meant to suggest dimensions to the South African story that have become lost in the clamour of the moment. The image of the Afrikaner flickering across the consciousness of the Outside is shallow, as all media images are, a mix of facts half understood and factoids that have taken on their own life, as they always do when journalists go on crusade. The path to understanding is more hidden than current events will allow, and without understanding there can be no true solution. Without understanding, Western policy towards South Africa will produce only unpleasant surprises. There are signposts along the way with which this book is concerned: the matter of *hiervandaan*, of being *from this place*.

The Afrikaners are now nearly 3 million strong, part of a white population of 5 million and a total of nearly 33 million (blacks 24, coloureds 3, whites 5, Asian less than 1). They were formed in the south, the product of their Calvinist past and their African present; they were shaped and exploited by a corrupt imperial trading company, withdrew to the interior, and ran headlong into the expanding Xhosa kingdoms; they were overtaken by the most arrogant imperialism of its time, the narrow, sanctimonious, supercilious culture of Britain; they withdrew again after war into the clean, open, endless air of the deep interior; they conquered the Zulu empires of Shaka's heirs Dingaan and Mzilikazi; they sunk their roots into the red earth of the open north; they fissioned into small and quarrelsome groups under local leaders, in the tribal way; after hundreds of years they had become a people of Africa and were shocked into tribal awareness when they were savagely attacked in their turn by the jingoes under Milner and Chamberlain and Lord Kitchener of Khartoum.

The subsequent history of the Afrikaners — and of South Africa to the present — has been the history of tribal manoeuvrings. It was the ethnic mobilization of a defeated people that governed policies chosen and options taken up: out of a deep and historic insecurity, the Afrikaners chose the route they believed would best lead to security, but instead it has led them to the abyss. Apartheid was a reaction to uncertainty, a grasping at the Tribal Now, a grateful sinking into the comfort of the group. The Afrikaner's history made a cross-ethnic class solidarity impossible: the tribe remained the tribe. What's happening in South Africa now is not colonialism but a post-colonial tribal power struggle.

The process is as unexpectedly fluid as tribes are, and as uncertain. There are no people with a greater dislocation between their political and private actions than the Afrikaners; their tribal reality is in conflict with their dimly remembered European past. Politically, they're intolerant, arrogant, determined to get their own way. Privately they are hospitable and want badly to be loved. It's their tribal history: they have had to withdraw so often, have been dispersed so often, have been attacked so often, that group cohesion has become the highest goal. Even dissidents — usually from the right — have invoked *die ware volk*, the real people, as the reason for their dissidence. Accommodation with other groups becomes anathema: integration is the end of the *volkseie*, of Afrikaner identity. This is true of all nationalisms, but especially true here.

If you define identity as the Afrikaner nationalists have historically defined it — with the highest allegiance given not to an idea or to a principle or to the individual or to a piece of geography or even to God but to *die nasie, die volk*, and its mission as an expression of God's will; and if this volk is defined in terms of its history and language and Puritan traditions and location and mission and stern Calvinism — if this is the way you look at it, then integration *is* death. And it's no good saying that its identity is doomed anyway — that the management of a modern capitalist state and racist society has already destroyed much of it and will destroy the rest in due course. No good either to point out that the very implementation of the vision perverted its nature. The Afrikaner nationalists are acting as primitives in charge of dangerous machinery always act; they will strip its gears and ruin everything for tribal advantage. The tribe must live. This is the dominant reality.

But only the Afrikaners' many enemies and Afrikaner nationalism's own propagandists maintain that the tribe is a monolith and indivisible: schism is also in the blood. The nationalists are not the whole tribe. Thus we have Afrikaners like the academic Jacques Kriel, who writes in the Sunday papers that the *toevlugsoord*, the escape from reality, is over and that "we must adapt to the new reality by becoming part of Africa in a real way." Thus we have Afrikaners like Beyers Naudé, who has held unswervingly to his Christian conscience through years of revilement and banishment. Thus we have Afrikaners like Kowie Marais, who travelled from his membership in Afrikanerdom's secret councils to a belief in an open society. Thus we have Afrikaners like my father, René de Villiers, who was born in the Boer heartland but who has long ago refused the Afrikaner's assumption to himself of all moral authority: he is part of a small but not forgotten band of Afrikaner liberals who reject the weird edifice of apartheid in all its forms. The tribe does not speak with a single voice. These Afrikaner liberals have been holding fast to their vision, which is that the Afrikaners have a place in the larger Africa, not just a refuge in their ethos of singularity — not just a mission to build a Calvinist fortress in the continent's Deep South.

My father was cast out by the spiritual leadership of the tribe because he believed in accommodation and respect between the races. That same tribe has made the cause for which he worked so long perilously unlikely — why should the blacks any longer care that some whites cared? When the time comes, to have been white is enough . . . It is a peculiarly Afrikaner tragedy, to revile those who would save you, and it's not likely anyone will ever pick through the garbage dump of history to see what the Afrikaner has thrown away. Will anyone care any longer to remember the spirit of compromise? Sometimes, in the decadence of the West, we are tempted to see even gentle liberals as cynically self-motivated — as "making friends with the crocodile so as not to be eaten first," as the Zulu leader Gatsha Buthelezi put it. South Africa is a crucible of raw emotion — there is plenty of hatred there, but it's a reminder, also, of the gentler virtues we are in danger of discounting: sometimes cynicism is itself a lie.

The Afrikaner liberals practise the politics of faith: archaic, perhaps, and useless, but reassuring in these times. When my father reminds us that violence always leads to terror and dismay, he is speaking for *'n deel van die volk*, a part of the people, a neglected and misunderstood part, that saw in the Afrikaners' Great Trek to the interior an adventure of the spirit and not a retreat from the future. My father is saying, One must do what one must, even if one is forgotten; and this puts him in his time and his place, and among his people. It is possible that in the heat of the events to come, in the grief and the rage that will culminate apartheid, when the system is swept aside, the rage will allow no pause to consider the white Afrikaner liberals who failed to deliver the blacks from the system. History will punish them for failure, but at least they will have proved that the Afrikaners are not all stiff-necked hypocrites who protect their identity with holocaust. Some, some few, will remember.

PART 1

Jacques and Abraham de Villiers: the establishment of the Way

———

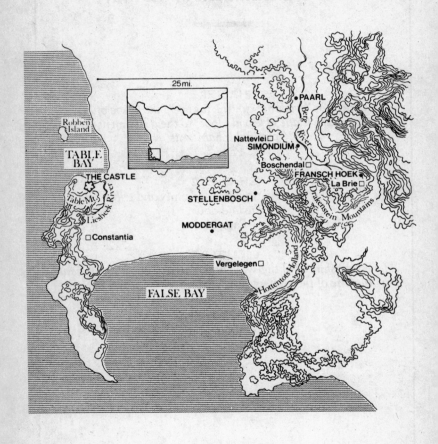

The Cape peninsula

Chapter 1

The arrival in "a country for the taking": the Cape of Storms becomes the Cape of Good Hope, to the bafflement of its original inhabitants

I

JACQUES DE VILLIERS WAS born in St-Jean-d'Angely, near La Rochelle in the French province of Charente Inférieure, in 1661. The town's main claim to fame was that its church had housed one of the two extant heads of Saint John the Baptist (the other, more successful, claimant was in Toulouse); a choir of monks stood vigil over it every Friday night for centuries until the more promotionally minded Toulousian diocese succeeded in convincing even the Angelynois that they were venerating a fraud.

Though probably not because of this hiccup in the faith, the town was a hotbed of radical Protestantism, as indeed was the whole province. Jacques and his brothers Pierre and Abraham grew up on stories of Richelieu's atrocities in the market port of La Rochelle, and when the Edict of Nantes was revoked in 1685 they refused to join the mass abjurations of the *religion prétendue réformée* pressed on them by the gleeful monks of the one true church; they abandoned their farms and headed to La Rochelle, whence they took ship for the Free and United Provinces of the Netherlands, where they could pray any way they wished. This was no small decision. They were not wealthy, but on the other hand Jacques's grandmother had married the sheriff of Niort, and their wine-holdings were far from modest. Nevertheless they abandoned everything they owned and joined the swelling tide of Protestant refugees called the Huguenots. There is a pretty family legend that describes the brothers departing by the back door as Richelieu's thugs enter by the front, but there is no evidence whatever that it's true.

Huguenots were fleeing France in all directions. Thousands made their way to Germany, more to England, many left directly for Quebec. The Dutch port of Texel became a gathering place for refugees from the French south and southwest; their arrival there was a happy coincidence for the Council of Seventeen of the Dutch East India Company, which had established a "refreshment station" at the Cape some 25 years earlier and was already growing tired of the cost of garrisoning and running the place. (A peevish note persisted in all Company correspondence with local governors until the very end, when the Company was swept aside by the British — the wretched place always seemed more expensive than it was worth.) The council had resolved to set up a farming population at the Cape to augment the meagre offerings from the Company gardens and the often erratic supplies of fresh meat from the wandering bands of skittish Khoikhoi.

The Company's first efforts at rounding up colonists had been rebuffed. Seven hundred refugees in Nuremberg had expressed a desire to depart for the Cape; they were to be provided with free passage, credit, agricultural implements, and food stores. This timid lot refused at the last moment to leave; "being averse to the sea and the long voyage, they have changed their minds and settled in Germany," as the council wrote to the governor at the Cape, Simon van der Stel. Later attempts found the would-be colonists more intrepid, and a few actually achieved their destination.

Pierre, Abraham, and Jacques de Villiers reached Holland safely and applied at the Company's offices in Zeeland for permission to depart for the Cape. They had virtually no property with them except their clothing, family Bibles, and a few rapidly devaluing French banknotes, which they traded in for Company *rixdollars*. Under "specie" on the emigration form, they wrote: None. They left on the *Zion* from Texel on January 8, 1689, carrying in their baggage a letter from the

Company's governing council at Delft, addressed to Governor van der Stel, which said in part, "We have permitted the following French refugees to sail to the Cape and earn their living as freemen, Pierre de Villiers, Abraham de Villiers and Jacob [Jacques] de Villiers, all three brothers born near La Rochelle. We are informed that these persons have a good knowledge of laying out vineyards and managing the same, and thus we hope the Company will acquire their good service. You are recommended to give them a helping hand."

The Company did acquire their service, and did give them a helping hand, but these were dissident Protestants from dissident France and a contrary lot, and matters did not always go so smoothly. As we shall see.

At first the Portuguese called it the Cape of Storms; later they optimistically (and on slight evidence) called it the Cape of Good Hope. It had been used since the early voyages of Vasco da Gama as a place to take on fresh water. By the 1600s it was so frequently visited that messages were left and exchanged under "post office stones" on the beaches of Table Bay, the future town's main harbour. The Dutch East India Company arranged for the first settlement, issuing strict orders that it was not to become a colony. It was to be used only for refreshing Company ships on the outbound and inbound voyages. The Company was determined on this — it already had plenty of colonies elsewhere, and they were expensive to run. But after Company crews had stripped their earlier refuge, the island of St. Helena in the deep Atlantic, of most of its vegetation and all of its wildlife, the Cape came to seem more desirable, particularly since it soon became clear there were cattle to be had there as well as fresh water.

The Company was a consortium of Dutch trading companies that came into being after the Netherlands muscled into the Portuguese trading routes. For almost 200 years from 1600 the Company held a monopoly on all Dutch trading in the southern oceans. It thought of itself as above the law and acted in all ways like a state, uncontrolled by any Netherlandish political power.

A Company ship, the *Haerlem*, was wrecked in Table Bay in March 1647, and the survivors remained there until the following year. They discovered the Cape had fertile soil, plenty of fresh water, and tractable natives; they argued before the Company's board, the Council of Seventeen, that — high praise! — the natives were *not* cannibals, responded to kindness, learned Dutch easily, could become Christians, would make good servants, and owned cattle, which they would barter. Citrus, known to be an effective counter to scurvy, could be grown there. And, as the Seventeen themselves pointed out, if they didn't occupy the Cape, "our public enemies, the Spanish and the Portuguese, might use it as a base for attacking our ships."

On March 25, 1651, the Company issued an instruction to "provide that the East India ships [may procure] herbs, flesh, water, and other needful refreshments, and by this means restore the health of their sick"; it also specified that "a general rendezvous be formed at the Cape of Good Hope." On April 7, 1652, an expedition of about 90 men, under the command of Jan van Riebeeck, went ashore at Table Bay, with orders to build a fort and a lodge near a freshwater stream running into the harbour, and to select suitable land for gardens and pasture.

Van Riebeeck had been fired from Company employ in Batavia (part of present-day Indonesia) early in 1648 for "private trading," a practice abhorred by good bureaucrats everywhere; this was his first post in his effort to reinstate himself in the Company's good books, and he was determined to make it work. His early dispatches, with this in mind, were whinings about the difficulty of the task: "On a parched, poor soil without a dwelling place and only some light material to build a fort, work had to be started with just 90 persons . . . just from a sea voyage, and suffering from scurvy. They were as raw as the whole world had ever seen." And, he pointed out plaintively, he himself had to work as "engineer, digger, gardener, farmer, carpenter, mason, smith, etc."

In truth, those 90 persons, "raw as the whole world had

ever seen," were less than impressive as a labour force. To their dismay, the Khoikhoi stubbornly refused to do an honest day's work, and they were forced to turn to themselves. Many slacked off, knowing they'd have to be paid anyway — this despite harsh discipline and occasionally savage punishments. (Robben Island, in Table Bay off the townsite, was early established as a prison; the worst offenders against propriety were blinded and put out there to pasture.) Many simply deserted. Some disappeared into the hinterland and were never seen (or at least recorded) again. Several were spotted with nomadic Khoikhoi bands. Only a few weeks after the van Riebeeck party arrived, the official journal recorded, somewhat wistfully, that the writer felt industrious Chinese would make successful cultivators there. There were slaves and servants in all other Company establishments. Why not at the Cape?

However, van Riebeeck was an able man, and the settlement got going remarkably quickly. Within a year the first visiting fleet arrived for victualling and was given meat bartered from nearby Khoikhoi bands, fruit, vegetables, and water. By the time van Riebeeck left in 1662, ten years after he arrived, the place was operating efficiently and had the feel of a town-in-the-making. A rudimentary hospital housed the scrofulous; there were houses, a granary, workshops, and gardens. A jetty was completed in 1659. True, the settlement was still small and its population meagre. It was not yet a colony, and van Riebeeck was mindful of his instructions to keep it that way. The Seventeen didn't want to spend any more money on maintaining the place than they had to. The budget deficit was severe enough without their making encouraging noises towards those who would expand the station beyond its limited purposes. There was, in fact, serious discussion about turning the Cape peninsula into an island by cutting a canal from Table Bay to False Bay. Van Riebeeck never attempted any more than a cursory survey of the hinterland, and to guard against Khoikhoi thieving and cattle raids he planted a thick hedge of almonds to enclose the 6,000 acres he considered proper for a refreshment station's needs — South Africa's first futile attempt at segregating the races.

The station was a success in its stated aim of succouring ships. An average 33 ships a year were supplied by the small garrison. The Cape hospital most probably effected cures more by the healthy climate than by any remarkable standards of medical care (a service that was in any case farmed out to company employees with depressingly small medical educations). Nevertheless the station was a drain on the Company purse, and van Riebeeck cast around for ways to diversify its economy. His solution was a kind of state-controlled monopoly capitalism. The first step was to stop issuing food to women and children. Instead, he offered land to married employees. Anything they produced on it above the van Riebeeck household's needs (effectively above "official" needs) they could sell — at Company-controlled prices. He soon transferred other activities to private hands, creating as he did so a class of freemen, or free burghers (spelled *burgers* in Dutch or Afrikaans), former Company employees freed from indenture for the purpose. Tavern-keeping, hunting, fishing, and practising medicine were then delegated to the free burghers as licensed monopolies.

As an extension of this practice, he argued to head office that the Company should get out of the agriculture business altogether, and rather delegate it to free burghers, who should, however, be tightly controlled — they should be able to sell their produce only to the Company at Company prices. It was well known, van Riebeeck argued, that freemen in other company stations had no interest in the general welfare: they wanted "merely to get rich by tavern keeping and return to Europe." He argued that they be bound to remain for at least 10 years and their children for 20, so they would "come in time to regard this country as their fatherland." The Company should support settlers, not tax them immediately, and supply them with slaves to get them on their feet. The Company, wary of getting into the colonist business but nevertheless happy to reduce the salary bill by creating as many freemen as plausible, agreed. With this in mind, nine Company servants were freed, given 26 acres of land each, and set up in business along the Liesbeek River, on what is now a golf course adjoining a Coloured area of Metropolitan Cape Town.

It was not a happy experience. Slaves were imported from West Africa by the Company for the freemen, but many simply took off into the interior, clearly hoping to walk home. There were scattered revolts and incidents of violence; most of the freemen, "fearing for their lives," returned their slaves to the Company. Testiness grew. The newly slaveless burghers, still forbidden to press Khoikhoi into servitude, finding them in any case unwilling and unsuitable for service, and finding themselves unwilling to tackle the manual work farming demanded, went on strike. As van Riebeeck reported home, they complained that "it [is] too hard that they are compelled to plant this or that . . . to refrain from following their own bent and from bartering all sorts of things from natives . . . to sell . . . to the ships," and they declared, "We will not be slaves to the company."

Four years after van Riebeeck departed, his successor, Zacharias Wagenaar, remained sceptical about the free burghers' freedom. Most of them, he reported in disgust, were too poor, too lazy, too dissolute to succeed. Most wanted only to be able "to set up houses for the sale of brandy." The burghers, in turn, continued to complain of rigid Company policies that discouraged initiative. In some cases the solution was perceived to be a freedom to trade and barter with whom they would, and a freedom to set their own prices. Some began to turn their gaze to the north, beyond the Cape flats, where possibly matters would be better: the Khoikhoi ability to vanish at will into the interior excited contemporary envy.

The establishment of free burgher farmers on the Liesbeek, traditional grazing grounds of the peninsula Khoikhoi, changed Khoikhoi bafflement at white ways to fury. Their occasional thievery escalated to organized raiding, raiding to skirmishes, and the skirmishes to what later became known as the First Hottentot War, in 1658.

II

NO ONE KNOWS WHERE the Khoikhoi ("men of men" in their own language) came from. Early assumptions that they migrated from the north-east have generally been rejected, and the most plausible explanation is that they originated in what is now Botswana. Their language is a complicated series of clicks; and although many of the early Khoikhoi learned Dutch with some rapidity, as far as we know the first Europeans to even attempt Khoikhoian discourse were the 19th-century missionaries. The early white settlers called them by various names, including Caffres, but soon settled on Hottentots as a generic. This name has since fallen into disrepute, and has vanished except for the Hottentots Holland Mountains near Cape Town, the self-disparaging "Hotnot" corruption, and a slight presence in Dutch (the longest word in the language is supposed to be *Hottentotstentententoonstelling-terrein*, a nonsense word meaning display ground for Hottentots' tents).

Since nothing has survived of the Khoikhoi culture, or indeed of its yellow-skinned people — their bloodlines blended with Malays, blacks from Madagascar, and Europeans to form what is today called the Cape Coloured population — knowledge of their politics and organization is meagre. Modern South African historians, perhaps trying to compensate for traditional racist disdain, are now playing down the primitive nature of their way of life. But this was not an advanced people. They were primitive pastoralists who scratched a meagre living from their environment. They owned cattle — sometimes significant herds — but had only meagre trade and hardly any manufacture apart from rudimentary working of copper. They had none of the rich arts of the northerly black tribes. They were not hunter-predators like the Bushmen (also called San) nor did they have the relative sophistication of the village-and-town culture of the blacks to the east.

What political organization the Khoikhoi had tended to be fluid; allegiance was given to clan units, with only vaguely defined deference (but not allegiance) given to senior lineages. These small groups shifted and split constantly, depending on the personalities of the clan head. A strong leader could easily form a new group from disaffected remnants of other clans; his group in turn would last only so long as his leadership was efficacious. Warfare was commonplace, sometimes with the even more primitive San hunter-gatherers and sometimes among themselves. There was no population of black Africans in the south at that time — a point often made by Afrikaner historians.

In southern Africa the peninsula Khoikhoi were a favoured lot, cut off by desert and mountain from the predations of the Bushmen — non-pastoralist hunters — and from the territorial ambitions of inland clans. The peninsula Khoikhoi were themselves divided into cattle-keepers and the so-called Strandlopers, scavengers who lived on the beaches and subsisted on seal, whale, and fish. The pastures around Table Mountain, in what are now the suburbs of Constantia and Rondebosch, were traditional grazing lands for the southern Khoikhoi, and they regarded the intrusions of the Europeans with understandable suspicion.

By the time van Riebeeck arrived in 1652 to build his fort, Europeans and Khoikhoi had a nearly 200-year history of sporadic contact, a history that had built up a 200-year reservoir of suspicion and distrust. From the Khoikhoi point of view, transient sailors were probably not the best ambassadors for Western civilization; whites came to be regarded as unpredictable and violent, though with abundant stocks of goods worth the risk of cautious trading. From the whites' point of view, the Khoikhoi were an unreliable crowd skilled in warfare — a judgment puzzling to later settlers, who found them timid and disorganized. Anthropologists now assume that Khoikhoi society was itself going through a long (and indigenous) cycle of decline, and that the white settlers triggered, but didn't cause, their catastrophic cultural collapse.

At first, ships intent on bartering for meat were encouraged. They were given prodigious quantities of cattle and sheep in exchange for goods precious to the Khoikhoi, such as iron and copper. Old barrel hoops and ships' junk would sometimes bring a hundred or more cows. In the early part of the 17th century the exchange rate abruptly altered; presumably the Khoikhoi demand for iron was sated, and even copper that once brought in 10 cows would now bring only a scrawny sheep. This made the Europeans very indignant.

As Richard Elphick has pointed out in his *Khoikhoi and the Founding of White South Africa*, in this long history of wary trading the Khoikhoi formed an opinion of white habits that was plausible but in fact completely off track. From time to time parties of Europeans would build small houses or mini-forts on the shore, usually in the path of Khoikhoi grazers. The idea that these curious creatures would actually settle down alarmed the Khoikhoi, but after a while they became reassured — they began to see a pattern. Europeans might stay a while, but they were by nature rootless and restless. They would always leave.

This preconception was reinforced in 1647 by the wreckage of the *Haerlem* in Table Bay. The stranded crew of 60 stayed more than a year, and while they were there they built a substantial fort. The local Khoikhoi chief, who was later to become notorious for his intrigues with and against the Dutch, was called Autshumato. He was known to the Europeans as Hadah, Adda, or Hadot and later, after English sailors had taught him English and taken him to Java and back, as Harry. Early in the year Harry came by to inspect the new fort, and by September he was convinced that, finally, the whites had come to stay. With an eye on the main chance, he promptly asked for an alliance against his inland enemies, but he was turned down. A year later the Europeans confounded his new confidence and disappeared, confirming to Harry and his people their transient nature. Thus, when van

Riebeeck arrived, it was some years before the Khoikhoi realized that he represented a permanent threat and not just another passing opportunity for gain.

By 1652, relations between natives and Europeans were almost equally balanced between peace and fighting, between co-operation and conflict. There were strong forces pushing for co-operation, notably the Dutch company's need for peaceful relations in order to secure access to bartered cattle and their consequent determination — and instruction to van Riebeeck — to treat the locals as a free people. That is, they were to be neither enslaved nor subdued but were to be treated with courtesy and respect. Van Riebeeck is on record as disagreeing with this assessment (arguing that he should, after all, be allowed to round them up, he wrote home: "They are not to be trusted . . . they are a savage set, living without conscience"), but he needed to impress his employers and did his best to carry out their policy. He offered gifts and services to those Khoikhoi within reach; he invited their leaders to inspect the fort and entertained them there; he punished whites who plundered Khoikhoi cattle; he took Khoikhoi into his home.

One of van Riebeeck's protégés, famous in South African history only as Eva, grew up in his household, learned fluent Dutch, wore Western clothes, became a Christian, and later married a Danish surgeon, Pieter van Meerhoff, in a wedding financed and blessed by the Company. Eva is famous because to generations of South African schoolchildren she has been used as a cautionary tale; in modern times the lesson of the tale is ambiguous. In later years Eva became a drunk and a prostitute, vacillating between two cultures alien to her. Rejected by both, she abandoned her children and died in prison on Robben Island, not the first and far from the last victim of racial confusion.

The Khoikhoi, fascinated and appalled by what they saw of European culture, suffered from their own misconceptions. European customs puzzled them. The idea of inheritable property was new; that land could be alienated from the tribe was found peculiar. The arrival among them of settlers with large stocks of apparently unused goods was often too tempting to ignore, so they tended to take it. This petty thievery, as the whites saw it, became endemic very early.

Van Riebeeck was irritated by Khoikhoi unwillingness to part with enough stock to feed passing ships and by their bland denials that they were harbouring escaped slaves from Java or West Africa when "everyone" knew they were. Van Riebeeck told head office he could solve all this by the simple expedient of enslaving the locals, but the Company continued to refuse permission. He resorted, therefore, to hostage-taking and threats, most of which worked — hostage-taking was an old Khoikhoi custom. Van Riebeeck was also an unwitting player in Khoikhoi politics; Harry, the Strandloper chieftain, used his knowledge of Dutch and his frequent presence at fort social gatherings to manipulate gains for his clan and to enrich himself personally.

It was the arrival of the white burgher farmers — however inept and unwilling — on the Liesbeek River that changed mutual suspicion to outright hostility and precipitated the first war in 1658. The conflict was not a grand event in military history. The Khoikhoi, under the leadership of a charismatic commoner called Doman, who had visited Java in a Company trading ship and felt he understood how Europeans behaved, launched an attack on the colony. Cunningly, at Doman's urging, the Khoikhoi attacked under cover of the driving Cape winter rainstorms, which Doman knew would cause the colonists' dangerous but erratic old flintlocks to misfire. They burned most of the colonists' farms, stole their livestock, and made off with what booty they could find, including metal farm implements.

The war ended in stalemate. The burghers withdrew to the fort, which the Khoikhoi had no way of capturing; the Dutch, on the other hand, lacked the manpower, mobility, and military savvy to mount a decisive counter-attack. Shortly thereafter Doman's unstable coalition began to come apart, and since neither side found itself able to harm the other, they concluded peace more or less from weariness. The treaty — Europeans always insisted on treaties — recognized the war's indecisive nature. The only clause worth noting — it was decisive for later events — was the Khoikhoi's forced admission that the free burghers owned the land on which they had settled.

By the early 1670s the Company in Holland was losing interest in the Khoikhoi. In van Riebeeck's day they were a threat to colony stability and to the food supply, but now the colonists had begun to spread into the fertile valleys near the Drakenstein Mountains, 20 or so miles to the east, and the increasing size of their own herds meant that Khoikhoi cattle were less essential. The concurrent disintegration of Khoikhoi political will and social structure meant that the colonists were free to mop up what was left of Khoikhoi resistance. As their society broke down, the Khoikhoi were drifting into service with Company employees and farmers as hired hands, partly because their own herds were depleted and partly because that had become easier than dealing with the constant sniping and stealing of the San hunters across the Hottentots Holland Mountains.

There was a Second Hottentot War (1673–77), but it consisted mainly of punitive expeditions by settlers against Gonnema, an influential chief of the last remaining powerful Khoikhoi tribe, the Cochoqua. These attacks were gleefully helped by Chief Gonnema's many Khoikhoi enemies, and by the time the "war" was over the settlers had shown — more or less effortlessly — that they had the power and the intention to stir into local affairs whenever they wished. Khoikhoi society never recovered its coherence. Some bands trekked away to the north; the southerners became "free men" — not slaves, but without resources of their own. They took work as cook's aides, runners, labourers, and domestic servants, and, as their avenues of escape declined and their alternatives shrunk, as herders of other people's cattle.

In 1713, when the deterioration of Khoikhoi culture was well advanced, a visiting fleet sent its linen ashore to be washed by Company servants in Cape Town. It bore a small-pox virus that was to kill hundreds of Europeans and black slaves; it spared only one of ten Khoikhoi. It came close to annihilating the Khoikhoi of southern Africa and destroyed them as an organized culture, but not before the master–servant pattern had been implanted in the Afrikaners-to-be.

Chapter 2

The beginning of hiervandaan: *the family and tribal patterns are laid down*

I
___

IN THE SANITIZED PROSE of the school textbooks of the Orange Free State when I was growing up, the Cape in the decades following the Huguenots' arrival was portrayed as an energetic, bustling port of hardy burghers-about-to-be-Boers; I always thought this picture of the Huguenots and other colonists made them out to be a sanctimonious lot. Here's a typical sentence, taken from *The French Refugees at the Cape*, by Graham Botha, published in 1919: "With what thankfulness must they not have lifted up their eyes and with their voices praised the One Being who had brought them in safety through perils to a land free from religious persecution, to a place where they could openly confess their faith before man!"

True, the books did hint that there were a few more than slightly villainous Dutch East India Company officials bent on enriching themselves at burgher expense, and they did acknowledge that the town was known throughout the Indies as the Tavern of the Seas (possibly on account of its equally villainous brandy). The Khoikhoi were barely mentioned, except as porters bustling about stowing the settlers' baggage, and that the town ran on slave labour from Madagascar was never mentioned at all. Most emphatically not mentioned was that most — or at least many — of the visiting sailors and arriving refugees gratefully spent their first night ashore at the lubricious pleasures of the Company slave lodge, which doubled as the town's semi-official brothel. Piety — and they *were* pious — never seemed to preclude bawdiness.

We have no idea whether Great-great-great-great-great-grandfather Jacques availed himself of the opportunity in 1689. He didn't confide in posterity. Very probably not, however; the family seems to have stuck together. Big brother Abraham, for his part, already had his eye on one of fellow emigrant Jean Gardiol's kid sisters (there were few women in the colony) and probably stayed in the barracks room the Company lent the arrivals. Jacques's notes, scraps of paper retained by the family, recall only being woken at intervals by what must have been the Rattle Watch crying the all's-well on the hour. The Rattle Watchers were burghers pressed into service as a citizen militia; their job was to watch for wandering "rogues," usually slaves bent on mischief.

Cape Town was a very small town in 1689, only a couple of hundred people, not counting the slaves, who didn't count as people. There were, nevertheless, a good many taverns, which catered to the locals as well as to the crews of the 30 or 40 ships that called every year at the Cape; the taverns served as hotels when the farmers from the new settlements at Stellenbosch and Drakenstein came to town. Many of these taverns were sited along the Heerengracht (what is now Adderley Street, Cape Town's main business thoroughfare), within easy staggering distance of the fort. These taverns themselves were rough-and-ready establishments.

A contemporary description: an unnamed house a block from the jetty. A lantern swinging in the south-easterly wind that they soon came to call, sardonically, the Cape Doctor. No sign or name-plate; just the smell of brandy-soaked wood and the shouts of the drunks. In the corner, a rack for firearms, flintlocks, and a few new breech-loaders. Tables made mostly from ships wrecked in Table Bay. A few Khoikhoi men in a corner. Most of the Khoikhoi who hung around the cities had given up *dagga* (a mild form of marijuana that had been their only traditional crop) in favour of the quicker fix of alcohol; and since the Company maintained what the burghers regarded as the fiction that Khoikhoi were a free people, they were allowed, though not encouraged, inside the taverns. Outside, on the streets and down by the docks, there were often a few Khoikhoi hookers plying their trade, usually not very successfully, since only the passing sailors, used to the state of shipboard sanitation, easily tolerated the Khoikhoi habits that disgusted the settlers, such as the smearing of animal grease on their bodies (a primitive cosmetic not to the taste of the Europeans of the time) and their way of eating lice. These Khoikhoi women were pathetic cases. The Khoikhoi penalty for prostitution, which they counted as adultery, was death by strangulation. The hookers were accepted by no one: they were South Africa's first racial outcasts. Self-esteem couldn't have been very high.

Most of the women in the tavern would be from the Company slave lodge, ebony blacks from Madagascar or Malays and Javanese from Batavia. Women were in short supply at the Cape. Only about a third of the settlers were married; Governor Simon van der Stel kept complaining to head office of the imbalance, and in the early 1680s, as a minimal response, a small group of orphan girls were sent out (their fate is not recorded).

The French refugees, to van der Stel's disgust, turned out to be mostly men, and most of the women on board had been "taken" by the time the ships docked. (Suzanne Gardiol was a case in point; she later married Abraham de Villiers, and her sister Marguerite married his brother Jacques, my direct ancestor, to start the South African line of my branch of the family.)

Liaisons with slave women were not all relationships of sexual exploitation. Many of the men were simply lonely and were trying to establish what relationships were available to them. Although attitudes towards the Khoikhoi were hardening, and the slaves were always just slaves, race relations were sufficiently flexible to accommodate long-term liaisons between Company employees or burghers and slave women.

Many of the women had "patrons," who would buy them finery and ply them with better food than that available in the lodge. Occasionally a slave's freedom would be purchased and manumission granted, usually after the birth of a child. Company statistics in the 1680s record that almost half the children born in the slave lodge had white fathers; these children became freemen, forming the gene pool for the "coloured" community of today; and though many of them drifted later into servitude many simply "passed" into the Afrikaner bloodlines. They can be tracked: the code-word in the genealogies is the name Maria, sometimes followed by a geographic designator — "Maria van Cijloen" or "Maria van die Kaap." (*Who is Maria de Villiers?* asked the title of one odd modern volume on the de Villiers family, and its delving into the family's ethnic background makes many de Villiers quite cross.)

Male slaves were another matter. The refugees soon realized the extent to which the colonists feared their slaves. With good reason: the campfires of runaways could be seen on Table Mountain at night; murder and drunkenness were frequent. Recaptured runaways were not let off with the relative softness of work on the blue stone quarries on Robben Island; they were generally flayed, then hanged. But the harsh punishment seldom deterred slaves bent on escaping, and they often committed violence in the process, sometimes in order to get away, sometimes in reprisal, and sometimes, the colonists felt, just for the sheer hell of it.

Relations between the slaves, particularly the East Indians, and the Khoikhoi were almost as bad as between master and slave. So much did the slaves despise the locals that in the First Hottentot War van Riebeeck had contemplated arming the slaves, until it became clear that their desire to escape exceeded — if only just — their desire to create mayhem among the Khoikhoi. The slaves from the sophisticated cultures of the Orient looked down on the rude Khoikhoi — a people who seemed at first glance to have no particular culture to speak of — as much as the Dutch did. They bitterly resented the freedom of such an undeserving people. This high disregard was returned in good measure: the Khoikhoi saw all slaves as cringing and servile and utterly without human dignity.

By the time the de Villiers family arrived, other social divisions were also beginning to emerge. There were already two classes of whites, Company "servants" (employees), who were forbidden to own property or indulge in private trade, and free burghers, who could practise their crafts but received no salary from the company. Each class looked down on the other. Company employees could be transferred at whim to Java or Madagascar or Madras, but they were town folk and made the rules; they regarded the burghers in the way a bureaucrat regards the subjects of his paperwork.

The burghers, on the other hand, saw themselves as unjustly restricted. They had left the Cape peninsula proper, crossing the 20 miles or so of sand flats to the east, and were living in the sheltered valleys beyond the first of the concentric mountain ranges that protected the southern Cape from the climatic extremes of the arid plains to the north. They were entitled to grow all the grain they wanted, but they had to sell it through the Company at Company-set prices. They could raise cattle — indeed, they were encouraged to raise cattle — but they couldn't take the easy way out and barter directly with the Khoikhoi, whose herds were rapidly becoming a Company monopoly. The colony was run by the governor-in-council, but to the burghers this "council" meant nothing — it excluded them and included Company employees, and so it was even more a source of grievance than direct one-man rule would have been. The Court of Justice did include two burghers among its eight councillors, but they couldn't rule on Company matters, only on cases that concerned burgher rights — another source of grievance. Resentment in the newly established hinterlands — soon to be called the *platteland* and to become a synonym for rural backwardness — was early and angry.

How much of this Jacques saw is not recorded. His own

scattered notes refer only to the taverns, the accommodations, and the supplies (meagre, as predicted) given them by the colonial government. Within two weeks, at the nagging of Abraham, the group departed with 60 others to the distant mountains beyond Paarl Rock, to the valley named Drakenstein. It was May. Winter was beginning. Rains soaked the valley and the Berg River, as the Dutch called it, was in full flood. It was a long way from the ancient stones of St-Jean-d'Angely.

II

JEAN GARDIOL, fellow traveller of the de Villiers brothers, took his sisters with him when they all set out from the Cape on the two-day trek to the great Berg River, to the Drakenstein Valley, which lay between Olifantshoek and the Paarl Hills. Marguerite, Jacques's future wife, was 15. The party travelled in a convoy of 12 wagons. The route took them through Moddergat (Mudhole) to Stellenbosch, and then on the laborious trek over the first low mountain range to the district the de Villiers brothers named La Petite Rochelle, later to be called Le Coin Français and eventually Fransch Hoek. Somewhat to their irritation, they discovered that Jean Gardiol, sisters with him, had been awarded a land grant some distance away, northwards towards Paarl. Gardiol ended up adjoining the farm of Jean Taillefert, whose daughter Marie Elisabeth married Pierre de Villiers within the year. The French refugee families had all been scattered among the existing Dutch farmers, an act of deliberate policy by Governor van der Stel, who had no intention of setting up a dissident minority in his midst.

On May 17 the brothers' wagon stopped at their temporary joint land grant, which they called, inevitably, La Rochelle. When they lowered their eyes from praising the One Being, they must have looked around them with some dismay. In a heap on the ground: copper kettles, tools, one plough, sacks of grain, two barrels, bedsteads for all, axes, canvas for tents; standing nearby: one glum slave, the oxen that had got them there, and a solitary horse. La Rochelle, in its stunningly beautiful valley, was untilled earth. It consisted mainly of tough scrub, with a tangle of bushes by the river, pierced with game paths. The nearest trees were on the slopes of the mountain, a mile or so away. There were the remains of a Hottentot kraal, half encampment and half village, by the river. Elephant sign — stripped trees, trampled mudholes, and formidable dung heaps — was everywhere. They had been told to watch for leopard, and they had their firearms at the ready. As far as they knew, there was nothing between them and Europe but wild beasts and savages.

Thereafter they were too busy to leave notes. There are only tantalizing glimpses, drawn from the archives, church records, and deeds on file in Cape Town. We know they lived for three years in a mud-and-wattle house. We know they joined the Reverend Simond for Protestant services in French every Sunday, walking the 14 miles to Simondium and back, taking turns riding their only horse. We know, of course, that Abraham and Jacques married the Gardiol sisters as soon as they were granted their own farms, which were situated on the Berg River and consisted of parallel strips of "58 morgen 400 roods," about 100 acres each, grants they regarded as somewhat meagre. Pierre eventually moved the dozen or so miles to Paarl, to be nearer his in-laws the Tailleferts; Abraham moved to nearby Boschendal; Jacques stayed where he was, on his farm called La Brie, but eventually bought the Boschendal farm as well, when Abraham ran into difficulties.

A scattered and not wonderfully reliable history of the de Villiers family, written by Dan de Villiers in the early part of this century, says simply of Abraham that he was "well known for his great services to the French community." Governor van der Stel saw his activities somewhat differently. In a report to his council in 1689, he made known "the many difficulties which he has been occasioned by certain supposed French refugees here, who, under the appearance of having left their King on account of religious oppression, escaped

from France . . . in order that . . . they might lead lazy and
indolent lives; and the Hon. Company, our Lords and Masters, having allowed some of them a passage here in their
ships that they might earn their living by agriculture or any
other industry, they have shown no prudence therein . . .
and have not come up to the expectations of the Company."
This diatribe was set off by a Huguenot demand, prompted
by Abraham, that they be allowed to settle together, have
their own magistrate, and build a church somewhat closer
than Simondium, 14 miles away, where they could have services in French. Van der Stel rejected all these "impertinent"
demands. A year later the governor grudgingly sent to Olifantshoek a schoolmaster who spoke both French and
Dutch, but he refused to allow a new church and made it a
deliberate policy to discourage the use of French anywhere in
the colony.

From what we know, Abraham seems to have spent more of
his time in local affairs than in farming. He was one of the first
deacons of the church and became a *heemraad*, a presiding
councillor in local government; he was referred to as "Mayor"
de Villiers, mostly at his own insistence. Van der Stel, a strong
and hot-tempered governor, was having his difficulties
with the Dutch burghers as well. They already outnumbered
the Company servants and were growing restless at not being
allowed to manage their own affairs.

The Huguenots were a quarrelsome lot, but they did make
some effort to ingratiate themselves with their Dutch
neighbours. Maurice Boucher, in his book *French Speakers at
the Cape*, recounts the case of Mathieu Frachas, a French
immigrant who had been hanging out "with thieves and
vagrants" and who was accused by several Khoikhoi of stealing their cattle. Their testimony, to the general fury of the
burghers, was believed by the courts in Cape Town. On the
other hand, no one much liked Frachas or his sentiments: to
his friend Pierre Dumont, a hunting mate of Jacques de
Villiers, he confided that "the Dutch had better take care,
there are French ships off the coast to attack the settlement

from the sea and he, Frachas, would make up a party to attack it from the rear." He would round up his friends, he said, and survive by thievery if necessary. Seditious talk didn't go down well with the Huguenot settlers; escaped slaves and runaway sailors were enough of a problem already, without adding revolution. They approved of the Dutch governor's sentence — that Frachas be deprived of his possessions, whipped, branded, and taken to Robben Island — taking care to dissociate themselves from Frachas's pro-France sentiments; they had after all fled the French government and had no burning desire to see the flag of the Bourbon kings fluttering over the Cape fort.

The early farmers were poor and ill equipped. They had little start-up capital. The market for their produce was meagre, and prices were tightly controlled by the Company. Visiting ships often spurned their grain, having their holds full of Batavian rice already. Cape wine, in spite of the de Villiers brothers' expertise (or maybe because it had been overstated), was of poor quality. Their herds were growing, but Khoikhoi cattle were freely available still, and a Company monopoly: the burghers could barely afford to sell to the Company at the Company-set low prices. Pierre de Villiers's will contains an inventory of household possessions (an estate of 10,000 gulders was at the time reckoned a pretty fair net worth; a good wage for a skilled artisan was less than half a gulder a day):

26 horned cattle at
24 gulders each,
big and small . . . . 624 *gulders*
180 sheep at
4 gulders each
big and small . . . . 720 *gulders*
3 men slaves
at 210 gulders each . . . . 630 *gulders*
1 old wagon
with accessories . . . . 90 *gulders*

1 plough with accessories	90 gulders
20 empty wine vats at 24 gulders each	480 gulders
2 leaguers of wine at 75 gulders a leaguer	150 gulders
2 leaguers of brandy at 180 gulders per leaguer	360 gulders
1 old brandy kettle with hose	45 gulders
2 copper kettles	30 gulders
Bedsteads and boxes	60 gulders
One table, chairs and benches	36 gulders
All household furniture	150 gulders
15 muids of corn at 9 gulders per muid	135 gulders

Governor Simon van der Stel did what he could to keep them going, deferring taxes, providing free seed, adding to their stock, giving them marketing advice, helping them with transportation. Justifying the subsidies in a letter to head office, he pointed out that "it would have been an absolutely impossible thing for a poor destitute people to have accomplished anything with empty hands, except with our encouragement." However, the "poor destitute people" were not any more co-operative than they had to be. Roads and local facilities were supposed to be provided by the heemraden, the local magistrates, paid for with locally raised taxes, and constructed by labour provided by the colonists as a condition of their original grants. Most colonists avoided paying taxes and delegated inept and unmotivated slaves to do the labour. Roads were therefore poor, services non-existent. The isolation remarked on by all early travellers set in very early.

Van der Stel's major contribution to the colony was the land-holding system he devised. He understood, in the economics of the time, that viable farms were needed and that capital and labour were lacking. He therefore substituted the one resource that was in plentiful supply — land. Livestock farming, subsidized by hunting, fishing, and, to a limited extent, lumbering, was the only way the colonial settlement could be extended. In addition to the 120-acre outright grants, each farmer was allowed a "common share" of up to 6,000 acres for grazing purposes. Boschendal's several-hundred-acre home farm — the original land grant — was supplemented by more than 2,000 acres of unclaimed grazing land — land that Abraham and Jacques soon came to regard as their own. By the turn of the century there were still fewer than 400 farmers in the entire colony; population density was about two to a square mile. The de Villiers brothers benefited from the land tenure system; it gave them control, if not ownership, of vast tracts of countryside for timber and for hunting. Their herds increased rapidly. The large land grants — later to become entrenched in even larger tracts — meant that the poor existing services were seldom improved, and this pattern of development led to growing isolation and alienation from authority.

The 180 Huguenots and the pathetic shipload of orphans from Holland had been the only organized immigration the colony had ever had. There were a few individuals who had arrived on their own — Jacques's neighbour to the south was a militant Protestant from Amsterdam named Combrinck; to his east, a German refugee from the Palatinate, whose name was not recorded. The rest of the burghers were either former Company servants who didn't want to go home or wanderers, the product of another of Europe's turbulent centuries, displaced by the Thirty Years War west of the Rhine or the Eighty Years War in the Netherlands. Unlike the Puritans of New England, who expected to look after themselves and who, within a few years, had constructed schools, town halls, and whole communities, the settlers at the Cape found that the Company provided everything. It became a habit of the settlers early on to complain about the Company, but also to make demands on it and expect it to provide a living.

Van der Stel never encouraged immigration. His assessment of the economic possibilities precluded it. The Cape was not a country ideally suited to settlement. The climate was, by colonial standards, benign, but geography was against productive colonization. On the slopes of Table Mountain itself there were good pastures, particularly in the valleys to the south, around Constantia. But these pastures were limited in size and, though well watered, prone to gales. Beyond that were 30 miles of sand flats, useless for agriculture. Beyond those were the mountains of the Hottentots Holland and Drakenstein, and the valleys of Olifantshoek and Waveren. These valleys were stunningly beautiful, surrounded as they were by mountains pierced by streams, but they were also at least two days' journey from the only market for thousands of miles. To the north of these fertile valleys lay more mountains, and beyond them the arid and unexplored plains of the Great Karoo; to the east, along the coast, it was known only that there was a black people much more numerous than the yellow-skinned Khoikhoi. The rivers that existed were mountain torrents and useless for navigation. There were virtually no commercially exploitable forests, except for some that were hundreds of miles to the east. The only really good harbour was at Saldanha Bay on the Atlantic coast, a hundred waterless miles away. Prospects for industry were nil. Van der Stel therefore discouraged all demands the burghers made for more European immigration.

The free burghers existed in growing isolation in their lovely Cape valleys. Their only real contact with the authorities at the Cape was in their rare forays to market. By this time their herds had increased to such an extent that they exceeded those of the Khoikhoi, or at least those Khoikhoi within a reasonable distance of Table Bay. But because land was freely available, the hunger for ever-increasing herds was hard to assuage. Many of the burghers turned from farming to a pastoralist life, not unlike that of the Khoikhoi themselves.

One of the early signs of failing Company influence was

unauthorized bartering; the colonists travelled a hundred miles and more to trade with the Khoikhoi of the interior. Stock theft by rootless Khoikhoi bands was becoming a serious problem. Even worse neighbours were the San, who roamed throughout the territory, owned no herds, hunted in small, efficient bands with bows and poisoned arrows, and tended to live in inaccessible places.

The San were not treated like Khoikhoi stock thieves, like criminals; instead they were given the same status rogue leopards had — from the early 17th century they were hunted as if they were animals. Unlike the Khoikhoi, they fought back ferociously. A poisoned arrow was one of the constant hazards of farm life, much more dangerous than the still-common leopard. Small hunting parties of burghers regularly set out, partly in search of game, especially hippos and eland, but also in search of San. The colonists developed a few eccentric offensive techniques. San arrows were deadly, but without much penetration. The hunters would advance behind a heavy woollen blanket and fire only at point-blank range. The blanket would afterwards be prickly with arrows. The white raiders would commonly kill the men and women and take home the children, who were "apprenticed" as farm labourers and usually called "tame Bushmen."

These posses were a kind of citizen militia, a rudimentary form of the paramilitary organization that was to become central to Boer society, the commando. They were used for protection and for punishment. They were virtually independent of Company control, though they were used to bring malefactors to Cape Town to be tried in Company courts (where, to the disgust of burghers, they were often let off). Bloody-mindedness among commando leaders was an early sign of free burgher independence and of their quarrels with the soft life at the Cape.

III

SIMON VAN DER STEL retired in 1699. Unlike his predecessors, he had no wish to return to Holland. He moved from the Castle, as the Cape fort had come to be known, to the splendid Constantia Valley on the south-east slopes of Table Mountain, and there he built himself the great manor house called Groot Constantia. The house was as splendid as the valley, the wine cellars more splendid yet. Even the slave quarters were splendid. There he devoted himself to farming, planting orchards and vineyards, many of them still under cultivation. He was the first — the de Villiers notwithstanding — to produce wine of exportable quality. Over the years the sweet Constantia wines gained high praise from Baudelaire, among other literary lions, and were drunk at the court of Napoleon. Administration of the colony van der Stel turned over to his son, Willem Adriaan.

Van der Stel fils was as committed to the Cape as his father. To prove it he began construction of an estate as grand as his father's, situated across the flats where the mountains of the Hottentots Holland slide gently into the sea. Vergelegen, as he called it, was built with burghers' taxes. Those burghers didn't much care for this; van der Stel, in his turn, didn't much care for them, this rabble of European cast-offs — weren't they there on Company sufferance? The market — and the governor — didn't need them. They were thieves and cheats. They robbed Hottentots in the guise of barter. They savagely beat their servants and ought to have been forcibly restrained. If they wanted to sell produce to ships they would have to get in line behind his, Willem Adriaan's, wagons.

The uproar that followed in 1705 involved most of the settlers and had an echo in a de Villiers family dispute. Abraham was the first to be caught up in it. Heemraad or no, captain in the burgher militia or no, arguments with the older van der Stel or no, he was widely regarded as a governor's toady.

The freemen had little respect for the Company, nor did they feel much allegiance to it. There were rumblings of discontent. Commandos started to form. Van der Stel attempted to head off a revolt by arresting those he believed to be leaders, locking some of them up and banishing others abroad. The incident is famous in Afrikaner history because it marked the first time a formal distinction was made between "Europeans," as represented by van der Stel and the Company, and "Afrikaners," a new designation, meaning people of that place. One of the arrested, Hendrik Bibault of Stellenbosch, is said to have denied the Company's right to arrest him because he was an Afrikaner and the Company men weren't. "Ik ben een Afrikaander!" he yelled as the sheriff arrived to flog him for "public rowdiness." It availed him as little then as similar defiant cries against the British a hundred years later did his successors. (The word "boer," which at first meant simply "farmer," is more complicated. It came to be used to describe Dutch-speaking farmers only, and among English-speakers it gradually took on a pejorative meaning, with connotations of backwardness and primitiveness. By the end of the 19th century the Afrikaners had stopped using it to describe themselves, for the most part. The term is no longer current.)

After the incident van der Stel made the mistake of banishing four men to Holland instead of to somewhere safely remote; they carried with them a petition demanding the governor's recall. Abraham de Villiers was one of the first to sign a counter-petition on behalf of the governor, but it failed: the Council of Seventeen in Holland listened to the first petitioners and ordered van der Stel's recall in 1707. The glad news was spread by young men on horseback. Most of the burghers were exultant, but not all of them. Four years later, after suffering considerable community opprobrium, Abraham de Villiers made a declaration: "I signed the petition in favour of Willem Adriaan van der Stel partly because of fear, and partly out of weakness, having many regrets for having gone to the house of Hercule de Pré where Starrenburg [the governor's agent] was staying. I had a feeling that something sinister would happen. I could well imagine that I would be asked to sign something false. I found that I had been deceived. When the document was translated into my own language I was ashamed that I had signed such a document."

Surprisingly, this weasly apology seemed to satisfy everyone. Abraham dropped out of public life and retired to two
farms called Lekkerwyn and Meerrust. His other place,
Boschendal, he turned over to his brother Jacques.

The famous victory over van der Stel and the forces of autoc-
racy didn't presage a reverence for democratic institutions at
the Cape. It did help to hasten the integration of the French
settlers into the Dutch community. It confirmed the burghers
in their growing belief that they had a right not to be pushed
around and in their contempt for the soft townies at the
Cape. It confirmed them, too, in other beliefs: that they had a
right to withdraw from alien influence and a right to use
whatever labour they pleased without interference. The only
intervention of Willem Adriaan that they cherished was his
issuance of free grazing permits for land beyond the settlement. This gave the burghers *de jure* rights over 6,000 and
more acres each, a number that was doubled in the decades to
come. The growth of the grazing lands was to become a form
of colonial expansion and was to further isolate the colonists,
both from their government and from the contamination of
fresh ideas emanating from Europe.

In 1717 the Company made a crucial decision. A report
from one of van der Stel's less pessimistic successors recommended relatively massive white immigration, arguing that a
greater population would make for a larger market, that white
artisanship should be encouraged, and that the economy
would thereby diversify agreeably. Company head office in
Holland decided that these arguments were specious. The
existing colonists were poor. The market was tiny. The only
possible exports were to the east, and the traffic between
Batavia and the Cape was minuscule. Cape Town was twice as
far from Europe as Boston was. Its purpose was still, after all,
to be a victualling station. Their decision: no immigration.

The disintegration of Khoikhoi culture and the decima-
tion of the tribe by smallpox prompted the Company to
encourage further the importation of large numbers of slaves,

and to extend credit to any farmer who wanted to buy them. It was a decision that would perpetuate a pattern already strongly imprinted on the colonists, that labour was something to be done by others. That same year, 1717, Jacques contracted with the Company for five male slaves, on credit, bought Boschendal from his surly brother, and commenced construction of a manor house of his own.

IV

ABRAHAM DE VILLIERS WAS born in 1707 on his father's farm, La Brie; he was named after his uncle, perhaps as a

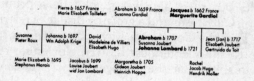

gesture of familial reconciliation. He was 10 when his father took over the farm at Boschendal. La Brie Jacques left to his eldest, Susanne, who raised cattle, vines, and vegetables there with her husband Pieter Roux. Jacques was by this time a prosperous farmer; an inventory shows he had seven slaves, 12,000 vines producing nearly 5,000 litres of wine annually, and many sheep and cattle. Jacques's net worth on his death was well over 30,000 gulders.

This kind of success wasn't at all common. Jean Le Long, the original grantee of Bossendaal, as the farm was then called, went broke; he had farmed there for 30 years but had never made a go of it, and his son Charles was a debtor to the Company all his life. Abraham senior, dispirited at the way his life had turned out, couldn't make it work either; when he sold to Jacques two years after he acquired it, he gave his wife Susanna a power of attorney to make the transfer — he couldn't quite bring himself to do the deed. He died two years later, in 1719; thereafter he drops out of Afrikaner history since he left no heirs.

The farming economy was evolving into two types. One was represented by Jacques: prosperous, bourgeois, pillar of the church, insular. The other — and the most common — was the cattle-rich poor, with a meagre home farm that was producing mostly unmarketable grains, with large herds grazing on free-lease lands, sometimes miles from home; they tended to be rootless, restless, and disgruntled, with a sense of grievance against the Company and the Castle.

The first group helped build new churches and pay the pastor's salary; the second wrapped their religion around them and took their Bibles into the bush. This group depended on the Company but hated their dependence — their ammunition pouches were stuffed with good shot from the Castle, but their aim was guided by a primitive and unwavering Calvinism and a growing dislike of restrictions of all kinds. That the Company's way of doing things seemed to guarantee their indebtedness didn't help: estate records in Cape Town show that the average debt of estates valued at 10,000 gulders was 4,170 gulders; the average debt on all estates was fully 78 per cent of gross assets.

There were members of both groups among Jacques's many descendants. A few became *trekboers*, the restless ones, "men with eyes turned north," and vanished into the wilderness. One grandson, Jan, and his heirs got Boschendal and the soft valleys of the Cape and seemed content to stay there. Abraham, from whom I come, represents the ambivalent middle: he too stayed to farm in the valley his grandfather had pioneered, but his mind, like the minds of his heirs, was always turned to the Afrikaner future in the endless north.

Jacques laid out the first manor house at Boschendal. It was built at the high end of a gentle slope. In front, he planted an avenue of oaks to frame the view down the valley of the Drakenstein; the neat vineyards at the rear contrasted with the deep folds in the mountains. Boschendal was an early example of the Cape Dutch style, a graceful amalgam that Ruskin, an admiring tourist to the Cape, later called "the only contribution to domestic architecture for several centuries." The style was consistent in all the old homes. Gwen and Gabriel Fagan, who restored the house in the 1970s and helped convert it into a museum, describe it in a pamphlet this way: "With wild country all around them, the settlers grouped the buildings into an ordered symmetry, binding them to each other and to cultivated land with linking walls and avenues of trees. It's the interlinking of manor house, outbuildings, opstal-wal [ring wall] and landscape that make Boschendal one of the most pleasing examples of the Cape Dutch style."

The style itself came from simple north European farmsteads, strongly influenced by Mediterranean building practices introduced by Provençal Huguenots like the Gardiols; this architecture gradually evolved to suit the warm climate of the Cape and the needs of an agrarian people. The Fagans wrote in their Boschendal pamphlet:

> The buildings themselves were simple structures, for they had to be constructed of materials on hand. The widths of the rooms were generous, six or seven metres, the length of obtainable beams. The traditional H shape was also dictated by available timber. Walls were massive; easily worked lime plaster allowed craftsmen, usually Malay slaves, to indulge in fanciful cornice work on the ever present gables. Everything was lime washed to keep out the drenching Cape winter rains; this unifying white gives the houses their most captivating characteristic.

Nevertheless, as many have pointed out, what impresses now is the spaciousness of these old houses and their grandeur, quite at odds with the primitive economy from which they grew.

Jacques and Marguerite lived in the manor house with their eight children. In the house also were a Malay houseboy and two Christian Hottentot girls. In a room of their own between the stables and the poultry yard were the estate cabinet-maker and craftsman, another Malay slave, and his wife, both freed later when Jacques died. Further back, towards the end of the *werf* (yard), were the dank quarters for the other male slaves. Hidden from the view of the main house was a small, squalid kraal of Hottentots, pastoralists without cattle, who had chosen service rather than retreat. Already they were no longer Khoikhoi, "Hotnots"; they were becoming *kleurlinge*, coloured people.

Relationships with these workers were still complicated by their origins and the legal fictions to which the Company still clung — that they were a free and independent people. The Boschendal group owed nominal allegiance to an offshoot of the Goriquas, whose chiefs were given a quasi-Company status when Cape Town formally recognized their accession. Estate "employees" could be fired and expelled from the estate, but "discipline" was still subject to Company monitoring; Khoikhoi could, and often did, resort to Company courts. It was a source of much grievance that the soft-living Company officials, who understood nothing of the demands of farm life, could take the word of idle heathens against free burghers. Occasionally a farmer would be whipped for maltreating servants, and once or twice offenders were actually stripped of their assets and banished for repeated offences. Nothing like this seems to have happened at Boschendal; at least there is no record of it, and the relatively high rate of manumission for slaves at the farm argues against it.

Chapter 3

The establishment of the Way: how the tribe became Africans; the lure of the endless blue horizons; first contact with black Africa

I

THE FAMILIAL PATTERNS are intricate, but revelatory of the state of the colony at the time. The family was already spreading out over the Drakenstein Valley, turning it into a sort of de Villiers fief. Jacques's son Abraham became heemraad in his turn; so did his brothers David and Jan. Later in his life, at a time when he was charitably called "elderly," Abraham was a captain in the burgher militia's Drakenstein company. For most of his life, he farmed at De Goede Hoop, within sight of the manor at Boschendal (already earmarked for his son Jan). Abraham married his first cousin once removed, Susanna Joubert, herself the daughter of first cousins. That wasn't all. When Susanna died in childbirth Abraham took as a second wife Johanna Lombard, daughter of his brother Jacobus's wife, Louise, from her first marriage. Abraham's other brother, David, had already married his first cousin, Madeleine de Villiers.

Abraham and Johanna had 12 children; no fewer than six of these married back into the de Villiers clan (Jan married Anna de Villiers; Izaak married Ester Maria de Villiers; Johanna married Pieter de Villiers, her cousin once removed; Maria Elizabeth married Jan de Villiers, her first cousin; Rachel married Petrus Johannes de Villiers, a mere second cousin once removed; and Magdalena married another Petrus Johannes de Villiers). Of Jacques and Marguerite's 32 grandchildren, 12 married back into the family. (The family

Trekboers in the western Cape

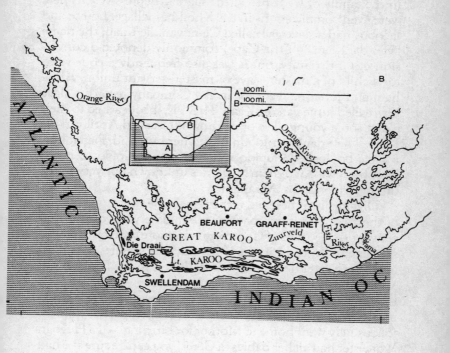

Trekboers in the Cape province

has not spent too much time mulling over the genetic implications of all this inbreeding, though Dan de Villiers, in his family history, did admit to having seen more than his share in the family of what he called "maniac depressives.") There were even complications in the Khoikhoi village. Louise and Jacobus had a slave girl called Clara van die Kaap; the name "van die Kaap" (of the Cape) commonly denoted a conversion to Christianity, but it was also frequently a code-word for a child of a master–slave or master–servant union. Abraham and Johanna recorded in the Company records a slave boy, called Junie van die Kaap. They also bequeathed to their eldest son a young slave of unknown sex called April van die Kaap. Their daughter Johanna and her husband, Pieter, kept a slave boy called Cupido van die Kaap; Cupido seems to have been willed to them by parties unknown but very likely, on the evidence, by Abraham.

Digging into these old records makes it easy to get a sense of the colony as it approached the middle years of the 18th century — 100 years of Company rule, more than 60 of *familie* settlement. Already, in the tribal way, the families were clustering into extended clans: the de Villiers in the Drakenstein Valley, the Hugos in Worcester, the Jouberts in Swellendam, the du Toits at Tulbagh, the van der Merwes at Ceres. Tracking the birth records makes the patterns obvious: the womenfolk usually went home to Mother for birthing — if a Hugo in Worcester had all her babies in Ceres, you can be sure she had been a van der Merwe.

A generation later the pattern became even more pronounced. There were de Villiers families everywhere in Drakenstein, Stellenbosch, Bottelary, and Paarl. Tax records collected by the local *veld-cornet* (a kind of sheriff's officer), C. A. Haupt, listed dozens of them, along with their slaves, servants, wagons, stock, and vines. The farm names soon changed from the nostalgic French to local Dutch. Haupt — who also married a de Villiers, Anna Gertruida — listed in and around the little village of Groot Drakenstein de Villiers farms called Lekkerwyn, Zandvliet, Goede Hoop, Dwars

Rivier, Papiermolen, Rustenvrede, Nieuwe Dorp, Wolvekloof; near Stellenbosch were Brandwacht, Helderenberg, Deel Versaagt, and many more.

The patterns have little in common with the self-assertive awareness of the American Pilgrims, who were already casting and recasting the ideas and the phrases that were to result in their declaration of the notion of inherent rights for all men. The farmers of the Cape, isolated, cut off from the intellectual development of Europe, tucked into their folds in the southern mountains, days from Cape Town, were yet irrevocably tied to an effete (and, to them, arrogant) bureaucracy in the Castle by their need for a market and by the cumbersome system of Company monopolies, maintained even after the departure of the unlamented Willem Adriaan van der Stel.

Drakenstein, Wagonmaker's Valley, Tulbagh, Paarl — the valleys slowly filled with farmsteads, pushing north to the Hex River and the passes to the plains of the Karoo. For another hundred years afterwards there were virtually no roads, and what few existed were little more than cattle tracks, climbing over projecting crags, descending abruptly to the riverbed, the wagons and their loads having to be dismantled on each crossing and strapped to the backs of the plodding oxen. A contemporary traveller wrote of the mountains that they were "huddled together and tower up overhead in grand and wild confusion — the cliffs, the peaks and crags seeming to topple every way." Cut off as they were, it made less and less sense to the burghers that the Company should have any say in their governance; it made less and less sense that they should be tied to the tidy slopes of Table Mountain, huddled around the very south of the continent, when the northern farmers were beginning to turn their eyes farther north and east, to the limitless horizon, to the lands open to a limitless future.

Travellers' tales were already spreading: a few had passed the Great River, as the Orange was called, and although there were tall tales of horror ("a leather thong left outside for an hour in the sun shrivels and falls to dust when picked up, so hot is it"), there were also wonderful stories of the open spaces and the hunting to be done (one traveller in the course of a week shot three elephants, two rhinos, a giraffe, and 10 hippos). Land seemed to go on forever. To these trekboers, grazers and farmers, any groping towards freedom would be freedom to be left alone, freedom to be ignored. Land was there for the taking, so they took it; sullen quarrels erupted if a farmer could see his neighbour's smoke on the horizon; it meant the neighbour had come too close. Farms were staked out by riding into the endless faded horizons and stopping when enough space had been established. There the patriarch and his family, his many sons and daughters, his families of Hottentot retainers, set up their wagons and then their mud-and-wattle huts, and unpacked their rifles and their Bibles.

Their way of life was little different from the ways of the Khoikhoi, who had been on the land for millennia: a nascent society already fragmented into clans, small, insular, fierce in defence of their territory, inward-looking and parochial, deeply identified with the land. Their religion reinforced their way of life. The Confession of Dort, a sophisticated abstraction by Protestant theologians of the essence of the revolt against the corrupt church, was in this endless, drought-prone landscape reduced to its elements. The patriarch doubled as theologian, and theologian as Arm of God. The word was law, and his was the word. One had only to fear the wrath of God and obey his commandments. More learning was not necessary. Only the Bible travelled. Other books were too much excess baggage; they remained in the Cape.

The country imposed itself on them. These were not the rain-drenched pastures of Table Bay or even of Fransch Hoek. Land was endless and so was pasture, but drought was a factor, and the search for water became at first a preoccupation and then an obsession. Some years the rains never came, the rivers and *spruits* dried up, the grasses shrivelled, the wild springbok vanished, the land faded, the sky turned steely blue, the earth cracked; sometimes the locusts came and the crops vanished. There were years when the horses abruptly died, the crops died, the grasses died; only the San and their poisoned arrows stubbornly survived. An anxious British traveller, George Thompson, returning across the platteland from the frontier town of Beaufort, remarked on how the Karoo was "most dismally parched up . . . so precarious are the rains in this quarter that none had fallen, as I was told, for three years." Then, in the good years when the rain came, the arid Karoo bloomed in a carpet of brilliant colour; the rivers ran and the *vleis*, the soft marshes, were filled with sweet water; the miracle of the wildflowers, the dusty plains transformed into a garden larger than a man's imagination, filled the farmers with fierce exultation.

II

AT THE CAPE, the Dutch East India Company continued its by now venerable practice of victualling passing ships, entertaining their sailors in town taverns and brothels, and justifying fiscal losses to an increasingly irritated home office. Company servants maintained their monopoly over commerce, though it no longer made any sense. Life in the kremlin at the Cape was less and less in touch with reality as it became more and more refined and decadent. The futility of their efforts to maintain any vestige of control over the trekboers melting away into the endless horizons had not yet been admitted. Still, the bureaucracy was confined to matters affecting the port; agents of the company were hard pressed to administer Stellenbosch, never mind the frontier with its extraordinarily low population densities. The land-grant system then in effect, the legacy of van der Stel fils, entitled each farmer to what was now regarded as a minimum of 6,000 acres; Company "control" by the middle of the century consisted mostly of recognizing the occupation of a new farm; the paperwork followed the reality by several months or even years, since it could take a farmer several months just to get back to Cape Town to register a claim. The trekboers' population density was even lower than that of their predecessors, the nomadic Khoikhoi, though their way of life differed only slightly. Even in the south-western regions, where the rainfall was steady, population density varied from one person per four square miles to one per six or seven square miles.

The trekboer withdrawal was no mass movement. There was nothing organized about it. Individuals and families simply exercised their restlessness and rootlessness and moved off into the yonder. The de Villiers family was torn; contemporary documents speak longingly of the north, and the family began to collect travellers' tales. Jacques's son Abraham remained a farmer at De Goede Hoop. His son Abraham, the third generation, moved only a few miles, and that in a south-westerly direction, to Klapmuts on the road to Stellenbosch, where he bought a farm he called Nattevlei. He moved south,

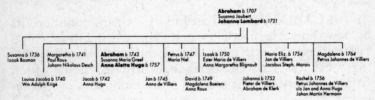

but his heart was always on the frontier.

He married into the Greef family of Stellenbosch, but Susanna Greef died childless a few years later and he remarried, this time into the prolific and restless Hugo family; his young wife Anna Aletta Hugo, a van der Merwe through her mother's line, was born at Tulbagh but her parents had already moved to the pass to the Karoo, at Hex Rivier, where they farmed at a place called Hartebeestekraal, on the slopes of the mountains they called simply Agter Hexriviersberge, or "behind Hex River mountain." The Hugos were already tied into the de Villiers family by several marriages, and the two families kept intersecting for the next three generations, preserving the restlessness of the young men — already by 1750 there were Hugos in the far interior, north of Beaufort on the approaches to the Orange River, and by the turn of the century Hugos (and the other families bound to the de Villiers by marriage, the Jouberts, Lombards, Rouxs, and van der Merwes) had made it to the north-eastern frontier region, near what was to be called Graaff-Reinet. The younger Abraham and his own sons followed their progress with fascination.

This progress was relentless. In the 1740s the trekboers had crossed the Langeberg Mountains; by 1760 they had pushed north-west beyond the Cedarberg and Bokkeveldberg mountains towards the Buffalo River, almost halfway towards the mouth of the Orange, and were on the Gamka River in the Great Karoo. To the east they were at the marvellous mountain amphitheatre called. Camdebo (later Graaff-Reinet) by the mid 1760s and had entered the Zuurveld, on the banks of the Fish River, by the late 1770s. There, for the moment, they stopped: behind the Fish and Keiskama rivers were the Xhosa, a black tribe of the Nguni group, an opponent more numerous and more formidable by far than the Khoikhoi or the Bushmen; by 1780 a conflict had been engaged that has yet to be resolved by the agents of apartheid and their heirs.

The trekboers were not quite free of the effete south. They lived off the land in a way unthought of by the first Huguenot settlers, but they needed some of the products of European civilization, notably coffee, salt, ammunition, tobacco, and sugar. And they still maintained a curious formal reliance on Cape paperwork. They might settle on a farm, but they always, in the end, demanded paper to validate it; they were individualists but they very early developed the fascination for formal process that was later to find its full flowering in the intricate codification of apartheid legislation. There were virtually no services in the interior, no schools, and hardly any churches; services were usually performed by the patriarch on the *plaas* (farm), and only occasionally some itinerant preacher would wander by. Marriages needed a licence from the Castle, yet the mores of the frontier allowed young cou-

ples to marry first and collect paper afterwards; there are
numerous files in the Cape archives in which veteran mar-
rieds registered their vows and the birth-dates of their many
children at the same time, up to a dozen years after the fact.

Here's a typical declaration, from the records in the Swellendam archives:

> We, Philip Lemmetjies and Maria van Deventer, here truly and
> faithfully swear that we, Philip Lemmetjies and Maria van
> Deventer, on the 15th day of January in the year 1824, or
> thereabouts, at Groot Swartberg, did with each other wed, and
> that we have had in this marriage 5 children with each other,
> namely,
>
> Kupido — 11 years old
> David — 9 years old
> Philip — 7 years old
> Put — dead
> Rachel — 7 months old
>
> Dated at Swellendam, 10 April 1839.
> Witnesses: G.F. Martins and J.G. Wuteen
> The married couple, their marks: Xs.

Paper was important, but clearly they were in no tearing rush
to get it. Other young couples undertook the three-week to
three-month journey to Table Bay to pick up their licences.
Early writers marvelled at the distances travelled; on the
other hand it must have been a wonderful relief for young
people, especially the women, to escape the drudgery and
hardship of frontier farming, if only for a while. There were
other reasons for the long journey too. Economically it made
little sense for farmers to spend months on the road, winch-
ing their wagons up and down mountains, just to get their
produce to market; but they needed the trade. For young
people, it was pure joy.

Abraham de Villiers, Jacques's grandson, was by then
living a settled life on Nattevlei (he had built a gracious
whitewashed homestead, almost as grand as Boschendal), but
what little of his own jottings survives mentions mostly visit-

ing relatives; the Hugos were already at Beaufort, and we know something of the way of life from fragments left behind and from the journals of travellers, now filed in the Cape archives.

That life was monotonous, a product of isolation and the rigour of the land. A family rarely saw anyone outside the immediate circle except on Sundays. The social graces were lacking because there was no time to practise them. Life was especially hard for the women. The men spent months in the saddle, supervising stock, hunting, exploring; the women stayed home, raising large broods and supervising the Khoikhoi who did most of the actual work; it had already become a fixed part of the natural order of things that physical labour was performed by others. Few family documents remain from the frontier: we have only a fragment, Anna Aletta's recording of a note from an unknown relative, that expressed a "bitter fear" on seeing a puff of dust on a distant horizon. Such dust, kicked up by a horse at full gallop, commonly meant evil news: either a report of a hunting accident in the far interior involving a husband or a son or, much worse, the appearance of a raiding party of "wild Hottentots," which usually meant San. Under such circumstances the arrival of strangers meant danger: the first response was to call in the servants and reach for the guns.

There were occasionally more pleasant visitors. There were tourists, even then, sometimes a Swede or two, or an Englishman, someone from France, maybe a German. All these outsiders commented on two things: the remarkable hospitality of the trekboers to strangers, and their poverty.

The hospitality was legendary. Travellers were fed as much local produce as could be found, mutton, curried beef flavoured with cumin and coriander, apricots, wicked fruit brandies — a frontier cuisine strongly influenced by Malay and Batavian touches. Anna Aletta's kitchen at Klapmuts, supervised by herself and run by Malay slaves, produced many memorable feasts for visitors, typical of the meals given travellers throughout the colony. For openers, a mutton curry soup, flavoured with cumin and tamarind. Another mutton dish would follow, accompanied by vegetable pickles called *blatjang*, and Indonesian preserves made from onion, small fishes, and hot peppers. Chilis were torn in shreds and scattered on the meat as seasoning; the Boers had robust palates. A roast bird or pig would follow, usually with preserved fruits as accompaniment. Small meat pastries and bowls of fresh fruit completed the meal — melons, grapes, mulberries, figs, bananas, peaches, and apricots were common, the fruit of the cactus less so. Oranges were still rare. Farm wine would always be provided except in the hot interior, when fruit cordials or villainous tea were the usual drinks. After dinner there was invariably a *soopie*, a tot of brandy, drunk neat: only the English, the saying went, murder good brandy by adding water. Visitors could stay as long as they wished — and they did, sometimes for weeks or months. Many took the chance to go hunting with their hosts — as with the Xhosa, hunting was a fierce passion among the young men that had only partially to do with putting food on the table.

A traveller from Germany, Henry Lichtenstein, has left an account of a tour he made later in the century (in the 1790s) through the Karoo from Graaff-Reinet in the north-east to Cape Town. Midway through his journey he arrived at a farm called Die Draai, where Abraham's daughter Johanna Susanna lived. She was married to a Bek (also spelled Beck, or Bekker); her mother-in-law was sometimes referred to as "the widow Bekker." "Our hopes of finding at this place, which was one of considerable note, the rest and refreshment we began very much to want, was cruelly damped on our arrival," he lamented. "Nobody was at home, everything was locked up, no bed, no supper was to be obtained, excepting by breaking the house open. A couple of slaves said that their master and mistress had gone out on a little ride. We inquired, whither?— the answer was, into the country of Zwellendam, so this little ride was a distance of perhaps 15 German miles."

Everywhere, Lichtenstein noted ruefully and admiringly,

people went on these "little rides," some of them lasting a week or more. "In fact, by this expression is to be understood the friendly visits made to connections and acquaintances, and such kind of journeys form the principal amusement of the colonists." The whole family, he observed, set out, the women and the children each having their own horses; they would travel 40 or more miles, visit for an afternoon, ride the 40 miles back. When at one point the traveller professed himself too exhausted for such a journey, his hostess told him blandly that "after every lying-in, and this had hitherto been an annual ceremony with her, she rode on the second or third Sunday herself with the child to have it baptized at Roode-zand [30 miles away]. She had a very safe horse, she said, which carried her so well over the mountains between her house and Roodezand that she could go and return in the same day, and she was never afraid of suckling her child even in the wildest parts." Lichtenstein later in his travels passed by another leathery old relative, Tannie (Auntie) Anna, the widow of a de Klerk (it was she who once had a slave castrated for impregnating too many female slaves); she was 75 when she last made the two-week trip to Cape Town by oxcart: she had been alone throughout the trip.

The German visitor was a sympathetic traveller, but he was pleased to get back to Cape Town. The rugged Afrikaner hospitality palled:

In a country where there are no places of amusement, where there are no popular festivals, no fairs, where there is not even such a thing as a tavern, and where dancing and all sports are everywhere, except at Cape Town and in its neighbourhood, regarded as inconsistent with decorum, scarcely any mode of recreation remains but such kind of visits. People amuse each other in the best manner they are able; relate all the recent family occurrences, lament the absent neighbours, and the like; and when conversation begins to flag, the scene is relieved by having recourse to the exercises of devotion. The whole company seat themselves around a table and sing psalms; or one reads a sermon, or some chapters from the Bible; a ceremony which is performed commonly each evening even when there are no visitors.

Every morning the scene was repeated: family, children, slaves, servants all gathered for the patriarchal homilies. Morning services, evening services, the patriarch's limited repertoire of sermons, the slaves hauled in to kneel for devotions — it all began to grate. Lichtenstein was relieved to be able to attend a wedding — "when the whole tribe [was] invited, and feasted for several days together." These clans were huge: so many cousins and uncles and sons were there, with so few Christian names to share among them, that the farmers were commonly called by their farm names to distinguish them: Jan Druk-my-niet, Abraham Natte Vallei, Jacobus Hierverdwaal . . . Commenting on the apparently endless Huguenot clans — the de Villiers, Rousseau, Joubert, and Le Roux families — Lichtenstein saw in them nothing of the "French national character": "Like all other settlers here, they are become entirely Africans."

The obverse of the hospitality towards strangers was an extreme individualism; quarrels with neighbours were frequent and seldom patched up. These quarrels were a long time in the making and conducted with old-fashioned gravity (many early travellers noted with amusement that the developing patois contained virtually no swear words).

Nevertheless, the sense of community was strong. It was expressed best in the *nagmaal* communion services held four times a year in the frontier towns. Everyone attended. People came for miles — sometimes travelling for up to a week to get there. At first these quarterly fairs were held on a neighbouring farm — anywhere from 4 to 30 miles away. Eventually communities, small towns called *dorps* in Afrikaans, sprang up. They played a crucial role in Afrikaner society. The rich and poor alike would be drawn to the dorp for nagmaal, as would the pious and the non-pious, the educated and the obdurate.

Andrew Murray, the influential Dutch Reformed preacher (and, typically, a relative: he was my grandmother's grandfather), left some notes on the curious citizens sometimes to be found at nagmaal. Commonly they would believe the earth to be flat, the blacks to be suffering the eternal torment of God's wrath (and, of course, serve them right, the cattle-thieving heathen!), and Canaan to be just *oor 'n bult of twee*, over a rise or two, within the reach of a determined man's wagon. All these people would be doing business in town, taking communion at least twice, meeting old friends and making new ones, eating and drinking hugely, indulging in *volkspele*, formal folk dances; nagmaal services were at the heart of the primitive Calvinism of the people, but the dances and the social occasions were as vital to their lives. What went on afterwards in the wagons, stables, and hayricks had little to do with religion and everything to do with the urgent need among the young to find mates; even funerals didn't attract this many people to one place, and for some young folk the nagmaal represented their only chance to meet others their age.

There was little for young people to do in the colony other than become semi-nomadic stock farmers. They had the skills and temperament that allowed them to thrive in the harsh interior, but those skills hardly permitted them any other outlet. A hundred years after the colony was founded, opportunities for the kind of intensive wine and vegetable farming practised by Jacques and his son Abraham were closed off; that kind of land had been taken up. There was nothing to do in Cape Town, and, because of the self-sufficiency of the Boers, there were few chances to practise as artisans. There were no apprenticeship positions open. Occasionally a need arose from the limited economy for a craftsman but the unlettered frontiersmen couldn't compete against an artisan imported from Holland, or against skilled slaves or free blacks. It was no longer possible to fulfil everyman's dream of van Riebeeck's day and become a tavernkeeper; a rich and self-perpetuating middle class of merchants had emerged and was dominating trade in the capital. Fishing, another possible outlet and a growing industry, had become the trade of free blacks. And manual labour . . . in a slave society like the Cape, physical labour was slave work and not open to free burghers.

The system therefore perpetuated itself. The trekboers, romanticized by Afrikaner historians into little more than sturdy, liberty-loving, hospitable individualists, in fact developed the worst kind of agriculture for southern African conditions, coming as they did somewhere between the settled farmers of the south (who had the capital, and developed the know-how, to improve and intensively cultivate their land) and the Khoikhoi (who were more truly nomadic and moved on before their stock-grazing damaged the veld). The trekboers built houses, rudimentary as they were, and stayed in one place long enough for their herds to cause severe damage to the environment. The contemporary reports that commented on the extreme poverty of the inhabitants often expressed shock at how the landscape had deteriorated. The Afrikaners' intense involvement and identification with the land was a love less for the land than for the idea of the landscape, with its endless vistas and apparently endless opportunities for withdrawal. Separation has always seemed to the Afrikaners a legitimate option.

III

THE FARM OF Abraham de Villiers fils and Anna Aletta at Nattevlei was, from the meagre accounts available, a gracious thing. Abraham had been left several thousand gulders and a wagon in his father's will, if little else; but by the time his children were teenagers the farm was prospering, selling wine in the barrel to factors from Cape Town and planting what were among the first apple orchards in the colony. The house was smaller than Boschendal's, though as comfortable. They lived in a house they built themselves, using furniture they made themselves, and ate food they grew (or shot) themselves. But it's clear that the family was restless; their lives didn't seem as settled as those of some of the prosperous burghers of the valley.

Abraham was often away. He went on several punitive expeditions against San stock thieves, one ranging as far as the Cedarberg Mountains in the north, where they pursued (and lost) the wily hunters among the gigantic boulders that littered the landscape. Another expedition was recorded to the Nieuwveld Mountains north of the arid flat called the Klein (Little) Karoo; several hundred cattle were "recovered" and a dozen "apprentices" brought back. The San men were shot. (In the last decade of the century, when the colony had been taken over by the English, George Thompson, the English tourist, was taken aback, as well he might be, at how common these raids were. He wrote in his journal: "July 2. In the afternoon I left Beaufort in a waggon drawn by six horses. I was accompanied by three boors [*sic*], one of whom informed me, in the course of conversation, that he had lately been out on commando against the Bushman, in which 30 of those unfortunate creatures were shot; namely, 26 men, two women and two children! This is truly a shocking system . . . still continued under the beneficent sway of England . . . ")

Stock theft was to be a major problem on the frontier beyond the century's end, beneficent sway of England or no. In 1780 there were still roving bands of Khoikhoi and San bent on stealing, and raids from Xhosa country were becoming commonplace. Anna Aletta was twice visited by female relatives who had accompanied their husbands to Cape Town on marketing expeditions lest they be attacked in the farmer's absence; all trekboers had neighbours or friends whose farms were raided or burned to the ground. It was a major source of grievance with the frontier farmers that the government — the Company and its servants — was unable or unwilling to defend its citizens against predators. Several times the anger spilled over into active revolt, as we shall see. Always it simmered below the surface. The Boers responded to provocation in two ways: by sullen defiance of the Company in its other manifestations (such as tax collecting) and by inventing a form of defence that was wonderfully suited to the country and that would a century later help them hold off a militarily sophisticated empire: out of their primitive citizen militias, they invented the commando.

The commando was a small, informal, strike force under the leadership of whatever local personality seemed appropriate. It was highly mobile, able to live off the land, to disperse and regroup at will, to melt into the landscape at need, to revert to being simple farmers when necessary, able to move swiftly and strike sharply at agreed-upon targets. There were overtones of feudalism in the system (service in a commando was owed by all burghers). It was also explicitly tribal in its clan linkages. The same tactics were adopted by some roving bands of Bastaards, the self-adopted name of clans of mixed European and Khoikhoi ancestry. The Boer commandos ranged widely afield, from the Cedarberg in the west to the Zuurveld in the east; they must have been a terrifying sight for the remaining peaceful bands of Khoikhoi clinging precariously to ever-diminishing free land; a commando that failed to find cattle thieves often took cattle where they found them. Who was to stop them? The Khoikhoi nursed their grievances but under the Company had few options.

There were also non-punitive forays to be made. Bands of Boer cattle traders routinely penetrated deep into Xhosa territory. As far as we know Abraham never ventured across the Fish River, the Xhosa boundary, but he did accompany a small party that pushed far into the interior and crossed the Orange River chasing after game; they found scattered bands of Khoikhoi and, to the east, rumours of larger kingdoms made up of substantial cities. These were presumably of the tribe anthropologists call the South Sotho, though there is no hard evidence for this. The party never made contact with blacks in the northern reaches.

By 1780 the restless Boers with their constant demands for new land were already turning their thoughts beyond the Orange River, hundreds of miles to the north. It was an old family dream to find the source of the Nile, though they seem to have had no inkling of how far it really was. Later settlers located Nylstroom (Nile stream) not far from Johannesburg; they truly thought they had discovered the headwaters of the great river. Whenever things weren't going well in the south, when frustration with the inept government of the Company boiled over, when fury at the ever-increasing Xhosa raiders could no longer be contained, when fear of San arrows and their quick death permeated the mind's landscape, the Boer imagination always turned to the north, where he could carve out for himself a home that was his alone, where he would be left in peace, where his fierce identification with the veld could be expressed; he looked always to some mythical republic of the imagination, to some imagined Land of Beulah where he would be master. And he looked also, of course, to a place where pedlars with lots of ammunition would frequently visit. The Boers didn't wish to be totally cut off from the products of civilization. They just wanted to damp the interference level and filter out the anxiety. It was the Zeitgeist of the tribe.

IV

IN THE 1760s racial attitudes in South Africa were still fluid; 30 years later they were considerably less so.

By the 1790s there were 21,000 free people in the colony and already more than 25,000 slaves. The number of Khoi-khoi servants is not known, since there was never any registry; their condition would have varied from that of clients, bound by a kind of loose allegiance in which work was exchanged for protection, to quasi-slavery. The colony was of course driven by slavery from the very beginning, a policy deliberately pursued by the Dutch, who were simply bringing to the Cape their experience in many other colonies (mostly in the East but also in north-east Brazil). It was the importation of slaves that complicated the Cape's ethnic mix, which to that point had been fairly simple.

The first two shiploads of slaves in the two decades after

the colony was founded were from West Africa (Angola and Dahomey), but thereafter most came from the slaving ports of Madagascar and Indonesia. Fully two-thirds of Cape slaves were Madagascan in origin, brought in after agriculture became established in the second half of the 18th century. Javanese slaves brought with them Islam, which flourished in the slave lodges. Caste hierarchies were soon established: West Africans tended to do the dirtiest, roughest work; the Indonesians were the skilled craftsmen. The lingua franca in the slave lodge was at first a patois of Portuguese and later the emerging version of Dutch that was to evolve into Afrikaans.

Also in the 1790s, a more complex stratification process was under way in Cape Town. About 10 per cent of urban marriages crossed colour lines, usually joining white men and the offspring of slave–white unions, and there were still numerous incidents where religion took primacy over race — the alchemy of Christianity converting black into white — but they were diminishing. Rules of racial conduct were beginning to emerge, and if the freewheeling population still paid little attention to the rules, the preconditions for codification were being worked out. White attitudes towards free blacks were shifting as the class system developed; the blacks were emerging as a proletariat. Attitudes towards the Khoikhoi were more complicated, since in town they were blending into an undifferentiated *kleurling* population, European in culture, urban in nature, imitative in character; here are the seeds of the Afrikaner attitude towards "coloureds" as "brown cousins," not very different but not similar either, an ambiguity of perception that persists into modern times.

By the 1790s a complicated society was emerging in the town, which was still clustered around the docks and the governor's house within the fort. At the apex of the social pyramid were the senior Company servants surrounding the governor. They spoke a modified low Portuguese and also a Dutch of an almost ostentatious refinement, considering that many of them by this time were not Hollanders at all but had been brought up in company stations in the East; most aimed to retire to estates in Java rather than to the Netherlands. Some had built magnificent houses on the Oranjezicht slopes of Table Mountain overlooking the harbour and the Castle. They formed a small, inbred clique, whose social arrangements were intricate, decadent, a complicated *pavane* of status-seeking and privilege. The Eastern influence was clear in the Malay workmanship of the gables of the new houses, and to some extent in the developing cuisine in which Oriental spices played a significant role.

Below this class was an emerging group of substantial merchants. On a social level with them were the wealthy farmers of the near hinterland; when Jan inherited Boschendal from his father, Abraham, it was already valued at 40,000 gulders, a pretty fair sum. The rest of the urban population consisted of the merchant class who ran the Tavern of the Seas — tavern-keepers, victuallers, hoteliers, brothel-keepers, tradesmen; free burghers who for lack of training drifted into shop-keeping; free blacks, some of them well off (some kept slaves of their own), who made their living as craftsmen, fishermen (even fleet-owners), middlemen, and tradesmen; the garrison; convicts, rounders, and rogues of every description; and, of course, the slaves. There were also a few Asian political exiles, some of them eminent Indonesian princes with a hundred and more slaves, who lived out their lives without much affecting the colony; there were two such estates on Robben Island. A larger group of Asians came in chains as convicts. Many of these did not live long enough to complete their sentences. Those who did generally joined the Cape's many rogues and trouble-makers. The law-abiding ex-convicts were just as much trouble. The Council of Policy, as the Company executive arm was called, demanded that they be taken back to their place of sentence: "After their sentence has expired they become free and remain free, competing with the poor whites of European descent in procuring their livelihood, and [are] consequently very injurious to the latter."

In the countryside around Stellenbosch and Paarl, which

included the settled and prosperous farmers of the Drakenstein Valley, attitudes were much more rigid than in town.
These substantial burghers looked down on the loose living
in Cape Town; they developed a society formal in its conser-
vatism, stratified in its social relations, orthodox in its Calvinism; it was a slave-owning population that treated its
Khoikhoi retainers as people without resources of their own,
to be looked after, disciplined, educated, and controlled.
Intermarriage and sex across the colour line were increasingly
rare, possibly because the sex ratios in the white population
were more nearly equal than in other parts of the colony. The
Khoikhoi came into contact with whites only as servants; the
aspects of European culture they assimilated most rapidly
were the craft skills useful in marketing themselves as labour
— masonry, plasterwork, carpentry, weaving, and others.

Almost every farmer of substance had slaves. Their pri-
mary tasks were domestic service and agriculture, but there
were specialist workers too; there are suggestions, though no
real evidence, that Boschendal had two musician slaves in
addition to a mason, a brickmaker, a wagon-master, and
others. The Madagascans were preferred in the countryside.
The Asians were unreliable. In 1767 the Company had forbidden the importation of any more Eastern male slaves after
a series of violent crimes in the hinterlands. These crimes
found an echo in old family documents. Charl Marais, who
married Abraham senior's cousin Marie, was beaten to death
by four slaves on his farm; a post-mortem report by the
French-speaking surgeon Jean Prieur du Plessis survives in
the Cape archives, describing in clinical detail the wounds
inflicted. Abraham's cousin Jan married Anna Hugo, cousin
to Anna Aletta, and lived on a farm at Vlottenberg in the
Stellenbosch district. We know nothing about them except a
notation in the archive: "Cruelly murdered by their slaves."

Slave escapes were common. Some simply enlisted as sailors on visiting ships, whose captains were usually desperate
for able-bodied help and were prepared to risk the penalties
for discovery, which included the confiscation of the ship's

cargo. Other slaves fled into the mountains; some eluded their captors for weeks, but most were hunted down by posses using Khoikhoi trackers. Slave-owners were required by law to report a runaway immediately, and punishment was severe for farmers who employed escapees. Slaves who informed on runaways were always rewarded, in some cases with manumission.

It's one of the commonplaces of South African history that in the early years the colony was segregated not on racial but on religious grounds; the example of Eva, the Khoikhoi who was baptized and married a white, was always trotted out as evidence. Even with the Khoikhoi this is only partly true. With slaves, matters were more ambiguous still. The idea of enslaving Christians was looked on with more and more revulsion in Europe, and in all Dutch colonies there were pressures to free baptized slaves. In 1770 the requirement to do so was made explicit. Instead of this leading to more manumissions, however, it led to fewer baptisms; farmers were not wonderfully keen, despite their explicit Christian duty to bring heathen into the fold, to do themselves out of a work-force. Commerce, as it usually does, proved a force superior to conscience.

Freed slaves became "free blacks," not free burghers — the colony maintained the Roman distinction between freemen and freedmen. Freedmen — and free blacks generally — had considerable rights. They could buy and sell property, own businesses, farm, borrow money, initiate court cases, attend church, have their own militia under free black officers. But if the law was officially colour blind, the practice was different. Farmers ran the economy and dominated society, and since blacks never established themselves as farmers, their influence was limited to town: they could do well enough in the Tavern of the Seas but never managed any real impact on the colony as a whole. (This also explains why Cape Town, a racially more freewheeling city than the towns of the stiff-necked interior, resisted apartheid longer than anywhere else.) There were numerous marriages between white settlers and free blacks (though only half a dozen between black men and white women), and the progeny of white–slave unions themselves frequently married back into the white community. By the second half of the century the visual distinctions were becoming almost as meaningless as they were when the apartheid Population Registration Act tried to sort them out 200 years later.

Until about the middle of the 18th century there is little evidence of "racist" thinking (in the modern sense of the word). And after about 1760, when it did start to appear, it was almost always in response to a perceived threat of social disintegration. At the same time, the official attitudes were becoming less tolerant: in 1765 a decree had prohibited free black women from appearing in public in "coloured silk clothing, hoopskirts, fine laces, adorned bonnets, curled hair or ear rings"; this was intended to prevent them from considering themselves not only on a par with "respectable burgers' wives but often even above them." By the 1790s another disturbing — and, to modern ears, depressingly familiar — decree was published in an effort to "control vagrancy": free blacks had henceforth to carry passes if they wished to leave town.

On the frontier, among the trekboers, things were very different. Their connections to European culture were tenuous and increasingly irrelevant. Company officials and visitors to the interior routinely expressed alarm at the rapidity with which the frontiersmen were abandoning everything "European"; visitors to Cape Town from abroad were regaled with often lurid tales of how the frontiersmen had already sunk to the level of the squalid Hotnot, and there were occasional schemes floated to save them from themselves by separating them from Khoikhoi or even — a radical notion! — from slave labour.

These not-yet-apartheid schemes, as separatist schemes so often do, entirely missed the point, which was that the trekboers had become Africans. Their economy was African. Their loyalties were to the place in which they found themselves, their dreams and songs were of the blue horizons of the north, their art, such as it was, invoked the landscape and their cattle, their hopes were for escape from the dead hand of the Company and the deadly predations of the San and Xhosa cattle raiders. Their houses were usually a few rooms with mud walls and a reed mat for a front door. Only their Bibles gave them a thin, tenuous link with literacy and the larger ideas of the outside world.

On the very fringes of the northern and north-western frontiers, the trekboers often lived in the open, or in their wagons; some set up house with a Khoikhoi wife. The trekboer culture merged with the Bastaards while it created them; even in the larger houses Khoikhoi and trekboers all lived together indiscriminately. They learned from the Khoikhoi matters of survival in the veld that would become essential items of frontier lore — the storing of milk in skin sacks, the sun-drying of strips of game later called *biltong*. Anders Sparrman, an 18th-century traveller who wrote in French, noticed how often sheepskin clothing was worn, and how the trekboers had adopted the Khoikhoi sandal made from cattle skin, which were called *velskoene*, skin shoes, later corrupted by the English to *veldskoene*, or veld shoes. There is at least one recorded instance of a trekboer marrying the daughter of a Nama chief in a Khoikhoi ceremony, and later conducting himself like a Khoikhoi ruler. But generally the trekboers didn't "go native" in the traditional sense of adopting native culture. Instead, they created their own *African* culture.

On the eastern and north-eastern frontier near the Xhosa vanguard, the farms were larger and more prosperous, and more settled. The trekboers here often had substantial investments in slaves; they were developing their own code of labour — and therefore interracial — ethics; the proper (though seldom attained) relationship between master and servant was one of courteous authority and respectful servitude. Their developing attitude towards the Xhosa, whom they could sense massing across the slender barrier of the great Fish River, was one of respect and some fear, though coloured by their already developed assumptions of superiority vis-à-vis native peoples, assumptions that had been formed by the way the Khoikhoi in the settled areas had collapsed under the combined weight of disease and a far stronger alien culture.

By the time substantial contact was made with the Xhosa masses, the preconditions for Afrikaner nationalism had been set: the rejection of cosmopolitanism from the Cape (seen as arbitrary rule based on foreign — that is, European — ideas); the notion that Boers and their descendants were by natural right entitled to as much land as they wanted and needed; the belief that political superiority was theirs by natural right; the by now developed notion that the land was "empty" and therefore ownerless; the idea that physical labour was not done by whites; the assumption that black cultures would give way before superior white will; the belief that retreat into the interior was the way to solve the problems of poverty and harassment by law and by native.

PART 2

Pieter Jacob de Villiers
and the Century of Wrong I:
the search for Beulah

———

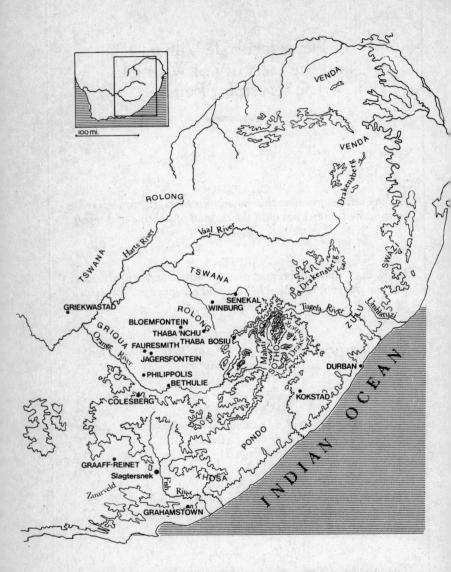

The opening of the interior and the intersection of the tribes

Chapter 4

On the restless frontier: the brown hills burn, the restless tribes clash, the family lives with the turmoil of fighting and revolt

I

PIETER JACOB DE VILLIERS, of the fourth South African generation, was also born in the soft valleys of the southwestern Cape. Anna Aletta Hugo gave birth to him at Nattevlei on January 30, 1785. He was one of 11 children born to Abraham and Anna Aletta; four of them married back into

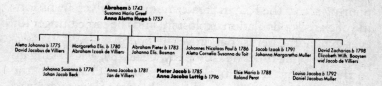

Abraham b 1743
Susanna Maria Greef
Anna Aletta Hugo b 1757

| Aletta Johanna b 1775 David Jacobus de Villiers | Margaretha Elis. b 1780 Abraham Izaak de Villiers | Abraham Pieter b 1783 Johanna Elis. Bosman | Johannes Nicolaas Paul b 1786 Aletta Cornelia Susanna du Toit | Jacob Izaak b 1791 Johanna Margaretha Muller | David Zacharias b 1798 Elizabeth Wilh. Booysen wid Jacob de Villiers |
| Johanna Susanna b 1778 Johan Jacob Beck | Anna Jacoba b 1781 Jan de Villiers | **Pieter Jacob** b 1785 **Anna Jacoba Luttig** b 1796 | Elsie Maria b 1788 Roland Perot | Louisa Jacoba b 1792 Daniel Jacobus Muller | |

the de Villiers clan, one married a de Villiers widow, two married Mullers, and Pieter Jacob was to marry Anna Jacoba Luttig, the granddaughter of a German immigrant. The Luttigs, like the Hugos and the Lombards, departed the Cape early and drew the de Villiers' attention to the frontier as they became increasingly disenchanted with the stultifying atmosphere of the Castle-dominated south-west. There were relatives spreading out through the north and the east for all of Pieter Jacob's life. He visited the frontier frequently with his father, listening to frontier stories and hearing his father in his turn deliver warnings about the venal ways of the Castle. There were relatives and friends not 30 hours' ride from the valley of the Fish, and Xhosa cattle raiders making forays into new territory were a constant threat. The farms in the frontier area were typically substantial — 12,000 acres was the common, and the few white farmers with their Khoikhoi retainers were hard pressed to protect any more than the homestead. Farms to the east and south of Graaff-Reinet were frequently set ablaze and their stock stolen by young Xhosa men on hunting parties out to collect the nucleus of their own herds. In these conflicts dozens of farmers were driven off their land. Some returned to the Cape, others relocated in the frontier villages. All the burghers, on the frontier and around Stellenbosch, listened to their travails.

These travails — and the anger they caused against the Company for not heading them off — were in the background for all of Pieter Jacob's life and were part of his early consciousness. The skirmishes started when he was just a baby. The worst year of all, the year the burghers called *die stormjaar*, the storm year, was 1787, when he was only two. Hardly a week went by without violence. The Xhosa began pouring across the Fish in greater numbers, driven by fissioning of clans, a population explosion, and the same hunger for ever-expanding herds that drove the Boers.

At the same time the Company, belatedly, was waking up to the fact that it was neglecting its errant charges on the frontier, and it set in motion the machinery of bureaucracy to bring them under control and under whatever protection it could offer. In 1785 they gave the name Graaff-Reinet to the north-eastern frontier district of Camdebo and assigned it a *landdrost*, a sheriff. (The de Villiers family was burrowing into frontier life too. Pieter Jacob had relatives there, and acquired more. For example Anna Eleanora Luttig, whose cousin Pieter Jacob married and whose own mother was a de Villiers, married Petrus Stockenstrom, whose father was Graaff-Reinet's landdrost. The elder Stockenstrom was ambushed and murdered by a party of Xhosa raiders in 1811.) But the Company was ineffectual, undermanned, bogged down in paperwork, cumbersome in its procedures after 150 years, and made only feeble efforts to prevent conflict between Boer and Xhosa, mostly by issuing edicts aimed at preventing contact. In a typically useless act, the Cape governor, Joachim Plettenberg, posted beacons along the valley of the Fish. The burghers were forbidden to pass the beacons going eastwards; those Xhosa who could be reached were instructed not to pass westwards. Neither side paid any attention to such edicts, or to the Company's equally feeble attempts to preserve its trading monopoly: the trekboers routinely made hunting forays for ivory into Xhosa territory and bartered for cattle when they could, stealing when they couldn't. The raids continued. War threatened along the whole frontier. In mid-year a Boer delegation petitioned the incumbent landdrost at Graaff-Reinet, demanding Company aid. The landdrost was Stockenstrom's predecessor, Honoratius Christiaan Maynier. He refused.

Maynier, who himself led a massive retaliatory raid considerably east of the Fish a few years later, is one of the most vilified figures in Afrikaner demonology. The farmers apparently found him *bedonderd* — wilfully contrary. Most contemporaries found him stubborn, imperious, excessively self-confident. His place in the Afrikaner memory is one reserved for appeasers, later to be called *kaffirboeties*, people whose sympathy lay more with black than with white.

But Maynier has been unfairly vilified. He was himself faced with the same bloated Company bureaucracy in Cape Town — it could take several years for them to make a difficult decision — and in any case his assessment of the politics of the frontier differed from that of the stubborn trekboers, whose constant demand for more land pushed the boundary ever eastwards: there were trekboers in the valley of the Fish itself only a year after Plettenberg's beacons went up. Maynier realized, from his relatively detached position as landdrost, what the farmers could not: that in the Xhosa they had met a population radically different from the San and the Khoikhoi they had met hitherto; that the Xhosa were a relatively stable people, their homelands densely populated, inhabiting land they considered theirs by ancestral right. Here were no nomadic herdsmen to be pushed ever further into the interior. Maynier's assessment of the ominous numbers of the Xhosa has reverberated down through South African history ever since.

He also understood, or thought he understood, another fact of Xhosa life: that here for the first time was a culture with a centralized decision-making apparatus. He believed (not altogether accurately) that the Xhosa owed allegiance to a king, and that if one could only treat with the king, accommodation could be reached. In fact the Xhosa political structure was not unlike the Boer republics-to-be — small, fractious, and changeable. Treaties were likely to prove unreliable instruments for peace, but Maynier didn't know that. There was another factor in Maynier's inaction: the barren plains around Graaff-Reinet had settled into a serious drought, which made the search for stability even more urgent. To the trekboers, Maynier's attempts to negotiate with the "kaffirs" meant he wasn't on "our" side. He ignored the Boers' "complaints and entreaties"; they, on the other hand, wanted nothing to do with the wretched company he represented, especially its monopolies and its taxes, except when they wanted protection.

A heroic figure to set against the contemptible Maynier then appeared, as heroes are wont to do when needed. Pieter Jacob, in his later years, was to remember Adriaan van Jaarsveld as all the Boers did, as a man who exemplified their virtues. He remembered him as a big man, powerful, strong of will, toughened by years in the saddle and dozens of forays against the San and the Xhosa, independent, devout, egalitarian within his own group, with a strong sense of the rightness of his cause and of his place in God's universe. In 1790 he was appointed — even the Company recognized his leadership — commandant of the eastern frontier districts.

Van Jaarsveld was a tough, no-nonsense leader; family members who were pressed into service in one of van Jaarsveld's commandos carefully remembered only his virtues and glossed over the many atrocity stories that surrounded him. It seems clear that he refined the informal commando system into a more disciplined fighting force: he is credited by some sources with the invention of the *laager*, the defensive circle of wagons that was to become a central symbol of Afrikaner life — it served them well against the Zulus, and afterwards became, as it still is, a political metaphor for Afrikaner tenacity and stubbornness.

In 1791 van Jaarsveld caused all the farmers in the Zuurveld, white and Khoikhoi, to draw their wagons into laagers, left men to guard them, and took off after the Xhosa. He is said to have opened his campaign by treachery, scattering tobacco on the ground in front of a party of Xhosa and having them all shot when they stooped to pick it up. On this campaign, family lore is silent. Van Jaarsveld vigorously denied the story, and Afrikaner historians have always ascribed it to missionary invention; nevertheless the incident lives in Xhosa oral history, where it is regarded not only as treachery, but as unmanly — a typically white kind of trick. Atrocity stories cut both ways: almost two decades later landdrost Andries Stockenstrom was murdered as he smoked a pipe with a Xhosa chief, which event marked a further deterioration in relations, since after that the Boers ceased simply stealing cattle — they burned homes and shot all who resisted.

Van Jaarsveld's campaign was successful, if only temporarily, and the Xhosa were driven back across the Fish. Pieter Jacob, then eight, remembered visitors to his father's farm: large, weary men, stained from travel, grim with stories of killing, filled with foreboding about the uncounted kraals beyond the great river, brimming with rage against the villainous Maynier and the efforts of the missionaries, who were said to be "stuffing the Kaffirs' heads with nonsense imported from England." As fuel to the fire, the newly imported German settlers near the Fish, trapped in a war they hadn't imagined, were spreading incendiary stories among the burghers, stories of the great events in Europe, stories of revolution and conquest, and of people taking control of

their own destinies — words that spoke directly to the
affronted Boers' hearts. The spirit of revolt was in the air.
Maynier paid no attention. The Company was on its last legs.
England went to war with France. Rumours of fleets at the
Cape travelled swiftly along the frontier. The Xhosa came
pouring back into the Zuurveld once again, burning and
looting. More than a hundred farms were destroyed, their
owners fleeing to neighbouring farms or to the landdrost's
seat in Graaff-Reinet — more kindling for the fires of the
burghers' discontent. None of Pieter Jacob's relatives' farms
were directly affected, but there were refugees from every clan
and family milling around the Paarl area.

II

AND MAYNIER? What did he really believe? Was he, as Afrikaner historians have always assumed, filled with Rous-
seauian innocence about the noble savage, a sentiment easy
to accept in European drawing rooms but harder to cling to in
Graaff-Reinet, where grim commandos could be seen every
week returning from skirmishes with the Xhosa? The Boers
always assumed he was readier to give a hearing to the feared
kaffirs than to any explanation of theirs, that because he was
mean-minded and penny-pinching he found it easier to
blame the farmers for every cow stolen, every man killed.
Boer delegations to the Castle were in vain; the Castle preferred to trust its landdrosts.

In truth, Maynier did try to keep the peace, he did try to
pacify the Xhosa with gifts of cattle and tobacco, he did try to
persuade the Xhosa chieftains to control their raiders, just as
he tried to control his own. No one listened. At last, in 1793,
Maynier called together a commando of his own. They
raided as far east as the Buffalo River, but in four months
succeeded only in driving the confident Xhosa back to the
Fish Valley. The unsuccessful campaign confirmed the Boers'
contempt; Maynier was either inept or treacherous or both.

For two more years the Boers struggled. San continued to

steal, Xhosa to plunder. The long march to the Cape market was hardly worth while; the Company kept prices artificially low, and ships were limiting purchases to necessities. The Cape rixdollar was distrusted by the farmers, and with good reason; half its value was arbitrarily wiped out by Company fiat. Most farmers were poor and could hardly afford to maintain their supplies of ammunition. There was a widespread belief that the sale of monopolies benefited only Company servants. Immigrants from Germany and the Netherlands continued to import and spread lurid tales of the great events in France.

The rough-and-ready mind of Adriaan van Jaarsveld put their stories together with the poverty of his neighbours and the refugees he saw every day from the outer fringes of the colony; in his mind the Company and its servant, the creature Maynier, became the Bourbon kings. He began to preach revolt at every farm he could visit. He passed like a storm through the platteland, his ideas infecting all the restless trekboers. A month later, in February 1795, an armed commando with the indignant van Jaarsveld at its head appeared before Maynier's house and drove him out. Some of the burghers nailed the tricolour to their farm stoops. The twin intoxicants of freedom and revenge proved irresistible. They declared themselves the Republic of Graaff-Reinet.

The de Villiers family had no part in this stirring event but the news was potent enough to infect Pieter Jacob, as it did all the Drakenstein burghers — notes and correspondence of the times are filled with the news, though few felt impelled to actually take part themselves. Many went from Paarl to Cape Town to see if they could catch a glimpse there of the hapless Maynier, but he was in seclusion.

A few months later, in June, the other frontier district, Swellendam, followed suit. Its burghers had neither the excuse of a Maynier nor pressing need for protection, but the "shrill cries of the Jacobins," as the historian Willem de Klerk put it, "reached even the blue heights west of Bruyntjeshoogte," and they finally shrugged off the dying husk of the

Company and declared themselves the Free Republic of Swellendam, professing themselves ready to risk their "last drop of blood for our beloved Fatherland." The local veld-cornet, who was a de Beer, named his first-born John Bonaparte and his second Nicholas Moreau. The heroes may have had European names, but after 143 years of Company rule, the Fatherland had become Africa. They had become Africans. In their own language, Afrikaners.

The Company at the Castle struggled on feebly and ineffectually. It arrested a few of the ringleaders, sentenced them to death, and then let them go. To Graaff-Reinet the Company dispatched a commission of inquiry, not having any soldiers to do the job. To Swellendam it sent word to await the results at Graaff-Reinet. No such results ever came.

In Europe, France went to war with Holland, and to prevent the French cornering the route to the East, the British sent a fleet to the Cape to take "protective custody." The fleet anchored not in Table Bay, to which the Castle's fixed cannons pointed, but in False Bay, at the other end of the peninsula and at the Castle's back. In September 1795 the British crossed the peninsula on foot and took the Castle from behind, without a shot being fired.

For the rebellious burghers their century of isolation was over. They had been left alone to do more or less as they pleased, and to invent themselves as a people. The land they occupied had been, for all intents and purposes, theirs for the taking. Now, at century's end, they were confronted not with the feeble Khoikhoi or the primitive San, whose small bands were no match for an organized culture, but with the formidable and unyielding Xhosa. To the north waited the Sotho and the Zulu; and to the south-west no longer an ineffectual trading company with its idiotic rules and inept regulators but an outpost of a global empire, an empire becoming utterly confident in the rightness of its ways and intensely curious about these odd citizens it had so abruptly acquired.

The Afrikaners had been allowed a century to settle into their land. Now larger forces were at work. In Afrikaner terms, the Enemy had arrived; the Afrikaners were about to enter their *Eeu van Onreg*, their Century of Wrong, which would open and close with war and defeat but which would serve to consolidate the tribe and form the *volkseie*, the fierce group cohesiveness, that drives them to this day.

Chapter 5

Black, Boer, and British missionary; mutual bafflement leads to war on the frontier; the rebellion and hangings at Slagtersnek

I

THERE HAS ALWAYS been argument in South Africa about who lived where, and when. The "kaffirs," the Xhosa, the Thembu, the Pondo — all the groups linked generically under the language group Nguni — who were they and where did they come from?

Afrikaner and black historians still indulge in an I-was-here-first, no-you-weren't debate exceeded in its silliness only by its earnestness. When I was at school in Bloemfontein we were told — the syllabus insisted on it though our teacher, Davie Marquard, my great-uncle, did his best to instil scepticism — that the interior of South Africa was uninhabited when the Afrikaners got there, that the black tribes were pushing south at the same time whites were pushing north. Since they actually met at the Fish River only a few hundred miles from Cape Town, this argument would seem to have limited utility for partition purposes from the white tribe's point of view, but they clung to it anyway. A pamphlet from the 1960s I have in my files gives the official (modern) nationalist Afrikaner point of view: "They had equal title to the country. The Voortrekkers . . . wished to live in peace because they had already experienced enough trouble in the Cape. But the Bantu were not amenable to reason. He [sic] respected only one thing and that was force."

By now a complicated ethnic mix has existed on the same land for more than three centuries, and sorting out who actually lived where is far from easy. The idea that the "Bantu," to use the discredited South African government term, were only recent immigrants from unspecified northern regions has been disowned by historians. Clearly, there were Xhosa in what is now Pondoland and the Transkei, on the Indian Ocean between the Fish River and Durban, by the end of the 1400s; archaeologists guess there were Sotho between the Vaal and the Limpopo rivers, the modern Transvaal, by the 6th and 7th centuries. True, they had not yet made their way to the south-western Cape, as the Khoikhoi and the San had. True also, large areas of the interior were virtually empty when the trekkers reached them. This was a contemporary — and temporary — phenomenon, caused by powerful forces set off by the abrupt rise of the Zulu kingdom to the north-east, but the trekkers had no way of knowing that.

There are two major language groups living in southern Africa: the Nguni, of which the best known sub-categories are Zulu, Pondo, and Xhosa, and the south Sotho, now centred in the modern state of Lesotho, founded by the astute king Moshoeshoe in the last century. There is also a northern Sotho group, the Pedi, and another subgroup called the Tswana. To complicate the ethnic mix further, there are the Venda and the Tsonga, whose languages are radically different from the main groups, and a variant of Zulu spoken in Zimbabwe (taken there by one of the Zulu tyrant Shaka's fleeing generals). Xhosa and Zulu are not different languages but merely dialects of the same language, much closer than, say, Italian is to Spanish. There are dozens more dialects; it's only because 19th-century missionaries wrote down these two that they became identified as "languages" rather than variants of a larger language, as the others are.

No one knows for sure where the Nguni originated; it's generally assumed they migrated in several stages and at different times from the northern reaches of Kenya, on the Somali border. But when they did this, or how long it took, no one knows. When the white settlers first began to push north, the Nguni heartland lay in the coastal regions, from the great Fish River to Swaziland in the north, taking in all of modern Transkei and the modern province of Natal, as well as the creature of apartheid called kwaZulu.

The Xhosa shared their territory with the Khoikhoi and the San for some centuries. There was some intermarriage, a good deal of linguistic cross-over, and modest amounts of cultural intermingling — for example San hunters furnished a group of travelling magicians, useful in time of drought. Not all was harmonious: there are derogatory terms for Khoikhoi in the Xhosa language, and warfare with San was frequent. Many of the larger clans had servants, some of them lifetime retainers, but neither the Sotho nor the Nguni ever used slavery.

Unlike the Khoikhoi culture, the more complex Xhosa culture had a developed agriculture: sorghum, corn, watermelons, pumpkins of various kinds, and plenty of tobacco of satisfyingly superior quality as staple crops. They raised sheep, dogs, goats, and cattle. As the trekboers did, they invested most of their energy and acquisitiveness in their cattle. Cows meant status and wealth; they were gifts at important times such as marriages; they were the most common subject of art — praise poems were made to them, just as they were in trekboer settlements. Most Nguni food came from milk and from game killed in hunting rather than from cattle slaughter. Hunting was a necessity and a great joy, a fitting task for men. Cultivating was women's work; men only tilled fields in the service of a chief, never voluntarily, and then only for tribute. Elephant hunting was common; control of the ivory supply was an important source of chiefly power.

Politically the Xhosa were a loose-knit federation of linked clans. There was no "paramount" chief, only senior lineages that lesser lines acknowledged as senior without necessarily submitting to their authority. The organization was not as scattered — or as chaotic — as that of the Khoikhoi, but this lack of a central power was a source of constant irritation to successive white governments, who often believed they had settled some point of dispute only to have agreements ignored; one of the main thrusts of later British policy was the search for a legitimate central power, and where they didn't find it they often attempted to invent it.

The clans were relatively fluid, with allegiances shifting according to clan fortunes and chiefly competence. This lack of centralized authority was a source of confusion within as well as without. A chief could recognize the seniority of another without in any way recognizing his authority; not surprisingly, there were disputes, inter-clan rivalries, skirmishes, and warfare. A chief's power was limited by the frequent splits caused by his senior sons setting up rival groupings. A mean-spirited chief could find his followers melting away; a generous chief would attract others. The poor commonly attached themselves to a chief's household and were given cattle in return for tending his herds. It was not uncommon in the early years of white settlement for shipwrecked sailors or army deserters to be absorbed in this way as chief's clients, family retainers; one Xhosa clan still traces its descent from a particularly memorable shipwrecked Portuguese.

There was seldom warfare for territorial reasons; clans that split simply moved to new land. Vendettas were virtually unknown; all early travellers among the Xhosa remarked on their universal acceptance of a rule of law, enforced through a system of chiefly courts. A chief unable to resolve a dispute invariably referred the matter to a more distant (more objective) and more senior chief.

Unlike the Sotho, whose towns could contain up to 20,000 inhabitants and whose herdsmen commuted to grazing lands, the Xhosa had a highly decentralized society. Senior chiefs could have as many as 10,000 followers, though seldom in one place. Towns, and even villages, hardly existed. Most Xhosa lived in homesteads ranging from 2 to 40 huts, depending on the wealth and prestige of the family head.

Trade was modest and sporadic, consisting mostly of

worked iron, medicines, grain, ornaments, and later ivory. The Xhosa were great travellers. Like the Boers', their hunting parties ranged far afield; Xhosa travellers were sometimes found several hundred miles away in northern Natal, and in the late 1700s groups of curious young Xhosa males would walk the hundreds of miles to Cape Town to see what the peculiar whites had perpetrated there. Most Xhosa homesteads of any size kept a hut for travellers, and food and drink was ungrudgingly provided. There were caveats, however; travellers were advised not to take with them iron or copper, which acted on the locals in much the same way an openly displayed cache of cocaine would affect some inhabitants of Lower East Side Manhattan.

Nor was everything bucolic peace. Religion had its underside among the Xhosa, as it did in contemporary Europe. Since in theory everyone was immortal, illness and disease were surely caused by malice. Trials for witchcraft were common and, as in Europe, ordeal by torture was the preferred way of extracting a confession. In the early years of white settlement the traffic of refugees was two-way: runaway slaves and deserters were given a home among the Xhosa; people accused of witchcraft occasionally showed up in the western Cape looking for work. A farm neighbouring on Boschendal had two such workers, who gratefully accepted indenture in return for sanctuary.

Like most peasant societies, Xhosa society was inherently conservative, despite the fluidity of its politics. Piety was equated with stability. Innovation was discouraged. It was only in periods of great stress that change came rapidly, periods such as the establishment and rapid expansion of Zulu military power, or the arrival of the whites and the resulting wars. From the point of view of the Xhosa, these wars rapidly changed in character, from the early cattle-raiding parties organized by adventurous young men to what they belatedly recognized as a fight not for a few cows but for their very existence as a people. Into this witch's brew of passion came the British and their missionaries.

II

THE LONDON MISSIONARY SOCIETY was the next of the demons the Afrikaners sought to exorcise from their lives by their withdrawal into the burning interior. The LMS emissaries, often simply called "the philanthropists," as if that automatically vilified them, were generally men of intellectual rigour, with a feeble spirit of compromise and the burning zeal that the newly righteous, even in England, were feeling in their campaign against the Church Smug and the Tory Complacent. The names of van der Kemp, Wilberforce, and the devil incarnate, John Philip, were known to every frontier farmer as men who were contributing to chaos and murder on the frontier by their single-minded championing of the kaffir cause.

There's not a communication, not a note that passed between the Mullers, the Hugos, the Rousseaus, and the de Villiers that didn't in some way mention the Troubles; the causes were always assumed to be the venality at the Castle (which persisted under the British) and the hypocrisy at the mission stations, where missionaries were learning "kaffir ways" and not troubling themselves with the problems of the Boers. It didn't help reduce the colonists' choler that many of the missionaries they knew best — those who stayed on their farms and ate their food — were corrupt and hypocritical. Dispatches home to London with glowing reports of the good works they were doing in the north among the heathen were frequently written from the comfort of an affluent Boer's parlour. Henry Lichtenstein was reflecting that distaste for missionaries when he wrote:

Most of these consider the voyage to Africa only as a means of leading a more agreeable life . . . Preparations were outwardly made for transporting themselves to the boundaries of the colony, but when it came to the point they seldom got further than three or four days journey from Cape Town . . . Marriages with daughters of the pious citizens came afterwards in the way, and then all idea of further journeyings must necessarily be abandoned . . . Living a fortnight with one colonist, a month with another, regularly receiving the salary towards which many a penitent sinner in Europe had contributed his ducats, under the pious idea of assisting in leading heathen from the paths of error . . . None of these holy messengers ever thought of crossing the Karoo . . . They boasted loudly, in letters to Europe, of the progress they had made in their task of conversion.

Lichtenstein grudgingly admitted that there were some, "especially the English," who "went among savages"; the de Villiers family considered these even worse. Among them, the London-trained Hollander Johannes van der Kemp was especially disliked. He made attempts to understand Xhosa culture and needs in a way still rare in South Africa. Van der Kemp lived at the kraal of the Xhosa chief Ngqika, learned the language, produced a Xhosa grammar, preached his Word, sowed a few crops, taught Xhosa men the unaccustomed and undignified virtues of agricultural labour, fought off accusations that he himself was causing a prolonged drought, and sought to understand the structure and meaning of Xhosa culture.

What he found was a society in deep turmoil, its naturally expansive ways abruptly halted by an alien culture small in numbers but infinitely superior in warcraft. The Xhosa were milling along the east bank of the Fish, anger boiling beneath the surface, suddenly overcrowded, their lands in danger of overgrazing, living in new and dismaying poverty, forced abruptly to confront and change their ancient ways; they were reacting then as the Afrikaners have always reacted — with an angry retreat into a "purified" tribal ethos. (Yet there were Xhosa then, as there are Afrikaners now, prepared to open up to accept alien ideas.)

Van der Kemp and the missionaries believed, and acted as if they believed, that the Xhosa were co-equal citizens of the country. The Boers naturally interpreted this unlikely notion as anti-white bias: it was *their* farms that were being overrun, after all, their stock stolen, their families murdered and abducted. And when a farmer sought to recover his cattle and sought revenge for the violence done against him, the missionaries lodged a complaint at the Castle, where the British governor now resided, or in London, or wherever the devil could find a compliant ear. It wasn't just the raiding kaffirs who were finding a newly sympathetic hearing either. The countryside was full of *skorriemorrie* — riffraff, vagrants, and roving bands of Khoikhoi, or San and Khoikhoi, or people of no known ancestry; these bands had no visible means of support except cattle theft, yet they all received missionary protection. The San up in the hills were not yet subdued.

Frontier life was a series of strikes and counter-strikes, violent reactions to violent acts. The Boers hadn't yet understood that the Xhosa were not the simple Hottentots of the old Cape peninsula, and they were still convinced that if only the place were governed right the problems could be cleared up.

III

THE LITTLE REPUBLICS of Swellendam and Graaff-Reinet didn't outlast the coming of the British, who dealt with them by paying absolutely no attention, simply proclaiming their right to govern everyone everywhere. The republics collapsed; the farmers didn't have time to argue, much less to govern.

If the British had wanted to push the emergent Afrikaner people into their Century of Wrong, they could hardly have chosen a better chap than their first governor, the Earl of Caledon, an arrogant young fellow of 29. Caledon was a creature of the High Tory reaction that governed Britain in the shocking (to the British) aftermath of the American revolt and the shrill excesses of the Robespierre Terror in France. The secret of governance was discipline and stability, he believed. Punishment for deviation from approved Castle — which meant English — ways was the method of achieving it. He and his successors didn't like the Boers much. They lived rude lives, caused trouble, wouldn't listen. They were poor, their contributions to the economy meagre, they were scarcely better than the savages, who at least had the virtue of being convertible pagans and therefore fodder for Britain's civilizing mission.

Sir John Cradock, Caledon's successor, believed as Caledon did. Cradock's most notorious attempt to bring the unruly farmers under the rule of law was the establishment of a circuit court in the district of Graaff-Reinet in 1811, a road show that rolled through the district, gathering notoriety and calumny as it went, stirring Afrikaner indignation to fever pitch, till every farm in the Cape buzzed with its doings and the tales of its excesses. Nattevlei, where young Pieter Jacob was now a robust 26, was no exception. His father Abraham was 68, a bitter opponent of the British and their ways. The family of Abraham's daughter-in-law Johanna Muller was soon to be embroiled in an event that was to generate a hatred that survived into the campaign rhetoric of the election of 1948: the insurrection that led to the hangings at Slagtersnek.

The reason for the circuit court's notoriety was simple: the judges heard with the utmost gravity the charges brought by Hottentots, vagrants, and thieves. The Black Circuit, as it came to be called, is by now so enshrined in Afrikaner myth that its actual sentences are less important than its mere creation and existence. There seems no doubt that the Reverends van der Kemp and James Read encouraged aggrieved Khoikhoi to complain to the court of maltreatment at the hands of the Boers; and there seems no reason to doubt, either, that the suddenly gleeful Hotnots seized the opportunity to get a little modest revenge, for many of the charges were thrown out of court as false, malicious, cooked up in conversations with other complainants and the missionaries themselves. On the other hand, a good many accusations were proved — hardly surprising considering the rough-and-ready attitude towards staff discipline that prevailed on most farms, where a sound thrashing was delivered for the most trivial offences; it was a system that gave virtually free rein to the brutal and the sadistic among the Boer population.

So deeply felt was the dislike the British engendered in a short time that a few malcontents actually considered ganging up with the kaffirs to drive them into the sea. It was known that there were Xhosa dissidents so furious at the loss of traditional ways and pastures that they were resorting to sorcery to get rid of the English, and the cantankerous Boers, while deploring their methods, approved their intentions. This bizarre alliance was attempted after a farmer, Cornelis Frederick (known as Freek) Bezuidenhout, refused to appear before the court to face charges of maltreatment brought by his servant, a Khoikhoi named Booy. (There is a neglected subtext here. Booy's wife and his friend, known only to posterity as Dikkop — Thickhead — were lovers, and some of Booy's "beatings" were in fact the result of Booy's finding the enamoured couple *in flagrante*.) After several toings and froings a posse was sent to arrest Bezuidenhout at his farm in wild country high up in the hills. He resisted and was shot dead by a "Hottentot bullet," as the story had it. He was 55.

Johannes Jurgen (Hans) Bezuidenhout, 57, the dead man's brother, lived on a farm owned by the Muller brothers, cousins by marriage to the de Villiers at Nattevlei. Bezuidenhout lived there with his brother-in-law, their wives, and multiple children by numerous women. (Few of the Bezuidenhouts ever bothered with formal marriage and Hans was no exception: he had many children by at least three women before finally "marrying" Martha Faber. Only one brother, Coenraad, made the formal commitment, and when his wife died he took up with a half-caste woman called Sara Cloete.) The Muller farm was on the lip of the Fish River; many of the men had made trading and hunting forays deep into Xhosa territory. Now they cobbled together an expedition to attempt an alliance with the Xhosa chief Ngqika — an attempt that severely limited Bezuidenhout's Boer following, at least for the short term. Ngqika in his turn expressed deep scepticism at this turncoat offer and refused it, but not before the British, alarmed at the prospect of another Xhosa invasion, turned on the rebels and threw those they caught in jail. Bezuidenhout resisted arrest, was wounded, and died. It was the year of Waterloo.

In the events that followed, the Boers forgave and forgot Hans Bezuidenhout's curious try at cross-racial alliance-making. Five ringleaders of the 70-odd Boers who took part were sentenced to be hanged: Cornelis Faber, 43; Hendrik Prinsloo, 32; Stephanus Cornelis Bothma, 43; Abraham Karel Bothma, 29; and Theunis Christiaan de Klerk, 32. They were all, in the tribal way, related. Hans Bezuidenhout's Martha was the sister of Faber. Another Faber sister had married Prinsloo, who was nicknamed Kasteel (Castle) and whose father had been sentenced to hang alongside van Jaarsveld after they had drummed out Maynier (the elder Prinsloo was reprieved). Both Bothmas had been related to the Bezuidenhouts for several generations, and de Klerk had married a Prinsloo — Kasteel's cousin. Theunis de Klerk's daughter married into the family of Johanna Muller, Abraham de Villiers's daughter-in-law. There was another tenuous relationship to the de Villiers family through the Jouberts.

The Slagtersnek "rebellion" was in fact a quarrelsome clan being quarrelsome — these were not liberty-loving patriots but mountain men of the wildest kind — but this was quite lost sight of in the Afrikaner consciousness, where they were soon given martyr status. The five condemned were taken to the gallows at Slagtersnek, with Martha Bezuidenhout forced to watch. The ropes of four of the accused broke at the first attempt, "to the screams of friends and relatives." The four men were dragged upright, new ropes fastened around their necks, and they were hanged until martyred. All the accused had relatives at Paarl, and the news electrified the colony; it was being retold and embellished in the parlours of the southwest within days. Slagtersnek became a synonym for the unforgettable and unforgivable; British became a synonym for enemy.

Chapter 6

Afrikaner eyes turn north, in longing, to the emptiness of Transorangia

I

THERE IS A CONTINUITY of sorrow. In the 15 years after Slagtersnek the troubles never ceased. Cattle raiding and random violence were endemic. The British authorities in Cape Town listened more to the insistent voice of empire. John Philip's missionary zeal only increased. The martyrs at Slagtersnek were a symbol. The way to the east was closed by the formidable Xhosa. Eyes turned north: to the north lay the untroubled dreaming of Africa, the horizons empty (or so they thought), hazardous and hard, but a refuge. The sentiment was in the air after the British arrival and the killings at Slagtersnek — not yet tribal, but in the air. It persisted into this century. I remember my grandfather, not a man who cared over-much for the church, rolling the words of Isaiah around in his mouth; the verse is underlined in all the old Bibles: "Thou shalt no more be termed Forsaken; neither shall thy land any more be termed Desolate: but thou shalt be called Hephzi-bah, and thy land Beulah: for the Lord delighteth in thee."

The incantations were spoken in all Boer homes. Isaiah's redemption spoke to the trekboers as Christ's could not; Isaiah turned chaos into myth and sorrow into the precondition for escape into Beulah. Christ's sophisticated alchemy, the conversion of pain into triumph, was not for them. From the fierce underscoring, Pieter Jacob remembered the words:

"Even the carcasses of men shall fall as dung upon the open field, and as the handful after the harvestman, and none shall gather them." In the aftermath of Slagtersnek the Children of Israel were their best hope: God had brought them here, God made them a people, God would deliver them, God would provide a refuge.

II

MY GREAT-GRANDFATHER, Jacobus Johannes Luttig de Villiers, was born in 1818 on his father's farm, Welgelegen, in Bottelary near Paarl, three years after Slagtersnek and a few years after the British Empire had turned its full attention to the Cape. He got his schooling at Paarl with the sons and gentlewomen of the great houses, but he never accepted their ways. His father and his father's father might be farmers; he would not be. His father had turned his attention north all

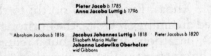

Pieter Jacob b 1785
Anna Jacoba Luttig b 1796

Abraham Jacobus b 1816   Jacobus Johannes Luttig b 1818   Pieter Jacobus b 1820
Elisabeth Maria Muller
Johanna Lodewika Oberholzer
wid Gibbons

his life; Luttig would do something about it. Throughout his boyhood he watched families selling off their farms, disposing of their goods, buying fine wagons and oxen, laying away ammunition — in the aftermath of Slagtersnek the sentiment called *trekgees* (the spirit of withdrawal) had infected nearly everyone. These auctions were to become major social events over the next 30 years. They commonly lasted three days and more, as the families disposed of generations of bric-a-brac. There were now family members in the far interior — Oberholzers at Beaufort, Hugos near the Orange River, friends of the family already settled in what was coming to be called Transorangia, for lack of a better name. Luttig watched one family leave — they were not related and their names are not recorded, but he watched them pack.

There were two wagons. Sixteen oxen. Two rams and 16 breeding ewes. Cattle for meat and milk. A bull to provide more oxen. Two young men — one was a Muller, though likely not a relative, the other a Perot — along for the adventure. Two young San maidservants seized in a raid and weaned by wet nurses in the Khoikhoi village. Hottentot herdsmen, mounted and armed. Spare horses. Saddles, tackle, spare harness for the mules, spare wheels, a new axle. Water barrels, topped up at every sweet brook (which became fewer and fewer as the party moved from the Drakenstein Valley into the Great Karoo). Food. Clothing. Blankets. Skins. Two ploughs and harrows. Shovels and axes. Blacksmith's and carpenter's tools. Lamps. Three books: the Bible, the catechism, and an ABC primer for the children. An iron cookstove. A wooden churn. Chickens. Salt. Yeast. Seed. Guns. Spare guns. Powder. Ammunition. More ammunition. Lead for making even more. Unlike the explorers who had gone before them, this was not intended to be a seasonal visit for pasture, or a hunting expedition. It was emigration. Most of the early trekboers had believed they were extending the frontiers of the colony, not evading them: they were critical of the way the colony was run but had never meant to set up a rival state. These emigrants, trekkers but not yet the "Voortrekkers" who would soon depart on the Great Trek, were different — they wanted out.

The route was straightforward: Klapmuts to Paarl, Paarl to Tulbagh, Tulbagh to Hex Rivier and over the Hex Rivier valley pass, north to de Doorns, Touwsrivier, Beaufort West. They crossed the Orange at Bethulie, where there was a mission station. From Bethulie west to Philippolis, from Philippolis north to Jagersfontein. West of Jagersfontein, 30 miles short of the Riet River, just outside what was to become Fauresmith, they stopped, four months after they had set off.

Luttig knew the exact route, not then but later, for he followed it many times. When he left school at 16 he became a transport rider running supplies to the farms and towns of the interior.

Most of Luttig's trips took him to the immediate hinterlands, but he visited the eastern and northern frontiers many times and often passed through Beaufort West. After 1841, when he married Elisabeth Maria Muller, he visited their relatives in Beaufort, Colesberg, and Graaff-Reinet and in the isolated villages of Transorangia. Elisabeth, not to be outdone, joined him as transport rider. Sometimes she would go even though pregnant; she would have her children where they came: Pieter Jacob was born at Paarl, Daniel Jacobus was born at Beaufort, Jacobus Johannes at Paarl, David Andries at Colesberg, Abraham David back at Paarl. They visited the Oberholzers in Fauresmith and the Luttigs in Senekal. Luttig de Villiers got to know Winburg and Bloemfontein, small villages where many family members would later settle.

Of all the land he saw, he loved the golden sun-drenched landscape around Bloemfontein the most. It is even now the place that most lifts the Afrikaner heart. To be sure, the geographers talk of the beauties of the western Cape, of the pleasures of the tropical beaches around Durban; and if asked, most Afrikaners who have seen it will say they'd rather live in the misty mountains of the eastern Transvaal. But the veld between the Orange and the Vaal is what we think of when we conjure an image of the heartland: endless plains made of the colours of Africa, faded purples and weary browns, the long grasses waiting for rain, the only trees the *doringbome* in the *spruits* (creeks), military green with cruel thorns around which the weaverbirds construct their intricate nests. The land is flat, made for wagons, the infrequent rivers frequently dry, the landscape cut with *dongas* (gullies), red earth washed raw by flash floods. Always on the horizon there is a *koppie*, a hillock hiccup, flat-topped, covered with scrub.

When I was a boy I would sit on the koppie behind my grandfather's house; I could see dust-devils for 30 miles, false storm clouds chasing each other on the horizon, the smoky dust of the herds, the arrow-straight track of a car on a dirt farm road. If I was still, the shy wildlife would emerge: the rock rabbits called dassies, the meerkats, the dog-sized deer called dikdik. Under rocks I could find scorpions; we always held dung-beetle races in the fine sand on top of the koppie.

In the middle of the last century the plains were swept by magnificent herds of every kind of game, in the way the Tanzanian reserves are now. The Boers took ruinous toll as they shot for the pot, for the trade, for the sheer joy of shooting. The beasts seemed so endless. In the 1860s, in one year, 300,000 wild skins were shipped to the coast, most of them destined to be cut into *riempies*, thongs used primarily for upholstering furniture. Eland biltong, sun-dried and tough but wonderfully tasty, hung from the settlers' wagons like a fringe. When I was a boy only a few farms had herds of springbok left; few eland had survived. The elephant and the predators of the early days had gone; there were no longer leopard in the hills, and lions had been driven to the game parks, where humans shot humans to protect them.

By the 1840s and 1850s, when Luttig and Elisabeth visited, the farms in the Fauresmith area were well established. There were flocks of fat-tailed sheep. There were already stands of young bluegum trees, a small dam, often dry, and a well. The houses were similar to the one Luttig himself built there later, which was similar to the one his son, my grandfather, built near Winburg. It was square in plan, with a thatched roof learned from the Khoikhoi, later to be converted to corrugated iron as the products of the industrial Cape made their way north via travelling *smouse*, or itinerant traders. These houses almost always faced east, unless there was a view towards water, in which case that took precedence. Typically, they were surrounded by wide stoops, on which most of the summer living took place, from the morning coffee in the first sun to the late-night pipe. The stoops were furnished with old benches. Often they would contain the house refrigerator, a coke-lined wooden box with a flyscreen door, covered in sacking kept constantly damp so evaporation would cool it.

The trekboers ate huge quantities of meat, typically three

times a day; breakfast consisted of lamb chops, eggs, and *boerewors* (a beef sausage spiced like biltong with coriander). *Kop en pootjies*, literally "head and feet" of a sheep, was a common evening meal, a stew that contained trotters, brain, tongue, even eyeballs — the Boers were not squeamish eaters. There was a small orchard on each farm, which not uncommonly died in the droughts.

Life was rough. Dentistry was done with the implements of the smithy. There were no doctors, but there was plenty of herbal lore; the Afrikaners had learned well from the Khoikhoi. Illness took many, often sweeping away whole families. The Oberholzers recall how a neighbour, a van Zijl, arrived weeping at their farm one day, all his family dead of the pox. He had burned the house to the ground with the bodies of his family in it. He stayed in the Oberholzers' fields for two weeks, retreating each time they dropped off food, so as not to contaminate anyone else. It was taken for granted. One of the hazards of a hazardous land.

A hazardous land it was. But it was *their* land. I can still feel it in my bones, the way they loved it. The north was *theirs*. It was the refuge into which they poured all their battered hopes.

Chapter 7

The vexed question of who owned what: Adam Kok and the brown cousins

I

MUCH OF THE LAND THROUGH which the emigrants had passed was relatively empty of people. The early trekboers knew little of the stirring events among the Zulus beyond the Drakensberg Mountains that were causing this emptiness; they only profited from it. There was land to be had around Fauresmith and elsewhere. However, it could not be said to be free, exactly. It was under the nominal control of the Griqua people of Adam Kok, and could be leased for insignificant amounts, usually in ammunition. Despite the long leases for small sums, this wasn't quite the paradise of Afrikaner dreams. For one thing, the wretched missionaries of the London Missionary Society hadn't been altogether left behind; their agents were active among the Griquas, attempting to convert them not to Christianity — they were already nominally Christian — but from their freewheeling lives of plunder and raiding to a more settled way of life.

The name Griqua was a recent coining. Charighuriqua was a (possibly mythical) Khoikhoi ancestor, and an LMS missionary had drawn on it to suggest the name Griqua as a means of ending the odium of mongrelization inherent in the name Basters, or Bastaards. The Griquas were remnant Khoikhoi from the southern Cape who had been pushed north by the expanding trekboer culture. They were in many ways trekboers themselves. The Khoikhoi physical type had long ago merged with the European; their language was a curious mixture of Khoikhoi and Afrikaans; their culture Afrikaner. There were agriculturalists among them, but most lived by hunting. They were armed, rode horses, and could travel considerable distances.

School histories still gloss over the Baster factor in Afrikaner history; it's not well known how much of the northern frontier was opened by "bruin Afrikaners," and it's only uneasily understood how much these brown Afrikaners *are* Afrikaners. Like the present Coloureds, the Basters were in fact Africanized Europeans. The fate of the Griqua represents a major lost opportunity in South African history; the possibilities were there for a free state in Transorangia managed and populated by the Griquas, in co-operation with frontiersmen of other races.

The first Basters, mixed-blood descendants of Khoikhoi, slaves, and whites, joined by manumitted slaves, settled on farms in the Little Namaqualand on the north-west frontier of the colony in the middle 18th century. Most had Dutch names — Kok, Bester, Brink, Diedericks, van der Westhuizen, Kruger, Pienaar, and others. Some became relatively wealthy. The best known and wealthiest of them, Cornelius Kok, had four farms and white *bywoners* (tenant farmers). Eventually they drifted over the colonial border, driven by population pressure, a strong push by white farmers, and increasingly onerous colonial laws drafting them into military service, an attempt to lump them in with "Hottentots" for the purposes of controlling vagrancy. They were also driven by the same restless search for new, open, free land that drove the trekboers — the Basters were among the very early trekkers, though they didn't call themselves that and Afrikaner histories ignore them.

They settled north-west of the confluence of the Orange and Harts rivers, around what was called Klaarwater and is now called Griekwastad. They had *de facto* ownership of the land; there were no other claimants, and their title was supported by the missionaries.

The evolution of the Griqua political entities closely parallels the Afrikaner mini-republics that grew in the same stubborn soil some decades later. Both grew out of a patriarchal frontier community whose characteristics were distinctively African and clearly tribal in their origins. This evolution was affected by the need to constantly look over their shoulders to the empire that had so abruptly appeared on their doorsteps. Griqua politics were further complicated by an ambivalence towards the Cape government. On the one hand, the Cape's increasingly dismaying inability to distinguish between Hottentot vagrants and settled Griqua citizens urged on them caution and withdrawal; on the other hand, they wished to maximize access to Cape markets and the Cape economy — they were as dependent as the Afrikaner trekkers were on ammunition and guns.

The Griqua leaders invited in the missionaries and treated them at various times as representatives of the Cape government and as their protectors from it, depending on their political assessments of the moment. The missionaries, in turn, used their ambivalent status in an attempt to create settled communities that could be used to develop self-perpetuating mission cadres; by controlling access to ammunition they effectively locked the agriculturalists into the mission stations. The Cape government, for its part, had hoped in vain that the missionaries would be agents of social order; missionary encouragement of indigenous political independence didn't go down well at the Castle. A commission of inquiry from Cape Town reported back favourably, however, on the Kok family's attitude towards the colony, and a supply of powder was allocated for defence of the community against Bergenaars, renegade Griqua predators.

Many of the Griquas were substantial land-owners, with considerable herds and flocks. Most had Khoikhoi and San retainers, living in small villages on the farms. Political power was exerted in the same way as among the Afrikaner trekkers. Large land-owners had prestige. Commando leaders who maintained the community fire-power exerted considerable political power also. Just as in the eastern frontier zones,

trekboer culture had vested enormous authority in the patriarch; farmers ran their domains like mini-empires, wielding
quasi-feudal authority only nominally controlled by the colonial government, freely punishing malefactors and rewarding
clients. There were other parallels. The fiercely independent-
minded — not to say bloody-minded — patriarchs in the
trekker republics were to have their authority challenged by
their legislatures, the Volksraads. The Griqua captains'
governance was similarly challenged by the appointment of
magistrates to oversee the lives and politics of non-land-
owners. The squabbles of these contending powers were
to form the similar political histories of the Boers and the
Griquas.

By the time the first trekboers arrived in the 1830s, the
Griqua community had split, in an ancient Khoikhoi (and
African — and Afrikaner) fashion, into rival chiefdoms:
Andries Waterboer and the West Griquas stayed where they
were, around Griekwastad, and Adam Kok drifted down to
Philipstown and Philippolis, settling on both banks of the
Orange a hundred miles or so to the south-east. Kok's group
called themselves the East Griquas, but they didn't last long,
beginning a long process of decay by leasing land to white
farmers who then came to "own" it, thus doing themselves
out of a patrimony. (Kok later led his people on their own
Great Trek, selling out to the Boer republics and trekking
south-east across the Drakensberge to the present Kokstad,
where they founded another East Griqualand, eventually to
be squeezed between the Sotho under Moshoeshoe, the
expanding Xhosa, and more white farmers. Griqualand now
exists primarily in memory.)

By the 1820s, though, when the first white settlers were
reaping their second harvest, the fate of the Griquas was
unsettled. Transorangia was still far from the control of the
Cape government. The governor did make sporadic attempts
to use the missionaries as his agents of control and also tried
political manipulation, by "recognizing" the captaincy rights
of certain Griqua chiefs — setting off at least one Slagtersnek-

style revolt. But the Griquas were to all intents and purposes autonomous: the land was theirs to grant. It's the major difference between the eastern and northern frontiers at the time: in the north, the wealthy land-owners, the employers and politicians, were predominantly non-white.

Why was the opportunity missed? Why didn't the Griquas, an articulate group with access through the missionaries to influence at the Cape, succeed in doing what the later trekker republics did, consolidate and gain independence? Why weren't they able to work out a real role for themselves in an independent Transorangia? Why couldn't the first non-colonial republic outside Swellendam and Graaff-Reinet have been one of land-owners, brown and white, instead of the exclusive white republic it became? The northern frontier was fluid even by tribal standards. There were small groups scattered along the periphery of Castle influence, from the small community of Afrikaners near the mouth of the Orange, in what is now Namibia, through the tribal groupings of the Tlhaping and Rolong in what is now Botswana, to the Griqua communities in Griekwastad and Philippolis and another group on the Harts River. In addition, there were white farmers at Fauresmith, Trompsburg, Jagersfontein, and Edenburg and in the countryside around Bloemfontein.

In the eastern sphere, near the Caledon River on the borders of Lesotho, there were Wesleyan missionaries who had attracted Basters, Sotho, a few Tswana and remnants of various other scattered tribes. Of all these groupings, the Griquas were the most organized. Most of the trekkers treated at least the major Griqua land-holders with formal courtesy as fellow emigrants. Yet somehow the Griquas failed to come together into a formidable enough group to establish community rights. The missionaries have been blamed — each station supported its own local chiefs, and they never worked out a system of dealing with the Griquas as a whole. The Philippolis Griquas, who were on the main trek route north, never therefore established themselves as part of a greater whole, and their land was frittered away. Others have blamed Griqua divisiveness, internal quarrels, their feuding and raiding; but in this they were no different from the trekker republics, which divided as readily as germ cells in a tissue culture. Possibly their military incompetence had something to do with it; they operated commandos, as the Boers did, but never with the same effect; they had no Adriaan van Jaarsveld, no inventive military tacticians, and their communities were never quite able to hold off the raiding parties of blacks that began to spill across the veld in the aftermath of the Zulu explosion across the Drakensberge.

The historian Martin Legassick has argued plausibly in *The Shaping of South African Society* that the Griqua failure was not the fault of the trekkers. The trekker leader Hendrik Potgieter wrote to Adam Kok, Legassick points out, calling himself a "fellow emigrant" with the Griquas, "who together with you dwell in the same strange land." Legassick attributed the Griqua failure rather to the British annexation of the Orange River Sovereignty in 1848, which led to a capital and political base at Bloemfontein, rather than Philippolis. It was in Bloemfontein that the constitution of the later Free State was written, a constitution that excluded the Griquas and all non-whites from citizenship. That constitution is a significant document in South African history. It guaranteed many freedoms — it was the first African constitution to guarantee freedom of the press, for instance. But it also represents a major opportunity lost.

Chapter 8

British politics on the eastern frontier; Ordinance 50 and Abolition; the first stirrings of trekgees

I

THE EXPULSION OF THE Xhosa across the Fish River in the 1790s hadn't brought peace to the eastern frontier. In Xhosa country, a state of armed truce held between various chiefs. The competition for land had led to conflict, but, as is common in tribal societies, neither side held sufficient power to subjugate the other.

On the west side of the frontier matters were scarcely more settled. Khoikhoi remnants still roamed the countryside, living on plunder. There were even centres of agitation that weren't part of the extended Bezuidenhout family. So-called *skelmbaster* kraals consisted of a volatile mix of army deserters from the Cape, Xhosa deserters from across the Fish (usually men accused of witchcraft), angry Hottentot families, a few Afrikaner sons bent on hell-raising, trouble-makers of all kinds. These kraals, besides talking rebellion, raided whose herds they could and contributed to the general uncertainty. The circuit courts were uncovering abuses of all kinds, "free" labour being converted into indenture by all kinds of swindles. Their punishment of white employers set off new rounds of resentment among the prickly and patriarchal Boers. John Philip and his fellow missionaries swam energetically in these turbulent currents, making waves where they could.

Official British policy assumed that the way to frontier peace was separation of the warring sides; in this they were merely following the precedent set by the Dutch East India

Company. As a refinement, they proposed a densely settled buffer zone between the stock farmers and the Xhosa, on the unproven assumption that the more densely settled the border, the less penetrable by raiders. With this in mind they settled thousands of hapless English immigrants along the Fish, having lured them to South Africa with promises that wouldn't have stood a chance in any truth-in-advertising litigation: they were offered "garden lots," virtual parkland, well watered and easy to cultivate; what they found was arid scrub suitable mostly for sheep.

No mention had been made in England of the Xhosa, either, no reference to any troubles or disturbances. Xhosa raiders enlightened the immigrants fast, and the Boers explained the facts of life that the Xhosa missed. Many of the new immigrants fled to the towns, in violation of their contracts, but many stuck it out and became sympathetic to the Boer cause. An unlooked-for consequence of the immigration as far as the government was concerned was the beginning of an irritatingly free press. The Boers, with no newspapers or printing presses of their own, used the English-language Grahamstown *Advertiser* to expound their growing grievances to the world.

These grievances, exaggerated by general economic depression, centred more and more on the relationship between master and servant. In the last years of the Company and the first of the British occupation, regulations had gradually come into force modifying the by now venerable attitude that Khoikhoi and free blacks were to be treated with theoretical equality. The Company had lost interest in the Khoikhoi and had left it to local interests to define their role. At the turn of the century it was decreed that "vagrant" Khoikhoi be set to work for periods of up to two years; vagrancy was gradually defined in terms of the absence of permission to be abroad. The first passes had been ordered in Swellendam and Graaff-Reinet; Governor Caledon had confirmed and extended the burden, requiring all Hottentots to carry a document signed by their employers. The penalty for not doing so was imprisonment. The British were much better at policing and maintaining racial attitudes than the Company had been, but the attitudes they enforced had been taking root for 150 years of colonial society, only gradually growing more pronounced; they were now being reinforced by unequal economic status and by the chaos of frontier life. It was these entrenched attitudes that the missionaries and the later British governments sought to undermine. It was these attitudes that the trekkers took with them to the north. It was these attitudes that controlled social development in the northern republics and shaped Boer culture there. It is these attitudes that govern apartheid.

II

ON THE BLACK SIDE of the Fish, the east, the Xhosa in their frustration were turning to the mystics and the diviners. Ancient Xhosa beliefs placed great store in visions and prophets; their faith in the visionary powers of young girls was positively Lourdesian in its intensity. Social tensions focused attention even more on the healing power of ritual: the creation of victorious armies through sacrifice, and ritual protection from the spells of witches. These beliefs were only sharpened by the activities of the missionaries; the part of the Christian myth that spoke most clearly to the Xhosa was the bit about the Doom at the End of the World, of redemption through destruction, of the dead rising at the End — the apocalypse struck a real chord, as it has in various parts of the Christian world through the millennia; here it fitted neatly into an already worked-out world-view. Many of the early Xhosa raids — through the teens and twenties of the 19th century — were led by holy men preaching the divine way.

Failures of the raids didn't discredit the notion, they only reflected on its current practitioner. The halting of the "natural" tribal expansion and the existence across the Fish of baffling numbers of baffling people nourished the belief that a true prophet, who would bring about true cleansing, would drive the interlopers into the sea.

Such a person was found later in the century; her vision, instead of causing — as the confused folk legend demanded — the arrival of black "Russians from the Crimea on marvellous horses" to expel the Boers, caused instead the destruction of Xhosa power and their subjection, continuing into the present era. The episode began in 1856 when Nonqose, a young girl, told her uncle she had seen a vision of strange people and cattle. Her uncle was an eminent diviner, Mhlakaza, counsellor to the chief; when he investigated her vision, he reported a confirmation that these strange people were indeed the Russians (known to him from reports of the distant Crimean War), among whom his long-dead brother could now be seen. They had commanded him to abjure witchcraft, to cleanse himself, to cause the sacrifice of all cattle in the chiefdom, to burn all grain, and to refrain from sowing new crops. If the Xhosa now did all this, a great black wind would arise to sweep the whites into the sea, and cattle would once again be as plentiful as the land on which they could graze. In a frenzy of religious enthusiasm, the whole population rose and executed their diviner's intentions, killing all their stock and destroying their grain. Within a few months of the slaughter the countryside was starving; entire chiefdoms dispersed, some members drifting to work on white farms, some to death from hunger. Nonqose survived, living long enough to see the Boers themselves subjected by the English in 1902.

III

A SIMILAR, THOUGH less apocalyptic, process was at work to the west, on the "white" side of the Fish, where the primitive Calvinism of the Boers, already tinged with mysticism after 150 years in the African sun, was more and more shaping the *volksgees*, the quasi-mystical belief that the tribe was there for a larger purpose than its own existence. The tribe itself had already come into being. Its existence was now in the process of articulation, shaped by the irritant of the raiders from the

east and by the imperial arrogance from the Cape and
Europe, in the form of a British presence whose governing
assumptions included the intrinsic superiority of their manners and customs over the rude people of the interior. The
Xhosa reliance on the Black Crimeans (and, in another
despairing rising in the 1920s, on "American Negroes in
airplanes") was matched in its intensity by the Boer identification with the travails of the Israelites (and, much later, of
the Israelis). Pieter Jacob de Villiers's search for Beulah gradually began to obsess all the Afrikaners along the frontier.
Trekgedagte (thoughts of departure) gradually became *trekgees*
(the spirit of departure).

The farmers were only partly tied to their farms in any
case; their obsessions were in the haze of the far horizons, not
in any particular *lappie grond* (piece of ground) or any farm.
Land in the south was no longer to be had for the finding;
regulations hemmed them in as much as the Xhosa did. The
horizons seemed jammed with people. Intolerable officials
jabbering in English demanded information, insisted on the
filling in of too many forms. Afrikaners now needed English
permission to visit their relatives, needed a pass to visit farms
in the frontier, needed a permit to take stock to market, were
forced to line up for hours just to talk to an English official.

Even at home there were troubles. The smoke from
neighbours' chimneys was everywhere insufferably close. To
the north, it was known, lay all of Africa. The *predikante*
(preachers) searched their Bibles for signs. For the Afrikaners
were a people, were they not? Forged from many peoples, their
governing spirit a dissent, a refusal to worship any way but
their own, refugees from European corruption. God had
surely brought them here. He had meant for them to be here.
Their destiny was under his control. Surely it was not his will
that their farms be burned, their cattle stolen, their free
spirits crushed? Parlour gossip was not all that different from
the grumbling in the kraals. These were natives of Africa, and
Africa seemed there for the taking. More and more, the sweet
grasses of the empty north beckoned, Beulah beckoned. It

was an easy conversion to believing that God was ordering them to depart into the blue distance.

The precipitating politics of the *trekgees* were of course more prosaic, filled — from the Afrikaner point of view — with the malicious presence of the philanthropist John Philip. Philip's 1828 tract, *Researches in South Africa*, caused a sensation in England and was a seasonal hit in the Reform Parliament of the day. In what would today be regarded as a first-rate piece of advocacy journalism, Philip's work was a thorough indictment of Afrikaner labour practices and an urgent plea for the legal protection of Hottentots. The Commons, filled with the easy zeal of legislators without responsibility, demanded action. The infamous Ordinance 50 was issued in Cape Town the same week.

Infamous in Afrikaner iconography, at least. The Khoikhoi, naturally, felt rather differently, but their voice went unheard in the colony. When I was growing up in Bloemfontein we hardly ever learned what Ordinance 50 actually *was*; we only "knew" it was an evil piece of business that had caused an indignant withdrawal from the colony. In fact much of the ordinance was positive and most of the rest inoffensive; it spent most of its clauses gathering in and collating ordinances that had gone before. The clause that stirred up trouble was the one that established equal rights before the law for everyone regardless of colour. Whatever the merits of the theory, the Boers knew what it would do in practice: it would free more vagrants to make more mischief.

The landdrost of Graaff-Reinet, Andries Stockenstrom, had agreed with Philip that such a law was desirable, but he knew enough about the frontier to understand that if enacted it would indeed increase vagrancy, theft, and violence, and he therefore urged that it include a provision that everyone, regardless of race, be forced to carry a pass. But instead of extending passes in a colour-blind way, the 1828 ordinance abolished them altogether, with predictable results. Lack of formal control meant that looting, burning, and killing increased, as Stockenstrom had feared. Racial attitudes hardened further.

The final precipitant of the Great Trek was the emancipation of the slaves in 1834. Abolition was effected throughout the empire; the English abolitionists' eyes were fixed on the massive slave-owning plantations of the West Indies, whose wealthy owners travelled frequently to London on business. It made some sense, therefore, for compensation — what little there was — to be disbursed in London. It made no sense to the Afrikaners, however, since few of them could afford the trip. Compensation when it did come was only about a third of assessed value; in addition, most of the Afrikaner owners got cheated by unscrupulous British free-lancers taking infamous commissions. Many Afrikaners ended up with nothing at all. Abolition at the same time precipitated into the "free" population a large and quite angry group of ex-slaves, for whom law and order was not high on the list of post-slavery priorities. The sense of Afrikaner injustice grew.

Some modern writers have dismissed the trekkers as people who pushed off in a fit of pique after being deprived of their slaves; but it's forgotten that slavery had been legal and now was abruptly not; many farmers were ruined, and the money they had borrowed to invest in labour was, in effect, expropriated. Still, it wasn't just the money. "These shameful and unjust proceedings," as Anna Steenkamp called them, affected entrenched attitudes as much as they did the purse. Wrote Anna, a heroine of the trek: "It is not so much their freedom which drove us to such lengths as their being placed on an equal footing with Christians, contrary to the laws of God, and the natural distinction of race and colour, so that it was intolerable for any decent Christian to bow down beneath such a yoke, wherefore we rather withdrew in order thus to preserve our doctrines in purity." The tribe was protecting its privilege, all right. Also, in anthropological terms, its endogamous nature.

The authorities knew something was in the wind despite the threat of prosecution hanging over would-be emigrants. Boer scouts had made several trips into the northland and had made contact with King Dingaan, Shaka's assassin and heir, in Zululand, north of present-day Durban; and Stock-enstrom noticed more than the usual restlessness among the frontier farmers. Trekgedagte were at first kept confidential; no burgher wanted to be accused of treason in a repeat of Slagtersnek.

Some half-hearted attempts were made to prevent the exodus everyone knew was coming; a regulation forbade farmers to take servants or "apprentices" out of the colony, but no one paid any attention. In farmhouse parlours the predikante marked the passages containing the exploits of Moses and Aaron; the parable of the plagues was widely — if loosely — interpreted. Wagons began to assemble. The future Voortrekker hero and martyr Piet Retief drafted and published a manifesto, complaining in detail of the "unjustified odium" cast upon them by "interested and dishonest persons under the name of religion," despairing of "saving the colony from those evils which threaten it" and promising:

> Wherever we go . . . we will uphold the just principles of liberty; but, while we will take care that no one is brought by us into a condition of slavery, we will establish such regulations as may suppress crime and prepare proper relations between master and servant. We solemnly declare that we leave this country with a desire to enjoy a quieter life than we have hitherto had. We will not molest any people, nor deprive them of the smallest property; but if attacked we shall consider ourselves fully justified in defending our persons and effects.

Retief's manifesto was the credo for the exodus. The wagons began to pull out. The Great Trek began, and the people who came to be called Voortrekkers were on the move. The tribe was on the move.

Chapter 9

The ravages of Shaka, the healings of Moshoeshoe, the search for Beulah; the working out of the tribal process

I

THE TRIBE WAS ON THE MOVE, but into what was it moving? The who-was-here-first tribal quarrels of South African scholars can be traced to the peculiar condition of the interior when the first trekker wagon trains pulled through. Scholars writing about African societies always assumed somehow that tribal societies changed, if at all, at a glacial pace, that the conditions that anthropologists found had held for centuries and would remain frozen until the glitter of Europe melted tradition. If this was ever true, it had nothing to do with the realities of early 19th-century southern Africa. The area had suffered a convulsion as cataclysmic as the rampaging through Russia of the Golden Hordes.

In the western part of Transorangia, the dreams of the peaceful Rolong and restless Griquas were disturbed by the eruption of marauding bands of who knows who, warrior bands bent on pillage and plunder, driven by some demon at their rear. The Oberholzers and their fellow farmers in Fauresmith heard the rumble of conflict and the smoke of rumour and occasionally took their guns and their horses on commando to cut off a band that penetrated too dangerously close. The trekkers heading north from the Orange River drew their wagons into the laager circle every night, the Hottentot retainers cutting thorn bushes to stuff between the wagon booms; they too dreamed uneasy dreams.

In the Maluti Mountains and on the plains of Thaba

'Nchu the trekkers found Sotho towns of considerable size sacked and deserted, their cattle byres burned; there were heaps of bones everywhere. The cattle of a cattle-loving people were absent; Boer outriders caught glimpses of scrawny herds on hillside pastures, but they melted away when they saw the wagons; the herdsmen were nowhere to be seen. Lone travellers approached cautiously, fearful of being shot. They warned of cannibals in the hills; a madness, they said, had passed through, turning family against family, angering the shades, turning good men into bad animals; often their own families had been butchered by others frantic with fear, or driven by revenge, or desperate for something, anything, with which to feed their own people. Decimated clans took to mountain fastnesses and hurled rocks at all comers. Whole tribes had disappeared.

Across the Drakensberg Mountains an iron peace prevailed, the discipline of the tyrant. To the south the Pondos, already made nervous by the growlings of Xhosa traditions disturbed, attempted buffers against the wind from the north. Tribal Africa was undergoing the convulsion let loose by the Zulus now called the *mfecane*, a word some have translated as "forced migration" but that resonates in tribal memories much the way the word "pogrom" does for the Jews. If the Afrikaners, for their part, had entered their Century of Wrong, the black tribes of the interior were undergoing their Time of Fear and Blood, which led to a defeat not yet ended. From the south, the Afrikaners were on the move. In the east, so was the great empire of the Zulus.

The trekkers entered the interior innocent of the cause of its emptiness, knowing only the results. Chaos seemed the normal condition, the people timid and afraid. In their vision of themselves, their role as pacifiers and civilizers took shape among the feelings of rejection and insecurity; one reinforced the other, their own tribal ethos reinforced by the tribal realities of the black peoples. Many South African blacks still feel Shaka and the Zulus have much to answer for.

II

NO ONE KNOWS how long the Zulus had been setting roots into Zululand. They were already on the northern Natal coast when the first Portuguese explorers set foot there in the 1500s, and recitations of lineages told to shipwrecked sailors indicated they'd been there for centuries. Even less clear is why they were transformed from a fairly typical Nguni tribe, run by small competing chiefdoms without any centralizing power, into a military state whose consolidation would cause consternation and chaos from the Fish River to well beyond the Zambesi. The whys are obscured by the legends that have grown up around the heroic figures in Zulu history, and particularly by the romanticization of Shaka the tyrant, aided and abetted by European fictionizers like the sympathetic E. A. Ritter (*Shaka Zulu*) and the atrocious Rider Haggard; popular perceptions of Shaka now make him a weird combination of Genghis Khan and Napoleon as written by Edgar Rice Burroughs. But if the whys are obscured, the hows are reasonably well documented.

The Zulu founding ancestor, Malandela, lived in the hills of Babanango north of the Umhlatuzi River, about 120 miles or so due north of Durban and, ironically, about equidistant from two places central to later Zulu history: Umgungundhlovu, the royal kraal where they murdered Piet Retief, and Rorke's Drift, where Zulu armies battled the British Empire. Malandela had two sons, Qwabe and Zulu. Qwabe, the senior son, settled near the coast; Zulu settled in the valley a little further inland. Zulu's son Mageba ousted his twin, Phunga, to continue the line through Ndaba, Jama, and Senzangakhona, the father of Shaka. Shaka was succeeded by his brother Dingaan, followed by the younger brother Mpande. The lineage from Mpande is Cetshwayo, Dinizulu, Nkayishana, and Cyprian Bhekuzulu. Chief Mangosuthu Gatsha Buthelezi, a controversial figure in South Africa now and sometimes denigrated as a jumped-up poseur, is in fact a grandson of Dinizulu; as well, his great-grandfather, Mnyamana Buthelezi, was chief councillor under Cetshwayo ("councillor" was generally a hereditary post). Buthelezi is also chief of the Buthelezi tribe, a sub-clan of the Zulus.

The man who began the Zulu march to empire wasn't a member of this royal line but merely the chief of an obscure Nguni clan called the Mthethwa, living near the coast at what is now Richard's Bay. Dingiswayo succeeded to the chieftainship of the clan in the closing years of the 18th century. Tradition has it that he had become fed up with the petty jealousies and tyrannies he saw around him and had killed his brother, then the incumbent, for incompetence. In any case, he took command. Dingiswayo then invented the system Shaka was later to perfect: he cut across ancient clan and lineage loyalties by ignoring the central bonding institution, the circumcision schools, instead merging them into age-linked military units that placed members of diverse clans in single regiments. This undermined small loyalties and created larger ones, bringing about a chánge in attitudes decisive enough to give his armies a crucial advantage; his power began to spread as he brought more and more small chiefdoms under his control. One of these small chiefdoms was the Zulu. It numbered fewer than 2,000 people. Its chief at the time was Senzangakhona. The chief had a lover outside marriage, Nandi of the Langeni tribe. In 1787 Nandi gave birth to an illegitimate child and called him Shaka.

A vast literature of lively and romantic nonsense exists on the life of Shaka. Even reputable historians can't resist some of it: the *Oxford History of South Africa*, for instance, noting that Shaka forbade his men to marry until their 40s, remarked that "sexual ardour was sublimated in intense military activity and discipline," thereby missing the simple point that sex and marriage in Nguni culture had very little to do with each other. Historians can't even decide on Shaka's own sexual performance. Ritter's legend has it that he was a great lover; others, noting he had no children of his own, thought he was impotent or a latent homosexual.

The basic facts of his career are well known. He made a name for himself at Dingiswayo's court as a soldier, was installed as leader of the Zulus at the head of an armed escort from the king, and proceeded to revolutionize Zulu life along the lines his mentor had begun. Clearly he was a military tactician of genius; he used spies and covert action of all kinds; disinformation was common; his discipline was harsh and efficient — well before Stalin, he knew the uses of organized terror. His major innovation was the addition to the armoury of a short stabbing spear; it was enough to give his armies yet another edge.

After Dingiswayo's death in battle — alleged to be brought about by Shaka's treachery — his influence expanded rapidly. He set about to conquer systematically the area of the present province of Natal and territory of kwaZulu, subjugating tribe after tribe and incorporating its people into his military system, usually killing its ruling family for insurance. Like that of many tyrants, Shaka's system worked because it worked — its success brought it more success, and dissent was stilled. His armies had prestige and ate well. They might own no cattle themselves — they all belonged to Shaka — but they had control over many, and endless supplies of milk. They were Men of Respect. Discipline was harsh but the rewards great. Only towards the later part of Shaka's reign, when the tyrant's disease called megalomania was in full flower, did fear supplant loyalty. By this time he was having people impaled for the most trivial offences — sneezing at the wrong time, not laughing or laughing too much at the royal jokes, not weeping sufficiently on the death of the tyrant's mother, who was killed by the tyrant himself.

His armies rolled south, and west, and north. To the south, many of the Pondo fled or were incorporated into the Zulu military system. To increase his insurance, he effectively depopulated the southern part of Natal; thousands of people were killed, grain fields burned, cattle stolen, home life in the whole territory utterly disrupted. Refugees poured into Xhosa territory, squeezing their resources even more severely.

These were the Mfengu, the homeless ones, whom the Xhosa grew to despise and whom the whites, not understanding their origins, called the Fingoes, as if they were a coherent tribe. The Xhosa themselves only escaped because Shaka had heard of the guns of the white farmers and wanted a buffer population between himself and their firepower.

To the north, there were pockets of resistance in the hills. The Dlamini clan, into which Nelson Mandela's family is married, resisted to the end; their reward was to become rulers of what is now the independent country called Swaziland. Refugees from the tyranny poured through their territory, depleting its resources, causing starvation and chaos. A renegade warrior band from Shaka's army descended on the Portuguese settlement at Delagoa Bay (now Maputo, in Mozambique) before subjecting and oppressing the local black tribes along the lower Zambesi. Another refugee band, growing as it went through conquest and intimidation, eventually reached Lake Tanganyika, almost 1,800 miles from its starting point; no one along its path escaped the chaos. The most famous refugee of all was Mzilikazi, one of Shaka's most trusted captains, who defied his tyrant and fled, cutting a horrid swath through Transorangia and eventually well into present-day Zimbabwe, where his descendants, the Matabele, still struggle with the Shona of Robert Mugabe.

To the west, small bands existed in the Drakensberg Mountains, their lives ruined, their cattle gone; they survived by foraging for roots and occasionally eating the flesh of unwary travellers. Marauding bands of refugees disturbed the peaceful Sotho chiefdoms of the interior, setting off further waves of destruction. In the high hills of Lesotho a young man of genius, Moshoeshoe ("the razor") founded a small clan at a stronghold called Thaba Bosiu and began to collect the wandering bands into the Sotho nation. Almost a fifth of Africa was affected in some ways by the *mfecane*; almost the only people who were innocent of it were the white settlers now pouring into the highveld; they paid little attention to black politics; they only knew what they cared to know, which was that much of the land they were entering seemed without centre, without authority, except for the organized empire to the east, of which lurid rumours had reached the frontier of the eastern Cape. They believed — their emissaries assured them — they could treat with that empire.

III

MOSHOESHOE WAS A contemporary of Shaka's, born at about the same time in a small village in the high mountains of northern Lesotho. He was the son of a minor chief who ruled little more than his homestead — not an uncommon thing in Sotho government, where there were dozens of competing chiefdoms whose domains ranged from one hamlet to major towns. A chief's authority depended only partly on his genealogy and substantially on his own ability to protect and counsel. Since defections from one chief to another were common and approved by custom, they were an effective brake on bad rulers and would-be tyrants. The Sotho chief's major function was to settle disputes; those who couldn't settle them satisfactorily lost adherents to those who could. Young men of ability commonly split off to found their own communities; the disputes caused by these splits lasted for generations. Politics, therefore, was extremely fluid in a society that was intensely conservative.

By the time Moshoeshoe reached manhood the catastrophic effects of the *lifaqane*, as the Sotho called the Zulu chaos, were well under way. Three times in the early 1820s large bands of marauders passed through the Caledon Valley and the Maluti Mountains, destroying cattle and grain as they went, killing where they could, driving tribal remnants to take shelter as the San did, in mountain caves and on sheer koppies. By 1825 there was hardly a village in Sotho territory that hadn't been sacked at least once. Major towns were simply abandoned, their inhabitants drifting off to take refuge in the hills, many dying of starvation. Bands of them turned up near Griekwastad, where they were driven off by Boer commandos.

The traditional raiding of cattle, practised by the Sotho as well as the Nguni, had been done more for joyous demonstration of prowess than for booty (though the more cows you had, the more desirable you were to young women and the more wives you could have — booty did have its uses). This joyousness disappeared, banished by the more serious warfare waged by raiders from across the mountains. A group of these invaders fell upon the village Moshoeshoe had recently founded below a mountain called Botha Bothe. Moshoeshoe lost most of his cattle and retreated to his father's village, where he was attacked again, this time by victims of the first raiders. The second attack he beat back, picking up as a bonus a couple of new wives.

Moshoeshoe's later tactical successes against the Boers were foreshadowed by the craft he now showed; he used a subtle combination of force and diplomacy, sometimes going as far as offering already victorious enemies even more cattle than they had demanded as a token of tribute and respect. His diplomacy won him considerable immunity from attack. He also built up a series of informal alliances that were to serve him well later. He was the only chief at the time to fortify koppie summits as protection against attack, to the dismay of his counsellors, who considered caves fit only for San and hyenas. Moshoeshoe always listened to his counsellors but trusted his own counsel most.

IV

THE KEY EVENT THAT marked the beginning of the end of the *mfecane* and the beginnings of black reconstruction was Moshoeshoe's Black March in 1824 to his final fortress home of Thaba Bosiu, an event that lives in the legends of Lesotho in much the same way as Mao's Long March does in the self-conscious mythology of the Chinese Communists.

Moshoeshoe undertook this now famous endeavour after a three-month siege of Botha Bothe by an ambitious chief called Sekonyela, who wanted control of the upper Caledon

Valley. Sekonyela's siege failed, but Moshoeshoe had seen the vulnerability of his home, and, with his family and two hundred followers, made a forced march of 70 miles to the south, where he had heard of a koppie that had perennial springs at the summit, a place more suitable for defence. The march was made in three days in the dead of winter, through frozen countryside inhabited mostly by roving bands of cannibals. Half starved from the siege, chilled by the frozen mountain air, they struggled through high mountain passes. Several of the old, including Moshoeshoe's grandfather, fell behind and were caught by cannibals. The party reached its destination late in the winter's evening; Moshoeshoe named it Thaba Bosiu, "the mountain at night," and set guards at the narrow fissures that pierce the cliffs and are the only way to the top.

He was to remain there for nearly 50 years, forming a constantly shifting network of *ad hoc* alliances, slowly expanding his influence, building his kingdom, defending it through diplomacy and war against Sotho and Nguni enemies, missionary seductions, Afrikaner predators, and finally the white Afrikaner republics, skilfully playing off contending forces against one another.

His survival had nothing to do with luck. He was a tactician of superior skill, fighting successfully all his life against enemies of superior strength. He was one of the few rulers of whatever colour to successfully manipulate Shaka and get away with it. Moshoeshoe's emissaries, bearing both gifts and crafty plans of battle, persuaded the Zulus to take care of most of their enemies without the Sotho having to lift a spear. The Zulu tyrant, always ready for military adventure, detached a regiment to help Moshoeshoe defeat his neighbour to the south, a runaway Nguni called Matiwane. The Zulu army passed through Lesotho like a hurricane, leaving a trail of devastation behind them, and leaving the ruler of Thaba Bosiu the dominant power in his area.

Although Moshoeshoe's legend has undoubtedly heightened his virtues and obscured his faults, there is enough trustworthy evidence to confirm his remarkable qualities.

Moshoeshoe and Shaka were almost invented by history to exemplify diplomat and warmonger, statecraft and tyranny; together they would have confounded Machiavelli, for the gentle man's virtues proved more lasting.

Shaka and Moshoeshoe were opposites in all things. Shaka was aggressive, restless, an illegitimate child who had a wretched boyhood; he never married and recognized no children of his own. He was blood-thirsty, capricious, and bent on conquest. Moshoeshoe had a happy childhood in a peaceful village; later in life he lost count of his wives and many children. He hated war and waged it only when he had to. Even in his diplomacy he was unusual, resorting to deceit only after many years of being lied to by the British. Shaka caused the *mfecane*; Moshoeshoe's calm strength gathered in the shattered remnants of the tribes, left them their customs and their chieftains, offered them the protection of the Mountain at Night, and put a stop to the new and disturbing habit of eating human flesh. It was typical of the man that when he captured the cannibals who had eaten his grandfather, he refused to put them to death. In an apocryphal phrase very Moshoeshoean in its humour and elliptical wisdom, he is said to have remarked: "I will not defile the tomb of my grandfather," and sent them on their way with his blessing and an injunction — strictly enforced — to abandon their ways.

At the end, faced with a choice between conquerors, he had the wisdom to choose the one who wanted him least; the Afrikaners to his west would have stripped him of his land and deprived him of his power; instead, by yielding to the British, he preserved his kingdom intact. The Boers, he knew, were a tribe like Matiwane's or Mzilikazi's; their intentions were to stay and to rule. The British attentions were distracted by events from beyond the borders; they could be counted on to depart, in time. They were not of that place.

V

THESE, THEN, WERE THE processes at work when the white tribe turned northwards. The Afrikaner dream of the empty interior, of the peaceful haven from predators (and their current myth that they took nothing from anyone that was not freely ceded), is as wrong-headed as the black legends, which look to the roll call of lineage leaders to provide sustenance for the comforting myth of endless peaceful occupation. In fact southern Africa was in turmoil, seething, restless, changeable, violent, set off by a long list of causes that included heroic leaders, the prickly yeast of an alien culture in the form of the Afrikaners, a population explosion caused in part by the cultivation of maize instead of sorghum (its six-month instead of nine-month growing season allowed two crops a year and therefore greater population density), a political structure that encouraged fission and opposed consolidation, and mutually antagonistic cultures. (I remember an old Sotho in Bloemfontein when I was a boy disparaging the Zulus as "cockstrutters" because, he said, they let their penises hang out. The Sotho, on the other hand, encouraged marriage back into the paternal line, which the Zulus thought was disgusting incest.) The Afrikaners took "their" land. But "they" had been taking each other's land before the whites ever got there. It is the tribal way.

The apartheid struggle is an outgrowth of the configuration that emerged as a result of the *mfecane* and the white tribe's restlessness. The configuration was caused by multiple tribal processes, happening — then and now — in parallel.

The Zulus, southern Africa's largest, most coherent, and most warlike ethnic group, had their process of consolidation, the process that was begun by Shaka, fatally interrupted by the appearance of the trekker wagons. By 1825 Zulu power was at its apogee, the most formidable military power yet seen in southern Africa. Three years later the great tyrant was dead, assassinated by his brothers Dingaan and Mpande. Dingaan inherited the dismal task of dealing with the trekkers; it was to be Mpande who would have to witness the dismemberment of the kingdom. Nevertheless, it was not the Afrikaners who dissected the corpse. The military system Shaka set up was overthrown not by the Boers but by the British; and Zulu power was not ended except by the slow attrition of 20th-century industrialization and the slow stagnation of the countryside. In a way, it exists yet. KwaZulu, the Bantustan bastard state, the creature of apartheid, is a pathetic remnant, its most important areas reserved for whites, its resources usurped, its access to the sea gone, its coherence destroyed. But on the Tugela River in the Zulu heartland they are beginning to sense that the white tribe that interrupted their dreams has itself reached its apogee. The Zulu process continues.

The Xhosa process of expansion, for its part, was interrupted by the strange white presence beyond the Fish River, and is now once again resurgent; it is likely no accident that the tribe with whom the trekboers had first contact is now leading the opposition to the trekboers' successors — the Xhosa will make sure they have their place at the victors' table. Meanwhile, they are divided. Some cling to the peculiar "homeland" called the Transkei, which has now deteriorated into petty squabbles and tyranny. Others go there only under duress, considering it a vacuous creature of apartheid. There is no doubt that in the times to come the Transkei's days will be numbered. There will likely be reprisals taken.

The Swazi nation's heroic age was its resistance to the great tyranny of Shaka. Its process of consolidation was at first fostered by its alliances with the Voortrekkers, but was put on hold by the arrival of the British, whose dealings with the Afrikaners rode roughshod over their erstwhile allies, as we shall see. The Swazi fate is still uncertain, preserving a precarious independence as they now do outside — but just outside — the boundaries of the apartheid state.

The Sotho process, set in motion by Shaka and consolidated by the tactical genius of Moshoeshoe in his mountain fastness, was stalled by the creation of the non-apartheid haven of Lesotho and is still on hold despite being surrounded by idiotic "homelands." What will become of Moshoeshoe's heirs in the post-apartheid dispensation is an intriguing question.

The creation of the Griquas was merely a temporary halt to the slide in Khoikhoi culture; no one believes the Griquas are or will become a factor in the politics of the change to come.

There are many other tribes. Some — the Venda, for instance, and the Ndebele — cling precariously to ancient cultures in the face of brutal Europeanization and potential Zulu hegemony; the Tswana, for their part, survive in the modern state of Botswana, set up by the British mostly to thwart the Afrikaners, but no one takes their independence seriously, either now or for the future.

And then there is the Afrikaner process, the dispersal into the Endless North of the white tribe. When they got there, as we shall see, they fissioned, as other tribes had, into squabbling chiefdoms. Their process of consolidation was begun again in British concentration camps in the Boer War, and yet again after the Great War of 1914. They won back their country. Their fate is the great question at the heart of the darkness to come.

No process comes to an end, except by apocalypse. Tribal manoeuvrings continue.

PART 3

Jacobus Johannes Luttig de Villiers and the Century of Wrong II: Blood River and the consolidation of the tribe

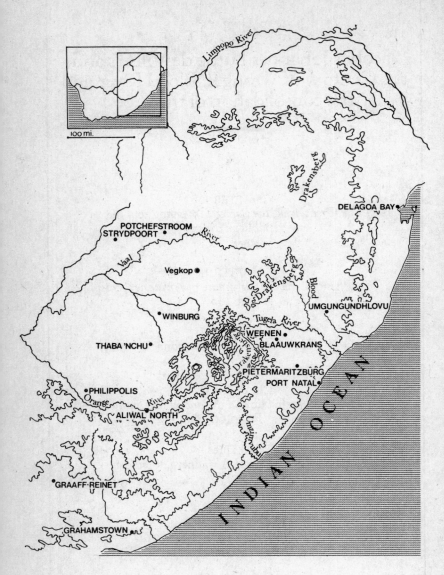

The Great Trek

Chapter 10

The Great Trek, the Sacred Covenant, and the republican dream

I

REPORTS FROM THE NORTH continually filtered down to the troubled Afrikaners in the eastern Cape frontier regions. In 1834 the wild country north of the Vaal River (now called the Transvaal) was still largely unknown, but Luttig de Villiers, only 16, was already accompanying convoys to Transorangia, where the trekboers had settled down temporarily in their endless search for new land. The young transport rider was soon to set up his own business; meanwhile, he made as many trips as he could with other convoys serving trekboer communities in the north. It was known there was a militant king of the Matabele, Mzilikazi, in the Transvaal, but the details were hazy — it wasn't yet known he was Shaka's most famous defector.

Wild rumours of the doings in Natal were published regularly in the Grahamstown newspapers. Shaka's exploits were followed closely through dispatches from the band of English adventurers who had set up shop at Port Natal, as the modern city of Durban was then called. Francis James Farewell, a superannuated naval officer, attempted twice to establish a colony in Natal, becoming a friend and confidant of Shaka's before he was finally murdered by a resentful Zulu vassal. Shaka's conquests — some of them in battles personally witnessed by Farewell — made lurid reading in the south, as indeed they still do today. What fascinated the Afrikaners most was the English description of the unpopulated plains from Port Natal to the Drakensberg Mountains, south and west of the Zulu heartland. Shaka was friendly with Farewell, but he was too shrewd a leader to confide classified information, and the lieutenant, a rough-and-ready fellow of great presence but not hugely gifted intellectually, had no idea that this depopulated zone was an act of deliberate, if brutal, policy, on Shaka's part, later carried on by Dingaan after Shaka's assassination. The frontier settlers sent a deputation to the Zulus to investigate the possibilities: unpopulated land with access to a port sounded irresistible.

The Uys Commission, under Piet Uys, a farmer from the town of Uitenhage who was to become a Voortrekker leader, travelled through the coastal zones to visit the Zulu capital. This commission has always been trotted out by Afrikaner historians as an example of the careful planning of the Great Trek, and of the law-abiding nature of the trekkers: they would take nothing they were not freely given. In fact, the commission is a lamentable example of the failure to understand black politics. Uys found the Xhosa chiefs through whose territory he travelled courteous in the extreme: they offered him endless land to their north, the homeland of the Pondos. The Pondo chief, Faku, received them courteously and pressed on them large tracts of land to his north. With remarkable innocence of human nature, Uys interpreted this as meaning there was land to be had for the asking; he missed altogether Faku's urgent desire to place someone — *anyone* — between himself and the Zulu predators. Of the fact that the *mfecane* still troubled black dreams Uys knew and learned nothing.

In Port Natal Uys stayed with the English, spending a week or two in their sprawling frontier town filled with sailors, their many Zulu wives, and dozens of refugees from as many Zulu sub-chiefdoms. The Zulus instructed Uys in some of the realities of Natal politics, the chief lesson being that Dingaan controlled everything, from the Drakensberge to the sea.

Dingaan, who had inherited and polished Shaka's espionage system, knew only too well they were there. He had no objections to whites at Port Natal. They knew many things the Zulus didn't, and could be used, but he had no interest in the settlement growing too large or too permanent. He knew about guns. Shaka had warned him many times that the whites were dangerous and that dangerous elements in the heartland were not to be tolerated. Dingaan dispatched a military escort of a hundred soldiers to take the Uys party to him.

Here events grow hazy. Most Afrikaner historians believe Dingaan confirmed his willingness to cede territory south of the Tugela, from the mountains to Port Natal. This seems improbable. The "conference," such as it was, was almost guaranteed to cause confusion. The party never did reach the king, since the Tugela was in flood. Uys was ill and sent his kid brother Jannie to treat for him. Messages were shouted back and forth across the river between Jannie and one of Dingaan's senior captains. It doesn't take a genius to realize the two parties were yelling to different agendas. From Dingaan's point of view, he had shown the courtesies and had missed the chance for a probing talk, and that was that. Uys, who had set out full of a sense of his own newly important mission, considered it well done. He returned to Port Natal having come to the firm conclusion that Dingaan had promised them all the land they needed.

It only took Uys's news to tip the already restless frontier farmers into emigration. They had been determined to go: Uys gave them a destination and a timetable.

The trekboers, and to a lesser extent the wandering transport riders, were in the vanguard of the exodus, but they had gone for different reasons. To do with frontier dissatisfactions, to be sure, but also as an extension of the Cape's restless traditions. What followed Uys's commission was to become a true exodus. The numbers were substantial. Within two years 5,000 Voortrekkers (the "before" trekkers or pioneers) departed the colony, crossing the Orange at Aliwal North. By the mid-1850s more than 15,000 people had headed north.

Mzilikazi, who had settled in the Transvaal, and Dingaan himself were to face their first serious military threat, to end in defeat: as we shall see, the Voortrekkers would in short order subdue the most powerful military machines and governments in all of southern Africa. And Moshoeshoe was to face a persistent harassment from his western flank that was ultimately to drive him to take refuge in the ample bosom of Queen Victoria's empire. The Afrikaners themselves, setting out to be a free and independent people in a free and independent state, had some of Shaka's skills but few of Moshoeshoe's: their incipient republics found fission easier than fusion, and the early years were a confusion of dynastic quarrels, clannish splits, and personal animosities reflected in governing structures; their fierce and militant individualism acted more strongly than their needs for collective institutions. They acted, in short, like the Nguni people in the now yearned-for days before the tactical inventions of Dingiswayo.

The Great Trek was the beginning of the second stage in the history of the white tribe, a stage that opened in war and victory, closed in war and defeat. But the Great Trek wasn't a revolution. The Voortrekkers didn't set out to create an entirely new society. They set out to recreate a traditional pattern that their African heritage had taught them was proper, and that the wars against the Xhosa and anglicization by the British had made impossible. Verwoerdian apartheid theorists later maintained that the trek was the first brick in a coherent structure of segregation — that the Afrikaners had first set out to segregate themselves. They did segregate themselves from the pressures that bedevilled them. And they certainly segregated themselves in order to maintain their newly discovered group identity. They also preserved in the north elements of the way of life in the south, and those included having people of other races work for them. The 5,000 Voortrekkers who left in the first few years took with them almost 5,000 servants. They were indeed yearning to be free; they were certainly yearning to be free from harassment and oppression. But they were also yearning to be free from having to do too much menial work. The white tribe's sense of itself was firmly in place.

II

THE FIRST TWO EMIGRANT parties, the treks of Louis Trichardt and Hans van Rensburg, crossed the Orange River at the beginning of 1836. There were, in total, only about a hundred people in a dozen wagons. They made the crossing at Aliwal North, headed west to the mission station at Philippolis and then north-east to the Rolong village of Thaba 'Nchu, where they camped. They were met in Thaba 'Nchu by a curious party of trekboer residents from Griqua country, 200 miles to the west. There is tenuous evidence that Luttig de Villiers, who was then 18, met Trichardt before that difficult man disappeared in the malarial country of the far north-east. But Luttig was well known as a yarner in later days, and the story probably persists only because a generation later the Ziervogel family married into the de Villiers line, and civil commissioner Jeremias Frederik Ziervogel had been Trichardt's closest friend in Graaff-Reinet.

Trichardt was by trek standards an intellectual — most histories of the period rely on the diary he kept for a look at the daily lives of the frontier people. He was also a controversial figure, having been accused by Sir Harry Smith, the peppery little governor of the Cape, of inciting one of the interminable border wars. This was probably rubbish — Sir Harry was notoriously a soldier first and a thinker afterwards, and he went off like a grenade every time someone crossed him. Trichardt was also accused of stock theft and maltreating his servants, and when he left the colony he did so with a price on his head. At the Orange River his party met with that of Long Hans, as van Rensburg was called, a fierce old patriarch nearing 60 who had spent much of his life on commando, most recently in the border war Trichardt was accused of starting. Van Rensburg dreamed often of a peaceful life far from the killing of the Xhosa frontier and was willing to put himself and his family to endless trouble to attain it; it was his personal vision of Beulah that drove the party northwards.

But a vision of the promised land was never enough to keep harmony among individualists this irascible; the temperamental Trichardt was constantly irritated at the way the van Rensburgs — who insisted on being out in front — would shoot at everything that moved, until one of their wagons was groaning under the weight of ivory. His rage spills over into his diary, where he confides that he warned Long Hans to hold his ammunition for targets that needed it. Van Rensburg, of course, paid no attention. They quarrelled about the daily routine, about the order of march, about the discipline of servants, and, most critically, about their destination. Both parties wanted to outflank the Zulus to the north and strike the coast near the Portuguese settlement of Delagoa Bay, but they couldn't agree on how to get there or, indeed, precisely where it was. The two groups finally parted company appropriately at Strydpoort, which would translate roughly as Conflict Gap. Van Rensburg pushed off into the north-east, through what later became the Kruger game park, and to the Limpopo River. There his party were set upon by the Magwamba, a runaway group of Zulus; as predicted, their ammunition ran out and they were overwhelmed and killed.

Trichardt hung around Strydpoort for a while longer, waiting for a larger party from the trek led by Andries Hendrik Potgieter to catch up. Instead, Potgieter himself arrived with a small scouting party, bent on exploring the country north of the Limpopo. Impatiently Trichardt set off on van Rensburg's path. Two years later he reached Delagoa Bay, at the river's mouth, and most of his group perished from fever.

Effective Voortrekker settlement in the northland began with the arrival of the first two substantial leaders, Potgieter and Sarel Cilliers. Potgieter was an imperious personage who was to cause endless trouble by his insistence on extending his patriarchal ways beyond the family to the community (he was also a military leader of note and entered Matabele legend as "the Scourge"). Cilliers was a Dopper, a Calvinist sectarian of haughty but narrow vision, the great puritan of the trek — he was in the north because he felt the trek had been ordained by God and that he had been chosen to implement God's will. It is a strain of Afrikaner thinking that often recurs; Cilliers himself referred to the trekkers in the northland — meaning specifically the whites — as God's tutors, with responsibility for the guidance and tutelage of lesser cultures.

Potgieter "bought" the land on either side of the Vaal River, now the Transvaal–Orange Free State border, from a compliant chief called Makwana. This "sale" probably wasn't as much a fraud as most such transactions; Makwana was a victim of Mzilikazi's patrols himself and was happy enough to set up a few guns between his home base and the Matabele leader. Potgieter's people settled down on this newly purchased land, but the leader himself, ever restless, trekked north on an exploratory mission to scout the land in what is now Zimbabwe for possible settlement. The trekkers, their numbers constantly refreshed by new immigrants from the Cape, spread out in the fertile grasslands between the village of Thaba 'Nchu and the Vaal River; they began planning the site of a town, later to be called Winburg. Living in a land they felt was freely given, they began to put down roots at last.

Mzilikazi, Shaka's errant lieutenant, watched these arrivals with a great deal of uneasiness. The main centre of Matabele influence was only about 100 miles to the north. Punitive Zulu regiments were still nipping away at his south-east flank; Baster commandos from Griekwastad, as mobile and uncontrollable as the Afrikaners, hit and ran on the west. An attack on Moshoeshoe's stronghold had failed. Mzilikazi had earlier prudently sent a lieutenant to Cape Town to sign an entente with the British governor, Sir Benjamin d'Urban (Sir Harry Smith's predecessor), but he didn't have much confidence in its value. What he didn't need was another threat so close to his southern boundaries. As he had done so often before in his relationships with other black tribes, he determined to secure his borders, by warfare if necessary.

Several incidents increased the tension. A farming family called Liebenberg was overrun on the Vaal River, the parents killed, and the children presumed abducted. This was just the kind of thing to whip up trekker indignation — a violation of the clan. Mzilikazi, for his part, was gathering reports from his scouts, and his alarm grew: these settlers were dangerous adversaries. A hunting party that idiotically entered Mzilikazi's territory without seeking permission was summarily wiped out; the old Dopper Cilliers, surveying the scene a few days later, recorded "a terrible murder and plunder . . . I found our laager in a melancholy state. Many were murdered, our livestock swept away by the Enemy . . . It broke my heart."

A few months later, in October 1836, a regiment of Matabele attacked a laager south of the Vaal, at a place enshrined in Afrikaner memory as Vegkop. The attack was beaten off and the Matabele had to be satisfied with cattle and sheep as booty. Potgieter's people withdrew to Thaba 'Nchu, where the sympathetic Rolong fed them and replaced their cattle. (Lot of good it did them: the Rolong were later devastated by being caught in the war between the Sotho and the Boers, and lost all their land.)

In the middle of January a large heavily armed commando under Potgieter and the newly arrived Gert Maritz, formerly a wagon-maker in Graaff-Reinet, retaliated, sacking the Matabele town of Mosega, killing nearly 500 people and stealing their own cattle back. Mzilikazi, his power seriously challenged for the first time, regrouped near the royal kraal. There the trekkers, under Potgieter and Uys, fell upon his soldiers and drove them north after an epic eight-day battle. Mzilikazi, doing for his people what the trekkers were doing for theirs, retreated across the Limpopo to withdraw from his enemies. When he arrived he savagely made war against easier prey, the native Shona, and founded a new headquarters, Bulawayo (meaning Place of the Persecuted One). The second most powerful kingdom in southern Africa had been decisively beaten; the Afrikaners considered the heartland theirs by right of conquest. Winburg was aptly named.

III

THE REMOVAL OF THIS major threat caused joy but no unity among the assembled trekkers. There were now four leaders milling around the Thaba 'Nchu/Winburg area. Each party was made up of extended family, retainers, servants, and hangers-on, usually people who had lived near the farm of the trekking leader. Each party was a self-sufficient clan under a strong-willed patriarch. Each believed the trekkers should unite into a *maatskappy*, a society of free and independent men, but each had his own idea of how that should be achieved, and where, and who should lead it. The four patriarchs were Potgieter, the most anti-British, the most arrogant, the most experienced commando leader; Piet Uys, who regarded himself as the natural leader after his triumphant and brilliant negotiations with Dingaan; Gert Maritz, almost as urbane as Trichardt and a great deal richer; and Piet Retief, perhaps the most magnetic personality of them all. Potgieter and Maritz were constantly at odds; Maritz wanted the trekkers to do a deal with Britain, which enraged Potgieter, whose idea of a new country was to outflank Britain entirely by heading into the far north-east. Uys and Retief wanted to proceed to Natal, Uys figuring they should do so under his leadership.

These contending forces were expressed in the elections to the Council of Policy, a burgher "governing body" made up of Voortrekkers at Thaba 'Nchu and some of the farmers at Winburg. In the first round, Maritz was elected president; Potgieter, logically, commandant. Uys got nothing, to his fury. However, when Retief showed up, he was elected governor, with unspecified and ambiguous powers, and also chief commandant, which cut out Potgieter. The result was acrimony and disputes. Hardly anyone took the deliberations of the council seriously.

By the end of 1837 the Potgieter party was patrolling gloomily about the highveld, and Retief had departed for Port Natal. The rest of the trekkers began to pour across the

Drakensberg Mountains, settling down in the well-watered plains of the foothills, which they found to be empty, and on both sides of the upper Tugela, where there were only small scattered pockets of settlement. Retief intended asking for a deed of cession for a huge stretch of land from the Zulu king, but in practice his people had already occupied it.

In Port Natal Retief learned that Dingaan had given the land away already, to the missionary Allen Gardiner. To this Retief paid no attention: of what use is land to a missionary? The land belonged to those who needed it and could best use it. In a provocative and ultimately fatal piece of politics, he requested the land from Dingaan and at the same time threatened him with the fate of his fellow Nguni, Mzilikazi. His politically confusing dispatch to Dingaan ended with this ambiguous promise: "If you desire to learn at greater length how God deals with bad kings, you may inquire concerning it from the missionaries who are in your country."

Dingaan for his part needed no such warning. He knew only too well what was going on. He had watched Mzilikazi's flight with interest; he had, after all, been trying to chase Mzilikazi off himself. Like Shaka before him, Dingaan had been careful in his dealings with "white people carrying fire," as the Zulu songs had it; he was wary of the implied strength of the British nation; he was intimidated by the achievements and the confidence of the white traders. The traders had now departed and the missionaries were no substitute: Dingaan had hopes of good powder, much preferred to the Word, and missionaries only jabbered. Dingaan was under pressure from his counsellors to drive the wizards off, and when Retief's people settled the land before permission was granted, the pressure grew too much to withstand. Still, he stalled for time. Some cattle had been stolen from him by a renegade chieftain, he told Retief. Get them back and we'll talk. Retief did the favour with an ease that troubled Dingaan, showing up at the royal kraal trailing his stolen herd and carrying in a satchel a document ready for his signature. In its innocent arrogance it demanded all the land from the mountains to the sea and from the Tugela to the Umzimvubu, including Port Natal itself.

The outcome was predictable. Dingaan yielded to his counsellors' urgings and determined to have the Retief party killed. He received them courteously, even putting his mark to the parchment Retief brought, entertaining them with vast quantities of beer and displays of regimental dancing. After 12 hours of this, the Retief party — some 70 Voortrekkers, one doomed de Villiers relative, and 30 coloured servants — were dragged to the execution hill and killed by being impaled on stakes. The scene was witnessed by the missionary Francis Owen, whose house, in a somewhat Shakan touch, had been placed to face the execution spot. Owen's diary has left us a gruesome eyewitness account of the Voortrekkers' lingering deaths.

I turned my eyes and behold! an immense multitude on the bloodstained hill nearly opposite my hut. About 9 or 10 Zoolus to each Boer were dragging their helpless unarmed victim to the fatal spot, where those eyes which awakened this morning to see the cheerful light of day for the last time, are now closed in death . . . Presently the deed of death being accomplished the whole multitude returned to the town to meet their sovereign, and as they drew near to him set up a shout which reached the [mission] station and continued for some time.

Trembling, Owen summoned his family and read them the 91st Psalm, but they were only missionaries and Dingaan didn't pay them any attention. His mind was on other matters. He failed, however, to destroy the deed of cession; it remained with Retief's corpse, waiting to be discovered.

Retief's murder was part one of Dingaan's plan. Part two was to destroy the existing Voortrekker communities and drive them out, as they had driven out Mzilikazi. This part didn't go so well.

On the morning of February 16, 1837, Zulu regiments abruptly descended on the Voortrekkers strung out along the Blaauwkrans River, killing some 500 people and stealing their cattle, an onslaught that has given rise to a millennium's worth of epic tales of bravery and resistance among the Afrikaners, most of them true. In point of fact the Zulus were thorough but not nearly thorough enough — Retief's own laager was missed entirely, and Gert Maritz's group managed to fight off the attack and even to dispatch a small expedition to recover some stolen cattle. In spite of these lapses, the Zulus were satisfied and returned north of the Tugela with their booty.

A few months later an expedition from Port Natal, consisting mostly of white freebooters and renegade Zulus, attacked Dingaan's army in revenge but was routed; in retaliation Dingaan sacked Port Natal, burning it to the ground and causing most of its inhabitants to take refuge in ships offshore.

Worse news for the trekkers was the disaster now referred to in Afrikaner myth as the Vlugkommando, the fleeing (or cowardly) commando. This was a punitive expedition under Potgieter and Uys, who assembled a group on the highveld and stormed across the mountains. It was the worst leadership combination possible. Neither man respected or would listen to the other. The commando was riven by dissent and acrimony and could agree neither on tactics nor on destination. It was ambushed by a Zulu general called Ndlela and humbled, and though most managed to escape, Uys and his young son Dirkie were killed. Potgieter, now facing accusations of incompetence and cowardice, retired in high dudgeon across the mountains back to the highveld. As far as he was concerned the Natal settlement was a lost cause, as he'd warned them from the start. He'd always known the promised land was not to be found near an established military kingdom or within the reach of the British octopus, and Natal was both. He'd warned them and now they'd seen.

Dingaan for his part missed his chance. The summer rains came and instead of consolidating his victory he savoured its fruits. He could easily have dispatched the remaining

Voortrekkers, sapped by defeat, weakened by poor crops and unexpectedly heavy rains, debilitated by lost leaders: Retief dead, Potgieter disgraced and gone, Uys killed, Maritz dead of a fever at 41.

But somehow the trekker spirit recovered, driven, it is said in Afrikaner legend, by the shrill threnody of women demanding a revenge in blood; near the site of the massacre at Blaauwkrans they founded a town called Weenen (Weeping) and determined to weep no more. Beaten and disorganized, they nevertheless turned to reconstruction, founding a capital, Pietermaritzburg (after Retief and Maritz), drafting a constitution, and even selling plots of land on the very borders of the patrolling Zulu armies.

In the Cape colony lurid reports of the massacre at Blaauwkrans created a sensation. Andries Pretorius, an experienced commando leader who was already intent on emigrating, and who had already made a swift exploratory pass through the northlands, accelerated his timetable and set off for Natal with a heavily armed group of 60 men, their wagons stuffed with materiel, including cannon. Pretorius's arrival brought decisive leadership to the disorganized trekkers for the first time. Within a few days he was on his way to the Zulu stronghold with a commando of some 500 mounted men. George Theal, a pro-Afrikaner historian, later wrote that the commando "resembled an itinerant prayer meeting more than a modern army on the march, for the men were imbued with the same spirit as the Ironsides of Cromwell, and spoke and acted in pretty much the same manner." On December 9 the commando vowed a blood oath, that they would build a church and keep the day as a covenant should God grant them victory. Which of course he did, and they did, for at Blood River on December 16 the commando routed and defeated a Zulu army of 10,000 men in a convincing display of the superiority of modern firepower.

The Day of the Covenant — now celebrated on December 16, the day the blood flowed — is still a national holiday in South Africa, though in my time we called it Dingaan's Day and cared naught for its significance. It still baffles the Boers that there can be dissension over celebrating such a famous victory — one that gave them temporary access to the Promised Land. They still seem unable to understand that to the Zulus Blood River was more than an honourable defeat in battle; it represented a furious assault on their homeland by an alien invader. Blood River's legacy is far from finished.

IV

AFTER THE BATTLE OF Blood River Dingaan abandoned his headquarters at Umgungundhlovu and retreated north of the Tugela. A disastrous defeat is never good for army morale; to an army as used to victory as the Zulu one had been under Dingaan's predecessor it seemed especially shocking. This defeat was particularly bad because of the disparity in numbers (10,000 to 500) and also because the Boers were widely believed in Zululand to be white deserters from their legitimate rulers in the Cape; the Zulu army felt strongly about deserters. Entire regiments began to drift away back to their homes; some of the clans conquered by Shaka announced their withdrawal from formal allegiance to the royal house, and Dingaan's brother Mpande began to challenge his authority openly. Dingaan sent an army against Swazi troublemakers in the north in an effort to hold things together, but when that raid too failed the Zulu nation began to come apart at the seams. Mpande, his jealousy now surfacing, made an alliance with the Voortrekkers, and a combined force was formed to put an end to Dingaan's power.

There was one more incident that for the Zulus has the same kind of totemic significance Blood River has for the whites. Dingaan, knowing of the planned invasion, sent two emissaries to Pretorius with presents, in a final attempt at generating an honest peace. Pretorius, at Mpande's urging, had them shot. For killing messengers under a flag of truce Pretorius was roundly criticized; but what affected Afrikaner opinion most was the manner of their deaths. They refused to plead for mercy, and only asked "to be killed by warriors, not by boys or small men," a request that struck a fierce chord among the Afrikaner commandos. Pretorius was later made commandant of the fledgling Voortrekker republic that followed the Zulu defeat in 1838, but his authority was never the same, and the trekker government at one point actually abolished his role as a gesture of disapproval.

Mpande's army under General Nongalaza thrashed Dingaan in a major battle; and as the Voortrekkers joined in, Dingaan's army, in full retreat, simply melted away. Dingaan himself was captured and killed by the Swazis, and Pretorius declared Mpande to be king of the Zulus and a vassal to the Voortrekker state.

This was not the end of Zulu power — that was left to the British to accomplish. Mpande was left with a rump kingdom, though still greater than the one Dingiswayo had ruled. And if Mpande's rule was introspective and uneventful, it was also a time of growth and renewal; in due course his son, Cetshwayo, the nephew of Shaka, rose with an army once more and inflicted a disastrous defeat on an imperial army at Isandhlwana. Only in 1879 were they crushed at the battle of Ulundi; that date marks the final dwindling of Shaka's dream.

V

THE VOORTREKKER REPUBLIC was short-lived. Born in blood, ended in débâcle, it is interesting now only to see what kind of institutions it created. In 1838 the Voortrekkers were faced for the first time with the reality of state-making, instead of the dream of Beulah. Their response was distressingly predictable. The Republic of Natalia was to be run by a Volksraad, which was legislature, executive, and judiciary all in one. There was no president, only a commandant of uncertain and ambiguous powers. The republic took in everything south of the Zulu heartland, north of the Umzimvubu, stretching from the Drakensberg Mountains to the sea. At

Pretorius's urging, the Afrikaner communities across the Drakensberge, at Winburg and at Potgieter's newly created town of Potchefstroom, were brought into the fold and given representatives on the Volksraad.

The voters' roll consisted of adult white males. In line with Retief's manifesto, which had been widely read by Voortrekkers since its publication in Grahamstown earlier in the decade, there was to be no role in government for servants. This was in harmony with the natural order of things, as the trekkers had experienced them in the Cape before the importation of English ways.

There was special provision for *uitlanders*, non-Afrikaners, whites who shared neither the trekkers' language nor their fierce adherence to Calvinism. They were to be treated with the utmost suspicion and allowed to vote only after proving unquestioned allegiance, not only to the Voortrekker state but to trekker ways. Their exclusion was a consequence of the trekkers' fear of the contamination of alien ideas. The theme was to recur often in Afrikaner history.

The Volksraad was never able to settle the case of the blacks native to the new republic. The trekkers had never understood that the land wasn't "theirs" by right of cession. Nor did they understand that the land had never been "empty" except by Zulu conquest and policy; they therefore regarded as interlopers the blacks who returned to their homes after Zulu power had been broken — remnants of many black tribes the Zulus had displaced, and remnants, too, of many Zulu clans that had taken to the hills for fear of the tyrant. The constitution of the Republic of Natalia maintained that blacks were not allowed in white areas at all, except as farm workers and servants — "surplus" blacks were to be moved south. At first they were encouraged to stay as servants, for a settled population of Boers had need of more servants than they had brought with them. And for a time, children captured on punitive raids against the Zulus were allowed as "apprentices." As the black population increased, the regulations grew more and more prescriptive; but the republic lacked the resources to do more than bleat, and the black population steadily grew.

A system of passes instituted for blacks was as ineffective as the modern one is in controlling movement; white society had (as it still has) a basic and built-in contradiction between the need for exclusivity and security on the one hand and cheap labour on the other. This wasn't, of course, the way they saw it. They believed fervently that they had been squeezed from their homeland, caught between savagery on the one hand and an uncaring, unknowing, arrogant imperial presence on the other. They had trekked because they could endure neither. In Natal, they had stained the land with their "own blood and the blood of savages" to secure their way of life; the land was theirs by right of conquest.

The imperial presence proved not so easy to escape. It loomed behind them menacingly wherever they went. It most certainly followed them to Natal. The early trekkers had no knowledge of British politics. They assumed England was united in wanting their subjugation. In fact the British colonists' attitude to the mass departure from their eastern frontier was a mixture of incredulity and apathy, their reaction a mixture of empty threats and cajolery; they certainly made no attempt to follow the trekkers into the apparently endless African interior. The trekkers didn't know this. They were constantly fearful of being overtaken. Now that they were masters of Natal, they wanted the British monster off their backs. Despite grumblings from old Potgieter at Potchefstroom, who believed they should ignore the British altogether, the Volksraad wrote to the Cape demanding British recognition of their independence.

It was a continuation of the habits of mind of the eastern frontier that led to the British refusal to do so and swung a somewhat reluctant colonial government behind missionary opinion that annexation of Natal had become inevitable. Governing was an addictive habit; the British believed they could do it better than the Afrikaners, whose treatment of native inhabitants in any case left a great deal to be desired.

Several widely reported incidents inflamed London and Cape opinion. Most of them involved Voortrekker mistreatment of black inhabitants. Many of these stories later proved to be fabricated. Some of them were true. The so-called Faku factor proved decisive.

Continued stock theft on the Umzimvubu, so reminiscent of the Xhosa raids across the Fish, persuaded Pretorius to form a commando to punish the offenders. As chief victim he chose a Bhaca chief well regarded by missionaries. When Pretorius attacked without warning, killing more than 30 people and stealing 17 children and 3,000 cattle, the Pondo chief Faku, backed by resounding missionary condemnations, asked for British protection.

The colonial governor sent a detachment to Port Natal. There they were besieged by angry Boers, but an epic ride by an Englishman called Dick King summoned reinforcements, and the British prevailed. After a small amount of more or less comic opera political resistance, including an angry petition signed by 400 Afrikaner women declaring that they'd "rather walk barefoot across the Drakensberge" than submit to the English, the Volksraad submitted to British authority in return for a general amnesty. Written into the articles of annexation was the missionary-inspired phrase "There shall not be in the eye of the law any distinction of colour, origin, race or creed; but that the protection of the law in letter and in substance, shall be extended impartially to all alike," a statement resoundly condemned by many Natal trekkers and dolefully broadcast by Potgieter as proof that any dealings with the British would end in dismay and defeat.

On August 8, 1843, the Republic of Natalia came to an end. The annexation did not, however, do very much to help the blacks who remained. British colonial realities were very different from philanthropic intentions. Boer and Briton proved not so very different after all.

The debate over capitulation in the Volksraad was typical of Boer politics: full of rolling oratory, round-house condemnations of one another, flights of rhetorical fancy, a complete absence of consensus. Shooting was avoided, though many of the men thumped the butts of their long guns on the floor in burgher-style applause. It was eventually Pretorius who carried the day. Logically he pointed out that the trekkers, no matter how heroic, couldn't fight both British and Zulu, especially since Britain controlled the one resource no one in the frontier could do without, gunpowder. The Volksraad, to the disgust of the women assembled outside, voted all but one to accept British sovereignty.

Commandant Pretorius carried the day, but it was not his words that lived in Afrikaner memory. It was the oratory of a gaunt, raw-boned widow called Johanna Smit, who laced into the astonished British envoy in his own office with two hours of bitter criticism, much to that man's discomfort. The envoy was an anglicized Afrikaner from the Cape, Hendrik (Henry) Cloete, who had quite lost touch with the manners of the frontier, and this large party, her hands callused by hot rifles (as she told him), both intimidated and horrified him. She was inspired, she said, by the Heavenly Bridegroom, and in his name she spoke. If the men were willing to yield, she declared, the women were not. "Yes," she said, repeating the words of the women's petition, "sooner to cross the Drakensberge on our bare feet to die in liberty, as death is dearer to us than loss of liberty."

Cloete, in the end, paid no attention, but the men of the Great Trek did. Smit reminded them of their God-given right to rule themselves in security and independence; if God didn't intend them to stay in Natal, they would depart. God had tried them and they had not flinched. God was not through with them yet. The spirit of the trek was revitalized. The trekkers began to pack their wagons, the clans gathered, the long whips were rebraided, the oxen harnessed, and they melted away in their second exodus. Their nomadic life began again. This time they knew where they were going. Far from the sea, where, as Potgieter had warned them, the British were always to be found. They would find a new home in the deep interior, in what they called Transvaal.

VI

BY THE TIME THE FIRST British lieutenant-governor of Natal arrived, there were only 60 Afrikaners left. It had all been for naught, the long and exhausting wandering, the arrival in the smiling valleys, the wars, the massacres, the blood oaths, the victory, the sour smell of defeat, the creation of a new order ranked by colour in the ancient patriarchal manner, the raids and counter-raids, the stealing of cattle; they had come and they left, interrupting by their presence the Zulu process and substituting, even if briefly, one of their own, creating a new pattern in the ancient tribal fabric.

As they melted back across the sharp-toothed mountains they had earlier crossed with such high hopes, they left the black tribes as they had found them, the Zulus much reduced in power, to be sure, but then clannish power shifts had always occurred without in any way disturbing the placid pool of the culture. The Afrikaners had paid no attention to black culture. They were too intent on their own collective spirit, wanting too much to be left alone; they were too defensive to want to interfere in any way with other peoples and how they ordered their lives. They were never an imperial presence. Mzilikazi recognized who they were, for they were not unlike him: he also made his way to a new place, twice, when conditions at home became intolerable.

The Afrikaners were reacting as Mzilikazi had, against a colonial presence, and were in their fibre anti-colonialists. They had come as settlers and turned to conquerors whose presence was, of course, destructive, but they never attempted cultural genocide. That was left to the British they despised and to their wretched missionaries. Especially the missionaries, who they believed wanted to dress everyone in the world in black suits and line them up before an endless series of Wigmore Halls to listen to endless series of lectures on the benefits of the Puritan way. There was nothing in the Afrikaner heart like the spirit of the Spanish looters who took South America, nothing even of the casual imperial assumptions of the American west, where the Indians were treated like wild ponies to be tamed and shut into paddocks.

The Afrikaners wanted only to be left alone to continue the life that had become part of their being, the life of the endless open, a quasi-feudal life of tenuous allegiances to outside authority. Then as later, the relationship of the Afrikaner farmer and the African farm labourer was, to be sure, patriarchal and paternalistic; it was also personal. Each had plenty of time, in the placid life of the frontier farm, to adapt himself to the other's ways. The mutual adaptation was to be hurried by the harrying presence of the British imperium and accelerated further by the discovery of minerals in the Transorangia territory and the consequent discovery of South Africa by the forces of Western capitalism. But the nature of Afrikanerdom survived even war with Britain and their own retaking of the whole of South Africa: their desire only to be left alone persisted when they were running the country, and it influenced in some measure the weird edifice they built out of scraps of ideas and called apartheid.

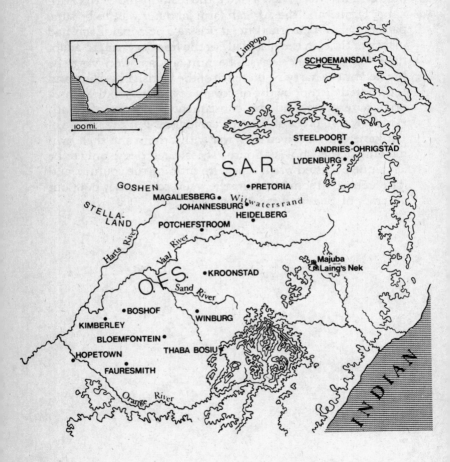

The Afrikaner republics

Chapter 11
Tribal fissions and the nightmare of Afrikaner schism

I

THE DESTRUCTION OF THE Zulu kingdom was left to the British, and the Afrikaner heart turned back inland. Transorangia split, as Afrikaner societies are wont to do, into two frames of mind.

The "softer" attitude was represented by the burghers around Winburg, in what was variously known as east Transorangia, the Orange River Sovereignty, or the Orange Free State, depending on the politics of the moment. At first, the trekboers who had drifted into the region in the years before the Great Trek had not bothered much with government. Some of them had joined with the Republic of Natalia, but many had simply leased land from Andries Waterboer and the Griquas and had kept to themselves, not apparently needing a Volksraad of their own. In 1842 a Voortrekker named Jan Mocke had made an attempt to get a republic going, but nothing much came of it. A circuit court judge, William Menzies of the Cape Supreme Court, tried to annex the area informally on behalf of the colony, but the attempt was disavowed by the British governor. The area remained without a formal name or a formal government until 1848, when it became the Orange River Sovereignty under the Cape colony.

These low-key burghers were used to dealing with the English; they were also confronted with the wise and formidable Moshoeshoe. In consequence, they turned away from old Potgieter and his fierce anti-British ways; they came to recognize that the English were among them for good and that the English people were not necessarily a dagger Europe was holding to the Afrikaner bosom. This accommodating attitude was helped in no small measure by the settlement among them of English people who adopted their own slow rhythms and cadences of life, immigrant families like the Murrays and the Mitchells, who were to become "Afrikaners" without ever learning to speak Afrikaans.

To the north, across the Vaal River, went the hardliners, the men like Hendrik Potgieter; and there also went the "freebooters" — the outlaws, the rangers, the anarchists, the dissidents who were to make up the citizenry of the future South African Republic that Paul Kruger, its president, took to war with the British Empire. The trans–Vaal River region, which later became the S.A.R. and is today the province of Transvaal, was a crazy-quilt mixture of stubborn mini-republics, enclaves run by visionaries, settlements founded and foundered by men of large egos and restless ambitions, held together by a universal desire to get away, to be left alone, and glued together also by their Old Testament view of their destiny. It was in the future Transvaal that Blood River was remembered and enshrined.

The two habits of mind eventually became two republics: an orderly republic between the Orange and the Vaal, and an anarchic republic north of the Vaal, the placid Orange Free State and the turbulent Transvaal (to give them their modern names). The gentler republic south of the Vaal is an example of how cultures can fruitfully mingle; north of the Vaal, on the other hand, the *volkseie* hardened into a mystic vision, and there the obsessive desire for freedom was perverted into a mindless insistence on rules, as it has been so often in human history.

II
—

POTGIETER, TYPICALLY, was full of told-you-so's on the

events in Natal. Early in 1839 his Potchefstroom group issued a proclamation dissociating themselves from any craven submission to the British and declaring their sovereignty over all the burghers from the Drakensberg Mountains in the east to the Orange River in the south, a piece of hubris intensely irritating to the many former trekboers in the southern regions of the domain he now claimed, including those who had struck deals with the Griquas at Fauresmith and who considered their lives reasonably well ordered. Many of the early settlers are on record as opposing Potgieter's homespun constitution, the Thirty-Three Articles, but the Patriarch of the North, as the old man now liked to be styled, simply ignored the nay-sayers and declared his Republic of Potchefstroom-Winburg.

Even that didn't satisfy him and his people. The British were still too close. Potgieter was feeling hemmed in. He paid a visit to the Portuguese and negotiated a deal for a settlement in the hinterland of Delagoa Bay, in the present eastern Transvaal. Potgieter persuaded a large number of Afrikaners to trek to the Steelpoort Valley, on the western slopes of the northern mountains, to a settlement he named Andries-Ohrigstad, after himself (his seldom-used first name was Andries) and a Dutch merchant from Delagoa Bay who had made extravagant promises about the amount of trade he would do with the Voortrekkers.

The settlement was a mess from the start, but Potgieter's pigheadedness wouldn't allow him to see its dangers. The farmers were wracked by malaria, and their stock killed by the tsetse fly. Nor was the area uninhabited: the Swazis and the Pedi regarded the intrusion with a marked lack of enthusiasm. There were, as usual, factional fights. Potgieter assumed command, but there were others who wanted to elect a representative body; it seems the primitive democracy in Natal had been catching. There were quarrels. They escalated. Armed commandos taunted one another. Potgieter furiously toured the farms, exerting the force of his remarkable personality. A rival group under a refugee from Natal, Jacobus

Burger, touting the virtues of people's democracy and bitterly criticizing Potgieter's high-handed ways, set up a government of their own. Civil war loomed. This encouraged the local Swazi and Pedi chiefs, who had been dispersed and demoralized first by Mzilikazi's epic pass through their country and then by the imperious whites with their wretched weapons. They rallied their troops, and raids on farms began again.

At this point a curious person named Doors Buys briefly enters the picture. Doors had been living with the Pedi as a sub-chieftain; he was a man of ability, with numerous wives, somewhat unconventionally drawn from many clans. He was the son of a white outlaw of Cape legend, a freebooter of larger-than-life style named Coenraad de Buys, a seven-foot-tall *alleenloper*, a loner, who had wandered north from the Cape, leaving a trail of children in a rainbow of colours to mark his path, before disappearing over the Limpopo and vanishing from history. (There is a Xhosa clan that still marks de Buys in its lineage tables.)

His son Doors, presumably seeing in the imperious Potgieter something of his father, followed him around with unctuous devotion, spying for him through his numberless wives, helping him steal cattle from the tribes, and generally causing mayhem. This shallow devotion turned to hatred after Potgieter refused to reward his activities by declaring him paramount chief, which is what he demanded. Doors thereafter used his formidable spy system to nibble away at Voortrekker morale. Adding to the uncertainty, war had broken out between Mpande's Zulus and the Swazis, and the turmoil threatened to engulf the settlement.

In 1848 Potgieter, after having had the Natalian Jacobus Burger arrested for crossing his farm, and then releasing him, gave in and departed in a rage, taking half the community with him. He founded a new centre in the Zoutpansberg in the northern Transvaal, settling on a farm he defiantly called Strydfontein (*stryd* means strife). This new site, at Schoemansdal, was even more unhealthy than Ohrigstad; the death rate was alarmingly high and the settlement, once again, was a disaster.

All hope of a unified republic north of the Vaal seemed to be slipping away. The rancour between Pretorius and Potgieter grew more intense; the victor of Blood River had an ego as large as Potgieter's, and his actions in and around Winburg led him later to defend or prosecute more than a dozen libel actions in Cape and Free State newspapers. Small tribal units had coagulated around the leaders: Potgieter in the Zoutpansberg, Burger in Ohrigstad, Pretorius in Potchefstroom and in Magaliesberg, and the old mystic Sarel Cilliers south of the Vaal near Kroonstad, now quite unhinged by his religion but still revered as the prophet of the trek.

However, the tide was turning against Potgieter, who had finally settled down in the Zoutpansberg with his fifth and final wife. Pretorius was living with *his* new wife on a farm near what is now Pretoria in a style unusually lavish for the Afrikaners (his house had wallpaper, the first north of the Vaal and a source of great gossip among the volk). He settled into the steady task of maintaining his reputation, firing off a long series of libellous letters, and with relish sending rangers to intercept the libellous letters of his enemies, including a few that accused him of selling out to the British in Natal. It was this "Boer swindler," as the trekker polemicist Jan Kock called him, who finally finessed a republic and signed an agreement with the British.

In 1849 Pretorius called a series of meetings. They decided, in Potgieter's absence, to elect a unified Transvaal legislature, or Volksraad (the word literally means "people's board"). This was duly done, and Pretorius became chairman. Potgieter ignored the whole affair; he didn't really care. After all, the Volksraad had adopted a version of his constitution, and he was prepared to wait it out, as he had before. Prudently, the new Volksraad had named no head of state. At a meeting in Potchefstroom its chairman, Pretorius, tried to get around this shortcoming by having himself elected commandant general; he submitted to the Volksraad a petition as evidence that to do so would be a submission to popular will. Since this was opposed by a counter-petition from his many enemies, the Volksraad remained sceptical. Pretorius thereupon resigned from the Volksraad and stalked out. Potgieter, for his part, petulantly continued to think of himself as head of state. The solution was a compromise. The Volksraad elected a Krygsraad, or war council, consisting of no fewer than four commandants (Pretorius and Potgieter, with two other trekker leaders, J. A. Enslin and W. F. Joubert, representing Magaliesberg, Zoutpansberg, Marico, and Lydenburg) with Pretorius as "acting commandant general," a solution that fooled no one but that worked anyway.

Potgieter continued to rule his fiefdom; he even sent envoys to his old enemy Mzilikazi in Bulawayo suggesting a treaty of "peace and friendship," and the two old despots met near the Limpopo, getting on over a pipe of tobacco in a way Potgieter had never managed with the other Afrikaners. As acting commandant general, in the pointed absence of a head of state and with the support of the Winburg republicans and, more obscurely, of Moshoeshoe, Pretorius was able to meet a British delegation at the Sand River with a fair simulation of a united republic behind him.

This was good enough for the British, who at this point wanted no more truck with these troublesome individualists. On January 17, 1852, they signed the Sand River Convention giving the trekkers the right to govern themselves north of the Vaal River. This of course they had been doing anyway; the British were just formally recognizing a status quo they had at the moment no interest in contesting. The South African Republic became official.

The convention contained two important clauses, both of which gave the British a decisive responsibility for deciding the future course of events in South Africa, including its race relations. After some boilerplate about the Afrikaners not permitting slavery within their borders, the British explicitly disclaimed all alliances with the "coloured nations" north of the Vaal. They also agreed not to sell arms or ammunition to said coloured nations, while giving the Afrikaners free access to supplies in British-held territory. That simple clause ended any hope of black recovery and consolidation.

III

BY THE MIDDLE OF THE century many of the black tribes dispersed by Shaka were returning to their homelands; sometimes they drifted back as families and individuals, but sometimes also they moved as villages and chiefdoms. In Natal the Zulus and the English were sufficiently organized to make the migrations orderly, but the Transvaal was another matter. The Afrikaners united were more than a match for the strongest black kingdoms, but when the danger was over and they returned to their farms they were unable to control much of anything. On the western borders, trouble was brewing. Parties of Hottentots and Griquas, dispersed over the centuries by Cape expansion, were once more restless. Migrations of other tribes forced the Bushmen deeper into the Kalahari.

Among the whites, some had settled onto their farms and into their villages. But especially in the Transvaal the *burgerstand*, the "society of equals," was haunted by fears substantial and unsubstantial. (The word is hard to translate, but it means some combination of kinship, community, and patriotism.) The primitive Calvinism that had been gathering force on the platteland in the century before the Great Trek had been one of the propulsive forces that drove the tribe north; it helped by giving them a sense of collective injustice — Beulah had after all been burned into their souls. They had trekked into the promised land, only to find there war, followed by their old enemies the British, who had dragged shut the gates to the vision. How could the promised land contain a grid of fences and boundaries? They searched the prophets and found only dire prophecies. *Trekgees* had been a true flame in the Cape; it had promised them deliverance from manifold injustices. There were some Afrikaners, especially in the Orange Free State, who saw it had done just that; it had made them masters in their own houses. And if those houses didn't have the limitless horizons of the Afrikaner dream, they were at least secure. For them, *trekgees* held true as a challenge and not a retreat; these Afrikaners seem to have vanished from international ken, but they are still there. (Some of them settled around Winburg, and we shall get to them presently.)

For others the *trekgees*, its intentions hammered at them by their Dopper preachers in bitter sermons, was beaten flat, its spirit bruised, until all that was left was the dry nightmare of alien ideas. This crippled *gees* was latent everywhere trekkers settled. In the Transvaal it expressed itself in fanaticism on the one hand and random violence on the other. In many places it was simply dormant, waiting for a later generation of Afrikaner intellectuals to give it direction under the banner of nationalism and give it shape under the ideology of apartheid.

In the western Transvaal, where Afrikaner settlement trailed off into groups of Rolong in the arid plains east of the coastal desert, matters were more or less chaotic. The area was vaguely and nominally under the jurisdiction of the Cape and its agents, the missionaries; the frontier region was beyond the reach of the Volksraad's limited controlling power. Throughout the 1860s and 1870s, hunting parties converted easily to commando raiding parties. Cattle theft was endemic: black from black and white, white from black, white from white. As the historian Cornelius de Kiewiet put it, the frontier was "loud with brawling and contentiousness." When war broke out between two rival groups of Rolong, one side called in white commandos, promising them the other side's land as booty in the form of 12,000-acre farms each. Alarmed missionaries sent dispatches to the government in the Cape demanding action. "The Boers are stealing cattle in all directions and burning villages," said an urgent note to the governor. The Cape took no notice. The Cape's whites were banned from mercenary activities, but the Transvaal Volksraad made no such prohibition on its side of the frontier. When the war subsided the "volunteers" duly moved onto the defeated party's land; but to the dismay of the victor, they also took his. Even the victors' own villages were invaded by thugs, under the notorious English freebooter Scotty Smith, and subjected to all the humiliations the fertile imaginations of such thugs could devise.

At the end of the 1870s Gert van Niekerk, who had been a farmer on the Harts River until farming palled for him, became the founder-administrator of the mercenary-run Republic of Stellaland, a tribal mini-state carved out of Rolong territory around Vryburg, on the S.A.R.'s disputed western frontier. Van Niekerk briefly bamboozled a naive Cape colonial servant by playing croquet with young girls on the lawns in front of his house — surely croquet and brigandry could not possibly go together? But van Niekerk was a brigand at heart; he named his new state Stellaland after a passing comet and set as his major national objective plunder and warfare. He governed his country from his farm and was finally to be brushed aside by Paul Kruger, by then president of the South African Republic, who gave Stellaland to the British as part of their corridor to the north in return for a promise of land elsewhere.

In the clear absence of competent authority, more freebooters emulated van Niekerk and in 1882 set up another minuscule republic around a place called Rooigrond, which was nothing but an armed camp. Its "president" was a farmer called N. C. Gey van Pittius. To the pique of the *predikante* they called it Goshen (or, in its proper Dutch, Het Land Goosen) and between cattle-thieving raids issued pious proclamations about their status as the Promised Land. Goshen, too, was eventually to be swatted by Kruger.

In another group of dissatisfied Afrikaners the *trekgees* became perverted as romantic vision combined with reformist zeal, always a deadly pairing. In the middle of the 1870s a group drew together in the central highveld to whom the broad ideal of the African horizon had been narrowed to a pinpoint vision: independence was converted to isolation, self-government to control, freedom to a messianic view of a land of ultimate rest, the search into a perpetual restlessness. Beulah festered in their minds until it was so clear they could sense it just beyond the next rise, *net oor die bult*. This group drew together their wagons and departed once more, melting away into the great beyond, crossing the Great Thirstland of the Kalahari, their bodies lost to Afrikanerdom but their spirit persisting, leaving the sour smell of disenchantment and defeat.

The Thirstlanders — led, ironically, by a coloured visionary from the Cape — departed into the Kalahari in a trek epic in its proportions but twisted in its intentions; that they ended not in their Beulah after all but 2,000 miles away on a high plateau in central Angola, surrounded by black Catholics instead of angels, is an inevitable irony. Fanatics can always endure hardship. It's in their nature. And fanatics always push themselves beyond denial into a contradiction of their own cravings. That's in their nature too. The Thirstland trek is important not because of who they were or where they went. The "great departed" are important only for the echoes they left on the platteland.

The sour spirit they left behind remained in the poverty-stricken hinterlands of the northern Vaal region, in the plattelanders brooding on their Bibles and their violent dreams, clinging to the Coming, underlining the prophets' call to apocalypse. They, and in the years to come their heirs, would be among the first to answer Kruger's call for the commandos to gather for war against the British interloper. They would be among the first to turn away from the broader and more tolerant visions of Jan Smuts and J. B. M. Hertzog and to listen to the new Thirstland vision of Daniel Malan, the prophet of apartheid. They became part of the *volksgees* and part of the *volkseie*, the way of thinking of the people: the iron in the Afrikaner's soul comes from many sources, but its grit comes from the Thirstland. The world sees the Afrikaners as if they're all Thirstland fanatics. But it doesn't see the danger in that misreading — that it leaves nowhere for the wagons to go, except into a descending spiral of impoverishment of spirit, ending in true apocalypse and holocaust. There is a strain, still largely dormant, that would welcome it. It's one of South Africa's many great perils.

Chapter 12
The opening of the heartland

I

MY GREAT-GRANDFATHER Luttig de Villiers had two brothers, and both of them joined him as transport riders in the years before and during the exodus called the Great Trek. None of the three liked the valleys of the Cape — too wet, too old, too closed, too close to the English: Luttig, as we have seen, had been making forays into the country north of the Orange since before the trek in the thirties; clearly he had been regaling his family with tales of the far horizons. By 1845 all three were making regular forays to the Transorangia territory, soon to be the Orange Free State republic; most of their journeys took them to Bloemfontein and Winburg, but their own attention was on the western part of Transorangia, at Fauresmith and Hopetown. Luttig himself eventually settled near Fauresmith; Hopetown was close to the Kimberley and Jagersfontein diamond fields, which had been discovered a decade before and were already attracting get-rich-quick capitalists from as far as California and Siberia: both Luttig's brothers bought land there hoping to strike it rich.

The de Villiers brothers' transport system ran both freight and passengers. In the 1850s the primitive ox-wagon, plodding along from skof (stage) to skof at two or three miles an hour, was still the mode of preference, especially for very heavy loads. These old carts would be pulled by spans of 18 or 20 oxen and could carry loads of five tons. They were large, clumsy-looking things, but well adapted to the terrain; they were exceptionally strong, and could be dragged up *kloofs* (ravines) impassable to more conventional horse-drawn traffic; they were essentially the same wagons used on the trek in the 1830s. Each convoy would have an accompanying flock, *voorlopers en agterryers* (vanguard and rearguard), who would scout the route, shoot game, prepare evening camps, watch for Bushmen, divert elephants, and do whatever else seemed necessary. Most of the passenger runs were made in large, roomy spring wagons with tent covers accommodating 10 or 12 passengers, drawn by teams of 8 or 10 horses. They made the remarkable pace of six or seven miles an hour, including stops. On quicker runs the Cape cart, decribed as a "tented dog-cart capable of holding three persons and a driver," made the journey from the Cape to Bloemfontein in 16 days; overnight stops would be made at farms along the way. The farmers never charged for accommodation or food, since they were usually glad of the company.

By the time Luttig retired in the late 1860s the railway had only reached Wellington, 40 miles or so from its point of departure in Cape Town, and the colony's engineers were still glumly patrolling the kloofs, looking for an easy way through to the easier terrain of the northern plains. The last trip Luttig and his wife Elisabeth made was by "post cart," a rapid transit vehicle with a well for mail and four seats for passengers, capable of a remarkable 500 or 600 miles without stopping except to change horses. But only 20 years later, in the late 1880s, the railway, financed by the gold of the Witwatersrand area and the diamonds of Kimberley, virtually put the transport riders out of business.

Luttig is remembered by contemporaries and in letters as a large, taciturn man, six-foot-three or more, bulky in the saddle, a man who exuded competence. Later in his life, when he lived near Fauresmith, he was occasionally to take on quasi-official duties, and though he was never made landdrost (sheriff) and never took any other paid government post, he was often called upon to settle disputes in the absence of proper order. His own sons remembered him later somewhat shrivelled by the sun, skin blackened to harness leather, his beard grizzled. He was frequently away on community business. A letter that survives simply notes of him that on some days "men would come [to his farm] and they would ride away [with him] never looking backward, to return [him] in their own time"; to his family these arrangements and excursions were always mysterious and their purpose obscure. It was always assumed, though without proof, that he was on state business of some clandestine kind.

Luttig spent as much time as he could on the northern farms. Between trips to and from the south he stayed with relatives in and around the towns of Boshof and Fauresmith. By 1850 there was still commando duty to be done in the western Free State near Fauresmith, for there were groups of Griqua renegades in the area. Luttig helped defend the community when he could.

But the farmers' anxieties had mostly to do with the slower rhythms of the landscape. Life there revolved around rain — too much in the rainy season, too little at other times. The houses looked as if they had been there forever, their roofs converted to corrugated iron, their wooden shutters, unpainted, weathered to a pale iron grey. Typically, rows of bluegums lined the road between the house and the *hoofpad*, as the road between the town of Koffiefontein and Fauresmith was called, still a dirt road on which cart wheels had worn two deep grooves, leaving a *middelmannetjie*, a hump in the centre that could easily tip a drunken driver. To the west, where the dust storms came from, there would be another grove of bluegums. Behind the house, where the farm dam was usually found, there would be the fruit trees — quinces, apricots, groves of mulberries, some *suurappels* for pies, a few trellises of vines. The farms would make no wine — the expertise in wine-making had been left behind in the southwestern Cape — and when a doppie was wanted the patriarch dipped into a barrel of stuff he'd distilled from apricots.

There was by now little cattle farming. Most places had only a small herd for meat and milk. The main crop was sheep. The shearing was done in the spring and the wool taken to Jagersfontein, where English merchants set up tents. Later these merchants moved to the new city of Bloemfontein, east towards Winburg, and sent travelling traders to the individual farms to strike deals; it meant the farmers never had to leave their own land.

The farm workers (or *die volk*, as they were now paternalistically called on the farms — there was nothing here of the *skepsels*, or "creatures," of the northern republic) were usually refugee Tlhaping from north of Griqua territory in what is now Botswana; they drifted southwards after a series of tribal skirmishes. They lived in their own villages on the farms, had their own modest flocks; they were paid virtually nothing except the natural increase of their own flocks, allowed to graze on farm pasture. Their children were looked after, the old folk cared for. The patterns of the south were repeated — it was all the Boers knew.

II

IN THE 1830S AND EARLY 1840S the stirring events of the trek and the Zulu *mfecane* had only dim echoes on the Transorangia veld; bands of riders in the night would occasionally pass; stories would be recounted from farm to farm; the merchants would bring news; but the slow rhythms persisted. By 1843, however, the world was once again beginning to impinge on this small self-contained universe.

John Philip, the infamous Philip of the eastern frontier, he whose polemics had had such an effect on British policy towards non-whites at the Cape, arrived at the London Missionary Society station at Griekwastad. Philip had already visited the Sotho king Moshoeshoe at his stronghold at Thaba Bosiu and had found him agreeable to some kind of treaty with the British. From Moshoeshoe's point of view a treaty that recognized his independence, albeit in a smaller kingdom than he would have liked, was a prudent investment. The Griqua leader Adam Kok was soon persuaded by

Philip of the benefits of similar protection; trekboer families in the area were gradually encroaching on Griqua territory, and Kok had grumbled to Philip about it. The Boers no longer saw the need for leases, he complained. They simply took what land they needed.

A compliant governor in the Cape, Sir George Napier, did as Philip wished. He signed treaties with both Kok and Moshoeshoe. Kok's jurisdiction over the greater part of the trekboer settlement was affirmed; he was awarded an annual salary of £100 and instructed to keep order in his domain.

Easier said than done. Griqua commandos, somewhat uneasily, attempted to settle several disputes and only succeeded in inflaming and uniting Afrikaner opinion against them. There were minor skirmishes; and when open fighting broke out a year later, in 1845, a Fauresmith commando penetrated deep into Griqua territory, where it was finally dispersed by British troops, dispatched by the governor for the purpose. Gloomily, the farmers returned home.

The settlement imposed by the British after this skirmish satisfied no one. Kok's jurisdiction was greatly reduced. But the area south of the Riet River (including Fauresmith and Jagersfontein) was declared "inalienable Griqua possessions," and Afrikaner farmers within it were instructed to vacate when their leases expired. A British resident was appointed to oversee the expected exodus and to mediate disagreements. But since the leases typically had 20 to 30 years to run, the exodus never happened, and the "agreement" had needlessly stirred up Afrikaner anger and uselessly inflated Kok's expectations.

The Afrikaners, who had built up their farms on the assumption of permanent settlement and who were now once again to be dispossessed, gathered once more in restless commandos, but they went nowhere. The Griquas, who had been expecting to move smartly back across the border, complained bitterly to Philip. Philip counselled patience, not having any other solution in mind. To make matters worse, the British presence in the area never really materialized; skirmishes and unrest continued.

In 1848, however, peppy little Harry Smith, temporarily finished with his warring on the eastern frontier and once again ensconced in the Castle as governor, popped up in the interior and declared the existence of an entity he called the Orange River Sovereignty, abruptly extending British dominion north from the Orange to the Vaal. The Griquas were to all intents and purposes expropriated. The Afrikaners were left where they were. But their independence, once again, was gone, their orderly and government-free lives changed with a flourish of Sir Harry's pen.

Smith proclaimed his annexation after solemnly affirming to the old Voortrekker leader Andries Pretorius that he'd take no action without prior consultations with the Afrikaners — or so Pretorius afterwards declared. Consultation, however, wasn't Sir Harry's strong suit; he did what he had to do without asking anyone's permission. (As it turned out, he hadn't really even asked the permission of the Colonial Office in London.) North of the Vaal, left alone, the Afrikaners in the S.A.R. brooded; in Winburg, a gathering of farmers called for an uprising under Pretorius, and the now ageing warrior put together a ragtag army of some 1,200 men and drove Sir Harry's regent, a non-entity called Maj. Henry Warden, and his three companions back across the Orange. But the military glories of Blood River were far in the past, and Pretorius's time had gone. At this point the Boers had no stomach for fighting the British. When Sir Harry returned full of vim and martial vigour at the head of a regiment of British soldiers, there was one minor skirmish at Boomplaats and the Boer army melted away, Pretorius dodging British patrols all the way to the Vaal and beyond.

III

IT WAS ALSO AN uncertain time in the regions east of Winburg. Moshoeshoe, whose spies kept him well informed of white politics, knew the Afrikaners had been humbled by the British. He also knew that the British were committed to a ferocious war with the Xhosa on their eastern frontier — indeed, there had been suspicions in Graaff-Reinet that Moshoeshoe had had some hand in fomenting the latest Xhosa uprising. Though no one was ever able to gather any evidence of his involvement, he surely profited from it. Henry Warden, back again to set up shop in the new capital of Bloemfontein, and fired with zeal by Wesleyan missionaries working with the Sotho, a few Rolong, and left-over Griquas at Thaba 'Nchu, east of the city, promulgated a new boundary line to the east, between the Sovereignty and Moshoeshoe. It gave the land between the Orange and the Caledon to the whites, as well as everything north of the Caledon Valley. This arrangement, he believed, would better protect the missionaries' protégés, reluctant vassals of Moshoeshoe. Moshoeshoe himself paid little attention to the grandly named Warden Line and instead gave permission to his people to spill freely over it. Warden thereupon put together an oddly composed army of Afrikaner loyalist farmers, coloured regulars, and black opponents of the laird of Thaba Bosiu; this army was soundly thrashed by Moshoeshoe at Viervoet.

Unlike the trekker emigrants, many of the trekboers living north of the Orange had until this point considered themselves loyalists, British subjects who owed allegiance to the Cape colonial government. But with Warden's collapse and the demoralization in Bloemfontein, even they refused any longer to turn out for commando duty as they had in the past. Moshoeshoe by his very success had endangered himself. He had tried simply to protect his possessions and his people, but he'd done so almost too thoroughly — he had caused a complete collapse of authority, which violated his own constant search for countervailing forces. In one far-fetched attempt at solving the problem he had caused, he even at one time invited the old Voortrekker Pretorius to see if he could achieve a settlement, an invitation that caused impotent fury in the Bloemfontein fort, where the British occupiers were installed. After all, it had been at least partly to head off a possible intervention by Pretorius in Sotho and

Sovereignty affairs that the British had kissed and forgiven the Transvalers at the Sand River in 1852, in a convention in which the British had formally recognized the South African Republic.

It wasn't long before the Colonial Office in London decided enough was enough and that they should do the same for the Orange River Sovereignty itself — that is, turn it back to the Afrikaners who wanted it. London had become fed up with Sir Harry Smith's autocratic ways and had recalled him; the new governor, Sir George Cathcart, had told the Colonial Office the territory couldn't be held without a garrison of thousands. They weren't prepared to spend the money and began to look for ways out.

There were a few things to be done first. Moshoeshoe soon learned that the British Empire wasn't going to depart without repairing the stain on British honour that the defeat of Warden's motley group represented. Cathcart dispatched a formidable force to Thaba Bosiu to teach Moshoeshoe a lesson. This placed the old king in an awkward position. He didn't want to be defeated, yet he didn't want to leave himself wide open to the much more serious problem of Afrikaner predations without some British protection — his old theory of countervailing forces. His solution was typically Moshoeshoean: his horsemen delivered a sound, but not too sound, check to the British in the high hills of Berea, and then Moshoeshoe sent a humble letter to Cathcart declaring his loyalty to the Queen. The letter concluded on a note transparent in its false obsequiousness to all, except possibly a British army mind: "I entreat peace from you — you have shown your power — you have chastised — let it be enough I pray you — and let me no longer be considered an enemy of the Queen. I will try all I can to keep my people in order for the future." This rubbish apparently satisfied British honour, and Cathcart withdrew. Moshoeshoe immediately set about preparing for war with the Boers.

IV

IN THE ORANGE RIVER SOVEREIGNTY, opinion was split between republicans, made up mostly of Voortrekker settlers, and loyalists, who were trekboers still looking to the Cape for their government. Fauresmith and Winburg were among the communities that elected loyalist delegates to meet with the British representatives. But the British didn't want loyalists. Loyalists were under the circumstances a big pain — where were the freedom-lovers when you really needed them? All the British wanted was a rapid and peaceful withdrawal; they wanted no conditions imposed on them by clinging colonialists. Affairs in Europe demanded their attention: warfare was coming between Britain and Russia. The third Napoleon was on the throne of France. There was economic depression at home. They wanted out, and fast; and when Sir George Clerk, their plenipotentiary, discovered he was facing a reluctant convention he simply dismissed them and appointed republicans in their stead, under the Voortrekker commandant Adriaan Stander. In February 1854 the Republic of the Orange Free State was hastily declared after the signing of the Bloemfontein Convention. The new state's eastern boundary was unspecified, much to Moshoeshoe's unease.

Even then, the Free State defied predictability and veered off from the hardline policies at work north of the Vaal. It elected as president not an eminent commando leader but a small-town lawyer named Josias Philippus Hoffman, a gentle man who, though badly crippled, had wandered all over the interior collecting botanical specimens. Hoffman was an old friend of Moshoeshoe's; his farm at Jammersbergdrift had been given him by the Sotho chief.

By 1854 both Pretorius and Potgieter had died. North of the Vaal the South African Republic had been inherited by a curious character named Marthinus Wessels Pretorius, Andries's son, who in defiance of all sense considered himself the political heir to all Voortrekker domains wherever they might be, and had as part of his agenda a political unification under his own person of the S.A.R. and the new O.F.S. What he actually governed was a country that was scattered, poverty-stricken, anarchic, idiosyncratic. In the south, Hoffman didn't last — he was driven out of office for giving a present of gunpowder to Moshoeshoe — but nevertheless the Orange Free State was to remain a model republic. Its golden age was brief — a mere 40 years — but it gave the Afrikaners for the first time, and possibly for the last, a well-ordered, relatively prosperous home in which they governed themselves without interference.

In some ways it was a fool's paradise, since to the east were Sotho who considered at least part of the land theirs; to the north was the slightly crazed government at the new capital of Pretoria, and to the south waited the British, whose destiny they shared. But the stability of the little republic drew immigrants from the settled farms and towns of the western Cape; it also drew English settlers from the turbulent eastern frontier of the Cape. Both Bloemfontein and Winburg grew into towns whose orderliness and stateliness impressed visitors from Europe (who tended to condescend somewhat). The Fichardts and Marquards came from Germany to settle; the Leviseurs from France; the Fischers and Steyns from the Cape; the Barlows, Barrows, and Franklins from the Xhosa territories. The de Villiers family, which settled finally in the Free State, created farms and built homes in Fauresmith, Boshof, Winburg, and Bloemfontein.

In 1858 Elisabeth Muller, Luttig's first wife, died in Paarl, and nothing more could hold him to the south. He moved to Fauresmith, where he bought a farm he called Klein Treurfontein (Little Sorrowful Fountain) in memory of his wife; and there he met the widow of the Fauresmith storekeeper William Gibbons. Johanna Lodewika Oberholzer, the widow Gibbons, became my great-grandmother. The children of the first marriage also journeyed to the Free State; Pieter Jacob became an assistant landdrost in Winburg, as did his brother Danie. New children followed. The family was at home.

V

FOR THE NEXT 30 YEARS Luttig and his sons lived in and helped run a number of small Free State villages — Fauresmith, Boshof, Winburg. Neither Fauresmith nor Boshof was at all prepossessing, even by the 1870s. A roving correspondent for the *Cape Monthly Magazine* in 1870 told his readers:

> Fauresmith [is] built of unplastered brick in a hurry, and never yet finished, nor meant to be, I imagine, till the question is finally decided whether it is English or Dutch. Even the pot-holes are left open for starlings to build in. Half the inhabitants have gone to the diamond fields; the others preparing to follow. It stands on the red Karoo soil between iron-stone koppies, at the entrance to Sannahspoort, through which a small streamlet languidly trickles, threatening to water some half dozen water erven [plots] owned by the church, which sows not, reaps not, gardens not.

The following year another wanderer reported to his eager Cape readers on a brief visit to Boshof. Or rather, through Boshof:

> Boshof is one of the border villages on the extreme border of the Orange Free State, and lay directly on our route from Bloemfontein to the Diamond Fields on the Vaal river. A cluster of dilapidated houses, a couple of stores, and a church form a centre for the widely scattered Boer population to congregate at on Saturdays and Sundays, and supply their material and religious wants. A ruinous-looking establishment offers "accommodation for man and beast"; but a few hours there convinced us that our host could only give us a minimum of comfort at a maximum of cost.

Effete southerners! They had no understanding of the magic of the platteland, nor of the strength of will of the population then slumbering there.

Winburg, of course, was different. Winburg had a church with a fine thatched roof. Winburg had a fort that boasted a small cannon dubbed Ou Grietjie. Winburg had a fine hotel, several bars, and a telegraph; even visitors from the Cape could feel at home there.

Luttig was to have nine more children, four of them born on Klein Treurfontein in Fauresmith, two in Boshof, and

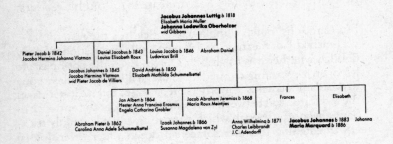

three in Winburg, including the last son, my grandfather Jacobus Johannes, born when Luttig was 65. Since most of his brothers were grown men, my grandfather usually called them by the Boer honorific Oom, or Uncle; he had remarkably little to do with them, and late in his life he would occasionally mention some other Oom that his children had known nothing about.

Luttig was careful to educate his children well; they can even now be distinguished in the Winburg landdrost's office documents by the flourish and flamboyance of their signatures. Young Jacobus Johannes, always called Jim, was the exception, possibly because he was born so late and spent his boyhood in a time of war; in any case he was somewhat proud of his lack of schooling and often boasted that he never wrote letters, even to his family. Luttig himself never became landdrost, but his family was very definitely in the business; at least two of them performed the office, which in the O.F.S. was a combination magistrate and sheriff, and one son, Jaap (Jacob Abraham Jeremias), who had been born in Fauresmith in 1868, went on to become the legal adviser to Presi-

Jacobus Johannes (Jim) de Villiers with the author on his farm La Rochelle, in the Afrikaner heartland near Winburg, in 1942.

The founder of the town of
Villiersdorp, Pieter Hendrik
de Villiers.

Hendrik François de Villiers
farmed Boschendal
in the 1840s and 1850s.

The Boschendal main house.

La Provence, home of Dr. Dan de Villiers, near Boschendal.

Family gathering of de Villiers prisoners of war in Ceylon, taken some time during the Tweede Vryheidsoorlog, as the Boer War was called.

De Villiers family reunion, Stellenbosch, 1932. Jim de Villiers is third from right in the front row; René de Villiers is second from left, back row.

Margaret and the Reverend J. J. T. ("Koo") Marquard with their family, taken just after the end of the Boer War. Maria is standing behind her father; John is behind his mother. Andrew is to the right, Louise is in front, Leo is on the chair to the left, and the baby, Davie, is at the centre. Leo, here a jug-eared kid with one sock up and one down, later founded the South African Liberal Party.

René de Villiers as a baby with his mother, Maria de Villiers, his grandmother, Margaret Marquard, and his great-grandmother, Maria Anna Ziervogel, at the family house in Drostdy Street, Stellenbosch, 1911.

dent Steyn of the O.F.S. and later chief justice of South Africa.

After 1860, when he settled in Fauresmith, Luttig himself rode no more on commando, though the politics of the two Afrikaner republics were still unsettled and there was still fighting on the eastern boundary with Lesotho. He lived for another 30 years and died in Winburg in 1894, living just long enough to see the first bicycles there and to pay a visit to the Volksraad in Bloemfontein, when the members and those landdrosts who could manage to attend saw a special showing of Edison's phonograph, "this latest up-to-date wonder," as *The Friend of the Free State*, the republic's only newspaper, called it. (The program apparently consisted of speeches, mostly incomprehensible, and recordings of brass bands.) Johanna Lodewika, "the widow Gibbons," lived in Winburg until 1901; she died that year when the town was under the occupation of imperial troops. Though she was far from ancient when Luttig died, she was thereafter and forever known to the family only as "old Mrs. de Villiers," who lived in one of Winburg's older houses and whose apricot jam was legendary.

By then the Afrikaners, like the family, had been at home in the heartland for as long as it mattered. It's what we all remember.

Chapter 13
The orderly republic and the anarchic republic

I

THE FREE STATE WAS to be a model republic, but its politics in its first few decades showed the typically tribal tendency to split and splinter. Josias Hoffman had been driven from the presidential residence in Bloemfontein after his gaffe with the gunpowder, and his successor was an Afrikaner who, like Pretorius, had remained in Natal after the coming of the British. Jacobus Boshof's loyalties were to the Cape rather than to the north.

This incited to wrath the unstable M. W. Pretorius, who descended on Bloemfontein to inform the startled Volksraad that he had inherited political power in both republics from his father, and Boshof was therefore out of office, as were the legislators themselves. Unsurprisingly the Volksraad took a dim view of this pronouncement and sent him packing. For a while, public opinion seethed; everyone scrounged recruits, Pretorius even attempting an alliance with Moshoeshoe, who prudently wanted nothing to do with him. Boshof, in turn, made a shaky alliance with Potgieter's successor as leader of the Zoutpansberg community, Stephanus Schoeman, who was, almost ex officio, an opponent of any Pretorius. Within a few weeks a Free State commando and a Transvaal commando faced each other on the Renoster River not very far from the spot where the Voortrekkers had defeated the regiments of Mzilikazi. War was narrowly averted, mostly through the efforts of the future S.A.R. president and respected commando leader Paul Kruger. This was not the first *broedertwis* (brotherly squabble) among the Afrikaners, and it was far from the last. Still, on this occasion a treaty of peace and friendship was signed, and everyone went home.

Pretorius was far from finished, however. He was still president of that happily anarchic state the South African Republic, and he went back to Pretoria to brood.

II

BOSHOF WAS HAVING his own troubles. When the British withdrew, they left the boundary between the Free State and the Sotho unspecified. The Afrikaners naturally took it to be Warden's Line, which gave them more land than any other document; Moshoeshoe, equally naturally, assumed that Warden's idiotic line had vanished with the British, and his people paid no attention to it. Boshof, somewhat reluctantly, raised a strong commando and sallied forth against Thaba Bosiu to teach Moshoeshoe a lesson, thereby following in the unhappy Warden's footsteps, with the same unhappy results: they were soundly thrashed by the Sotho horsemen and retreated in confusion.

C. J. van Rooijen, a burgher pressed into service by a commandant named Senekal, later wrote an account of his part in the débâcle in the Free State journal called *De Boeren-vriend*. A commando from Winburg was to rendezvous with others on the Sotho border. They took along Ou Grietjie, the cannon, with the schoolmaster, an *uitlander* called Rozema, as cannoneer. After two days' travel but before they reached their destination, they saw a party of Sotho horsemen.

We were naturally eager to get after them because none of us had yet fired a shot. About 150 stout fellows with good horses took off after them, also Rozema with Ou Grietjie, drawn by 10 black oxen. As we charged, the Sothos fled. We followed them into the mountains. But they were there to lure us in, lure us away from our laager, and it wasn't long before they were falling on us from all sides. A person can understand, we jumped on our horses and fled through the Sothos to the laager, miles away. We thought there were 30,000 Sothos on horses, and they chased us as hard as they could. You can imagine how we felt. The Sothos were armed with assegais, bows, some with guns. Everyone thought we'd never make it. But through some effort of God's we escaped the bloodhounds and reached the laager, except those who were shot dead or badly wounded. Everywhere you looked afterwards were dead men, corpses, the wounded, Sothos, horses, dogs, saddles and bridles. You could hear the cries of the wounded. The following morning we made a great hole in the ground and laid the dead in it. For three more days we were attacked, and then we retreated to Ladybrand. (my translation)

The schoolteacher and Ou Grietjie were presumably lost.

For a period the Sotho fate was uncertain. The Cape government, which was feeling its oats and which didn't want the Colonial Office in London meddling any more than it had to, tried to raise a regiment to take control of Moshoeshoe's stamping-ground, but never pulled it together. For a delicious few years, the whole matter deteriorated into farce. The Cape decided to import the Grand Solution, none other than Col. Charles Gordon, freshly dubbed "Chinese Gordon" after his triumphs in the Tai-ping rebellion, to pull them out of an embarrassing hole.

This famous man got it all wrong. Instead of letting the Sotho fight it out among themselves, as they had been threatening to do in the aftermath of their victory over the Afrikaners, he rigorously kept the peace. The Cape dwellers were furious — they *wanted* civil war in Basutoland, as the British called Sotho territory. "The man is unhinged," said a telegram from the colonial secretary, after learning that Gordon had urged brotherly love on the Sotho. In fact, it hadn't been brotherly love he was urging. It was just that he declared himself against small clan fights. He wasn't against the great clash: "Let them crash grandly together as an entire tribe," he cried. When no one seemed to appreciate him, Gordon departed for Egypt, decrying the small-mindedness he saw everywhere about him. After a while Cape Town simply gave up and resigned itself to allowing Moshoeshoe to allow himself to be governed directly from Britain. For the Sotho, it was the very least of a long list of possible evils.

III

ON THE FREE STATE'S western frontier matters were about as chaotic as in the Transvaal. The incredible diamond fields around Kimberley had attracted men of ability and energy, like Cecil Rhodes, the future Cape prime minister, and Barney Barnato, who was to become the biggest tycoon of all. They also gave a home to the riffraff of Europe, disaffected Boers, brigands, and politicians of all stripes. Luttig's young son Pieter Jacob, the deputy landdrost of Winburg, was killed in a diamond fields fracas near the little town of Boshof, to which he had been sent to keep order.

In 1870 a British drifter called Stafford Parker, an exseaman who had been eking out a living making bricks, got lucky and found enough diamonds to set up a small town, a canteen, a brothel, a music hall, and sundry other businesses. So successful was his "town" that he also set up a hospital, a police force, and a sewer system; then, emulating the woollier freebooters to the north, he declared himself president of the Diggers Republic. Said republic lasted only a few months before an English magistrate put a stop to it with little trouble. Nothing speaks better of the prudence of the Orange Free State republic than its washing its hands of the entire region of the diamond fields. The revenue from diamonds would have been wonderful for the exchequeur, but the rabble the same stones attracted was horrendous for morale and hell on law and order: the Free State sold the fields to the Cape for £92,000 sterling, and as they redrew the maps to jig their boundary around Kimberley they thought themselves lucky to get the money.

IV

MATTERS NOW BECAME complicated. Boshof was discredited
— partly as a result of the débâcle with Moshoeshoe — and he
resigned. Who should pop up from the Transvaal as declared
candidate but M. W. Pretorius, who saw a joint presidency as
one way to bring about the unification he craved. To the Free
State's own astonishment, he was elected. But now opinion
turned against him in the Transvaal, where the sterner isola-
tionists, backed by the Dopper church, feared the contamination of British ideas; they also feared, probably correctly, that
a unified Afrikaner republic would attract British reprisals.
They therefore disowned Pretorius, telling him to choose one
presidency or the other. Pretorius chose the Free State, but
instead of resigning himself to the loss of the Transvaal he
made an unlikely alliance with his old enemy Schoeman,
whom he caused to disavow the Pretoria Volksraad. For several years there was more than the usual Transvaal anarchy,
and two rival governments set up shop in the northerly
republic: the Volksraad, represented by W. C. van Rensburg
as president and Paul Kruger as commandant, and the erratic
"government" of Schoeman acting as Pretorius's stooge. The
Volksraad was supported by the Doppers, Pretorius by the
heirs of the Voortrekker predikante.

This was *broedertwis* at its worst. The Volksraad was
strong at Potchefstroom and Lydenburg but had supporters
everywhere; so did the other side. Families were split. There
were alarming reports of brother firing at brother. The commandos, reluctantly, gathered once more, Kruger with his
staatsleer (state army) ranged against Schoeman's *volksleer*
(people's army). They lined up one steamy dawn in a small
valley and yelled Calvinist psalms at each other for more
than an hour, singing the militant hymns of their heroic
times, seeking to squeeze one more drop from the banner of
Blood River. Then they opened fire. Within the next hour
the war was over. Seven were dead, some 30 wounded. Most
unlikely of all, Pretorius emerged as peacemaker, resigning

from the presidency of the Free State and (only in the Transvaal!) promptly being re-elected president in the north. The Free State, freed of his presence, elected as president Jan Brand, an anglicized Afrikaner who was the son of the speaker of the Cape legislative assembly. Brand was to rule over his model republic for 24 years (1864–88) and to bring to it an enviable stability.

V

TO THE NORTH, the Transvaal, erratic to the end, once more retreated to its patriarchal fiefdoms and, when Pretorius's term ended, left the government in the hands of a man almost completely at odds with everything it stood for, a liberal free-thinker from the Cape who had been drummed out of the Reformed Church for heresy: Thomas François Burgers, rationalist pusher of secular faith, follower of John Stuart Mill. Burgers ran for election against the afrikanerized Englishman William Robinson and won by 2,964 votes to 388.

It wasn't much that Burgers had inherited. The country was bankrupt. There were no schools (although Burgers appointed a superintendent of schools, there was nothing to superintend, as the historian George Theal pointed out). He imported other grand functionaries as well, among them Jeremias Ziervogel, Louis Trichardt's old friend and my great-great-grandfather (through my grandmother); as much as anyone, Jeremias played a significant role in keeping the tottering republican government in Pretoria going. He died in 1882 and is buried in Pretoria.

The tottering government itself kept no books at all for several years. The Afrikaner patriarchs on their immense estates paid little attention to Pretoria anyway, preferring to hold periodic *braais* (cookouts) for several hundred people at a time and going off on immense elephant hunts far north across the Limpopo. Many of them treated their black servants atrociously; missionaries who complained were sent packing.

There were new gold diggings at Lydenburg, and Burgers had several coins made up with his likeness on them, but the diggers ignored Volksraad demands for tax money. The new British and German immigrants who were beginning to make their way across the border from the Free State acted as if the government didn't exist. Burgers toured Europe trying to raise money for the Transvaal dream of a railway line to Delagoa Bay, but the £60,000 he raised was spent on rolling stock, most of which never rolled out of Europe.

In the northern Transvaal the Venda, recovering from the shock waves caused by Mzilikazi's rampages, were beginning the process of reconstruction. In the north-east the Pedi, first under Sekwati — who gathered tribal remnants into a mountain fastness in the manner of Moshoeshoe — and then under Sekhukhune, were becoming a formidable force. At one point, after a series of minor skirmishes between the Pedi and the Lydenburg farmers, Burgers gathered a commando and went off to punish them.

It didn't work. Sekhukhune had been quietly collecting firearms, some of them purchased from missionaries, others from hunters in exchange for ivory, most of them acquired in raids. The white tribe could always and easily thrash black tribes when the blacks used shields and spears; guns were another matter. The white attack was beaten off and the commando, in part attributing its loss to Burgers and his godless ways, disintegrated; its members drifted back to their farms, there to gather in massive displays of Afrikaner revelry and solidarity, leaving the government to its own devices.

Burgers, it seems, was privately coming to the conclusion that the only thing that could save the Transvaal from complete collapse was intervention by the ancestral enemy, the British; only the British could bring to bear the administrative skills to fuse these fissionable particles into a coherent nucleus. Not that he consulted the particles; far from it. And not that he needed to do any inviting — the British had developed more or less the same idea, inflamed by sensational press reports in London about mismanagement and maltreatment of blacks by whites, and also by exaggerated reports, from Rider Haggard among others, of the extent of the gold to be had for the asking.

They didn't, on the other hand, really want the Transvaal — who did? But the Colonial Office had conceived a scheme for federating all the odd polities of southern Africa, which would then enable Britain to withdraw from the responsibility of direct government, just as it had already done in practice in the Cape. Annexation would also help to ensure that the Afrikaner republics didn't cut the British off from access to the north. Afrikaner legend, of course, misses the complexity of motive. In the legend, annexation is annexation, its motive clearly to suppress Afrikaner liberties.

Annexation appeared in the person of Sir Theophilus Shepstone, the British governor of Natal. In 1877, accompanied by Rider Haggard in some quasi-official capacity and 25 mounted police, Shepstone arrived in the shabby little capital of Pretoria. After three months of lobbying (raising the spectre of the Zulu renascent, among other tactics) and of grand partying in an imperial style, Shepstone finally had Haggard run the Union Jack up the Volksraad's flagpole, signifying a merciful end to a thoroughly wretched experience in self-"government."

This meant war, of course, but not for a while. Matters were to move, but slowly. After due and somewhat deliberate mulling, the Volksraad protested, in the voice of its newly appointed vice-president, Paul Kruger. Burgers himself issued a muted protest too, but he soon took a British pension and went gratefully off to the Karoo to farm. News of the annexation travelled slowly through the platteland, eventually reaching the fiefdoms of the highveld. Shepstone's capricious and inept rule brought Afrikaner anger to the boil. Even before the British arrival morale in the hinterlands had been very low; now it was worse. The government had been a joke. The people seemed to have become lost in Africa, living feudal lives on their vast estates, living for the moment and for the *familie*, isolated and culturally bereft, dependent even more than ever on their own fierce interpretation of the Bible, apparently cut off even from their brethren south of the Vaal.

The British cause wasn't much helped by Shepstone's inept attempt to suppress King Cetshwayo's newly resurgent Zulus; the governor had wanted partly to strengthen his hold on Natal and partly to impress the Transvaal with his ability to control events. A sensational British defeat by the Zulu army at Isandhlwana (and the fall there of the Prince Imperial of France, on loan to the British army to polish his military skills at the expense of a few primitives) aroused not only Afrikaner anger but Afrikaner contempt — to see the mighty British humbled gave the Afrikaner souls a great deal of fierce pleasure. Gatherings on the huge farms drew Boers from considerable distances; at each massive gathering speeches were given, petitions written, quarrels patched up.

These *volksvergaderings* — gatherings of the volk — continued to gain momentum for three years, while the newly installed British garrisons in the small towns of the Transvaal paid little attention. Indeed, they hardly seemed to notice: the prospect of a rising was never taken seriously. At the end of 1880 a *vergadering* of 6,000 people at Wonderfontein declared its intention to boycott all British institutions; Shepstone's Crown colony government was to be considered null and void. Commandos started to form in the north, aided, ironically, by a British victory over the Pedi, which enabled most of the Boers to leave their farms unprotected without fearing for their families' safety.

The Volksraad reconvened. A triumvirate was appointed with Kruger in effective charge. At a time of their own choosing they precipitated war. A farmer, Piet Bezuidenhout — of the same family that had set off the rebellion a century earlier at Slagtersnek — was arrested for refusing to pay his taxes. It was the sign they were waiting for. An armed party of Boers freed him and returned his confiscated property. On December 16, 1880, the Vierkleur, the republican flag of the Transvaal, was raised once more, at Heidelberg; the symbolism of choosing the day of Blood River was deliberate. British garrisons woke up to find themselves surrounded by hostile commandos. Most of them surrendered; those that didn't were overcome. Some 2,000 burghers occupied Laing's Nek, the pass that controlled access from Natal.

General Sir George Pomeroy Colley, the British commander, led his men on a series of inept charges at Laing's Nek and later at Majuba, where some 90 British regulars were killed, and only one Afrikaner. It was the last fighting of the First War of Independence, or the First Boer War as the British called it. The empire retired in confusion, and at the Convention of Pretoria the Transvaal acquired, somewhat ambiguously, "complete self government, subject to the suzerainty of Her Majesty," a phrasing that completely satisfied no one and somewhat satisfied everyone.

The First War of Independence had done what none of the Afrikaner leaders had been able to do: it created out of the fierce individualism of the northern patriarchs a sense of common purpose. Beset a century earlier by a hostile black mass and an arrogant imperial presence, dispersed into the African continent, followed and harassed despite heroic victories over the peoples of the interior, dispersed once more into the endless horizons where they subsided into a long slumber, a white tribe dreaming a dream not yet soured, they were awakened again by the British enemy and brought together into a defensive laager against uitlander influence. It was the definitive creation of Afrikaner nationalism. It would drive them through another war and 80 years of ambiguous peace.

Chapter 14

In the Cape, stirrings of Afrikaner nationalism

I

IN THE GREAT MANOR HOUSES of the Cape, too, nationalism had been stirring. While the Voortrekkers were retreating into the blue beyond, Luttig's great-uncle Paul de Villiers at Boschendal and the de Villiers and Mullers who had inherited part of Nattevlei (and renamed it Weltevreden, or "well satisfied") continued to farm in the old ways. The English were everywhere, but there were also forces in the secret Afrikaner heart that resisted them. These forces were to become part of the Afrikaner Bond (Afrikaner Society) movement, founded in 1879 by a Dutch Reformed minister from Paarl, S. J. du Toit; the Bond was to play a significant role in Afrikaner politics and was crucial in the formal evolution of the Afrikaans language from its Dutch roots.

Paul and Anna had completed their house — the present Great House — in 1812, when Pieter Jacob was farming at Welgelegen, near Bottelary, and lived there until 1839, by which time Luttig was 21 and had already made four trips to the deep interior. We have only scraps of information on what they possessed and how they lived. There is mention in one inventory of "sofas, easy chairs and dining chairs with horsehair upholstery, mahogany-framed mirrors, a grandfather clock, cabinets with silver inlay, sideboards, paintings with gilded frames, several dining tables, a fourposter and other bed with drapery, carpets, curtains, cuspidors and kettles, a large collection of silverware and cutlery."

At the end of 1839, when the last of the slaves had gone or been freed, Paul and Anna moved to Paarl, where they became neighbours of Luttig's brother, Abraham, before he too left for the north. They transferred Boschendal to two sons, Jan Jacobus, then 35, and Hendrik François, 17 and newly married. The brothers farmed jointly for three years before the younger bought out the elder for £1,000. Hendrik then farmed Boschendal for 20 years before ill health forced him to resell the property to Jan Jacobus, who was the last of the family to own Boschendal; he farmed there from 1860 until 1879.

By this time Boschendal was one of the great estates of the Cape. It was close to 600 acres, many of them under grapes and other fruit trees — the farm was a major supplier of fruit to Cape Town. It made Jan Paul, as he was always called, one of the substantial landed gentry, a relatively wealthy man, and he became famous in peninsula society for his gentlemanly bearing and his garb, which usually consisted of exotic dressing gowns in silk and knitted nightcaps with fancy tassels. He was a horse breeder of substance and helped found the Cape Turf Club, which was much patronized by the British dandies of the era. In a way, it was horses that eventually killed him. He went out one night into the chill Cape winter air to investigate a "commotion" in the stables and contracted pneumonia. The resultant ill health caused him to sell the farm in 1879 and move to Paarl, where he died shortly afterwards. The selling price was £3,700; Jan Paul gave the new owner, Daniel Jacobus Retief, a mortgage of £3,000, with 20 years to pay.

But the Cape had fallen onto economic hard times; the Cape economy was too small to be self-sufficient and too weak to make demands on the imperium, and the world-wide depression affected it particularly severely. Retief went bankrupt seven years later and sold the farm to a member of the Myburgh family, Jan Gert, for half the price he paid for it. In 1889 Gert Myburgh, in turn, went bankrupt and the Great House was picked up by an agent for Cecil Rhodes for virtually nothing.

II

FOR WELL OVER A CENTURY the Cape Afrikaners had been mostly spectators to their people's struggle — on the frontier and in the platteland — to maintain their identity. They were looked upon with a certain disdain by the grim farmers of the eastern frontier; the remote burghers of the north hardly thought of them at all except when anglicized Afrikaners appeared among them pushing ideas of a larger *eenheid*, or unity. But the events in the north stirred their blood nevertheless; Jan Paul's cousins at Paarl (where some of the family still own farms and make wine) were Afrikaner nationalists; so was Jan Paul himself, but in his last years he was a follower of J. H. (called Onze Jan, "Our" Jan) Hofmeyr, who was developing his own, somewhat broadened, definition of an Afrikaner, in reaction and partly in opposition to the Afrikaner Bond.

To du Toit and the Bond it was self-evident that an Afrikaner was a person who, among other things, shared those things that historically defined Afrikaners: their religion (their version of the Confession of Dort), their opposition to alien authority, and their language — Afrikaners used the vernacular, Afrikaans, and not the High Dutch still used in pulpit and newspaper, in their daily speech and also in their writing.

To Hofmeyr, this was altogether too narrow a vision. To him, an Afrikaner was anyone who chose to be an Afrikaner; that is, anyone who truly shared what he took to be the central reality of life in southern Africa, which was a love for the land and a determination not to be governed by others. English-speakers could therefore be Afrikaners too; they were welcomed if they committed themselves to Africa, as the Afrikaans-speakers had done. Like Hofmeyr, Jan Paul held no animus against the British; the governor, Sir George Grey, always stayed at Boschendal when visiting the Groot Drakenstein area.

There was a cousin, Jonk Paul (Young Paul), in the group

that gathered around the Reverend du Toit in 1875 when he formed the Genootskap van Regte Afrikaners (Society of True Afrikaners), a precursor of the Bond whose early purpose was to push for the formal recognition of Afrikaans as an official language in the Cape. The language was from the start and by its nature overtly political, an expression of a tribe's political destiny, and, more narrowly, of its resistance to anglicization. In 1879 du Toit's Genootskap published a history of South Africa in Afrikaans, *Die Geskiedenis van ons Land in die Taal van ons Volk* (The History of Our Land in the Language of Our People), that made explicit the tribal dream: that the Afrikaners had been selected by their God to become a distinct people within their own fatherland, speaking a language ordained by God. Implicit in *Die Geskiedenis*, if left unstated, was the belief that to the Afrikaners was given the further destiny of ruling the entire fatherland and "civilizing" its native peoples — the first conversion of 19th-century withdrawal into 20th-century ideas of exclusivity and privilege. In European terms this kind of perversion was familiar — an intellectual's strained reworking of a peasant reality. Many revolutions have been made in this way.

Du Toit's romantic notions were also promulgated in the pages of his newspaper, *Die Afrikaanse Patriot*, a daily of virtually unreadable mysticism that struck one brave note: it supported and applauded the Afrikaners of the Transvaal in the First War of Independence against British imperialism, a position that won the paper, and the Genootskap, adherents on the platteland of the Cape and in the northern republics.

Its tone on this issue was unusually trenchant, the Reverend du Toit occasionally escaping the confines of his theological-school literary training to get off a few good lines about "timid Bondsmen, who are against the separation of the Colony from the Empire, believing that the withdrawal of the British flag might bring the fleet of Switzerland or Monaco or some other formidable power to take possession of the Cape." And occasionally his "cruel seditions," as the Cape prime minister once called them, were extraordinarily

specific: "There must be no English shops, no English sign-
boards, no English advertisements, no English bookkeepers.
Then a national bank must be started to displace the English
banks. Next manufactories of munitions of war must be
started in the two republics . . . So must we become a nation."
And again: "We have often said it, there is just one hindrance
to Confederation, and that is the English flag. Let them take
that away, and within a year the Confederation under the
free Africander flag would be established. But so long as the
English flag remains here, the Africander Bond must be our
Confederation. And the British will, after a while, realise
that . . . they must just have Simon's Town as a naval and
military station on the road to India and give over all the rest
of South Africa to the Africanders."

But Afrikanerdom is never as united as its modern leaders' rhetoric supposes. There was a competing vision of Afrikaner destiny at work in the Cape. This was the inclusive
vision of J. H. Hofmeyr, which recognized that "Afrikaners"
could be drawn from outside the narrow definition of the
volkseie, could include not only those born into the volk but
also those who shared its love of the land. This competing
vision was important then, and it is important still, because
those Afrikaners who share Hofmeyr's views cling to the
possibility of opening up not only to people of other languages but to people of other colours: the men and women
who hold these views could still save the Afrikaner from
himself. Hofmeyr's political and intellectual heirs are, in fact,
still a part of the Afrikaner body politic, virtually invisible to
the outside world, buried as they are in the tidal wave of
condemnation faced by the tribe. But Onze Jan's inclusive
spirit does live on. My father counts himself among its believ-
ers. So do many others. The *verligte* (enlightened) Afrikaners
still occasionally draw their nourishment from Hofmeyr. The
tribe, as I have said, does not speak with a single voice.

In the Cape of the 1880s, Onze Jan carried the day, at least
temporarily, until Alfred Milner and Cecil Rhodes made the
Anglo–Boer War inevitable and thereby brought all Afri-

kaners together, from the Zoutpansberg Mountains in the far north to the Constantia slopes of Cape Town.

III

HOFMEYR DIDN'T SPRING from nowhere. The Afrikaans schools in Cape Town and Paarl had their share of liberals, just as they did of anglicized Dutchmen; it's easy to be hard on the British South Africans, but English liberalism had its converts among the volk. Hofmeyr got his public start in journalism, becoming at the age of 16 a founding member of a small daily of strong Calvinist leanings called *Die Volksvriend*, a paper that to the modern reader seems overly preachy and narrowly focused, but that carved itself out a niche in the intensely competitive newspaper market of the small city. (Cape Town, whose population at this stage was no more than 30,000, supported seven daily papers, two in Dutch and five in English. One of the Dutch papers, *Die Zuid Afrikaan*, was later edited by Hofmeyr.)

Hofmeyr's superior tactical skill enabled him to effectively take over the Bond and defeat du Toit through lobby groups such as his Boeren Beschermings Vereeniging (Farmers' Protection Association); in the Bond his vision of the Afrikaner nation was to prevail, however temporarily. The political version of this vision shouldn't be overstated: it did believe in an inclusive nationalism, defining an Afrikaner as any person who was truly committed to South Africa, regardless of language. But Hofmeyr also believed in colonial institutions, in working through the existing system, and he agreed with Cecil Rhodes on the civilizing mission of the whites to the blacks: his definition of Afrikaner had no room for tribal blacks. On the question of the coloureds, on the other hand, his mind was made up: they were his constituents when he was finally elected to the legislature, he defended their rights, they spoke Afrikaans, they should be accorded full membership in the community.

The annexation of the Transvaal by the British and the

ensuing mini-war sharpened Hofmeyr's point of view and Afrikaans opinion within the Bond. Hofmeyr had condemned the annexation in *Die Zuid Afrikaan* but had never supported the growing demand for an Afrikaner resort to arms — partly, as he confessed later, because he didn't have much faith that the northern patriarchs could be stirred from their slumbers. He had believed that "if they ever decided on war . . . the next morning would find that they all had important business at home . . . and that therefore the taking up of arms was both suicidal and mad." He was convinced that an uprising was just what British officials in Pretoria wanted "as a pretext for military despotism." This attitude didn't exactly endear Hofmeyr to the Cape British either; it was widely believed that he had been responsible for inciting the Transvalers to revolt, and as a report in the *Argus* put it, "the windows of his office were thrown in by a hostile mob and the mention of his name in the Theatre was the signal for a demonstration of extreme hostility."

Hofmeyr ran the Bond as if it were a political party — it never formally became one — and from 1884 it usually controlled a third or more of the seats in the House. He himself accepted a Cabinet post once, though with great reluctance, and only after being guaranteed "freedom from the cares of administration."

His instinct was right. He should have stayed out. He hated governing and the constraints it brought with it, and he was never very good at it. For instance, he wanted to introduce a motion making at least Dutch if not Afrikaans an official language in the Cape, but the Cabinet of which he was a member wouldn't go for it. Hofmeyr therefore had to have the measure introduced by a private member, one Willie de Villiers, a Dutch Reformed clergyman from Malmesbury. De Villiers, a distant cousin only to the Boschendal de Villiers, duly put the motion, and to Hofmeyr's disgust another member of the Cabinet actually spoke strongly against it.

A year later he set off on a speaking tour of the platteland towns of Robertson, Montagu, Heidelberg, and Oudshoorn and there discovered how far he was distancing himself from the plattelanders' concerns. In the curious phrasing of contemporary newspaper reports came this account of his speech at a meeting at Montagu:

> If he thought of the shameful violation of the rights of the Transvaal by Great Britain then his pulse beat fast within him. Yet he could never advise them to take up arms, because he feared the power of England too much. He had done all, that was in his power, to arouse the sympathy of other nations, and to provide for the widows of the slain and also for the wounded, and had succeeded by means of an appeal to the charitable feeling of the country in collecting several thousand pounds. He had used all his influence in the direction of peace, and yet, in spite of all this, he was still suspected by many, and there were some who doubted his uprightness. At one time he was taunted with the reproach: "You are bathing yourself in Jingoism." At another time: "You are working yourself up to be King of the Africanders . . ." He would go forward undeterred to defend courageously the rights of our language, of Transvaal, and his fellow countrymen, but, the oath of allegiance to Her Majesty, once taken, he would never violate.

The plattelanders hooted and booed. This oath of allegiance was a touchy business. How can an oath be an oath if it's forced on you? How could Hofmeyr accept it so easily? How could he swear fealty to a power attempting to suppress his own?

Somewhat shaken by the vehemence of platteland feeling, Hofmeyr resigned a few weeks later after a furious public argument with the premier, John X. Merriman, closely calculated to win him back some of his wavering compatriots.

IV

THAT DONE, HOFMEYR turned his attention to the two great questions that were to plague South Africa for the rest of his life and that to some extent plague it still: relationships with the English-speaking South Africans, and "the native question," as it had come to be called. Of course it is the "native question" that obsesses the world today, but at first the question of the English was dominant; the imperial presence still hovered.

On the English his views never wavered; they persisted, and persisted in getting him into trouble with his people. He was, he declared, in favour of Africa for the Afrikaners, from the Cape to the Zambesi (a slogan then current among the members of the Bond, and a thread that ran clear through the Free State before snagging in the highlands of the Transvaal, where they couldn't care less about the Cape). But he refused to count out the English. His policy was well set out in a speech to the Bloemfontein Volksraad, which he visited in order to generate Free State sympathy for his abortive plan for the Cape, instead of the Colonial Office in London, to take over the Sotho territory.

> I have been exposed as a crafty diplomatist, whose striving it is, with all kinds of sly dodges, to keep the Englishman and his language out of South Africa. I must be mad if that were my aim! . . . I understand only too well that, even if the country became independent tomorrow, it would be impossible, yes, suicidal, to drive out that third part [who are English]. I know that, whatever the future of South Africa may be, the English element will have to be tolerated along with the Dutch. And I am quite content with that. But what I say to my English fellow-Colonists is this: Do you love your language, we love ours; you have national prejudice, we too are not free from that; therefore grant us the same rights in language and nationality as you ask for yourselves. Only when that demand is granted, not with grumblings and complaints, but willingly and readily, then shall we see a reconciliation between the two elements in South Africa. This reconciliation and rapprochement is the foundation of my hopes.

The speech was well received in Bloemfontein and Winburg, whose English minorities were already well integrated. (Hofmeyr's Sotho policy went down less well; the Free Staters believed that if anyone other than themselves were to inherit Moshoeshoe's territory, it wouldn't be the Cape. It also didn't go down very well among the Sotho, who were content to be ruled by London rather than the Cape, since the British were more remote and less likely to want to manage their lives too minutely.)

Oddly, the logic of events drove Hofmeyr the Afrikaner nationalist into the arms of the arch-imperialist, the immensely wealthy capitalist who was soon to be premier of the Cape, Cecil Rhodes. It was not Rhodes's mystical pan-Britishism that fascinated Hofmeyr but his vision of a territory united from the Cape to the distant northern horizons. And when Rhodes, frustrated in Bechuanaland by British military ineptness and by the irritating presence of the freebooter republics Stellaland and Goshen, decided that unification should take place under the control of the colonial, rather than the imperial, government, Hofmeyr saw in his vision an echo of his own. (Even du Toit was won over, as much by Rhodes's "immense and brooding spirit" and his romantic visions of a unified future as by any specific policy.)

The presence of the Boer republics was awkward for Hofmeyr to fit into his scheme — why a long-term plan to bring independence when independence was already half won? The peculiar antics of the Transvaal government helped; it was easy to see them as an obstacle to union rather than a source of it. The pace of the north might be that of an ox, but its attitudes were mulish. Hofmeyr much preferred the quick mind and international connections of Rhodes, helped by Rhodes's unwavering commitment to and love of the Cape. (Boschendal was not the only great house he bought and saved from ruin.) His determination to live out his days in the gentle valleys of the Cape won Hofmeyr's Afrikaner heart, and the two became fast friends. Rhodes's first government as prime minister included members of the Bond and had Hofmeyr's support; in return, Rhodes was to support the intentions of the Bond and the Afrikaners. Jointly they would push the borders of the Cape to the Limpopo and beyond.

V

THE "NATIVE QUESTION" WAS more intractable. Modern historians, reacting against the simple-minded assumptions of the past, have tended to dismiss Hofmeyr's views as primitive racial chauvinism. Thus Leonard Thompson's view, in the *Oxford History of South Africa*, was simply that Rhodes and Hofmeyr "agreed in regarding the African tribesmen as 'barbarous' people who should be prevented from obtaining a foothold in the political systems of the colonies and republics." Well, yes and no.

Hofmeyr, in truth, was ambivalent. His commitment to Bond members did, at least at first, drive him in irrational directions. In 1881 there was another in the long series of skirmishes and small wars along the Fish River frontier, a series that had started with van Jaarsveld and Maynier, as the expanding trekboers met the expanding Xhosa nation. After the British asserted control of the frontier around the 1830s, these wars for possession of disputed Xhosa and Thembu territory were usually dignified with names, and the various battles were grouped, for convenience' sake, into "Kaffir Wars" I through IX. Among black nationalists in South Africa today these have been renamed the Wars of Dispossession, which is what they represented to the Xhosa clans. In the 1881 affair, many Thembu were driven east to the Keiskama River, and in the manner of the trekboers of old, farmers came flooding in from all over the country to apportion the land among themselves. But the Cape government, for the first time, treated them not as legitimate settlers but as squatters. They were ejected and "their" land sold. Hofmeyr objected strongly. His arguments can most charitably be described as specious.

The substance of them was this: where a stretch of country is left vacant after a war it was not unreasonable that it be open for colonization, as this process did not involve the ejection of any owner. The sophistry of the argument seems to have escaped commentators of the period. From Hofmeyr's point of view the squatters had in fact conferred a service on the colony, for by settling on the land they prevented the Thembu straggling back, or, worse, the land becoming an "asylum for all the worst characters in the colony."

Over the next decade Hofmeyr's ideas became considerably more sophisticated, though still coloured by an ingrained paternalism that grates on the modern mind. They are worth setting out in some detail, since it was against his views that the early theoreticians of apartheid were reacting, and it is a version of his views, though couched in more modern language, that so-called *verligte* Afrikaners began pushing in the 1970s.

He believed that in their "ordinary state," by which he meant a preliterate tribal state, the "natives" were politically and socially inferior, and as such needed paternal treatment. He believed a corollary as strongly: the obligation lay on the more sophisticated culture to give the less sophisticated every chance to adapt, and that as soon as adaptation had taken place "then let [the native] be accorded his full rights due to his position as a fullgrown man." Hofmeyr's was a cultural, not a racial, chauvinism, which at least allowed room for escape.

In the politics of the Cape at the time, he said, there was a danger in a system that gave a full franchise to a majority of tribal people still smarting from serial defeats in war. "There is a grave danger of a system, whereby men of both colours vote together, in that eventually politics may become a struggle between the races." Hofmeyr was nervous that the complicated Xhosa patterns of clan and chiefly allegiances wouldn't translate well into parliamentary-style democracy; yet he was in favour of "native representation." At the same time, he considered the franchise qualification too low — the Cape constitution act giving the colony self-government stipulated that any man who owned £25 was automatically an elector. Hofmeyr finessed the difficulty by securing the passage of a bill declaring that "communal" property didn't count. Since all tribal property was communally held, this effectively excluded most of the tribal blacks. The bill passed after strenuous objections from the missionary lobby.

But was this merely a device to prevent blacks from ever voting? Hofmeyr insisted he was interested not in a colour bar but in a "civilization bar." He pointed out that there were on the books dozens of acts of what he called "class-legislation," acts that discriminated against blacks by placing them in an inferior class. He argued that these acts were inconsistent with granting the franchise to blacks. To be consistent, he said, the acts should only be applied to those blacks who didn't qualify for the vote. "As long as these restrictive laws remain on the statute books, the natives are logically not entitled to vote. But I am a supporter of the native franchise; it is not possible, therefore, that I vote for its abolition. My resolution, tabled here, gives effect to the principle that, in so far as all these natives . . . are deemed fit and qualified to vote [they] should also be deemed fit and qualified to look after themselves without the restriction of class legislation."

Hofmeyr proposed that black electors be exempt from the pass laws (which had been in effect in various forms since the early days of British conquest and which from the 1870s applied to most blacks), from the liquor act (which made it an offence to sell intoxicants in native areas), and from other minor acts such as those that refused to recognize tribal succession rights. The effect of his proposed changes would have been to create a multiracial electorate, still dominated by whites, to be sure, since they were the affluent group, but at least an electorate based on some criterion other than colour.

Not surprisingly, the English-dominated legislature found his suggestions too rich to digest and defeated them. (Their attack was frivolous, failing to deal with the real issues; they claimed Hofmeyr was pushing his bill as a thinly disguised way of creating a market in native areas for the Paarl brandy makers he represented in the legislature. Hofmeyr merely responded that there was in any case no great evidence of crime caused by drunkenness, and "it is ridiculous to think that a notice in the *Gazette* will have the effect of converting the Kaffirs into Good Templars.") But in the Cape colony, the effect of many wars and the patterns of two centuries were too strong to overcome. Hofmeyr couldn't prevail. The "native areas" were the "homelands" of the day.

VI

IN OTHER WAYS HOFMEYR was truer to his Afrikaner past. The flame that burned brightest in him was the tribal one, and he spent most of his considerable energy on the kindling of nationalism. The Cape Afrikaners, he saw, had come to think of themselves as second-class citizens, and though he himself admired the British, he despised second-hand Britishers. In a speech to a Bond crowd in Stellenbosch he declared: "I venture to hope of you that you will set yourselves in opposition to that anti-national spirit of cosmopolitanism of those who love all nationalities alike because they are equally indifferent to all, who know nothing of the life-giving, strengthening influence of a pure patriotism, and who are left as cold by the deeds of their forefathers as by those of the Laplanders or the people of Kamschatka."

But nationalism makes an uncertain fire. Hofmeyr's words smouldered in the theological seminaries of Stellenbosch and only burst into flame years later, with the emergence of the politics of fear under the nationalist leader Daniel Malan, who in 1948 was to capture the country. The heat Hofmeyr generated was real, but in the short term it was overwhelmed by the veld fire about to engulf the Transvaal, precipitated at last by the follies of Cecil Rhodes's lieutenant, Leander Starr Jameson.

Chapter 15

The coming of war

I

TO THE NORTH, THE Orange Free Staters were going about the business of running their model mini-state, having settled the question of Moshoeshoe on the one hand (they gave up trying to get the British to let them take over) and the Griquas on the other (the Griquas were, in the end, overwhelmed by the diamond diggers of Kimberley). Beyond that, the Transvalers finally acquired a leader fit to govern them: the patriarchal figure of Paul Kruger. It was 1883.

Kruger was the grand figure of his time. Just when the Afrikaner society, fractious and quarrelsome and lost to the civilized world in the distant horizons, was being shaken awake by the predatory forces of 19th-century capitalism, Kruger brought them together and spoke for them all. For the first time, the volk had a leader worthy of them. Just in time.

The outside world came to the highveld with a vengeance when word of the gold-fields reached Europe in 1886, and the slow realization followed that here was not just another California, another Australia, but a deposit unique in the world. The Transvaal was paced to the rhythms of the patriarchs, or, as the historian de Kiewiet put it, to "the splendid stepping of the ox"; suddenly they had to deal with freebooting English capitalists, rogues and brigands, entrepreneurs of every stripe, loose-livers, pedlars of all kinds, lawyers, engineers, bankers, foreigners. Deep anxieties surfaced. Was the second exodus, too, to be in vain? Were they about to be engulfed again by foreigners, free-thinkers, aliens, uitlanders? Were they never to be left alone?

The Witwatersrand, as the gold-fields came to be called, lay in a crescent not far north of the Vaal River. People poured in from all over. The Venda and Tswana and Sotho and Ndebele began drifting to the exploding city of Johannesburg as labourers, settling in stinking slums on the city's outskirts. Poor whites, until now invisible as *bywoners* (tenant farmers) on the platteland farms, appeared on the streets, their faces drawn and anxious, their clothes in rags, unable to compete, forced to live between the "kaffirs" and the unimaginable riches of the outside world, as represented by the English and their capitalists. Over all this Kruger's influence settled, an immense and brooding spirit to match that of Rhodes in Cape Town, a Calvinist fierceness to match the messianic Anglo-Saxon vision of empire. Here was a man rooted in his place and his time.

S. P. J. Kruger was born in the eastern Cape in 1825 and went north with Potgieter's group on the Great Trek in 1836, at the age of 11. His family settled in the Transvaal, and the young man became a prominent commando leader, making successful raids and counter-raids against Venda and Tswana; it was Kruger who led the exodus from the Zoutpansberg after the Venda eruptions and the abandonment of the northerly settlements. He had helped the Free State against Moshoeshoe. He calmed down the unhappy Marthinus Wessels Pretorius, and his presence at the Free State–Transvaal confrontation was credited with heading off civil war. President Burgers was anathema to him, and he spoke strongly against him, but after the British annexation he rallied to the republican cause. When the volk gathered in large numbers, Kruger was there to speak to them, to reassure them, to rouse them to resistance when resistance mattered.

II

IN THE FIRST ELECTION that followed Majuba, in 1883, Kruger was elected president, and he remained president to the end of the South African Republic — he was finally ejected, exiled, and martyred by the soldiers of the British Empire.

It was the main folly of the British that they turned Kruger from the leader of the backward Transvaal into the embodiment of his volk. On the face of it this homespun peasant, unlettered and governed completely by the narrowest of Calvinist visions, was an unlikely candidate to appeal to the men of the south, to the cultivated and sophisticated debaters in the Cape legislature, well-read and well-travelled men like Jan Hofmeyr. And yet Kruger was in many ways a true distillation of everything the Afrikaner had come to be.

He ran his country the way the trekboer patriarchs ran their farms. He sat on his stoop to receive his counsellors and his people. His house was open to all citizens, and they made free use of it. They would take their problems directly to Oom Paul, who would know what to do, and Oom Paul always did. He listened to the Volksraad and he listened to his family, but he made up his own mind, and when he made his decision the Volksraad fell into line. At one point he simply fired the chief justice when that dignitary attempted to act on his constitutional right to test Kruger's powers.

Kruger was an orator in the old Boer style, full of orotund phrases and long pauses; his speeches would last hours and would be filled with Biblical references obscure to outsiders but familiar to his listeners. His religion had nothing to do with guile and everything to do with an extreme fundamentalism. He was convinced of the God-given mission of his people. He spoke often of the *volkseie* and the *volksgees*; he understood completely the deep anxieties of his people, who had withdrawn and then withdrawn again, each time confronting their enemies and defeating them, yet each time being driven out once more. He understood the people of the northern landscapes; he understood people who looked to the laager, the last stand; he understood the *bittereinders*. To outsiders he looked and sounded like the unlettered peasant he was: he had no formal education at all. But he was used to command and his hold on his people was visceral and profound. He was easy to underestimate.

When he became president after the triumph at Majuba against the British, the republic was once again beset with anxieties. There was an enemy within, a viper at the bosom, and there was an enemy without, the English enemy, represented by that jackal Rhodes. Kruger correctly saw that the internal and the external problems were closely linked. The *gif* (poison) in the body politic was the uitlander problem, the problem of non-Afrikaners among them. The explosive growth of Johannesburg as a mining centre had its advantages — the Transvaal was rapidly becoming the strongest economy in southern Africa, a pleasant change from the poverty-stricken administrations of the past. The disadvantages were equally clear — a massive influx of outsiders, godless, unruly, arrogant, worldly, competent in matters of which the Afrikaners knew as yet nothing, disruptive and subversive. They came from the Cape, from Britain, from Germany and the other countries of Europe, though the English predominated.

The Witwatersrand (White Waters Reef) gold-fields were unique. Not just in size, but in their character. The seams were deeply buried and couldn't be reached with primitive technology. Sophisticated technology demanded pools of capital. Capital in turn meant the talents of men like Barney Barnato and Cecil Rhodes, the mining magnates who, in that special 19th-century alchemy, managed to translate unswerving purpose into pure money. They naturally came into conflict with Kruger. They believed the gold to be the natural booty of capitalists. Kruger, on the other hand, demanded volk control of the wealth: what was in the earth belonged to the people. And in this he anticipated the state socialism of many modern economies, including that of South Africa itself under his Afrikaner successors. The uitlander poison would run its sure course, Kruger knew. The uitlanders would soon outnumber the Afrikaners, and control of the republic would be yielded to those who had no sympathy for it and no understanding of its nature.

Kruger's solution was to refuse to grant uitlanders the franchise; and when pressure forced him to concede, he demanded a 14-year residency qualification. In another grudging concession, a "second Volksraad" was set up for uitlander participation; but Kruger took care that it had no real power. In fact most of the political pressure came from the Cape legislature, under Rhodes's prodding, not from the uitlanders themselves. Most of the uitlanders were there to make money, not to vote, and could not have cared less about the Volksraad and its doings. Much more important was the price of dynamite and what they believed were the criminally high customs duties levied on foreign goods. To these complaints the Afrikaners paid no heed. They remembered the English at the eastern frontier. They remembered the English in Natal. They remembered that Shepstone and the incorrigible Haggard had been welcomed to Pretoria by the English who lived there. They believed they understood the English nature, which was to denigrate and control. The weight of the evidence is on their side.

III

SO MUCH FOR THE internal poison. The *buitelandse gevaar*, the outside danger, was, of course, the British, represented by the hated and ill-understood word "suzerainty" and by the arch-foe Cecil Rhodes. At a conference in 1884 that resulted in the London Convention, Kruger got the word suzerainty dropped from the draft agreement and, more important, succeeded in removing a proposed clause that gave Britain the right to intervene in the Transvaal's treatment of its native people. But he lost as much as he gained.

In the west the unruly mini-republics, Stellaland and Goshen, had been needling Rhodes with their tiny but extremely provocative and irritating presences. Du Toit, the suzerain of Goshen, actually annexed himself to the Transvaal, running the republican Vierkleur up his farmhouse flagpole before being told by a testy Kruger to desist. In London Kruger finally put an end to du Toit's little empire by ceding control of all of Bechuanaland, including Goshen, to Rhodes and the British.

To the north, the traditional sight-line of the trekboers, Kruger was cut off by Rhodes, whose emissaries did a deal with Mzilikazi's successor, Lobengula, doing him out of his land and everything that was underneath it in the name of a new commercial venture, the British South Africa Company. Thus Rhodes got the passage to the north he so badly wanted to fulfil his grandiose vision of a "map red [British] from Cape to Cairo"; and he got a country, however temporarily, named after himself (Rhodesia, as we now know, didn't last; Zimbabwe it had been for centuries, and Zimbabwe it is again). Kruger didn't protest too much; he felt he had a special relationship with Lobengula and had no stomach for occupying his land. But he wanted a port under his own control, and that meant looking east. Potgieter had been right all along.

There were not many avenues open. The Zulu homeland was closed to the Afrikaners by the British, who had turned on their erstwhile ally, the Zulu king Cetshwayo, annexed his territory, and then, when he raised an army to retaliate, finally got their revenge for the defeat of the imperial army at Isandhlwana by crushing the Zulus at Ulundi, in Natal, on July 4, 1879. Zululand became a British colony. To the north were the Portuguese; in between was a narrow strip known as Tongaland; it was here Kruger focused his attention.

Rhodes and Hofmeyr didn't want Kruger to have his escape hatch; Rhodes because of his dreams of Anglo-Saxon empire, Hofmeyr because he wanted the Transvaal drawn into a customs union with the Cape as a first step to a pan-Afrikaner republic. Negotiations were undertaken between the Cape and Kruger's emissaries. The outcome was a convention that gave Kruger land-locked Swaziland (the Swazis, of course, were not consulted). But because he refused to be drawn into a customs union, Rhodes and Hofmeyr wouldn't allow him his corridor to the coast and coaxed Britain into annexing the corridor called Tongaland. Kruger, in retaliation, pushed through his railway line to the Portuguese-controlled port of Delagoa Bay anyway. It was completed only two years after the line to the Cape, and Kruger's heavy tariffs on Cape goods diverted a good deal of commerce east.

The Afrikaners had finally outflanked the English, an attainment of an old Voortrekker goal that Kruger acknowledged by invoking all the great trekker leaders in a roll call of honour at his ribbon-cutting speech.

This was not of course the end. Rhodes didn't like the northern republic eluding him. Germany's growing interest in the gold-fields and its encouragement of the Portuguese to stick it out in Delagoa Bay made him even more anxious. Pulling the Transvaal into a customs union as a first step towards a political union seemed less likely now. The Portuguese spurned his offer to buy them out. The entrepreneur in him began to supplant the politician. He *must* have a deal.

IV

THE THIRSTLANDERS, THOSE who couldn't still their yearning for escape, had departed into the blue yonder, but still *trekgees* had not abated. The population pressures in the Transvaal were acting in the old way. Where once the patriarchs couldn't bear to see their neighbours' smoke, now the farms were divided and divided again, the massive farms becoming smaller farms, the smaller farms becoming plots. A man with ten sons could no longer expect them to vanish over the horizon. To be sure, a few made their way into the alien atmosphere of the Reef, the Witwatersrand, and a few apprenticed elsewhere, but many simply stayed. Rural poverty and dissatisfaction grew apace. The idea of another trek, this time into the rich lands north of the Limpopo, simmered on the platteland. Rhodes's claim to the north they dismissed out of hand. And Lobengula? He was after all only the son of the defeated Mzilikazi. Why should he enjoy a kingdom as big as the Transvaal itself?

Kruger and his commandant, General W. F. Joubert, did their best to cool things down. Joubert wrote to Lobengula, urging friendship between the two peoples, and in 1888 Kruger, anxious to do a deal over Swaziland, let Rhodes have his way in the north. But even Kruger, with his visceral hold on his people, didn't govern the *trekgees* — treks were independent of governments. The emotions the idea of trek generated in the Afrikaners were now as irresistible as the swarming instinct among bees. In 1885 and again in 1886 men gathered on the northern farms, their wagons packed, but after a while they went home; in 1890 Kruger dispersed another group. The following year the call went out again through a manifesto published in all the Transvaal newspapers, urging the gathering of the tribe and the departure from British influence into the true north. Its leaders claimed to have gained from the "true and lawful owners" of the land north of the Limpopo a cession of land; "the God of heaven, who administers all things, can alone put a stop to this trek, but men cannot."

The provocative declaration, issued by one L. D. Adendorff, previously and subsequently an unknown farmer, was clearly a call to establish another republic, and this in a place Cecil Rhodes had staked out for himself. The Adendorff Manifesto read, in part:

The men who wish to go to their new land, not in their own strength but in the power of the Lord, who has made Heaven and earth, and still administers it, propose to go as a lawful and law-abiding people under law and order, and they choose as the basis of their legislation, after the best of all law books, also for their earthly and temporal government, the Grondwet [constitution] of the South African Republic of 1858 and of the Orange Free State of 1854. Their government and judicial body shall be regulated and chosen in accordance with that, as soon as the trek has got outside the borders of the South African republic, or inside the territories of the promised land, where these laws and the laager law shall be proclaimed.

That the "cession" from the "true and lawful owners" was largely spurious made no difference to the fervour of their intentions. The Banyai tribe, from whom Adendorff wrung his concession for who knows what price, were only vassals of Lobengula; they cheerfully gave away a lot more than they ever thought of owning. Why not? Giving is cheap. Spurious or not, the manifesto stirred Afrikaner hearts once more — one more time, O Lord! into the distant blue, this time where no one will follow, to the Zambesi if necessary, and maybe beyond!

At the same time, in a speech to a Bond meeting at Kimberley, Rhodes was declaring his intention of incorporating the northern republics, the South African Republic and the Orange Free State, into a South Africa "united to the Zambesi." And he added: "If I had my way I would abolish the system of independent states antagonistic to ourselves south of the Zambesi"; he declared that he had undertaken the development of the Zambesi regions "as a Cape colonist." Imperialism no longer from London but from Cape Town! It was scarcely to be borne. The editor of the Transvaal *Express* reacted typically by firing off an indignant letter, not to Rhodes but to Hofmeyr, sympathizing with him for being in the company of "such a man who would, according to his own confession, blot the Republics out of existence, and whose aim is to limit and enchain our legitimate sphere of influence." The Afrikaner was once again feeling hemmed in.

The Adendorff crowd was enflamed. The call went out. Set off at once! The farmers of the republic, convinced as always that the God of battles was on their side, gathered for the move. Some 2,000 people in several hundred wagons assembled on a farm just south of the Transvaal's northern boundary, the Limpopo River. General Joubert himself was there, and so was his son-in-law, Ampie Malan. The brother of the editor of the Cape *Patriot*, S. J. du Toit, was one of the leaders.

But life was no longer as simple as it once had been, and it was never to be as simple again. The great emptinesses of the African interior were only illusion. Geopolitics was against them. Even at home, the people who egged them on the most were speculators who wanted their land at bargain prices and agitators from Natal who wanted to stop Rhodes for their own purposes. And in the Cape, the formidable Jan Hofmeyr threw himself into the fray on Rhodes's side. In a call to the Afrikaner Bond, he argued essentially that if Rhodes didn't develop the north, the imperium itself would do so directly; that the devil you can control is better than the devil you can't; that a trek would lead inevitably to an armed clash the trekkers couldn't win; that if "Afrikaner and English be set against each other the land would be filled with bitterness and the economy dealt a telling blow."

Paul Kruger himself ended real hopes of a major move by throwing his influence against it; he was intent on the east and saw the hopelessness of the northern cause. He rammed through the Volksraad a proclamation threatening trekkers with prosecution if they attempted to leave; this effectively killed the trek. True, 112 Boers presented themselves at the Limpopo, their wagons packed, their farms sold, their lives uprooted, but when they attempted the crossing at Floris Drift they found there a detachment of British South Africa Company police, who politely informed them that they could cross only on signing a deed of submission.

This was the real end of *trekgees*; most of the burghers drifted away to become disaffected bywoners on the farms of others. Some emulated the Thirstlanders and in a similar quest for a hopeless goal signed the deed and left the republic anyway, in individual wagons, as families, drifting into Mashonaland and Matabeleland. A few even crossed the Zambesi and trekked slowly across the great plains of Tanzania to end up at Eldoret, north of the equator on the highlands of Kenya, where they remained, isolated, until the Mau Mau rebellion against the British in the 1950s. Some remain yet under Kenyan rule, adapting to the status of a tiny and exotic minority, tolerated on what used to be called the White Highlands, now a part of the tribal mosaic in Masai- and Kikuyu-dominated politics.

V

THE NET RESULT OF the Adendorff trek, as Hofmeyr had predicted, was to foment a sullen anger on the platteland — not against Kruger, who had stopped it, but against Rhodes, whose personal police had taken possession of something the Afrikaner wanted. The *Graaff-Reinetter*, among other newspapers, commenced agitation against the chief director, as they insisted on referring to the Cape premier. Hofmeyr, in a series of platteland speeches, argued forcefully if somewhat wistfully for all Afrikaners "to lay aside disputes and step forward, firmly bound together as one man," as one of his less felicitous phrases had it. In the republics, indignation against the uitlanders merged with indignation against the jingoes represented by Rhodes.

Rhodes himself paid little attention to Adendorff but much to bringing the Transvaal into the South African system. Before he was 30, Rhodes had succeeded in amalgamating the unruly fortune-seekers and freebooters on the diamond fields into one formidable enterprise, owned by himself (at one point he personally controlled nearly 90 per cent of the world's diamond output). Amalgamation of the diamond diggings had brought clear profit to himself and had ended the anarchy among the diggers. He saw no reason now why amalgamation of the unviable mini-states wouldn't have the benefits for South Africa that diamonds had brought him. In the diamond fields he had moved forcefully and audaciously. Would the same swift tactics not work in politics?

For a man of subtlety, Rhodes's preparations for bringing

the Transvaal republic into the South African federation were oddly clumsy. When he asked the British colonial secretary, Joseph Chamberlain, for a piece of Bechuanaland "for a railway," it was widely known in the Cape that he really wanted it as a gathering-place for mercenaries. The South African League, a pro-British group in the Cape, was in regular touch with uitlander groups on the Reef; that the uitlanders were plotting a coup was common knowledge even in the Free State; that Rhodes was behind the plot was the talk of the legislature. The Afrikaner Bond dealt with the rumours by denying them and hoping they weren't true.

Chamberlain, of course, knew the plans in detail: the uitlanders were to rise; a British agent would be sent to Pretoria to mediate; the Transvaal would extend the vote immediately to all uitlanders, who would vote in an anglicized government; a customs union would be proclaimed; and the subcontinent would be satisfactorily British. What the Transvaal's commandos were supposed to do — or not do — during the uprising it never occurred to Chamberlain to inquire.

The plot was conducted with all the finesse of a subcommittee of Goshen. The uitlander plotters fell out among themselves; Chamberlain tried to stop Rhodes; Rhodes tried to stop his chief lieutenant, L. S. Jameson; Jameson ignored him. Nothing worked. Jameson "invaded" the Transvaal with a ragtag mob of fewer than 500 mercenaries. As soon as they appeared, the news was rushed to Pretoria by bicycle courier, and before they had got very far they were surrounded. They surrendered without a fight at Krugersdorp. The uitlanders, too late, took over Johannesburg but promptly opened talks with Kruger. The British representative went to Pretoria after all, where he was received with enfuriating magnanimity by the president. The Transvaal plotters were sentenced to death by a Transvaal court, but Kruger commuted the sentences — no Slagtersnek here. Jameson was handed over to the British for punishment (he got 15 months). Rhodes resigned as premier in the Cape but kept his seat; he was no longer to be a factor in South African politics, and eventually he retired to his fruit farms and a small cottage overlooking False Bay. His memorial still stands on Table Mountain above the university, looking wistfully northwards. It's now used mostly by students as a trysting place.

Whether the Jameson Raid led inevitably to the Boer War can't be known; British intransigence and Afrikaner stubbornness would likely have taken them there anyway. But it certainly hastened the war. It turned the Cape Bond aside; Hofmeyr could no longer argue for Anglo-Afrikaner cooperation. English-speakers were turning against the Afrikaners; the South African League, which had been the English-speaking political equivalent to the Bond, became the home of the most radical of jingoes. They felt humiliated and urged Britain to annex the Transvaal without delay. In the Cape, the electorate split. Few Afrikaners any longer remained loyal to *diè Engelse*. A few English-speakers resisted the slide to the pornographic temptations of ethnic hatreds; the far-sighted few who did, the Cape politicians W. P. Schreiner and John X. Merriman among them, at least kept communication open, but they were swamped by ethnic antagonisms. The raid also confirmed the Transvaal burghers' already dismal opinion of the British. You couldn't trust them. They were by nature people who hated independence. Free peoples everywhere were their enemies. It was no good fleeing. They would follow you wherever you went.

In the Free State the harmonious community began to polarize. Winburg, paradigm of a model small republic, divided into them and us, though not always along language lines. The Dutch Reformed minister in Bethulie and later in Winburg, "Koo" Marquard (whose daughter was later to marry Jacobus Johannes de Villiers, my grandfather), cast his lot in with the Dutch; so did the English-speaking Murrays of Graaff-Reinet and Winburg. Izak and Jaap de Villiers, Luttig's sons, rode in 1898 with President Marthinus Steyn on commando to the Vaal River to demonstrate solidarity with the Transvaal. (The following year the two republics were to sign a new treaty; henceforth, if one were attacked, the other would respond.) Young Jacobus Johannes (Jim) de Villiers, who was just 14, was caught up in the emotions of the time. He remembered later keeping his saddlebags stuffed, just in case. He was ready to die for the cause. Dying was in the air. Parliamentarians like Jan Hofmeyr could smell it, and despaired.

But even so, war was not inevitable. Afrikaner feeling was far from unanimous. The Bond was still active; Hofmeyr and Abraham Fischer, an eminent lawyer and adviser to the O.F.S. president, were moderating forces. So was the republican government in the Free State. So was the way many Free Staters lived. Even in the Transvaal there were forces for moderation at work. Jan Smuts, a worldly Cambridge-educated intellectual, was a factor in Transvaal politics; he was the republic's attorney general. There were uitlanders who believed they could work out an agreement. Afrikaans journalists were sometimes sharply critical of Kruger and his old-fashioned ways. The most articulate and the most brilliant was Eugene Marais, editor of *Land en Volk* at 19; he would later turn to mysticism, become one of Afrikaans's major poets, write two seminal works of biology (on baboons and on termites), and, in the end, addicted to morphine, commit suicide in rage and despair at his inability to make anyone understand. In the Cape, in the comfortable south, the grand farmers of the Drakenstein Valley saw no need for war; they had coexisted with the English now for more than a century and still maintained their language and their culture. They saw real benefits from the English association.

The Boer War — or the Tweede Vryheidsoorlog (Second Freedom War), as the Afrikaners call it — had a clear beginning. War could have been avoided had not the colonial secretary, Chamberlain, been prone to the jingoism of his time and had he not chosen the chilly personality of Alfred Milner for his South African representative. The Boer War is still sometimes called "Milner se oorlog" (Milner's war) in South Africa.

Milner was the classic case of the wrong man at the right time. His test for South Africanism was loyalty to the British ideal. "If I am an imperialist," he said, "it is because the destiny of the English race . . . has been to strike fresh roots in distant lands." For such a man to conduct delicate negotiations with a ruler like Kruger, who was intimately connected through two centuries of blood and travail with the central myths of a majority of his people, meant almost certain failure. And it's still far from certain that Milner wanted to succeed. Paul Kruger, the shrewd old despot, said of him after an abortive meeting arranged by Steyn at Bloemfontein: "It is not the franchise he wants, it is my country." Even when Hofmeyr and the Transvaal state secretary, Francis Reitz, managed an announcement that Chamberlain's call for a five-year franchise for uitlanders was to be met, Milner rejected the proposals, invoking the long-discredited concept of suzerainty.

In an eerie precursor of the debates in the 1980s, Chamberlain still believed that strong and steady pressure from Milner would cause the Afrikaners to cave in; the jingo lobby had his ear, and they had never really understood 200 years of Afrikaner retreat and withdrawal and the extent to which they were bound by ties of blood to the land they now inhabited. The British never understood that it was their presence that turned Kruger from country despot to national symbol; that Afrikaners in the Cape and the Free State would be forced by ancient ties to rally to his side. They never understood the need of the *volkseie* to be free from contamination. They never understood how group identity and group cohesion and a *gees*, a spirit of solidarity in the face of outside pressure, had become part of the Afrikaner soul. They never understood the Blood Oath, the covenant sworn before the victory over the Zulus.

Because they lacked understanding, war became inevitable. The Afrikaners imported arms in large quantities. Reinforcements were sent to the Cape from imperial stations everywhere. Chamberlain's memorandum to his Cabinet declared that British influence and prestige around the world were at stake. The Afrikaners heard him. They were convinced the British wanted to destroy them. To strike before the reinforcements arrived, Kruger and Steyn issued an ultimatum. The British were to cease all their activities in the north and withdraw all claims and arguments against the Afrikaner republics. The ultimatum expired on October 11, 1899. Jim de Villiers was 15. Maria Marquard, his future wife, was 13. The village of Winburg, too, was at war. Despair and defiance were the predominant moods.

PART 4

Jacobus Johannes de Villiers and the Century of Wrong III: the bitter defeats

———

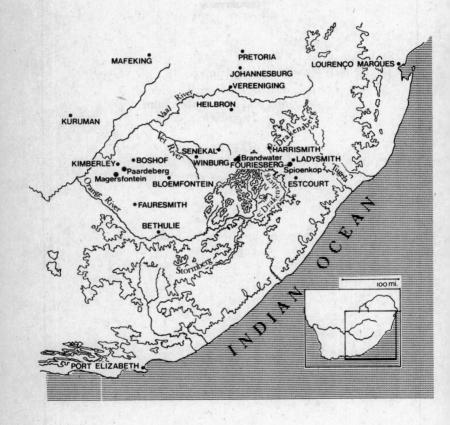

The Boer War

Chapter 16

The volk at war: the Boer War diaries of Margaret and Maria Marquard

THREE YEARS EARLIER, on New Year's Day, 1896, the day Leander Starr Jameson was arrested by the Transvaal commandos after his aborted "raid," the Marquard family of Winburg went on a picnic to Bell's Pass, a pleasant *kloof* in the low hills an hour or so from town. On their way out they passed the post-cart from Senekal, an event they remarked on, since there was usually no cart on this most restful of midsummer holidays. They were still close enough to town to hear the horn announce its arrival in the square, but they didn't return: the post could wait. Driving the Marquards' cart was J. J. T. Marquard, the Dutch Reformed dominee (parson) of Winburg and the moderator of the church in the Orange Free State, known always to his wife Margaret as Koo. Margaret, a daughter of John Murray, professor of theology at the seminary at Stellenbosch, was next to him. In the back, with the picnic provisions, were the Marquards' five children, Maria, who was 10, John and Andrew, 8 and 6, Louise, 4, and Leo, 2. Also crammed into the back were Jim de Villiers, just 12 and a classmate of Maria's, and his friend Klasie Reitz. Jim's father, Luttig, had died several years before; Jim stayed with his mother in Winburg about half the time and spent the rest in the country with a farming family, the Steyns. The Reitz kid was there for no apparent reason.

Nothing further is remembered about the picnic itself. Jim only remembered it because Maria was there; the others recollected mostly their return, when they were greeted with the astonishing news from the Transvaal, which sent shock waves through the little town. Winburg was not yet on the railway line (that came in 1898, in the form of a branch line from Theunissen, which was more grandly on the main route to the north), but it was hardly isolated from the world. Not only was there the three-times-a-week post-cart, but there was, of course, a telegraph office, which connected Winburg to great matters of the world stage.

When I was a child, Winburg was a slow, dusty little town hardly changed at all from the turn of the century. I remember mostly the old houses, their broad stoops shaded from the afternoon sun, their corrugated iron roofs painted silver. The houses were low and cool, the streets very wide — presumably to allow easy U-turns for the oxen spans still sometimes seen even in the '40s of this century. There were a few sleepy little country stores that sold everything such country stores sell everywhere, plus the Afrikaner specialties — *koeksusters* (a sweet sugar pastry), *biltong* (sun-dried venison), *boerewors* (spiced sausages), and more. My great-uncle Leo Marquard, who grew up in Koo's parsonage in Winburg, described the town of his boyhood. It was much as I remember it being 40 years later.

The town was laid out, like most platteland towns, around a large plaza almost always referred to simply as the Square. Everything radiated from the square, along the sides of which were the town shops, the Dutch Reformed church erected by Koo Marquard, two banks, two hotels, the town club (modelled after the grand men's clubs of St. James Street in London), the landdrost's office, where Luttig and several of his sons had worked, and a few of the larger private houses. Behind the eastern boundary of the square ran a nondescript street on the banks of the spruit, the creek, which was usually dry but capable of sudden flooding. Behind that was open country in which were two tennis courts made of beaten clay from termite mounds, a soccer field, and grazing land for cattle. Six streets emerged from the square. To the north, over a stone bridge, was to stand the railway station. To the west was the cemetery, where one headstone bore the skull and crossbones, which Leo and his friends firmly believed designated a pirate's grave. Near that was Winburg's school, and behind that the schoolchildren's favourite building, a lemonade factory. None of the streets except fashionable Victoria Street had names — *by die ou de Villiers huis* or *by die drostdy* (town office) was designation enough.

No blacks lived in town. In the aftermath of the Sotho wars the Sotho had withdrawn behind the boundaries Moshoeshoe had won for them; the only blacks near Winburg worked on the farms or in town as domestic servants or manual labourers. They lived in the "location" (it was usually called just that, "the location") set aside for their use. In the early part of the century it was a pleasant place, with fruit trees and small gardens, poor but not shabby.

The parsonage was immediately south of the square. It was a long, low house with a covered veranda giving directly onto the street; at the back were the outhouses, stables, and wagon house; beyond that was the garden, bordered by a quince hedge and containing mulberry trees, figs, a sour-apple, peaches, plums, apricots, walnuts, and a large vegetable patch. The household produced all its fruit and vegetables, its butter and cream, its eggs, and most of its meat.

The town was typical of its time and its place; the Free State had by the end of the century become in its own small way relatively cosmopolitan. In Winburg Kaestner the shoemaker and Weber the watchmaker were German, Koendrink the carpenter was a Hollander, and Lucas, the skilled baker, came from England. Family names to be found in town included Schultz, Dobinson, Gubbins, Bergstedt, Mitchell, Ford, Fendick, Beatty, Kaplan, Pincus, Zimmerman (the tailor), and Bell (the blacksmith). There were English, Scots, Irish, Welsh, Jews, French, German, Dutch — Leo even recalls a Manxman, Carmodie, who lived by himself in a small house quite hidden by tall trees; he was widely believed, for no good reason, to be a sinister character. There were two doctors: Gillespie, a Canadian, and Schnehage, a German whose main claim to fame was that he was rumoured to have played cricket in England.

The main diversions of the town included hunting, soccer played among the thorn bushes of the veld, the quarterly visit of the Circuit Court, always a time of high local drama, and the annual circus, of which Marquard strongly disapproved, partly because of the "immoral life" led by the performers and partly because the circus travelled on Sundays. (Marquard was responsible for seeing to it that Free State trains never ran on Sundays, and indeed until 20 years after his death, in the 1930s, trains never actually commenced a journey in the province on Sundays.)

The town existed mostly as a trading centre, not as a farmers' market. In later years Jim de Villiers did make a modest living supplying fruit and vegetables, especially strawberries, to Winburg, but most farmers' income came from maize, onions, potatoes, wool, skins, and meat sold to brokers from Johannesburg or Bloemfontein. The banks were instruments of farming policy; in a country where droughts were common, helpful bankers were as essential as sturdy ploughs. Farmers ate well but made little money. Jim bought his 3,000-acre farm after the war with a substantial mortgage of £2,500, and when he died 35 years later his estate still owed the whole amount — he never did manage to pay any principal.

In the Free State, where Dutch was the sole official language and the language of the church, and where Afrikaans was the language of the farms, educated people communicated mostly in English. Like the younger generation in the Transvaal such as Jan Smuts, most educated young people went to British universities and knew the details of their professions in English only. The people who spoke Dutch in the Volksraad, and who argued persuasively against allowing English an official foothold, frequently spoke English to their friends outside and even to their spouses.

President Steyn, who married a Fraser, the daughter of a Dutch Reformed minister, always wrote to his wife in English.

So did Abraham Fischer, Steyn's secretary of state, who married a Robertson. The war later polarized opinion but had little effect on this most civilized of pockets. Margaret Murray naturally spoke English to her husband Koo, whose preaching was all in Dutch; her daughter Maria grew up largely in English but married Jim de Villiers, whose language was Afrikaans. Their children, my father and his sister, were spoken to only in English by their mother and only in Afrikaans by their father; all their lives they spoke to each other only in Afrikaans but always spoke English to their cousins. My father married an English-speaking woman, a Franklin, whose father had been the *burgermeester* (mayor) of Afrikaans-speaking Bloemfontein.

Into this relatively harmonious scene the announcement of Jameson's Raid in the Transvaal dropped like the bombshell it actually was. The remarkable thing was not the bombshell but the limited effect its detonation had on these small-town Afrikaners: they went on talking to the English and treating them like *familie*, family — pacts were made so that *broedertwis* would not be allowed to interfere. Their neighbours were not automatically converted to enemies. The Afrikaners would wait and see. Meanwhile, they looked to their weapons.

II

THAT BRITAIN WENT TO war in 1899 light-heartedly and without anxiety to preserve the imperial honour (or, as Joseph Chamberlain put it, "the position of Britain in South Africa and with it the estimate formed of our power and influence in the colonies and throughout the world") meant nothing in Winburg. O.F.S. president Steyn's call to arms, reminding his burghers of old grudges (particularly the British support of the Sotho), struck a chord but moved few hearts. The Winburgers, like Afrikaners everywhere, were defending their homes and their place, that was all; they met the future with foreboding but some resolve. From the point of view of the Winburg Dutch Reformed parsonage, the great events swirled by, but there was little illusion. This was to be a bitter war. They would try to maintain the civilized virtues, though their hearts were torn. From the Boer parsonage in Winburg my great-grandmother Margaret Marquard, five days after war was declared, wrote in a letter to her mother that was never mailed:

Monday October 16 1899. There are almost daily visits here from the simple country folk who are not "of the clever" enough to make out the official news day by day at the Kantoor [the landdrost's office]. A very generally expressed sentiment is pity for the unfortunate soldaten [meaning here British soldiers; Boer soldiers were referred to as "commandos," or sometimes simply as part of a laager — "Daan de Villiers of the Heidelberg laager"]. A queer story is told of two of them in a sorry state finding their way to the boer laager near Riet River, and expressing their thankfulness at the kindness of the boers, who however, after helping them with warmth and food, urged them back. Mr Lategan had dinner with us yesterday, & was telling us of the flippant way in which the Transvalers talk of fighting the English: "{You fire a few shots throughout the night — keep them on the go the following day, keep them awake the second night again, and the next day you can catch the lot. If only you keep them awake two nights, you can catch them easily}." — as if they were talking of some innocent animals whom you have only to confuse and weary a little and you catch them alive! Still I do not care for that strain — it takes away from the spirit in which I think many of our men have gone.*

Two days later she wrote:

Koo had a most helpful letter from Mr Minnaar of Heilbron who is with the Heilbron Commando in the Drakensbergen: he speaks of the earnest mindedness of the greater number of the

---

* Parts of the letters and diaries enclosed in curly brackets — { } — are in Afrikaans in the original. Margaret and Maria switched between English and Afrikaans without a second thought.

men — two services a day are well attended, while evening prayer meetings amongst themselves are a regular thing . . . My dread is for the colonists who are one with us, and who may be tempted to rebellion: the horrors of another Slagtersnek loom before one! Koo is casting about whether he should go [on commando] . . . I think he grieves most sorely for all these things, loving the Free State and its people as he does.

The "colonists" she referred to were the Afrikaners of the Cape, which was nominally self-governing but still a British possession. For the Afrikaners of the north the war was war; for the Cape people, to fight the British would have been considered treason. Still, many of them dared it anyway. Two of Luttig's sons who were living in the northern Cape near the Free State border slipped across to join a commando; another of Jim's elder half-brothers took his horses and his guns into the hills. I still have a photograph of 21 members of the de Villiers family, posed stiffly for the photographer, in a British prisoner-of-war camp in Ceylon; most wear the slouch hats of the Boer commandos; two had adopted the British pith helmet. About half of them appear to be no more than teenagers. Close family members from Fauresmith, Heilbron, Winburg, Bloemfontein, and Boshof went off to war, gathering with their compatriots in commandos, as the Afrikaners had so often done before. After all, guns and horses were always to hand; danger coming *oor die bult* was bred into the Afrikaner bone — it was part of the landscape and always had been.

The Boers were large and raw-boned and tough in fibre; they were an intimate part of the country through which they rode. It is easy to romanticize this now, but there were plenty of British tommies of the time who spoke of the fell appari- tion of grim commandos emerging from nowhere with their Mausers and bandoliers of bullets, killing, melting away into nothingness . . . Winston Churchill, among others, recorded a chill moment when he heard above the beat of rain the voices of the commandos raised in their evening psalms, sounding more threatening than uplifting, more grim than joyous. Koo Marquard recognized the mood in foreboding messages to his family back in Winburg: on commando against an enemy endless in number and resources, the Afrikaner called on his God, reaching deep into the old anxieties and hungers and angers. The moods were retribution and rage, the emotions implacable; they took no joy in their hymns, but out of their Africa-born angers they made mostly a fierce contempt. It took them through the long nights. Koo himself shared the iron mood: preachers who rode with the commandos could have no room in their hearts for pacifism.

The country took to arms easily because it always had. It was nothing extraordinary. The farmers formed naturally into small commandos under known leaders, many of them experienced in the Sotho and Matabele wars. As Thomas Pakenham put it in *The Boer War*, the commando "was not a majestic fighting machine, like a British column. It was a fighting animal, all muscle and bone." It was mobile, swift-moving, independent, could blend into the civilian population at need; its members needed no training for this kind of warfare. The British, on the other hand, seemed to have learned nothing from Crimea. They advanced across the veld in serried rank, waiting for set-piece battles that never happened, cut down by snipers, demoralized by an enemy that killed without being seen, cut off from their leaders by the rigid class system of Victorian England, not caring for what they fought, not understanding at all the high-minded principles of high imperialism. The Afrikaners, however, were fighting for their land, which was their place, which was part of the *eie* and etched into their soul.

The early part of the war, the first few months, went badly for the English. The swiftness of the commando movements and their frightening fire-power overwhelmed the cumbersome imperial armies as they moved north across the Orange into Boer territory. Snipers cut down the tommies from the ridges, but when patrols went to investigate there was no one there. Supply trains were blown up by unseen hands. Horses were stolen, ammunition vanished. Commandos from the Orange Free State, from Heilbron and Fauresmith, invaded Natal and the Cape colony. Within a few weeks the Afrikaners once again held the Tugela, the river that contained so many memories of blood and travail. In the north-eastern Cape, several commandos briefly merged and met an entrenched British army under General Sir William Gatacre in the Stormberg Mountains. Gatacre was overwhelmed. The diamond centre of Kimberley was surrounded and besieged, with Cecil Rhodes inside it. The Bechuanaland capital of Mafeking was encircled; a British force under Robert Baden-Powell was trapped. At Magersfontein 8,000 Boers under Koos de la Rey and Piet Cronje thrashed an army of 12,000 heavily armed British. More than 1,600 British died at the Tugela, the heart of the country of Blood River. At Spioenkop came the first heroics of the British side of the war. Jim's half-brother, Oom David de Villiers, was with a commando under Louis Botha, later South Africa's prime minister. Botha's men held a key ridge, pinning down a substantial British force. The ridge was taken in a brave charge; Oom David was killed by a British bayonet. (Yet the charge proved, in the end, futile; Botha's commando was victorious and accepted the white flag, taking hundreds of prisoners.) Another British force in the little town of Ladysmith was besieged. The British made efforts to relieve the sieges of Mafeking and Kimberley, to no avail. In London, the jingo press was becoming hysterical. For the Afrikaners, the war was going well. The telegraph lines carried the news to Winburg.

There was another small voice recording events. My grandmother Maria Marquard was 13 in 1899, still a long way from the woman who was to marry Jim de Villiers and live on the farm called La Rochelle in Winburg's hinterlands. Maria's diaries are far from a history of the Boer War — the great events were filtered through the mind of a schoolgirl caught up also in girlish matters; her "history" was the one regaled to her by visiting men from the commandos come to pay a courtesy call on the dominee's family. But there is a flavour of the time.

She wrote: -

Maria Marquard

> Winburg
> January 1900
> Diary
> rather journal
> m. marquard

Winburg. January 1. Fight west of Colesberg. 7 men on our side wounded. Enemy's loss unknown. Early this morning I wished mother, auntie, father and John a "Happy New Year". Mother got an invitation for next year to auntie's for dinner! We have been hearing of different victories at Colenso, Dordrecht and Swaziland commandos. 450 burgers against 750 Cape police, Brabant's Horse and volunteers: nobody wounded on our side. 8 or 9 prisoners taken. (I hope Willie Collins is among them!)

January 4. We have received the news of a complete victory of Kuruman . . . Sterkstroom and Indwe are isolated. Also after fighting a whole day at Malopo [Mafeking] not one burger was wounded or killed . . . Boers have repulsed two armour trains near Cyfer-gat. Campbell is waiting at Indwe with 1700 Kaffirs. We read in the paper of 4 donkeys in a circus in Holland representing England, Holland, France and Germany. At a given sign all except "England" go out; he stands any amount of blows until a clown cries out "{here come the boers!}" at which he flees. Hurrah.

And a week later: "January 13 . . . We have heard that the English are bombarding Colesberg without having given notice to remove the women and children. Is that the work of a civilized nation or of savages? WHEN will this cruel war end?" But other matters pressed; the war didn't occupy all the young girl's attention: "Louise [her young sister] has the promise of a dassy [a rock rabbit] from Mrs du Plessis. Alas!"

III
___

"THIS CRUEL WAR," as Ouma Maria called it, happened in three stages of uneven drama and unequal duration: the sudden and dramatic commando triumphs, the inexorable sweep of the imperial armies, and, finally and unexpectedly, the heroic resistance of the "people on commando," the gallant but ultimately futile guerrilla warfare countered by scorched earth, concentration camps, disease, and death.

The first phase, the flush of Boer victories, lasted only the first three months, until the turn of the century. But the flush was real, the victories true, the mood on the platteland briefly exultant. The British armies moved in on the republics on three fronts: from the Cape, taking the route the Voortrekkers pioneered; from Port Natal, now called Durban, following once more the route the departing trekkers had taken over the Drakensberge; and from the west, from the British protectorate of Bechuanaland on the fringes of the Thirstland, the offhand by-product of Cecil Rhodes's dream of a continental corridor from the Cape to Cairo. But the British, as we have seen, met an enemy nowhere to be found in the military manuals of Sandhurst — elusive, mobile, ruthless, fighting by no known rules, with devastating firepower from the latest German armament factories. The imperial advance ground everywhere to a halt. They were trapped in the towns, and on the veld they found no one who would stand ground and fight. Instead they were cut down by snipers, their cannons useless, their brave charges futile. All they saw of the enemy were the horses vanishing over the ridges and the sinister winking of the heliograph mirrors among the hills as Boer commandos passed messages in some unknowable code. On the platteland, the sense of aggrieved righteousness was reinforced; in the villages of the O.F.S., and in the parlour of the Winburg parsonage, they allowed themselves some hope.

But by January 1900 the overwhelming superiority of imperial numbers was already having its effect. The Afrikaners were fighting for their place and their soul, but they were also outnumbered, 200,000 to 88,000. And the British were helped — traitorously! — by "volunteers" from among the Afrikaners of the Cape, regiments drawn from the settled and prosperous burghers of the south-west who had turned, so it seemed, against their kin — anglicized Afrikaners, renegades against the *eie*. The English controlled the sea, even the Portuguese-owned harbour of Delagoa Bay. The republics themselves were encircled; the laager appeared universal, the enemy inescapable.

And for the Boers, the virtues of the commandos contained also their flaws. Discipline was non-existent. When a Boer was needed at home for the reaping or the shearing, he went. If he thought the battle had gone well, he went home, simply riding off into the bush with no one to say him nay. The patriarchal habits died hard: individualism had its price. Koo, working the commandos as *veld predikant*, field chaplain, tried to maintain morale and instil a discipline of the spirit, but it was hard. Attempts to label *wegloopers* (walkaways) as deserters had only minor results: the Boers were too used to coming and going when they pleased, and there was little odium to being labelled a deserter.

The commandos had no real stomach for sieges, unless they were the besieged; but on the other hand the Boer leader, Commandant General Piet Joubert, resisted all attempts to make him lift his siege at Ladysmith and drive for the coast, where he might have been able to force the isolated British force at Durban to take to the boats. He decided he liked pinning the British down. He wouldn't take orders. There was no one to persuade him of the big picture. He wouldn't budge. There were other commando leaders who acted as he did. The tide began to turn.

Lord Roberts of Kandahar, the supreme British commander, pushed relentlessly north, with his executive, Lord Kitchener of Khartoum, mopping up behind him. The commandos were forced into measures that went against their nature and their skills. They were forced into set-piece battles in an attempt to stem the advance. The sieges of Ladysmith, Mafeking, and Kimberley were relieved, Bloemfontein, Johannesburg, and Pretoria captured, Kruger driven into gloomy European exile, whence he would return only on a bier.

In the little village of Winburg, they watched the great events in dismay. From the point of view of the parsonage, in fact, the evil news began early in the war. Only eleven days after fighting began, on October 23, 1899, Margaret confided to her diary: "Yesterday before evening service the terrible news of very heavy fighting and loss of life at Dundee [in Natal] arrived: the effect on many women you may imagine. Now the few remaining men and boys are being commandeered to be in readiness to go to Norvals Pont [a commando staging post near Winburg]. Mrs Josef du Plessis told of a classmate of Maria's who has been aangezegd [drafted] too, and when I said 'but he's a child', she said, "{My dear Mrs Marquard it looks as if they don't care about that any more: if it wears pants, it must go}."

The following day Margaret wrote: "Today's news . . . of our Winburgers driving off an armoured train on this side of Ladysmith again raises the courage and hopes: — we mourn bitterly the horrible loss of life on the English side: may the decisiveness be unmistakeable and make the end the sooner. Our faith forbids us to expect anything but that God will not allow the yoke of the Capitalists to be put on the Afrikanders." To the Winburgers, the war had been waged by the empire on behalf of Cecil Rhodes and the major mine-owners in the Rand; in their minds jingoism and capitalism were inextricably mingled.

On January 15, there was this entry in the diary: "It is touching hearing from the dear ones of those who had fallen particulars of the end. The Vet River burgers speak so well of our old friend Veld cornet Willem Pretorius . . . In one of those three first sore battles near the River he gathered his little band and under the bullet rain they sang, {trust in dire and dreadful days . . .} — ach — it's too — " Here her diary entry stopped; she was herself overcome with dread. This had been the battle hymn of the Voortrekkers, and here they were taking comfort in it once more, this time facing an enemy without end. The defeats, too, seemed without end:

April 9. The clash and din around seem so deafening to the gentler voices of the spirit. It is a very sacred cause to many, this suffering and fighting for their independence, for the Holy Birthright of Liberty to rule themselves and be free from foreign power. We do pray and believe that God will preserve it to us: but there are such grievous failings yet among our men! . . .

May 4. Boers have had to retreat to Vet River — heaps of them are fleeing! As I write Koo is packed up ready to start at a moment's notice to get out of the way of the enemy who may arrest him if he stays. All this morning one could hear the boom of the artillery in the distance. The shops are all closed, though in the morning the place had been teeming with burgers. Now deserted. These all were past. Alas, alas!

By mid-year, Lord Roberts could understandably consider most of his work done. He made plans to return home to England. His armies had taken Bloemfontein, and the Winburgers could hear the thump of the cannons. There were battles that were evil signs of what was to come. At Paardeberg and other places the commandos were forced to hunker down in trenches for long battles of attrition against superior forces and fire-power. The field hospitals filled with shattered bodies and dismembered corpses. The clean heroic death from a single bullet ("the small blue hole in the forehead," as the saying went) turned to carnage and mud — a gruesome rehearsal for the Great War to follow a decade or so later as Europe itself deteriorated into madness. The "fighting animal" of the commando turned instead to men fighting as animals, spearing each other in the guts with bayonets. For this, the Boers had no heart. In the end Gen. Piet Cronje surrendered his entire laager at Paardeberg rather than face the madness of mutual annihilation. For this, the Boers could not bring themselves to revile him. They understood and condoned.

Maria, who had turned 14 on February 18, was still keeping her diary, but the news had turned grimmer and it was hard for her to find solace. The news of the Paardeberg disaster had reached Winburg. On March 1 she wrote: "We have got the most awful news that Gen Cronje with his whole laager of about 3000 men has been taken prisoner. And there are a lot of women there also. May the English show mercy." A week later she noted:

> The Boers have retreated to Abraham's Kraal, our last standpoint father says. Dear Father! I feel very sorry for him, after hearing of Hans Naude's death the family cried, he says, it's so sad all these fine men dying. The Winburgers have been fighting bravely. This evening the news came, specially mentioning that every place was "alles stil en rustig" [everything quiet and peaceful]. Father says they must be negotiating or something. By the end of next week all our burgers will have retired to their borders and the English to theirs! Then o! then! how beautiful to think of.

But peace was more than two years away, and the weekly prayer meetings in the platteland churches did nothing to hurry its arrival. On March 20 President Steyn, defiantly on commando with his counsellor Jaap de Villiers at his side, issued an order that "every burger who does not take up arms and proceed to the front will be arrested for high treason" — individualists would no longer be tolerated. There was now a "front" — which was wherever Roberts had reached last. A council of war was held at Kroonstad; all the commando leaders were there. The resolve: to fight on, to the bitter end. Defeat was unacceptable, unthinkable. "Hands-uppers" (an English word sometimes spelled *hendsoppers* in Afrikaans, used to denote those who betrayed the *volk* by giving in to its enemies) were condemned in the name of Blood River and the Oath of the Covenant.

On March 20, Maria merely recorded: "Jim de Villiers came to say goodbye on Saturday."

IV

JIM CAME TO SAY GOODBYE because he was off to the war. He had just turned 16, plenty old enough for commando work, in his opinion. That the Afrikaners were pressed into using "young lads and greybeards" is no surprise; the disparity in numbers was too great. That the lads went should be no surprise either: we are used in our times to wars driven by the implacable and undifferentiated hatreds of the very young; in the South African townships now even the radical elders have been threatening the whites with the uncontrollable wrath of the young.

But Jim wasn't pressed into battle. He ran away to war. He went because going was irresistible: all his friends had already gone. Jim had his horse and his gun, as all the Afrikaners did, and had learned to use both when he was a small lad. He had clothes and food. There seemed no reason for him not to go, though to be certain he told no one except Maria — especially not his mother. He simply saddled up and rode east towards the Drakensberge; it was common knowledge in Winburg that most of the local men were on the Natal front. Jim certainly knew that Koo Marquard, Maria's father, was with a Boer general called Leo Roux on the Natal border, in the mountains near what is now Golden Gate Park.

In his later years Jim liked to tell the story of how he was indirectly involved in the capture of Winston Churchill. The incident took place near Estcourt in Natal, when the coach in which Churchill was travelling as a war correspondent derailed, and he was taken prisoner. As Jim de Villiers told the story, Churchill was slightly injured, so a Boer doctor, one Dr. Visser, skilfully bandaged his hand while a young Boer subaltern, none other than Jim himself, handed him bully beef and biscuits. Jim's kids used to listen to this anecdote with deep scepticism. It was much later that René read Churchill's book *From London to Ladysmith via Pretoria* and found that Churchill's version differed hardly at all from Jim's.

In 1934, when my father, René, was in London, he got a letter from his father (written by his mother, since Jim refused all his life to put pen to paper) urging him to visit Churchill and remind him of the event, and perhaps get some biscuits in return. "I was too diffident to do so and six years later when Churchill became prime minister my father never failed to remind me of the opportunity I'd missed in meeting the great man."

In the towns and villages of the Boer heartland, life changed as the imperial juggernaut gathered momentum. Maria's diaries tell first how the village turned out to see passing English prisoners of war being taken through. Then suddenly the English were everywhere: at Bloemfontein. Bloemfontein fell. At Senekal. In the surrounding countryside. Marching on Winburg. On May 1 the entry in her diary reads:

Alas!! This morning we heard the firing of cannons here quite distinctly. This afternoon the English are an hour and a half from here. Father is ready to leave for as he says he has no desire to go to Cape Town, for the English will most probably arrest him. Really when Bloemfontein was taken it was an awful day, but today the suspense anxiety and everything else are most terrible. We have bought a lot of condensed milk as we are afraid that if the English come they will commandeer our cows. Yesterday at Cornelius Uys the English made the women go out of the house and then set fire to it! Those savages! I wonder whether our people are going to be punished very much and then get the victory? Right not might shall rule mankind and we are more right than our enemies. Love your enemies is hard at present. It is too awful thinking of all this bloodshed, onschuldige bloed [innocent blood]! . . .

May 5. Never have I lived through a more sad day than this, and I think father must be feeling something like it also. This morning everybody was on the move, there was no quiet sitting down, hourly the English were expected. At about half past ten mother said I must go and get some oranges for father — I went and soon Minnie called me to hurry. Then came goodbye to

dear, dear father — oh, to me that was the hardest goodbye . . .
[but] I am glad he was not here to see the English take our village.
Before dinner an officer came and the keys were given over and
after dinner the troops began to come, and I don't know how
many have come since then, and also how many cannons they
have here which of course cannot be intended for Winburg
alone. They must have 50 cannons. Oh dear! This morning
there was a slight skirmish outside the place and a French doctor
says that several Germans were killed . . . Several Tommies have
asked for bread and mother has given them some . . . Mother
says I must not be bitter against them, it is not their fault.

Winburg's school was requisitioned for soldiers, the church
for a hospital. Soon, the village was run by a military adjutant. Food and horses were routinely seized. Arbitrary rulings
by petty officers were common. Despondency was on every
face. Now it was Boer prisoners who were taken through
Winburg, their faces grim; the town turned out to see them
pass in silence. "Military plunder," in Margaret's phrase, went
on daily. Even farmers dependent on carts and horses had
them taken by the British army. Those who refused had their
houses burned, and they were moved to squatter camps in
the towns, the precursors of the notorious concentration
camps that were to follow.

By the end of 1900, Lord Roberts had annexed the two
republics under the names Transvaal and the Orange River
Colony. Even by the middle of the year reverses for the
Afrikaners were hardly news, though they were interspersed
with small victories. The mood is clear from the phrases that
recur in Margaret's diary: "I suppose one will somehow get
used to it . . . but the verslagenheid [despair] is on every
face . . . The state of plunder under martial law goes on . . .
The ceaseless story of bullying . . . Cattle taken away . . .
Farmers are frightened to come to town for fear of their
animals or cash or wagons being taken . . . "

On June 3, writing as Lord Roberts was on the point of
taking Pretoria, Margaret recorded:

This aft. at the prayermeeting I read from *Die Kerkbode* the hints for a Prayer Union for peace . . . I do not think the spirit of the thing was caught by many. Mrs Daantje [de Villiers] is redhot — no no — there must be tooth and nail resistance — let Paul Kruger shut himself up and hold out at Pretoria — the breaking of faith here is too scandalous etc etc. She feels bitterly the pillage, the plundering under orders of the farms around. But Mrs de Kok is so anxious they should toch [so] give over Pretoria, for she says as long as resistance is offered no peace can be proclaimed and so long does this utter ruining of the country go on.

Phase two of the war, the turning of the tide, was already half over. The British generals and their armies pushed relentlessly northwards; the Boer armies, such as they were, scattered once again into commandos, remaining in the field as long as they could, sustained in the way they always had been, by the women and the volk back at the farmhouse, blending into the civilian population, living off the land. Pretoria, indeed, fell. Soon few cities remained under Boer control. The only charismatic leaders still at large were the extraordinary Christiaan de Wet, of whom more presently, and the O.F.S. president, Steyn, who continued to slip through English hands. The English seemed to be everywhere.

From Maria: "May 18. Everything is in English hands. The day before yesterday Mrs J van Rooijen said to me "{All you can see is English and dust}". This morning I went to Schultz [the local general store] but it is just empty of groceries."

In June:

We have in a way got news from father. On Friday Mr Nel and Jim de Villiers came back. Jim says on Thursday he saw father. But he says it's bitterly cold, and they have to endure hunger also. He says father walks nearly the whole night while the commandos are going forward. Father is with Mr [P. A.] Roux. Jim de V. says the only carts are father's, the ambulance and the

ammunition waggons. Well, this morning we receive the startling news that Mr D Roux, Mr Kahts, Mr Nel and Jim de Villiers
have been put in prison. It must have been informers. They are
afraid Mr Davie Roux will be sent away. I feel so sorry for them,
for it is bitterly cold and it has been raining most of the day. This
is a sorrowful world.

V

JIM'S WAR HAD LASTED only three months before his older
brother Jaap found him with Leo Roux's commando and sent
him home to look after his mother, much to his disgust. He
returned home with a "poor white" called Nel, headed
straight for the Marquard home to see Maria, and was
promptly locked up by the British. But only for a night or so
before he was released; even an officious adjutant found it
hard to believe the young man was a serious enemy agent.
Maria recorded his release in her diary, though it took somewhat second place: "June 20. I had such a lovely dream last
night about the boers coming back to take Winburg, and
father being with them, I do wish it would come true . . . Mr
D Roux, J. de V. etc released!"

Jim was set free and went home, but shortly afterwards his
mother died and Oom Jaap, suspecting that he would run off
again, caused him to be sent to Stellenbosch "to finish his
schooling." (He didn't get very much even so. His two years in
Stellenbosch accounted for half his total education.) Oom
Jaap was later wounded in the hand himself, captured, and
packed off to Darrell's Island, Bermuda, where he sat out the
rest of the war — much to his irritation, since many of the
other de Villiers POWs had been sent to camps in Ceylon,
and his close friends were at yet another camp on the remote
Atlantic island of St. Helena (still remembered for holding
Napoleon in his final exile). The family still has the letters
Jaap sent home, stamped "passed by the British Military
Censor." Most of them deal with mundane matters, since the
censor took out all references to politics. About half the
letters nag Jim about doing his lessons.

VI

"AUGUST 6. FATHER IS HOME! Well I don't know where to begin and where to end! . . . Father told us how it was he was here. The other side of Fouriesburg the Boers were, and Prinsloo coolly surrendered two thousand of them, including Gen [Leo] Roux of Senekal, father, and many other brave men who never meant to surrender till the end . . . " At this point Maria, in frustration, drew a noose symbol into her diary to symbolize what she'd like to do to the unfortunate Prinsloo.

Father and Mr P. A. Roux each got a pass from Gen Hunter "to return to their clerical duties". One Englishman asked Mr Roux if he thought the war was over, so Mr Roux said, "No, P. Kruger will take you into the fever country where you will die like rats." They then said he was the most bloodthirsty minister they had ever seen. And Mr Roux said, why man if we had your 800 guns and 254,000 men we would throw down our arms and run and throttle you all. Father says one thing, the country will not always be English. He says the lies they tell are awful, simply shocking.

Surrender. Prinsloo, the Boer general Marthinus Prinsloo, wasn't supposed to surrender at the Brandwater Basin, on the reaches of the Drakensberge. He was supposed to split his army in two and slip away, as President Steyn had done a day or so earlier. But his men were weary of battle, weary of the endless slaughter, weary of the unending enemy, and they wanted to go home. *Huis toe, kêrels!* Let's go home, fellows! *Huis toe* spread through the armies and infected Prinsloo himself; there was nothing Koo could do.

Surrender, and flight. Even Christiaan de Wet, safely away from the Brandwater in his laager south of the Vaal, though he called Prinsloo's surrender "an act of murder against the Boer nation," slipped camp and headed north when his scouts told him of an overwhelming English force heading his way.

The war, indeed, seemed lost. It certainly seemed to Roberts that he had won. He returned to Cape Town to take ship for England. There seemed nothing much more to be done.

VII

ROBERTS GOT A HERO'S welcome home to England; with the enemy surely defeated, the war was most obviously over, and the empire transcendent once again. Of course, the British generals entirely missed the point. This wasn't an army war but a people's war, and the people were to find it in their fibre to continue. These days it seems so obvious, but it was new then. When Joanna Brandt, one of the "petticoat commando" of Afrikaner spies, told a British soldier, "Ons het net begin" (we have only begun), echoing the firebrands of the wars in Natal two generations earlier, it must have seemed only bravado. But for the Boers the struggle — the struggle that was to result in the *burgerstand*, the final coming together of the Afrikaner nation — was far from over. Phase three of the Boer War was about to begin, and it would last another two grim years.

The citizen army was a new phenomenon. It might disintegrate after victory, it might lack discipline, its argumentative ways might irritate its leaders — but it could survive in the field where others couldn't. The Afrikaner gathered about him his long history of withdrawal, isolation and retreat, and found he had no more place to go but into the laager once more. A new kind of laager, as defensive and prickly as the old, but now internalized, the wagons converted to hatred, the guns to rage. The British policies of the next two years caused scars where they were hardest to heal, on the bruised psyche of a whole people.

The commandos of Generals Roux, de Wet, de la Rey, Smuts, and Botha stayed in the field, refusing to give up. Most stayed close to their home bases, seizing British supplies, eroding their confidence, sniping at their soldiers, nipping at their armies, harassing their supply lines. The Afrikaner mythology has been peopled by small deeds done in small places, but also by the arrival of heroes to replace the now-vanished pantheon of the Great Trek, represented by the aging Kruger in his Swiss isolation. The new heroes had their roots in the past of the endless horizons, but they were also part of the new age.

There was Jan Christiaan Smuts, the Cambridge-educated lawyer whose commando staged daring raids in the highveld north of Johannesburg. When the Transvaal was annexed, Smuts and his men scattered, but they gathered near Winburg in the eastern Free State and regrouped, whence they set off on a ludicrous and heroic 2,000-mile sweep through the Free State and the Cape, eluding capture, harassing the English, struggling through bitter winter weather in the high mountains, ill from scurvy, at one point surviving a disastrous illness caused by poisonous fruit. They never even considered giving up and even solemnly debated whether they should attack the coastal city of Port Elizabeth. They pressed on through the Great Karoo to the far west, where the commander allowed those many Boers who had never seen the sea to plunge into it, yelling and shrieking, before setting off once more on a grim foray inland.

There was Gen. Christiaan de Wet, the most elusive and tantalizing of the Boer generals, whose reputation grew almost magical among the war-weary and discouraged British regulars who plodded gamely through the veld after a foe they could hardly ever see, let alone capture. At intervals he would simply appear, strike quickly, and disappear with his booty. Attempts to follow were always fruitless. De Wet was a blunt, brutal man, neatly dressed with no hint of a uniform, marked as a leader more by the case of heliographic instruments he refused to surrender to aides than by his demeanour. His style of leadership was harsh — he would whip recalcitrants with a *sjambok*, a whip made of rhinoceros hide, and a sentry's penalty for falling asleep on the job was to be tied down over an anthill. He attracted to his side men as hard as he was, roughened country people expert in the field and with guns; a de Wet encampment could be at full gallop ten minutes after a scout sounded an alarm. He was also a tactical genius, hitting and running and slipping through cordons that were supposed to be tight, with a knack for the feint and a eye for an enemy's weak spot. He utterly captivated the Boers. Margaret has left us a few verses of a song the Afrikaners used to sing in Winburg, in English to infuriate the occupiers, to the tune of "Bonnie Dundee":

> De Wet he is mounted, he rides up
> the street
> The English skedaddle an A1
> retreat!
> And the commander swore: They've
> got through the net
> That's been spread with such care
> for Christiaan de Wet.

> There are hills beyond Winburg and
> Boers on each hill
> Sufficient to thwart ten generals'
> skill
> There are stout-hearted burgers
> 10,000 men set
> On following the mausers of
> Christiaan de Wet.

> Then away to the hills, to the
> veld, to the rocks
> Ere we own a usurper we'll crouch
> with the fox
> And tremble false Jingoes amidst
> all your glee
> Ye have not seen the last of my
> mausers and me!

De Wet's capricious journeys through the land — to the Transvaal, the Free State, the Cape, back to the Transvaal —

helped inspire the resistance. Even the English grew to admire him.

And there was old Koos de la Rey, of all the Boer leaders the most like the heroes of old, like van Jaarsveld of Graaff-Reinet, like the patriarch Potgieter, like Andries Pretorius of Blood River. De la Rey operated in the western Transvaal, home to the most stubborn of the old patriarchs, and there he remained, unbeaten, till the end. He operated in his own way, in the old style, taking inspiration from the Bible and orders from no man. Towards the desperate end, when hands-uppers were marching into the towns in defeat, and typhoid was sweeping away women and children, de la Rey captured the British general Lord Methuen; after treating and bandaging him, he sent him to a British hospital. When his men remonstrated, remembering the farms destroyed and women imprisoned, he simply said, curtly, that it was his Christian duty.

There was also President Marthinus Steyn of the Free State, who passed through Winburg so often with Koo and Jaap in attendance. Steyn was a peacemaker who failed, and after his failure he tried no more for peace but lived in the veld with de Wet, his uncaptured presence a constant reminder to the British that they had not yet won and a constant source of inspiration to the commandos.

Of course, things were more complicated than romantic tales of inspired commandos and dispirited tommies. The Free State had been annexed by Lord Roberts on May 24, 1900, and there were many Afrikaners who believed further resistance was useless, that it would bring only grief to combatants and to the *volkseie* itself, permanently grinding them into poverty. From time to time efforts were made by prominent citizens, in Winburg as in other villages, to contact the men on commando and induce their leaders to ask for terms. These petitioners almost always acted from a genuine belief that the war was over; nevertheless their actions were perilously close to treason and irritated their leaders as well as the men in the field. Two men somewhat idiotically involved

Margaret Marquard in such an attempt, much to her uneasiness — it could have compromised her husband's position on commando. She wrote to her mother:

> November 7. This aft. Mr Bergstedt and Mr Roux called to ask would I accompany them to the country tomorrow — they were going with Swanepoel to try to meet some of the boers and confab a little — to see if they could not induce them to some asking of terms . . .
>
> November 8. Started 5.30, drove in direction of Zand river to Izak Haasbroek's house. Mrs H and her daughters received us rather mystifiedly but I think were glad to see me. After some waiting about the people from the laager began to come. Well, that was a pleasure, to see men you had been thinking of so long! The talk among the menfolk came to little — Mr Bergstedt's arguments were met by Sarel Haasbroek in his bragging way. Teewie Wessels says if he gets caught or shot he is satisfied but a voluntary surrender on his part would be too palpable an act of ongeloof [faithlessness]. They say no, don't pity us: I said, ah but think of the sufferings of the women and children, so old Izak — who is very grave — said "{Miss, they must endure. It's so in all wars: it's they who must continue to pray aright}." Their contempt is great for all the handsuppers, many of whom are in town for protection and getting scant courtesy there either. Mrs H. says her volk are keeping so *getrouw* [steadfast]. They are dreadfully determined and bitter.

VIII

LORD KITCHENER HAD taken over from the departed Roberts. He was a soldier who devised a soldier's solution to a guerrilla problem, with the predictable results of alienation and bitterness. If the commandos couldn't be found, he would scorch the earth to smoke them out; if combatants blended with non-combatants he would make war on them both.

He built up the army of occupation to a quarter of a million men. He accelerated Roberts's policy of deporting captured commandos to camps in St. Helena, Ceylon, and

Bermuda. After some months, Johannesburg was subdued and the mines placed back in production. Kitchener ordered the construction of a network of mini-forts, blockhouses, a mile or so apart along all the major lines, manned them with soldiers (and their servants), and supplied them with telephones. He then deployed his armies to herd the commandos against these fences.

To shut down the commandos' supplies from the farms, Kitchener took the most controversial decision of all, the one that was to bring on him calumny from an aroused Europe and the universal hatred of all Afrikaners: he burned homes, set fields ablaze, and confiscated stock, then herded women and children, the families of the men on commando, into what he came to call concentration camps. There was one in Winburg. My great-grandmother Margaret visited it when she could:

December 20. So the days go on. The farms are "cleared", the corn unreaped, the cattle brought in. This afternoon going to see some sick people I saw droves and droves of cattle towards the race course — "{stuff that was brought in today}". Mrs Ph. Fourie tells of being here without milk — begging the British for only two of her cows, her youngest of nine children is only 14 months old — "no". The typhoid among the civilians is distressing . . .

January 29, 1901. Last week I visited the over-the-spruit Camps . . . The hospital for these deported women [is] in those stone buildings . . . In each house a girl is down with typhoid . . . What confusion . . . The state of health is distressing — Mrs Jan Scott has lost five big children in the space of about a month: in nearly every hutch [of the camps] there is fever, or the sign of it, or diarrhoea among the children . . . In one tent lay on a narrow stretcher a Mrs Linde from Brandfort with her youngest, say 3 yrs. — on some sacks on the floor a boy of 14 — the only "well" one a little chap about 12. The attempts at orderliness and comfort are astonishing — a tiny table neatly laid for the children to have their meal at. I am allowed to get soup and milk through daily — they are very strict about allowing any food articles through — a little basin of pumpkin sent for Mrs Koot Niemand's boy was sent back by a surly gatekeeper.

This was Margaret's last entry. The following week she, Maria, and the other children were given permission to rejoin Koo, who was by now on parole in the Cape Town suburb of Green Point, and the diary entries and letters stopped.

But in the north the war went on: more than 27,000 women and children died in the concentration camps, more than six times the number of men killed on commando. More than one in five who entered never left. The British nurse Emily Hobhouse, a heroine to the Afrikaners still, ministered to the victims in the camps, her letters home ringing like a crystal bell in the jingoistic heart of the British Parliament, slowly — too late! — turning imperial pride to self-disgust. But the killing didn't stop.

Chapter 17

The bitter defeat: Afrikaner nationalism emerges from the fires of Britain's scorched-earth policy

I

WHEN I WAS A BOY IN Bloemfontein we would be taken by bus once a year to the small rise outside town on which stood a simple stone obelisk; there we would be subjected to a memorial service of suffocating boredom and a sermon of interminable length; we were all infected by a desire to disappear *oor die bult*. But on the other hand we all understood why we were there. The obelisk was a memorial raised to the women and children who died in the camps. It is perhaps the most emotional symbol the Afrikaners have, transcending the massive Voortrekker monument in Pretoria or the monument to the Afrikaans language erected outside Paarl. The Vrouemonument (Women's Monument), as it is called, is a symbol of oppression; it is a symbol of the hatred of the world, of the imposition of alien ways, and most of all it is a symbol of how the outside world, the British and Milner in particular, misunderstood the Afrikaner spirit.

We understood viscerally as children that the monument was not merely a stone expression of the evil that outsiders do; it is a symbol of how the *volkseie* is fundamental to a people's identity: outsiders, people outside the *burgerstand*, foreign to the fundamental thought patterns of the people, will always try to do you harm. The only solution is a tight solidarity. You must control events if you can, resist if you can't. It is the ultimate internalization of the laager.

These attitudes were formed in the long centuries of isolation, but they were shaped by the British in war and given an outlet by the deaths in the camps. It matters not at all that hardly anyone was deliberately killed in the camps, that most of the deaths were caused by typhoid, malnutrition, and lack of hygiene: we "knew" perfectly well as children that the British put ground glass into the camp food to cause internal bleeding, diarrhoea, and death . . . There was always someone with a vial of the stuff kept as a "souvenir" among the diaries, the letters with St. Helena stamps, the buttons torn from an enemy's bloodstained uniform. We "knew" all this was true despite the best efforts of the Afrikaner liberals — Leo Marquard, Maria's brother, and René de Villiers, Jim's son and my father — who took from defeat the same deep desire for liberty but looked for its nourishment to reconciliation. Their vision, they believed, was the true heir to the endless horizons — the grander vision of a larger inclusiveness. Mostly, we didn't much listen. We knew what we knew: the British killed women and children and that was that. The evidence was there for us to see.

The war ground on, Kitchener sweeping the producers off the land, filling the camps, keeping the prisoner-of-war transports moving. The women in the towns and the camps remembered the Voortrekker heroes: it was their nourishment. Jim de Villiers remained in Stellenbosch, where he had been sent to school; later he would return to the Free State to farm, to work with animals, to keep his rifle oiled, to run his small world, turning his emotions to the soil that preoccupied him for the rest of his life, convinced despite the evidence and the testimony of his brothers that the great capitalists of the Rand and the empire would always conspire to keep the Afrikaner poor.

In the field, through the final days of 1901 and into the early months of 1902, the hands-uppers increased as more and more burghers realized the war was a lost cause, and though there was never a general collapse (a fact that sustains the Afrikaner nationalists even today), the fighting forces had dwindled to little more than 20,000 exhausted men.

The governments of the old S.A.R. and O.F.S., such as they were and where they could be found in the field, had spurned peace feelers from Kitchener early in 1901. President Steyn in particular had urged the burghers to continue the battle. But when Kitchener tried again a year later, in April 1902, the Boer leaders agreed to negotiate.

The Afrikaners' first two proposals — that their republican independence be restored and maintained but that uitlanders be allowed to vote, and then that the Rand and the gold-fields be carved off by and for the British from an independent Transvaal — were rejected out of hand.

On May 31, 60 representatives of the commandos met, under a British safe-conduct, at Vereeniging, where they voted 54-to-6 in favour of accepting British terms. The Peace of Vereeniging was signed that same night in Pretoria by Milner and Kitchener on the one hand, and by representatives of the republics on the other. The old enemies solemnly shook hands, Kitchener saying to each Boer as he passed, "We are good friends now"; perhaps he even hoped it would become true if he said it often enough. De Wet, for his part, smashed his Mauser across a rock and left the pieces lying for others to pick up.

II

THE WAR WAS OVER, the peace not yet contested. *Een Eeuw van Onrecht*, the tract issued during the war by the O.F.S. chief justice F. W. Reitz with an assist from the lawyerly Smuts, had referred to the 19th century as a Century of Wrong. It had been a century of defeat, retreat, defeat, withdrawal, filled with heroic figures who vanished and heroic victories that turned to ashes; first the Company, then the Xhosa, then the Zulu, then the British — against each the Afrikaner struggled, then withdrew, until the laager became the definitive symbol of his existence. Now the century was over. The tract, written in the heat of battle, expressed confidence the republican flag would fly again, and "Africa for the

Afrikaner" would succeed, from Simon's Bay to the Zambesi. But the Afrikaners had been forced to turn in their Mausers and retreat to their farms, and now, in the 20th century, there was no more place to go.

The century had thrown up a pantheon of heroes — Retief, Potgieter, Pretorius of Blood River, and Paul Kruger, the Scourge of Majuba and the ultimate patriarch — and these in turn had given way to the generals, Koos de la Rey and Christiaan de Wet, and the men of the modern era, Louis Botha, Jan Smuts, and J. B. M. Hertzog, the Free Stater who later broke with Botha and Smuts over their "accommodations" with the British. But now the Afrikaner's heroic age was over. D. W. Kruger's history, *The Age of the Generals*, concluded with this paragraph: "For a century and more Afrikanerdom had managed to preserve its life through heroic action. It now thought to prolong its existence by heroic thought against the whole world. The Age of the Generals was past and done with forever. Afrikanerdom would endeavor to maintain its existence through the age of the politicians."

The politicians and the bureaucrats together would throw up an entirely new kind of laager; they would take control of the machinery of state and erect a much weirder edifice made up of law and regulations and orders-in-council — out of their rage and their bitterness and the ashes of defeat they would make Afrikaner nationalism and apartheid. Military solutions and the attempt to flee had failed. The Afrikaner would turn to manipulating constitutions.

Milner had forced South Africa to war to preserve British supremacy, and to establish it where it hadn't yet been maintained. As anyone now familiar with peoples' wars of liberation could have told him, coercion is futile as a way of winning hearts and minds: what do you do after the peace treaties have been filed away in government cabinets?

Here and there were hopeful signs. In 1904 Jim de Villiers bought his own farm near Winburg and called it La Rochelle; he built a dam back of the house and went courting Maria when she returned with her family to Winburg. Koo Marquard returned as quickly as he could. As he told his daughter, the war was over; it was futile to sit back and bemoan the past or to allow vengeance and hatred to distort the present. The important thing was to build for a happier future.

There was much to be done. On many of the farms only a burned shell remained; people had to be resettled, food production restored. Relief had to be distributed, orphanages established, schools built. For Marquard, above all, the spiritual life of the people had to be quickened. A new church was built on the town square, where it still stands. When the government established a network of state-supported schools in which English was dominant — Milner's policy of anglicization at work — Marquard took a leading part in establishing Christian national education, in which Dutch was to have its place. Marquard was the Winburg agent for the Pretoria-based General Boer Relief Fund.

Milner himself stayed in South Africa to supervise the reconstruction; he was determined not to let the victory vanish in colonial bungling, and wanted to ensure a society loyal to the British Empire — self-governing, but definitely British. The methods he chose to accomplish these goals turned him, in the historian Leonard Thompson's phrase, into "the greatest recruiting agent [Afrikaner nationalism] ever had." The Cape liberals of the late 19th century, Hofmeyr and the Bond, had been pushing their inclusive definition of the Afrikaner and working towards a unified (white) population. The Jameson Raid put paid to that, and the Boer War, followed by Milner's aggressive English jingoism, pushed Afrikaner thinking even in the Cape towards narrower ethnic definitions. Instead of extinguishing the Afrikaner nationalist, Milner fostered him. As former president Steyn put it, the *Boerevolk* of the northern republics had to be defeated in order to create a new and larger Afrikaner nation.

Smouldering anger predominated on the platteland. The unfortunate Piet Cronje, loser of the battle of Paardeberg, caused a scandal and was ostracized by his people for re-

enacting the defeat for the edification of the crowds at the St.
Louis World's Fair early in 1904; he died still in disgrace. Paul
Kruger died in Switzerland in July the same year, and his
body was brought back to Pretoria for burial. In a last message
to his people he had returned to his credo: Look to the past,
he said, for all it contains that is fine and noble. The outpour-
ing of sentiment that followed his burial was a signal: impoverished and defeated, the Afrikaners were never demoralized;
they maintained their fundamental belief in their own rightness and in the God-given justness of their cause.

III

IN CAPE TOWN, HOFMEYR converted his Bond into the
South Africa Party, with the aim of a unified Afrikanerdom.
In 1904 Louis Botha became the first of many Boer War
generals to turn to politics; in Pretoria he founded a political
party he called Het Volk, the People, with the expressed aim
of "full self-government" for the two former republics. In
1907, in the first Transvaal election with adult male white
suffrage, Botha's movement defeated the Progressives, as
Milner's supporters called themselves, and formed a government. His Cabinet included two more of the heroes of the
resistance: Jan Smuts and Koos de la Rey. In the Orange River
Colony the local version of Het Volk, the Orangia Unie, won
30 of the 38 seats, and Abraham Fischer, Steyn's former
attorney general, became prime minister.

For the next eight years, the years leading to the formation of the Union of South Africa in 1910, Afrikaner politics
took place on two quite separate levels. The realities of the
gulf that emerged were obscured for more than a generation
by the extraordinary stature of some of the participants,
particularly Jan Hofmeyr in the Cape and the two generals in
the Transvaal, Jan Smuts and Louis Botha.

Hofmeyr had spent the war years in Europe; as a British
subject of the Cape he would have risked treason charges if he
had fought for the Boers, but he couldn't bring himself to

help the British side. By 1902 he had returned and was shrewdly directing things behind the scenes; in spite of his undeviating demands for the parity of Afrikaners, his spirit was one of compromise in the Cape and conciliation with the north. Smuts, whose intellectual breadth was unique in South African politics, shared with Hofmeyr and Botha one extraordinary trait: he refused to harbour bitterness or to give in to demands for retribution. Botha particularly knew the British connection had become inevitable and he wanted to use it as much as he could on behalf of the Afrikaners. Why not make the Afrikaners part of a world-wide civilization?

Conciliation was the central faith in their politics. All three men worked for conciliation within the *burgerstand* — reconciling the Transvaal bittereinders with the hendsoppers or, even worse, the "joiners" — the Afrikaners who had made common cause with the British in the war, such as the Cape Volunteers and the National Scouts. In the north, Botha also recommended reconciliation with the uitlanders of the Transvaal. With this in mind he emphasized again what most Afrikaners already "knew" — that it was the great capitalists of the Rand who had been responsible for war, not every English-speaker.

The English-speaking leaders responded in kind. John X. Merriman, the premier of the Cape and a Hofmeyr loyalist, had been alienated from Britain by imperial excesses and wanted nothing more than a South African nationalism. At the National Convention in 1909 that summoned delegates from the Cape, Natal, the Orange River Colony, and the Transvaal to discuss the creation of a new unified state, he made the extraordinary gesture of officially and publicly renouncing any ambitions for the prime ministership of the new country in favour of Louis Botha, so as to ensure the "bringing in of the Transvaal."

The National Convention was filled with the same generous spirit as Merriman's. Delegates included not only the Boer War heroes but Leander Starr Jameson, he of the infamous raid, as well as several raiders who had once languished in Transvaal jail cells. Even the choice of a capital, or rather capitals, signified the spirit of conciliation. Pretoria was to become the "administrative capital," where the machinery of bureaucracy and government was to reside; Cape Town was to be the "legislative capital," where Parliament was to sit. This cumbersome arrangement — whereby the entire appa-ratus of governing, as well as the entire diplomatic corps, uprooted itself twice a year to shift to another capital a thousand miles away — was believed an essential reinforcer of the new national state. (The old O.F.S. was not left out entirely: it was awarded the Supreme Court. Natal, the only truly tropical part of South Africa, was never taken too seriously by the English and was generally disliked by the Afrikaners; it got nothing.) A formal luncheon at Buck-ingham Palace to celebrate the successful conclusion of the convention included Jameson, Steyn, Botha, Smuts, and Hertzog; Botha's first Union of South Africa Cabinet, in 1910, included ex-Republican Afrikaners, Cape Afrikaners, and British. The undeniable fact that the imperial govern-ment in London, in full flight from its recent imperial past, seemed inclined — even eager — to grant virtual self-government on whatever basis the local delegates desired seemed vindication enough of the conciliation policy.

IV

BUT THE VINDICATION WAS only apparent. Two groups were left out of consideration: the blacks and the poor of the Afrikaner platteland.

In all the deliberations leading to union very few people paid any attention to the black majority; the last wars against the blacks were fewer than 30 years in the past, but the black tribes had become virtually invisible politically. The Zulus had been dispersed by the British, and their king, Cetshwayo, exiled; the Xhosa had been finally crushed in the 1880s and their leaders reduced to petty chiefdoms; the Sotho alone retained independence though they no longer exerted any influence. Most black chiefdoms had respected both sides' admonitions not to intervene in the "white" war (though Britain made some attempts to stir up the Sotho), and while a few independent but minor chiefs continued sporadic attacks on whites throughout the war and well into this century, they were never considered significant.

Attitudes to race prevailing in Britain and America weren't very different from the attitudes in South Africa: "exceptional" blacks might attain European standards of culture, but political and general cultural equality were unthinkable — blacks weren't "ready." Hofmeyr alone sounded a warning: in a speech arguing against locating the national capital north of the Vaal River, in Pretoria, he said, "If the capital once goes to Pretoria then it will not return before the gold mines are exhausted or the great native upheaval of the interior is in full swing . . . Cape Town will appear to be the last stronghold of the European settlements in South Africa." No one else believed in a "great native upheaval" or cared to envisage the conditions in which it might occur — had not the upheavals already taken place, and been taken care of? So no one listened and no one worried: the English were preoccupied with self-government and the Afrikaners' whole attention was turned to working their way with the victors of Vereeniging.

In the past when they determined constitutions in southern Africa the British had not allowed a franchise colour bar. The Cape colonial government, partly at Hofmeyr's urging, had manipulated the land ownership provisions to ensure a white majority but had never envisioned cutting blacks off from the franchise altogether, much less the Coloureds, as the Hottentot/Dutch/Malay hybrids were now finally and legally known. In Natal, the British-run colony passed stringent rules governing access to the vote but never went so far as to cut non-whites off completely. In the northern republics the franchise had always been restricted to white adult males. The British could have changed this after their victory, but they did nothing. At Milner's urging the British postponed the question of "native rights" until after the self-governing dominion was a reality, in effect postponing a decision until they no longer had the power to take it.

The act of union was on Britain's part an act of revulsion against its own imperial past; the British generously gave in to the vanquished on many fronts, and in doing so virtually guaranteed the continuing segregation of the blacks. Milner must have known this, but there is no evidence he cared. He seems, on the contrary, to have shared the most conservative Afrikaner attitudes towards race. The British could have headed off the Union of South Africa's colour bar and didn't. They didn't think it important. It was not the first time they had intervened decisively on the white side.

V

NOR WAS THE AFRIKANER proletariat satisfied. In the villages and on the farms of the platteland were the rural Afrikaners who regarded themselves as the dispossessed; they had lost the war to the English, their cities to foreigners, and now they were losing their heroes to alien ideas. Smuts the cosmopolitan and Botha the urbane, heroes of the war, had lost touch with their people. They might strike a chord in Winburg, where Koo Marquard set about the work of reconciliation in the last few years before his sudden death in 1904, and in parts of the Cape. But the camps, and the deaths of the women and children, were not forgotten that easily, nor the slights of the English jingoes who denigrated the Afrikaner and his language. The resentment simmered.

The post-war recession bit deep; the former commandos were trying to rebuild their burned homes with no resources. The government, they felt, was more concerned with bringing in new uitlander immigration than with its own people, the defeated poor of the platteland.

The anger first found expression in the fastnesses of the old patriarchies of the Transvaal when a band of bittereinders under one Ferreira, who had taken refuge in German South

West Africa, erupted into the western Transvaal in 1906 in an episode known as the Ferreira Raid. Ferreira passed through the platteland like a whirlwind, stirring up opposition, rousing the spirit of Graaff-Reinet and van Jaarsveld and Stellaland, invoking the heroes of the past — Potgieter was his mentor. A few commandos gathered on the larger farms. But the episode didn't last. The time for heroes really was past, and vain dreams of conquest were no substitute. Hofmeyr, using his own prestige as well as that of the old Afrikaner Bond, eventually put a stop to the sorry business by sending dispatch riders around the affected districts, pointing out that the Afrikaner volk would not support an uprising. Ferreira was isolated and banished.

There were also more serious figures at work — and at least one tragic loss. In the Orange River Colony, which became the province of the Orange Free State after union in 1910, Gen. James Barry Munnik Hertzog was becoming more and more prominent. He had been Steyn's education minister and had been asked to join Botha's union Cabinet. He believed conciliation to be wrong-headed; the task was to preserve Afrikanerdom first and worry about getting along with *die engelse* afterwards. When Smuts pushed through an education bill limiting the mandatory teaching of Dutch to the third grade, his suspicions that Smuts had sold out deepened.

And at the Cape, a more modern and altogether more formidable figure was beginning to make his influence felt. Daniel François Malan, like Hertzog, appealed to the Afrikaners' historical claim to have founded "South African civilization"; he also went further and delved into the fertile ground of Afrikaner Calvinism. Malan was a dominee in the Dutch Reformed Church and a graduate of the influential seminary attached to Stellenbosch University, and his writings, appealing as they did to the mystical and apocalyptic nature of the plattelanders, held an almost metaphysical appeal. The Afrikaners, he wrote, had been divinely appointed to their task; national unity (by which he meant the unity of those who spoke Afrikaans and shared the Afrikaners' world view, not some kind of Bothaist duality of English and Afrikaner) was a God-given right.

The Century of Wrong meant something. The Afrikaners had been tested and found acceptable: God was satisfied with their conduct, but they must not allow themselves to be led astray . . . It is familiar quasi-mystical stuff, but it struck a chord on the platteland, where they knew there had to be some reason for it all. Malan's influence increased when, in 1909, before the National Convention could meet, Onze Jan Hofmeyr died suddenly, leaving the South Africa Party (the former Bond) and the Afrikaners of the Cape without their leading moderate intellectual and most influential politician.

In the years after union, Malan built up his body of mystical theory; Hertzog, in his impassioned defence of the *eie*, was a champion of the plattelanders who felt themselves ignored and dispossessed in their own land. Afrikaner nationalism was finding its modern political voice.

Chapter 18

The nightmare of schism returns

I

THE BRITISH POLICY OF anglicization failed, as the Boer War did, to extinguish the idea of a separate Afrikaner identity tied into the land and distinct from all other groups, racial and linguistic, who inhabit South Africa. But while they failed to extinguish the idea of the volk, union in one government failed to extinguish the ancient tendency for Afrikaners to split into quarrelsome factions, each governed by a hero, a leader of substance. In the Cape, the majority of Afrikaners continued to believe they could work out their destiny within the British Empire; Smuts and Botha seemed to them natural leaders. In the O.F.S. and the Transvaal the talk of Afrikaner *volkseenheid* (people's unity) turned through the efforts of General Hertzog into ambiguous talk of Afrikaner separatism.

Hertzog joined Botha's first post-union Cabinet because it would have been unthinkable not to, but neither man was happy about it. The coalition consisted of the former Bond in the Cape, now called the South Africa Party and without its main rudder, Jan Hofmeyr, who had died in 1909; the former Orangia Unie party of the Free State, Hertzog's base; and the Het Volk party of Smuts and Botha himself, based mainly in the Transvaal. After union this loose coalition began calling itself the South Africa Party, or SAP for short. In opposition were the Unionists, primarily English-speaking and without much political direction.

If Hertzog was unhappy with Botha, Botha was distraught at some of Hertzog's speeches. In a series of addresses across the nation, Hertzog articulated his "two-stream policy" of separating the two language groups. In essence this was a policy of primitive apartheid within the white group: by separating English-speakers from Afrikaans-speakers, Hertzog declared, Afrikaans culture, language, and religion would be maintained intact. The two streams should run parallel in national life, neither inferior to the other, the two languages given equal weight in national affairs. South Africa is to be ruled by Afrikaners, he insisted over and over, but he convinced very few English-speakers that he meant them too — or at least those among them who were committed to South Africa and prepared to turn their backs on the imperial centre. Hertzog's later history proved he did in fact mean them — his definition of an Afrikaner was not so far from Hofmeyr's, which had allowed inclusion in the volk of any who put its interests and South Africa first. His concern of the moment, however, was narrower. There were rumblings of dismay from the jingoes in Natal, more muted rumblings from the anglicized Afrikaners of the Cape.

Hertzog's attacks on his own government became ever more strident; and finally, in December 1912, at a small railway siding in the Transvaal called De Wildt, he let loose a broadside against the policies of his own party and its leaders. At the same time he gave articulation in more precise form to his conception of Afrikaner nationalism. "South Africa first!" he declared. "I am not one of those who always talks of conciliation and loyalty because those are idle words which deceive no one. The time has come when South Africa can no longer be ruled by non-Afrikaners."

Botha, whose idle words of conciliation and loyalty those were, had to react. English-speakers were decamping from his government in protest. He disbanded the government and rebuilt his Cabinet; Hertzog was out. The following November in Cape Town the split was formalized: the congress of the South Africa Party voted with Botha, and Hertzog stalked out of the hall and the party, taking his followers with him — among them the legendary old general, Christiaan de Wet, who stopped at the door to call out his farewells, then slammed it shut behind him.

Out of the schism the dissidents formed the National Party, the forerunner of the modern party of the same name that governs South Africa still. At the heart of its credo was the urgent search "for a powerful conception of national self-sufficiency." As my father wrote many years later in the *Oxford History of South Africa*, its success from the start, and its longevity, "must be ascribed to its skill in persuading Afrikaners, and particularly non-Nationalist Afrikaners, that *die party is die volk en die volk is die party*, or as Dr Verwoerd was to assert almost without challenge while he was running the government, 'The National Party was never and is not an ordinary party. It is a nation on the move.' "

The depth of the split became distressingly clear the following year, when on the Day of the Covenant of Blood River, the Vrouemonument was unveiled in Bloemfontein. This was to be a day of solemn celebration for all Afrikaners (if a day of ambiguous pleasure for the English, not to mention the Zulus, who had cause to regret this constant harping on December 16; it was, after all, the crushing defeat of the imperial Zulu army that was being celebrated). The crowd of some 20,000, among whom were Jim de Villiers and some of his friends from Winburg, gave the old warhorse de Wet a rousing cheer; but when Botha spoke, the crowd turned its back and was silent. This was not a time for conciliation; Botha was becoming the enemy, the lackey of the Rand ("Botha's brokers," the Winburgers called the grand capitalists of the gold mines), a toady to empire. Botha gave his speech anyway, his words banging against his burghers' sturdy and stubborn backs, but it was no use; they would not listen.

II

THERE WAS WORSE to come. Less than a year later the Great War broke out in Europe. Botha had to risk a decision: the English South Africans were clamouring to enter the war on the British side, but to do so could mean an Afrikaner revolt. For a few weeks he and Smuts agonized: a decade earlier they had been in the field, defending their homes from empire, their women and children dying in British camps. Now there was an honourable peace. They decided that conciliation with the English-speakers was important enough a principle to risk revolt by the Afrikaans-speakers. They opted for empire. (It's worth remembering that the Afrikaner is capable of stubbornness in causes other than his own privilege.)

In September 1914 the government formally decided to invade the German enclave of South West Africa. The commandant general of the armed forces, Gen. Christian Beyers, immediately resigned in protest. He and the old patriarch Koos de la Rey headed north to their former stamping-ground to raise the alarm. Between Pretoria and Johannesburg there was a road-block. The impetuous Beyers refused to stop. The police fired. Koos de la Rey, hero of the War of Independence, was killed instantly. And it was all a tragic mistake: the road-block was not for the rebels, as they came to be called, but for a gang of hit-and-run thugs who had been staging Bonnie-and-Clyde-style raids on the small towns of the Rand.

The new South African army began to disintegrate. One of the commando leaders who had been with Smuts to the end of the Boer War defected with his brigade to the Germans. Beyers raised a commando in the western Transvaal. The magical de Wet surfaced: he would raise a commando and the Vierkleur would fly again over Pretoria . . . He was soon in the field again. General Jan Kemp, another relic of the old contests, also entered the fray. The news spread: the commandos would ride again; a nation was to be in arms; the defeats would be wiped out. This was the last chance: it was now or never; the bittereinders would triumph at the end; God willed it. The old issues surfaced. Maria Marquard, now Maria de Villiers of La Rochelle near Winburg, with two small children of her own, took up her pen once more.

III

ON OCTOBER 24, 1914, Maria wrote in a small black school notebook a "to whom it may concern" letter, putting down her tumultuous thoughts, trying to make sense of the way her people were being torn to and fro.

Jim had been off to the Middelveld (the north-western Free State) and he heard there that commandos were in the field again and urging the farmers to join up.

On Sunday evening we heard that commandeering was going on here — everyone had to be in town "{with gun, horse, and mouth-provisions for three days}". On Monday afternoon a small Kaffir brought Jim's "commandeer briefie", written in pencil on a scrap of paper. By this time those who had gone to Winburg were returning. Harley and F. R. Cronje [who were both Botha loyalists] addressed them, and said that those who would should surrender their guns and go home, but if they would [the loyalists] would be glad were they to stay and help them.

An assortment stayed in town to "drill" — all Hertzog people of course came out [left town]. That day a telegram was read saying de Wet had captured a train and disarmed the Defence Force contingent on it. Evidently commandos were forming in the north of the OFS. Then we began to hear things of the "reign of terror" in Winburg. Bergh, the head of the Kaffir scouts in the last war (who has never been heard of since, till there is dirty work to do) gave out passes the first few days. Old Theunis Wessels had to valuate oxwagons. Young Theunis bought horses. Jan Maree, Piet Joubert etc were officers. Sentries were put at the gates and everybody drilled.

On Sunday 1st November we heard Gen Hertzog had passed from Winburg to Bloemfontein and that on Thursday there was to be a conference at Onze Rust [ex-president Steyn's home]. During the next week we heard that Harrismith had peaceably surrendered to de Wet. We also heard that de Wet did not intend firing a shot; Conroy has a commando, Bert Wessels, van Schalkwyk and others.

On Tuesday . . . five of de Wet's men turned up here. On Monday they had held a meeting: de Wet had sent them to recruit: they forced no one, but whoever didn't come was to give his gun and usable horses. Well! I think Jim thought that without either gun or horses it would be rather dreadful, so (very half heartedly though) he sort of said he'd go. I said to this Nel (heading these men) "{Do you want the German flag here?" "No, we want our own flag." "But we can't, we are too poor}." He then said that the republics had started poor etc and that we were getting deeper and deeper into debt — "now again seven millions."

He said de Wet's object was this: to gather "die volk" together as far as Cape Town, and then to show Botha that there was a people whom he must consider — whom he can't pass by. (His eloquence rather took me as well as his undeniable good looks, but Jim wasn't much impressed by him!) He had seen de Wet last on Friday, and his last words were "{Don't be irresponsible. Don't even fire one shot}". The idea was evidently a bloodless revolution. But how can they think of getting their independence back? It seems too futile to discuss even — we were stolen to fill the capitalists' pockets. Botha's brokers won't let us go. There's something recklessly courageous about these men — and yet with so many it's just adventure. Yesterday afternoon Jim drove over to see Mr Steyn and when he came back was quite decided not to go — certainly not till Hertzog calls, which is remote.

Steyn (Jim's neighbour Steyn, from whom he learned farming, not the president) had visited the presidential residence at Onze Rust and been put somewhat in the picture. Botha had asked ex-president Steyn to help him contain de Wet; Steyn in turn had sent Hertzog to Christiaan de Wet with a letter urging calm. Prime Minister Botha broke faith with them both by having his defence forces attack a de Wet commando; back to square one. Steyn refused to sanction de Wet but refused to condemn him either. Hertzog, clearly, felt the same way.

On Wednesday morning, Maria wrote, sadly: "So now we know nothing and are nothing — till when? I only wonder what we'll have left when this is over. De Wet is said to be moving with 4,000 men — fancy how much they'll need to eat." Jim did a little guard duty later, glumly standing at a railway trestle, rifle propped against a culvert, stick of biltong in hand, but other than that he took no official part in the rebellion.

The first "battle" of the "armed protest" took place only a few farms from La Rochelle, and it was a pathetic affair. About 150 "loyalist" or "government" Winburgers, including the despised F. R. Cronje and Jan Maree, set off for de Wet's headquarters. They approached the de Wet encampment on Daan Erasmus's farm under a white flag with their hands up, but 20 yards from the camp they abruptly opened fire. De Wet was shot in the neck, his horse dead under him, his son Danie killed. Five died on each side before the Winburgers withdrew; and a day later de Wet entered the town and stripped its stores of provisions in retaliation. A grim de Wet would only say that he preferred his son to fall in this cause than in the service of the English.

De Wet gathered his men and rode south towards Bloemfontein. In a dreary little place called Mushroom Valley, the two sides finally met. The legend has it that Botha, waiting for the commando to arrive, saw mounted men approaching and announced: *Die engelse kom*, the English are coming. On the de Wet side, Jim's friends referred to the encamped Botha army as *die tommies* — the English. Once again, as so often in the past, the Afrikaners were riding to battle, not for the first time against one another, but no one could quite bring himself to believe it: both sides invoked the ancestral enemy. The other side *must* be *die engelse* . . .

The fight was soon over, but its consequences persisted. A note Maria received from a Mrs. van Zyl gives the flavour:

"{Frikkie Cronje sits next to General Botha in his car, oh how terrible, it's almost unbelievable, they transport the English here and other Boers to shoot our loved ones dead and shatter them with cannons and they follow them with a great army there near Korannaberg and Marquard, oh what will come of the poor Boers, it looks as if the dear lord has forsaken us, can you believe that Botha and Cronje, two Boers like us, fight with a huge army and cannons against our own people, their brothers.}"

Maria herself wrote, acidly:

To Frikkie Cronje thus comes the double honour of having fired the first shot in the OFS and of lusting for his brothers' blood . . . Of course, de Wet is a so-called rebel, and we may be taking a one sided view of things, but de Wet did NOT want to shed unnecessary blood, of that I am convinced from everything I have heard. How pitiful the whole thing is — how unnecessary — how terrible. WHY couldn't Botha have tried and tried alone to stand high in the estimation of his fellow Afrikaners instead of always playing to the English gallery, or why didn't he go to the country to see how he really stood, when he found he had not the confidence of the whole SA Party? Thus far I have not had much sympathy with the rebels, but now of course . . .

Maria the careful diarist, the recounter of events, viewed the future herself with unaccustomed foreboding. And she let slip a little the tight rein she kept on her emotions:

How can love of empire really actuate and move men like Botha, Smuts and Cronje, who FOUGHT for their independence, who saw their kinsfolk bleeding and dying before their eyes, who saw their flag taken, who saw their mothertongue in danger of anni-hilation? By the treaty of Vereeniging they owe England duty and allegiance, and I would lie to say I hated all Englishmen — but WHY this continual pandering to England and English capitalists — England gave us self government, but what did she take from us, from them? We honour the other nations who told in story and song of their fight against the oppressors — why should we forget so easily? England can't expect a nation to change in a day.

Even in conciliatory Winburg, the mistrust surfaced. The curious characters who emerge when bullying is to be done reappeared in town; farmers who drove to market had their horses commandeered, and they were issued "permits" to return home. More than in the War of Independence, as the platteland called the Boer War, families were torn in two. Maria wrote:

> Robbertse Schwartz is with de Wet, his brother with the govt. — feeling is frightfully tense, relations strained. I still hold the govt. responsible for all this — after all when one hears of rebellion in other lands one always blames the govt. (what about Slagters Nek?) I'm afraid de Wet is headstrong and from what I can make out he is relying on the Germans — what beautiful childlike trust! But I do grow so impatient when I think of what it will mean to the country . . . of course, de Wet did not want to fire a shot, but of course his enemies will say, "why then did he have a gun?" But all this petty tyranny in Winburg (I don't know if it's in the other villages) of course embitters feeling terribly. I'm going to stop writing; if only one could see a single ray of light in this terrible darkness, but one does not see a way out.

At this point young René de Villiers, then four, makes his first and only appearance in direct quotations in Maria's diaries. Cute quotes of four-year-olds are usually appealing only to their mothers, but there is a certain pertinence here: he asks his father if so-and-so is an *oorloger* (a "war-rer") and then asks plaintively: "Pappie waar is neutraal, waar bly hy?" (Where is neutral? Where does he live?) The search for *neutraal* has dominated my father's life ever since.

IV

ON NOVEMBER 14, 1914, the young woman returned to her journal to set down her considered thoughts.

> In a letter from Aunt Charlotte she says, what is de Wet after? Does he really contemplate independence, or is it primitive man

fighting Botha? I think it is a mixture of both. With due respect to all of you who are going to read this and in all modesty but I really think of you all I have come to know more of our people during these last few years than any of you: I live among them, and in passing hear more of their opinions and feelings than those who don't. I'll first repeat as nearly accurately as I can the "gezegte" [ponderings] of old Oom Jan Scott, who was here on Saturday 7th. (You know quite near him lives Cornelis Bruwer, a National Scout [Afrikaner volunteer in the British army] during the war, now a great Botha man — who has been having free use of the Galloway telephone, and who told one of de Wet's spies, thinking he was a govt man, he couldn't give his horses. "{It's the only way I've got to report to Winburg}".)

This is what Oom Jan Scott said: "{Since the war I've had it with these sort of people. Who killed my children in the camps? I'm not talking of those who fell in battle — he got a bullet like a man, but in a newspaper we smuggled into Ceylon Red Paul Botha wrote: 'As long as you leave the women and children on the farms you'll never catch the boers. I know because I was for seven years member of the volksraad and my wife farmed better than me'.}"

Well I think none of us, however deeply we felt with our people can realize what the feeling is of those who lost sons AND daughters to "die soort mense" (the national scouts) and, it seems to me, that Botha and his followers, who are always so anxious to propitiate all Englishmen, who are in such favour with the jingo press, with the opposition, are looked upon with suspicion. De Wet and Botha fought together — it must be galling to the former to see Botha's feelings . . . He is always ready to concede so much . . . these things have been accumulating and causing bad feelings — now the last straw is this most unpopular declaration of war. Feelings of this kind I think animate de Wet and many others. Many — whom I could name — are with him for adventure, and the idea that it is noble as Afrikaners to be on the side of those who support Hertzog rather than Botha! Then, sad to say, there are those who go out of strong dislike for Botha or a strong dislike (first political now alas! grown in many cases personal) for their representative in parliament. As regards independence, I personally see no hope, nor do I long for it particularly. But stranger things have happened.

What followed the Boston "tea party" may follow in SA, who knows? Old Naasie du Plessis has just been here — he tells us de Wet is past Virginia, past Bultfontein . . . where? One of his clan is with de Wet. Jim says I MUST put in my diary that we had green beans on the 20th of November! Well! We are justly proud of our early vegetables. I don't say much about them in my letters for fear they'll be commandeered! How I wish my next entry could be *peace* — but I fear not.

V

RENÉ DE VILLIERS'S very earliest memory of life in Winburg had to do with war. Seventy years after the event, he recalled, "I didn't see any fighting but I remember being taken to a neighbouring farm at night and hearing the government troops banging on the front door. I hid under the bed in a back room and only emerged when the all-clear was given. What they were looking for was my father's two cart horses, which they needed for their own purposes. I remember being on the farm without transport for several months. My father had little enthusiasm for the whole thing. I remember clearly his return from standing guard at a railway crossing of the Modder River not very far from our farm."

Maria's last diary entry of the period followed a week or so later. Her final paragraph was a cry: "That the rebellion has been a mistake I don't deny — that it is a sorrowful thing is certain — but that doesn't make the government right, and that they are all adventurers is a LIE."

There was one more pitched battle in the rebellion, and it was over. Beyers was drowned trying to swim the swollen Vaal River. Kemp and others were imprisoned; Manie Maritz, another Boer War general, took refuge with the Germans and ended his days in exile. De Wet surrendered, a broken and defeated man. Christiaan de Wet, the magical leader, the hero of the war against the English, the man who had kept alive the deep emotions of the plattelanders, who had seemed most in tune with their dark history, was locked securely into the Johannesburg fort. Many rebellious leaders would follow him there in the high days of black nationalism.

PART 5

René de Villiers and the creation of the sacred history

——

Chapter 19

The great experiment of Fusion and its failure

I

THE TWO BOER WAR GENERALS, Botha and Smuts, spent the next few years in the service of the empire and its allies in the war against the Germans — though not without taunts and disillusion at home, and not without some scepticism about what they were achieving; Botha particularly was filled with foreboding over the treaty of Versailles. Vereeniging was not so long ago; he understood only too well the trauma of defeat and what it would do to the Germans. He had been there, after all, and understood the anger that humiliation generated.

Within a few months of the end of the Great War Botha died, after a brief illness, and Smuts returned from the imperial war councils to South Africa to take over as leader of the South Africa Party and prime minister. He found that in his absence the Afrikaners had been slipping away from him. In fact, the platteland was slipping away not only from the cosmopolitan Smuts but away from any leader whose worldview wasn't focused tightly on its own alienation; it was also slipping away from its own heritage and its own past — reservoirs of rural poor were building up in the hinterlands, and the traditional subdivision of land could no longer contain them.

Nor were the solutions of the past any longer valid; there was nowhere to withdraw to. They had lost the war, seemed to have won the peace, now everything was going sour again

— how many more times could defeat be borne? In the councils of the Dutch Reformed Church there was fretting about their fate, fear that they would become so spiritually demoralized that they'd take themselves out of reach of salvation. From the perspective of the platteland, there was only one road: to become exiles in their own land and emigrate to the burgeoning cities, where the English — moneyed, sophisticated, competent, discriminatory — were in control.

The freewheeling frontiersmen were transformed into an urban proletariat — "poor whites" drifted past all the farms in the years that followed the war, seeking hand-outs, odd jobs that had more commonly been done by the black labourers. By the early 1920s, a government commission reported that nearly 20 per cent of all Afrikaners were living marginal existences, in penury. In the cities they founded slums on the periphery, unable to adapt, brooding on slights, made to feel inferior because shopkeepers sneered at their language. Even in the old Afrikaner capitals of Pretoria and Bloemfontein English was the language of commerce; life seemed to be run by "foreigners," by the former enemy; in the minds of the new proletarians, the defeat after the war seemed without end. Most of the disinherited took refuge in the mines, where they did semi-skilled and unskilled work under the supercilious direction of English-speaking pit bosses. And in the background, as yet inchoate but a presence that filled the horizons, was an even larger alienated proletariat, the blacks.

The first confrontation came to a head in 1922. The economy was in a bad way; there was drought on the platteland that drove even more rural poor to the cities. A falling gold premium prompted the capitalists of the Rand to cut costs by eliminating the already traditional colour bar in mine jobs — the black proletariat would work for lower wages than the whites, would complain less, and were marginally more competent, partly because their bedrock culture had not suffered disillusion and defeat. True, black politics had been overturned, black armies crushed, tribes had even lost their homelands, but in the kraals and the far hinterlands the culture remained as it had been for centuries, unaffected by the kind of sour disillusion and pinched vision that disturbed the Afrikaners' dreams. To the mine-owners, this made the blacks better workers. To the Afrikaners it was just one more proof that foreign capitalists, "the Jews and the English," were bent on cultural genocide.

Anger swept round the white slums; those with ties to the platteland brought in horses and guns; commandos formed again amongst the broken-down cars and shabby tenements of the unedifying city, as much bewildered and out of place as threatening. For a few days most of the Rand was in the hands of the rebels; there was talk once more of a republic and of ejecting uitlanders; surely the platteland would rise, would see the vision, would see the need . . . would see that foreigners would use blacks to estrange Afrikaners. When nothing was forthcoming from the platteland, the rebels flirted with local agents of Moscow's Third International; representatives of international Communism had already made inroads in some of the Johannesburg unions, and the Marxist rhetoric made as much sense to the white dispossessed as it did in the many countries of the Third World where it subsequently took root.

Smuts, who only two years earlier had efficiently put down a rising by the Xhosa in the eastern Cape (by a breakaway sect called the Israelites, whose messianic message had been threatening to get out of hand), called out the Defence Forces once more. This time Afrikaners showed little compunction in shooting other Afrikaners, and the rebellion was put down with dispatch. Within days the inflammatory English press, always as ready with alarums about the Afrikaners as it was by now hysterical about the agents of international Communism, was calling for an investigation into "collaboration" between Hertzog's National Party and the "bolsheviks" in the English-speaking Labour Party opposition.

In theory, class solidarity should have prevailed. The real divisions in Johannesburg were not between black and white workers but between mine-owners and an exploited, unskilled proletariat of whatever colour. But the old ties proved too strong to allow the ideology of the Third International — foreigners, after all! — to take real root. In spite of the blandishments of Marxism the "womb of ethnic collectivity," as the political scientist Hermann Giliomee called it, proved stronger than the lure of international brotherhood — to the blacks because they lacked a history of crossing tribal boundaries and also because they lacked that crucial resource, the vote; to the Afrikaners because they were only on the fringes of the modern world, not yet a part of it. A brief alliance that Afrikaans workers made with the militantly pro-white English-speaking labour unions didn't survive the old calls of blood and language. The English were too recently the victors and the Afrikaners the vanquished for them to feel comfortable in an alliance in which the English naturally dominated.

Nor did they — yet — feel the menace of that other proletariat very strongly; in this period blacks were at the periphery of Afrikaner consciousness — they had, after all, been dealt with in the past and no doubt could be again. The English were still the problem, not part of the solution. It's true that the effect of Afrikaner industrial action was against black participation; but its intent was a ferocious effort to preserve what collective security was left, aimed not so much without as within. In the future the intent and the effect would grow closer; *die swart gevaar*, the black menace, became a potent rallying cry in later National Party election manifestos. It's also true that the black presence had arrived in "white" South Africa and would not leave again. But for the moment white politics took the blacks for granted; they were not the cause of quarrels.

As for Smuts himself, he had been marked in the rural areas as *engels*, one of Them, and the voters began to turn away from him.

II

IN HIS DRIVE FOR POWER Hertzog used the Labour Party opposition, even though its English-speaking character got him accused of managing a "dirty alliance" with the former enemy. It took a fairly cynical attitude to bring it off, in any case, since the thrust of his opposition to Botha, and now to Smuts, was what he considered their rolling over and playing dead to the forces of English capitalism and culture.

Still he had to find allies somewhere; he wanted a parliamentary majority and in his first few tries he had fallen somewhat short. In the 1915 general election, the first it had contested, Hertzog's National Party had won 27 seats in a Parliament of 131; only five years later it had emerged from the election as the single largest party, with 44 seats — better, but not yet sufficient. In 1922 a feeble attempt had been made in Bloemfontein to heal the rift and end the *broedertwis*, but Hertzog and Smuts could not agree, and the attempt failed. It was at that point that Hertzog gritted his teeth and put aside, temporarily, his Afrikaner republican sentiments to make a marriage of convenience with the English-speaking Labour Party; at least both sides could agree that "big finance" (by which they really meant the mine-owners' efforts to attain ever cheaper, which meant black, labour) was the common enemy.

It was a bizarre marriage, but in the next general election, in 1924, the coalition was swept to power. "Dirty alliance" or no, the disinherited stayed with Hertzog; his personal authority and integrity helped, and so did Labour's militant defence of white proletarian interests. The Dutch Reformed Church, which approved the priority of economic consolidation over redemption, was silent. Smuts was personally defeated, his government in tatters. Afrikaner nationalism had finally been given its first chance at real power, its first real chance, Hertzog considered, of "winning the peace." Only in the seminaries of the south and in the coffee-houses of the Cape were dissident rumblings still to be heard: the Afrikaner was not yet finished with schism.

In the 1929 election, with the South African economy already in the throes of a depression (anticipating the Great Depression that was to engulf the world), Hertzog won an outright majority and was able to dispense with his coalition partner, which he somewhat brusquely did. Immediately he set about putting the Afrikaner house in order: a nationalized iron and steel industry, a nationalized railway, a state monopoly of the new trucking industry, official recognition at last of Afrikaans, as opposed to Dutch, a single-minded use of the railway system to employ the otherwise unemployable Afrikaner refugees from the platteland, a national flag to end the daily petty harassment of seeing the wretched Union Jack of the conqueror. Hertzog wasted no time. He helped wrench the South African economy onto a new path: in the depression that South Africa shared with the rest of the industrialized world, he anticipated the New Deal by creating vast state-run projects in irrigation and drought control, measures designed to soften at last a hard land, to make it a fitter home for his people. In the process, of course, he made sure to protect them from their fellow proletarians, the disinherited and displaced black tribes from the hinterlands, who were collecting in the "white" cities in large numbers. He called this his "civilized labour policy." "Civilized" and "white" were now synonyms in the Afrikaner lexicon.

All along Hertzog had been pushing for his "two-stream" vision of what made an Afrikaner; like Hofmeyr before him he was prepared to accept into the volk those whose language was English but who made the kind of commitment to the motherland he believed was in the blood of the Afrikaners. He believed, however, that the streams should be kept separate — it was the only way to protect the nascent Afrikaner identity. He had split with Botha and Smuts on the issue, because he believed they were out of touch with his people's needs — their stream was only one stream, an integrationist one, and it wasn't the Afrikaners': they would be bound to swamp the Afrikaner in a culture stronger and less defensive.

Now he himself was being overtaken by others using the same reasoning. There were those in his party who considered his attitude of relative acceptance towards the English dangerous heresy. Their dislike of him grew when it became clear that Hertzog, after six years or so in power, was beginning to see that there were still virtues in Smuts and the conciliators. For his part Hertzog was increasingly worried by Daniel Malan's different and fundamentalist Afrikaner vision of the future; and the economy in 1930 was in a catastrophic state. Hertzog's clinging to the gold standard long after the British had left it damaged the economy in fundamental ways. World-wide depression had cut markets for South African grain and wool and virtually ended the wine industry. The country was in the grip of a savage drought: the thirst for water obsessed everyone. Hertzog grew weary of the burden.

In 1933, after a few days of seclusion on his highveld farm, Waterval, he approached that other highveld farmer, Smuts, and proposed a coalition of his National Party and Smuts's South Africa Party. The "great experiment" of Fusion led to the formation of the United South Africa National Party, or United Party for short, with Hertzog and Smuts as joint leaders. Fusion was the intent; fission was the result.

III

SCHISM IS THE continuing nightmare of Afrikaner politicians. The Afrikaners have always been prone to schism — a tribe that follows heroes always is. Their history was full of divisions: free burghers and Company servants. Trekboers and settled farmers. Luttig de Villiers, the transport rider, and Paul, the master of Boschendal, frontiersman and stay-at-home. Trekkers and accommodationists. The Cape and the north. Potgieter and Pretorius. The Orange Free State and the Transvaal. Hendsoppers and bittereinders. De Wet and Botha. Hertzog and Smuts. And now that Hertzog was with Smuts: Hertzog and Malan.

Hertzog and Smuts began as allies in the Boer War,

became opponents, now were allies again. Malan was the enemy of the new vision. For a while under the new alliance matters went well. The Great Depression lifted, the mines went deeper and brought out more gold, foreign investment returned, jobs were created.

But Hertzog, immersed in his Fusionist idea and caught up in the tangled politics of running a multilingual and polyethnic state, lost touch with his people as Smuts and Botha had done in their turn. His heart had been tempered in the great events of war, and he had little understanding of the new classes of Afrikaners who were appearing in such alarming numbers in the cities. He had begun with sympathy for the disinherited of the northern platteland. He understood their clannishness and their clinging to their own, but he did not have sufficient understanding of their fears and insecurities. He had no sympathy for and even less understanding of the petit bourgeois functionaries and academics who inhabited the towns, seminaries, and academies of the Cape (to all of which he gave the shorthand notation: Daniel Malan).

To Hertzog they were second-rate minds with little knowledge of the real world, the world of war and politics, a world with a stage large enough to accept large men with grand ideas. He rejected their narrow definition of Afrikaner and their manipulation of the symbols of Afrikaner history to suit their own purposes. He rejected their deviousness and their penchant for secrecy; the emotions generated in their endless discussions in the coffee-houses of the Cape seemed to him unhealthy, a festering far from the clean lines and honest emotions of the platteland. To be attacked, as he was, as an *ou kêrel van die verlede* (an old chap from the past), as the "poor old general," was humiliating and infuriating. His opponents, on the other hand, wrote him off for his association with the crafty Smuts, who they were convinced would dilute Hertzog's nationalist principles. His idea that there was no longer need for two separate parties because the Afrikaners' interests were now secure they regarded as early evidence that Smuts had, indeed, bamboozled his new ally. The poor old chap from the past would have to go.

Daniel François Malan was himself born on the platteland and spent the first few years of his life there, but he was educated in Stellenbosch and in Utrecht in Holland. He had been in his 20s during the Boer War but had taken no part in the fighting: his interest was that of a politician and an academic, not a warrior. He graduated with a theological degree but took as his trade a more secular proselytizing — he became editor of _Die Burger_, an influential Cape journal that was the country's first Afrikaans daily newspaper. Malan's journalism was propaganda of a very high order; his Calvinist training and fundamentalist inclination combined with a mystic temperament to give a theological cast to his secular writing — he set out to make a theology of Afrikanerdom, to create for his people a sacred history. He was far from the first — old S. J. du Toit's Afrikaner Bond had done the same thing before Hofmeyr deflected it — but he was by far the best. He collected about him disciples who were to control the Afrikaner's destiny to the modern age: T. E. Donges, Charles "Blackie" Swart, Hans Strijdom, Hendrik Verwoerd.

Malan argued that Fusion was a material and spiritual threat to Afrikanerdom. The United Party contained large numbers of English and had the support of the Rand capitalists who had precipitated the war against the republics. Where capital flows, it governs. Where capital governs, its interests supersede those of any volk. The disinherited would be disinherited again: capital would allow them to be undercut by cheap black labour; Afrikaners would be split in two and the last chance for an Afrikaner-run country would wither. Nor would capital allow the nation to withdraw from the empire, as self-respect demanded. The Afrikaner would lose his history, which meant losing himself. In this definition, Fusion was a betrayal, a renunciation of principle at the hands of expediency. Hertzog, who had propounded it, was a hendsopper after all. The volk wouldn't allow it.

Malan's purified nationalism was articulating for the tribe

its own notions of itself. He was also drawing his own nourishment from the tribe, tapping into its collective memory, shaping but not creating its civil theology. Hertzog fought back, but he was another generation; he attacked Malan in the old way, personally, as a leader: how could a man who had sat out a war criticize its heroes? Hertzog was missing the point. You can't attack a religion — even a civil religion, a political ideology — by criticizing its leaders: revolutionary ideas are not stopped in that way. Attacking Malan wasn't going to help.

The political strategy of Fusion was the principle of full equality between the two white language groups. Only in this way, Hertzog had come to believe, would the Afrikaner be able to take his place as a full partner in his own country. Malan's strategy was based simply on the fact that the Afrikaners formed more than 50 per cent of the white population, and forging them into a single party would guarantee that they would control their own destiny. Fusion, Malan saw, meant competition with the English. The disinherited could not compete: the fear he tapped was the fear of being swamped — first by the English and then by their agents, the black masses. The politics of fear proved decisive in the ethnic mobilization of the Afrikaners.

IV

LONG BEFORE 1948, long before Malan finally came to power, the South African statute books were filled with laws that were racially, culturally, and linguistically discriminatory. The architects of apartheid weren't inventing a policy from thin air. They changed an accumulation of *ad hoc* lawmaking into a system, changed a long series of small acts aimed at petty matters into a comprehensive scheme as radical, as far-reaching, as thorough, as exhaustive, and as single-minded as the Bolshevik remaking of Russia — but they didn't invent discrimination, or differentiation. The two northern republics had never accepted non-whites as citizens with any rights;

the Cape, though it had a limited non-racial franchise, never-theless had a pass system and a system of residential segrega-tion, much of it laid out in statutes introduced by the British colonizers that predated the union government in 1910. In Natal, the largely English-speaking colony had devised a sys-tem virtually as complete as the Transvaal's; the Zulus were given no voice at all in the land of their birth.

Hertzog, too, did his share. The old patriarch Potgieter had defeated Mzilikazi by horse and gun from his base in the laager. The politician Hertzog used the internalization of the laager and the rhetoric of the moment, combining the tradi-tional and emotional support for the *eie* with the politician's fly-blown oratory: as we have seen, he proclaimed himself in favour of "civilized labour" and set about energetically erect-ing the industrial colour bar to supplement the social one the country had inherited from the republics (which in turn had derived it from the old colony). *We are not against blacks. But we must defend ourselves. The black proletariat is prepared to work for wages a white wage-earner cannot accept — not even the disinherited, who are still part of the volk. We must therefore protect ourselves.*

Some of the legislation onto which the apartheid system was later grafted was Hertzog's: the Wages Act of 1925 and the Mines and Works Act of the following year reserved certain jobs for whites and set up the hierarchy of salaries only now being dismantled as President P. W. Botha begins to pick apart the job reservation system.

On the campaign trail in 1925, Hertzog had declared that the admittedly pitiful number of black voters in the Cape province represented a threat to the whole country, presum-ably because they could theoretically cast deciding votes in swing constituencies and therefore affect policy; to Hertzog, the accumulation of property and education necessary before a black man could qualify as a voter were not at all sufficient to make such a man civilized overnight — this would take time, in an always unspecified amount.

Later, during the 1929 election campaign that brought his

party to full power, Hertzog officially declared himself in favour of keeping South Africa a "white man's country" — it was one of the first signs of the switch from Afrikanerness to whiteness — and tried to pin on Smuts, and particularly on the brilliant J. H. Hofmeyr (Onze Jan's first cousin once removed), Smuts's deputy prime minister and heir apparent, the odium of "swamping" the whites with black voters. This was tricky to counter: Smuts knew that stripping their meagre power away from non-whites wouldn't play in the world of the League of Nations, which he had helped found and which he still considered one of his constituencies though he held no official position there; but failure to answer vigorously with a defence of discrimination would cost him on the platteland.

He vacillated, until in 1936 he could vacillate no longer: Hertzog, prime minister of the Fusion government of which he himself was a member, introduced a bill to strip voting rights from blacks in the Cape.

The rhetoric of the debate was pathetic. First Parliament took away the franchise. Then it granted the "right" for blacks to elect three (white) members of their own; it then set up a puppet Natives Representative Council on which blacks were the minority and which had no power anyway. And while MPs were doing all this, they still managed to pretend to themselves that they were in some unspecified way defending "native rights." It makes depressing reading today. "The defence of European civilization" was a phrase much used by both sides. The concept of trusteeship — of guardianship "until such time" as blacks were "ready" — was used to soften the ugly reality. Only Hofmeyr, though a member of the government, felt impelled by what he said was his Christian duty to vote against the bill, to Hertzog's fury. The Malan people were already using Hofmeyr's name as a bogeyman on the platteland; Malan's disciple J. G. Strijdom particularly, "the Uncompromising Lion of the North," as he liked to hear himself called, linked Hofmeyr to the doom of the Afrikaners. Hertzog, by implication, was doom's employer.

The bill, which of course passed, was merely one in a

dismal series. It was important mostly for two speeches made during its debate, one by Hofmeyr and one by Hertzog.

Hofmeyr's opposition, delivered in his crisp, measured tones, was a cry across the years to the future. He was appealing to his people to break down the laager, to emerge into the world, to consider the consequences. Look at what you're really doing, he appealed, look beyond the discredited notion of white trusteeship, beyond "let the native develop along his own lines," look at what this really means. Having the blacks communally elect a certain number of members implies a racial divergence of interests. "But there is a far greater community of interests in this land. We have on both sides a contribution to make to the welfare of South Africa, and the weakness of this bill is that it emphasises differences, stimulates hostility and pays no regard to the ultimate community of interest." It would push educated blacks into the bosom of a peasant community in disaffection and revolt, he warned. The bill was born of fear, of the desire for self-preservation. You cannot preserve civilization in this way. The future cannot be built on unreasoning fear, and the bill was built partly on sentiment based on tradition, and partly on fear.

Having put his finger exactly on the cause, Hofmeyr then went on to show he was as blind to the future as any other of his time: "I know perfectly well I am speaking against the feeling of the overwhelming majority of the House. I know I am speaking against the feeling of the great mass of the [white] people of this country . . . I believe there is a rising tide of liberalism in South Africa. It is mostly the younger people who are in the forefront of that tide. It is they who are the custodians of the future."

The English-speaking press showed themselves even less perspicacious. George Heard of the Rand *Daily Mail* wrote: "[Hofmeyr] represents a new outlook in South African politics — a liberal outlook that is foreign to the fear-conditioned politics in our country. The old battle cries do not stir him; they belong to an age that is passing. Mr. Hofmeyr belongs to a new age that is just coming to birth. The young men in Parliament will, I believe, be with him in the day of its fulfilment." A decade later Malan came to power.

Hertzog's speech was equally significant, a cry not to the future but to the tribal past. Uncertainty, he said, was "a canker eating into the soul of the white population." Uncertainty about what? "The two great fears of South Africa are the intermingling of blood and black domination"; the fears he brought into the open had been transmogrified by history and magnified by defeat. Here he was right: they were a canker eating into the Afrikaner's soul; even the liberals, as we shall see, were overawed by their fear of the inarticulate, unknowing, unknown, and frightful black masses, steadily migrating to the cities. This bill was necessary to excise the canker. And those who claimed it contradicted Christian teaching and Christian charity were wrong. Reaching deep into the past, Hertzog told the assembled white parliamentarians that self-preservation was a sacred Christian principle. Was not the principle of sacrificing one's life for one's nation in time of war approved by all Christian nations? Was not national self-defence therefore a sacred Christian principle too? This was also self-preservation; a people for whom the *eie* was supreme had the supreme duty to preserve it against all attack and all attenuation; "it is the only principle, that of self-preservation, that of self-defence, by which humanity itself and Christianity will ever be able to preserve itself."

Here was the basis for apartheid-to-come; Hertzog's elevation of survival into a Christian virtue was to infect all South African governments from that time, and though each would define survival differently, none has come close to accepting that Hertzog's inclusive white South African-ness — a concept that could encompass outsiders if they accepted the Afrikaner world-view — could also be translated into a larger and colour-blind national identity, or that survival could best be assured by that other, somewhat neglected Christian virtue called generosity.

V

ALL THIS RHETORIC and emotion was being expended to get rid of 2 per cent of the electorate, which is one measure of how visceral was the Afrikaner's fear of being swamped; it may seem to outsiders like mere institutional racism, but the ancestral memories of the black sea pressing against the meagre Afrikaner breastworks troubled many a platteland dream and were expressed and articulated by their political leaders. Without the rigour of control, the Afrikaner would again become lost in Africa; there would be no more chances.

And what of Smuts, as the bill passed? He supported it, at the end, because the existence of a few native representatives and the idea of a natives' council preserved at least some political voice for blacks. Rather that, he said, than nothing at all. It was a position he could defend abroad, but it gained him no adherents at home.

In passing Hertzog managed to dilute the Coloured franchise in the Cape by more than 50 per cent. He did this in two measures designed to evade the entrenchment the Coloured franchise enjoyed in the South African constitution; a direct assault on the Coloured vote would have had to obtain the approval of two-thirds of both houses, and he had nowhere near this amount of support. In 1930, over the protests of many members of his own government, he extended the vote to all white women in the country, thereby doubling the white electorate. Coloured women remained without a vote. A year later he acted again. The vote in the Cape was a qualified vote given only to men (and now women) who met certain property and educational qualifications. Hertzog simply extended to whites the unqualified franchise already in place in the two northern provinces.

Even this didn't satisfy the purified nationalists under Malan, who would in their time launch a furious assault on the entrenched clauses of the constitution, including the Cape's Coloured franchise itself. Hofmeyr, of course, voted against both bills. The Malanites took that for granted. Hofmeyr was too de-tribalized ("anglicized") an Afrikaner to be able to understand the intensity of the need to be free of contamination by any other group of whatever colour except, as Alan Paton put it in his biography of Hofmeyr, "those things that God in his Providence had made it inevitable to hold in common, like air, disease and currency." Hofmeyr spoke Afrikaans, but he was not regarded as a *ware Afrikaner*, a true Afrikaner.

In the late 1920s and throughout the 1930s the statutory obstacles in the way of black movement became ever more severe. And yet the movement went on because it had to, because the blacks had no option. The drought in the "native areas," the population expansion, the lack of cash income in an increasingly arid landscape, the soil erosion and stock starvation — all these forced the blacks off the land, as they were forcing the "poor white" Afrikaners. The "locations," segregated townships, set aside for blacks overflowed; outside every city and every location shanty towns grew up, made of tin, sacking, cardboard, scraps of anything unburnable, without heat in the highveld winters or much fuel, without water, light, sanitation, uncontrolled by any government, their only authority the *de facto* power brokers made up of the few churchmen who ventured among them, the heads of the dozens of Christian splinter groups, the occasional clan chief from the rural areas, a huge amount of good will and good sense, exhaustion, and *tsotsis*, gangs of young criminals. These shanty towns exist still; they exist in the teeth of the most rigorous attempts by the state to end their existence; they exist because their inhabitants have been given no other alternative. In the 1930s they grew for the same reason, and the government response then was similar: control the movement and pay no attention to the reasons why the movement occurred.

Hertzog's Native Laws Amendment Act, another in an apparently interminable series, was a foretaste of the apartheid legislation to come. Malan himself could hardly have done better. Its express purpose was to control the movement of blacks to and within the towns. It would henceforth require a permit to move, a residence permit, a job permit. It would require permits to go on holiday. It gave to petty functionaries and the police complete power over the lives of families, for if a man lost his job he lost his residence permit and he (and his whole family) could be made to move back to "homelands" they had never seen and in which there was no work: it tended to make people very cautious in making protests to authority, since that authority could radically affect their lives at whim. Hertzog also shifted 15 million acres from white ownership to the "homelands," which allowed some politicians to feel generous, but in truth it changed little: there was still no work there, and no black organization powerful enough to insist on its creation. Ninety per cent of black convictions in the 1930s were for offences whites couldn't commit if they tried; every year one out of every dozen family heads was convicted.

The white Opposition voted for the bill virtually unanimously, justifying it on specious grounds that amounted mostly to tidiness; the government justified it on the grounds it was necessary for white survival: defence of the *eie* now depended on suppression of the black masses; security of the volk was synonymous with entrenchment of Afrikaner privilege. You didn't hear too many English-speakers kicking and screaming either — not about Hertzog's native policies. They worried mostly about the dumping of the Union Jack as the national flag; this was not their finest hour.

Hofmeyr, of course, voted nay. Again.

VI

MALAN WAS A MEMBER OF a controversial Afrikaner organization known as the Broederbond, or Band of Brothers; it is assumed, though not known — since the Broederbond is still a secret organization whose activities are not open to public scrutiny — that he shaped its ideas as it shaped his policies. In any case, the Broederbond and Malan shared a mystic view of the Afrikaner's destiny, controlled and governed by a militant Protestantism.

The origins of the Broederbond are obscure, but it is known it started as an Afrikaner self-help organization to deal with the problems of alienated Afrikaners in the "English" cities. There have been attempts, mostly by recent Broederbond members, to portray the organization as little more than a kind of Afrikaner Rotary Club, an American-style service club giving hand-outs to the needy and inculcating self-respect among the poor. No one takes this self-definition seriously. Because of the narrowness of vision of its members, because of the role they saw Afrikaners playing in the governing of South Africa, because of their purified definition of an Afrikaner, because of their success and the power they wielded, the Broederbonders played a sometimes decisive role in national politics. Every Afrikaner prime minister after Hertzog has been a member; the extent to which the Broederbond controlled the prime ministers is still not known for certain; it is assumed, however, that its influence is now greatly diminished.

Whether Malan created the Broederbond or was its creature hardly matters: the Broederbond was a revolutionary organization, tightly knit, secretive, militant in its righteousness, fanatic in its Calvinism, determined to secure the Afrikaner's control of his own place. Its members agreed: the Broederbond was to assume responsibility for *all* Afrikaners — they must assist the poor in the cities, help farmers, shape Afrikaner corporations, create Afrikaner banks and loan associations, control Afrikaner political parties — must help the Afrikaner control his own destiny. The Broederbond's use of Malan's sacred history was its triumph; its achievement was to direct the mobilization of the tribe to a single idea, and to articulate the idea, already inherent in the tribe, that survival depended on tribal cohesion.

Hertzog had carried three of the four provincial National Party congresses with him when he proposed Fusion with

Smuts; only Malan and the Cape opposed him. The old warrior thereupon launched a furious assault on Malan and the Broederbond, fuelled no doubt by their long sniping at his patriotism. He first accused the Broederbond of subverting the idea of a larger unity between English- and Afrikaans-speaking South Africans; he then accused Malan of demanding Afrikaner domination over the rest of the country — an accusation the wily Cape leader was only too happy to have flung at him, since that was, indeed, precisely what he wanted.

Once again Hertzog had missed the point: he couldn't see how much Malan represented the tribal longings of his people. Fusion represented dealing with the traditional enemy, the enemy that was even now running the cities. Dealing with the enemy meant a watering down of principle; any watering down endangered the volk. The line of reasoning was clear: survival of the Afrikaners meant absorption of the individual into the group; schism was not to be permitted; Afrikaners were not to be allowed to exploit other Afrikaners; the volk must move as a tribe to secure its future.

By the 1933 election, Malan had not yet formally split with Hertzog; he took part as a member of the Hertzog National Party and then, after Hertzog won, took his own group into opposition as the Herstigte Nasionale Party (Renewed National Party). What followed was hidden from public view: Malan and the Broederbond waged a ferocious battle for control of the political grass roots — the branches, constituency committees, candidate selection committees, provincial committees. Malan won most of these contests: his will was stronger, his ideology more militant, his political attention not distracted by the exercise of power. He left Hertzog with only the trappings; he had stolen the National Party away. And in the years that followed, he began his and the Broederbond's drive to capture the nation and secure it for his ideas in the same way.

Part of his conception of group cohesion was self-help; the bosses must be prevented from driving a wedge between poor

Afrikaners and the wealthy; *volkskapitalisme*, people's capitalism, was the answer — Afrikaner-owned enterprises employing Afrikaners, dealing with Afrikaners, selling to Afrikaners
at fair prices. The means of production must be Afrikanerized. Investment pools of Afrikaner capital must be created.
The Afrikaner poor must be helped to end their own poverty,
not through charity or welfare but through being given the
resources of an aroused volk.

Malan wanted the volk to "capture the capitalist system
and . . . transform it to fit [our] ethnic nature." Along with
economic aid for the poor went concern for their spiritual
nourishment. The "economic renaissance" of the volk had to
be accompanied by a cultural rebirth based on the ideas of
Christian nationalism, which made explicit the God-given
role of the Afrikaner in the African continent.

Malan's strategy worked because it exploited the deep
insecurities of the disinherited in the face of the English and
their growing fear of being overwhelmed by the blacks massing in the cities: Christian nationalism was a program for
survival and a licence to permit self-respect. It allowed them
to feel the superiority their history had both promised and
denied them; the "civilizing mission" allowed them at last to
allow the racial superiority they had felt but never needed
before. It was the tool Malan had sought in the drive for
ethnic mobilization; it was the agent that transformed the
tribe into a modern political movement.

Even so, his success was not instant. In the 1938 general
election the purified National Party won 27 seats, increasing
its strength from 20, but Malan was disappointed; he had
hoped to do better. The volk hadn't yet listened. Too many
were still following the cosmopolitan, Smuts, and his creature, Hertzog. They had not yet altogether abandoned their
heroes for Malan's radical assumptions; redemption was yet
to come. He could wait. He would wait.

Once again the outside world was to intervene at a cusp in
Afrikaner history. National Socialism's birth in Germany
and Hitler's furious assault on the ideas of democracy and

equality had dangerous echoes in South Africa. National socialism sounded not too alien to the socialist nationalism of Christian nationalism. Hertzog himself was fooled. His romantic blindness (and the advice of some of his inner circle) led him to draw peculiar parallels between the New Order Germany and the orderly republic that had been the Orange Free State. For his part, Smuts saw the danger at once, but Hertzog saw only an opportunity to subvert and destroy Malan and his party by opting for an "aware and sympathetic" neutrality; let the English-speakers just make this one concession to Afrikanerdom and sit the war out, and the two language groups would be welded into one South Africanism; Malan would be undercut, the need for his ideas would evaporate as fast as a pond in a platteland drought.

It was naive. He let his lifelong opposition to fighting "England's wars" blind him to the reality of the Nazi regime, and he argued against intervention. Smuts, on the other hand, demanded it, and eventually had his way in Parliament. South Africa was once again fighting at Britain's side and Afrikaners were once again hopelessly divided. The experiment of Fusion was over. Hertzog resigned, leaving Smuts as the United Party's sole leader, and in an emotional gathering of over 70,000 Afrikaners at the Voortrekker memorial in Pretoria, he clasped Malan's hand in a fervent display of solidarity.

But Hertzog was too straight an arrow to understand Malan's seminary-driven deviousness; nor would his straightness permit him to compromise when understanding finally came. At a congress in Bloemfontein of the Herstigte Nasionale Party Hertzog finally came to see the nature of those who had opposed him and were now his temporary allies. He saw they wanted not a broader South Africanism but Afrikaner domination. As he had done more than 20 years earlier, he once again walked out of a party congress. That earlier time, he had the old warrior Christiaan de Wet at his side. This time he left with only a small band of loyalists. As he departed, he turned to the assembled delegates, who were grinning at his discomfiture, and left them with a final thought: "We remain Afrikaners. Let us do nothing which is unworthy of the volk or which will lead to its downfall. In time all will come right again." Then he strode out into political oblivion. A year or so later he was dead. He walked unaided into a Pretoria hospital and had himself admitted for "exhaustion." He gave his occupation as farmer. The admitting clerk failed to recognize him. The Afrikaners were in a new era.

Chapter 20
Life in the Afrikaner heartland

I

THERE WERE OTHER and gentler developments at work too: the platteland was not all grimness and mean-mindedness. René Marquard de Villiers was born two days after Christmas in the year of union, 1910, in a sparsely furnished room in his grandmother Margaret's house in Winburg. Maria

delivered her children at her mother's house because although running water and electricity hadn't yet reached Winburg, it was considerably more civilized than La Rochelle, where Jim was still struggling to pull a farm together from the spare and dusty veld. It was a long way from a Europe apparently descending into savagery, and a long way too from the revolutionary ideas fermenting among the Afrikaner intellectuals of the Cape.

While more and more landless plattelanders poured into the cities, life in the formerly orderly republic of the Orange Free State went on much as it had in the past. In the O.F.S., now a province of the Union of South Africa, the broedertwis of the rebellion had subsided, and while the

Broederbond made its inroads in the towns and cities, attempting to wrest the Afrikaner to its own ideas, the sleepy little former republic minded its own business. In Winburg, where the widow Marquard now lived (Koo having died of pleurisy), life had resumed. Jim de Villiers, would-be soldier, half-hearted rebel, and full-blooded Hertzogite, was devoting all his energies to his beloved La Rochelle.

He had found his farm on the rolling grasslands 18 miles from Winburg. The first thing he did after buying the place was to cover every acre of his 3,000 on horseback, looking for a house site and planning the fields. Around the site of the homestead, he planted the groves of bluegum trees without which no Afrikaner farm is complete. There were no indigenous trees at all in that part of the Free State, and the bluegum provided shade for grazing stock, a wind-break against the constant dust storms, and a home for birds. The four-room homestead he built himself from brick and stone. It faced east, and there was the usual stoop on three sides. He built two thatched-roof cottages beside the house as separate bedrooms, a stone house for a cold-water shower by the windmill, and five outbuildings: a *waenhuis* (wagon-house), a separating shed, and three unroofed stone kraals for pigs, sheep, and cattle. Water was piped to the back of the kitchen from a borehole but had to be taken inside in buckets.

La Rochelle was a mixed farm, part stock and part produce. There was fruit of all kinds, especially strawberries, and many vegetables. There was maize for human and animal consumption, a bit of wheat, barley, and lucerne. There were cows for milk, oxen for ploughing and transport, sheep for meat and wool. Maria made butter to be sold in town. The creamery took the milk. The flock of 700 or so sheep was the farm's main cash crop, bringing in around £400 a year. The wool was bought by merchants who travelled the countryside picking up farmers' clips, transporting it by ox-wagon to the railhead and selling it at the coast. Jim never had enough money to buy his own ox-wagon and borrowed from neighbours when one was needed.

In most ways the farm was typical of Boer farms in the heartland, but Jim was often experimenting with crops and livestock. One time he acquired a kind of fish none of his neighbours had heard of and bred it successfully in his mud dams. He also kept a small flock of peacocks, but these were unpopular with his workers as well as his neighbours, most of whom looked on peacocks as birds of ill omen. No one but Jim would eat them or tolerate their noisy but flamboyant presence.

Jim always loved the soil and was a good farmer in the sense that he never exhausted it, carefully rotating crops and letting it lie fallow when needed. But he was an indifferent businessman, and the farm never made much money. In the few years after he started, the rural economy was in one of its boom periods; rains and crops were good. There was therefore money to be had for expansion and improvements. But Jim, who had never managed to pay off any of the money he'd raised for the mortgage, resisted borrowing, even from his stepbrother Danie, by then a prominent auctioneer in the eastern Free State with "large sums" to lend to anyone on liberal terms. La Rochelle limped along, Maria helping where she could.

Danie wasn't the only member of his family Jim had little to do with. Most of his brothers and sisters were considerably older than he was and he felt little affection for most of them. His parents, he said, used to talk to each other of "my children, your children and our children." René remembers his father once reading in the Bloemfontein newspaper *The Friend* of the death of a half-sister of whom he was very fond, but with whom he had lost contact even though she lived only 50 miles away. In 1929 Jim and René undertook a pilgrimage to the western Transvaal to look for grazing land for his cattle. When they got to the little town of Parys, Jim suddenly said to his son, "One of my brothers lives here."

"Who is he and when last did you see him?" René asked, never having heard of this particular relative before.

"Oh," Jim replied, "it is Izak and it was after the war."

"What war?"

"The Boer War."

Maria, used to the cultivation of the parsonage, made what she could of farm life, giving her children lessons and books to read, and introducing them to music and culture. That the farmhouse never had electricity or running water did not bother her; the civilized virtues could be inculcated anywhere. There were of course limits: when young René suggested to her he'd like to be a farmer, she told him very firmly: "There's been enough poverty in the de Villiers family for generations. You go out and earn a good living."

René's first schooling was from his mother on the farm; later she ran a small school for the children of the district, mostly to help make ends meet. From the farm he went to Bloemfontein and spent the first two years at St. Michael's, an English-language Anglican girls' school where his aunt Louise was teaching. His memories maintain he was an indifferent student (once achieving a zero score in arithmetic, which prompted a postcard from his mother on the farm calling the score "disappointing" — surely the parental understatement of the year).

Of the nine farms in the area where Jim farmed, seven spoke Afrikaans, one a mixture of English and Afrikaans, and one English only. The English were Catholics. The Afrikaners were all Dutch Reformed of various sects: by the 20th century they were prone to dividing into sects of all kinds, reflecting in their religion the schismatic tendencies of their politics — and of course reflecting in their politics the schismatic tendencies of their Protestant heritage. The institution of the quarterly *nagmaal* communion services had died with the birth of the motorcar. Prayers were still a feature of family life. They were still held morning and evening, still included the servants — or at least those who professed interest — and took place around the dining room table, with everyone kneeling. The family prayers were simply known as *boeke vat* (literally, "take the book"). The old psalms were belted out, usually without musical accompaniment but sometimes with a family member playing an accordion.

Jim's farm was an exception. Although Maria came from a deeply religious family and practised her faith all her life, religion played only a small role in the family's life: this was a long way from the Doppers, and the fierce Calvinism of the Afrikaners survived mostly in the Transvaal highveld. Jim was not at all interested. René believes that what disillusioned him about religion was the split in the Winburg congregation during the 1914 rebellion — a split that took one group into the nationalist camp and the other into the non-nationalist camp. "My father had strong nationalist sympathies, but he would not tolerate being dictated to, by churchmen or others. He certainly wouldn't be told where to go to church."

A feature of the religious life of the Afrikaners was *huisbesoek*, preacher's house calls, in which the dominee, accompanied by a church elder, would visit parishioners in their homes, almost always, in the rural areas, staying overnight. These visits were an opportunity to remind the Afrikaners of the spiritual heritage; they were also a way of warning political heretics. In the Free State, orthodoxy was no longer as sure as it had been. The ancient Calvinist doctrines had become a part of the fibre, but the Free State had begun to draw a line between formal religion and the rest of life. Jim used to tell a story of a rainy-season *huisbesoek* trip made by a dominee and one of his elders, a local farmer. The cart and horses and its two occupants got stuck in a stream. The current grew stronger and stronger, and the water rose steadily. "Broer" (brother), said the dominee, who was becoming increasingly anxious, "we must pray for deliverance." Replied the farmer, "No, Dominee. This is not the time for prayer — this is the time to thrash the horses like hell to pull us out of danger." It's a story with more than one moral, but mostly it speaks to the Afrikaners' pragmatic side. Yet it's still true that the Afrikaners on the farms believe in their special links to God. "The Lord will help us," they said and still say. They say and believe that God has a plan for the Afrikaner, that he will not let the Afrikaner go under. Even now, no party political congress is held without the chairman reminding God of his obligations.

Jim was an Afrikaner nationalist and a fervent Hertzogite — at least until Hertzog refused to take South Africa into the Second World War, when he switched his allegiance to Smuts; he died a staunch Smuts man. Maria was never a nationalist and took a moderate course in politics, as she did in most things. René remembers an incident soon after the formation of the National Party in 1914, when his father returned from a meeting sporting a colourful lapel badge. In his innocence, he asked his father what the setting sun on the badge denoted. Jim exploded. "That's not the setting sun! That's the rising sun of Afrikaner nationalism — a sun that will never set!" Maria watched the outburst with tolerant amusement; she had little interest in party politics and knew her Jim would always return to the soil.

II

LIFE PROCEEDED AT a sleepy pace. A cart and horse went to town once a week to buy and sell provisions and to fetch the mail. Until the 1920s there was no telephone in the district except at a little store called Galloway; people would travel 15 or 20 miles to give or get phone calls, and the Galloway shop at times resembled a small waiting room. The shop stocked staples like sugar and soap and paraffin for heating. It was largely a barter trade. Black men and women from the district would barter there as well as the farmers — a few fowl or some eggs would be enough for a small parcel of groceries, and a sheepskin would get a sackful.

These are small matters, but not unimportant: the life in and around Winburg represents the other face of Afrikanerdom, what René calls "the true South Africanism that might have been." The freebooters and hardliners and racists of the north are a true part of the volk, and so is the apocalyptic flavour of their rhetoric and the uncompromising nature of their politics. But nearly a fifth of Afrikaners have never voted for Afrikaner nationalism or Afrikaner domination: some of them took another road. Even now they can be found in villages and farms all over the country, in the Transvaal as well as the old O.F.S., in the gentle valleys of the western Cape as well as the steamy reaches of tropical Natal. These snapshots of the gentler way of Winburg represent authentic Afrikaner memories, as authentic as the fevered dreams of Daniel François Malan:

— Hawkers and pedlars were a minor but interesting feature of country life. These traders, the *smouse*, used to travel from farm to farm in a small two- or four-wheeled cart selling things like oranges or salt (usually for animal feed) and the odds and ends lonely farmers needed. Nearly all were Jews from eastern Europe, refugees from persecution there. They were useful to the Boers, and a cordial relationship existed between them and the farming families, who always linked them to the heroic tales of the Old Testament. Usually the *smous* would stay the night with the family.

— It wasn't only merchants who travelled the country. One night a Catholic priest showed up at a farm in the Winburg district to ask shelter. Inside, the priest noticed a large head-and-shoulders portrait of Pope Pius XI on the wall. Surprised that an Afrikaner farmer had a picture of the Pope in his house, the priest asked the farmer for an explanation. "But that's not the Pope," the farmer said a little testily. "Yes, it is," insisted the priest. "That's my spiritual father, and I know." Flummoxed, the farmer thought for a moment. Then he said, "And to think that bally *smous* sold it to me and said it was a picture of Dr. Malan!" (Malan and the Pontiff shared shiny bald pates; possibly the *smous* was himself confused.)

— René's sister Margaret hurt her foot late one afternoon, and the family set off to town by cart to see a doctor. Night fell when they were only half way, so they turned into the nearest farm, where they were put up for the night, fed on mutton and farm milk, breakfasted the next morning on chops and boerewors (farmer's sausage), eggs and strong coffee, and reached the doctor the next morning at sunrise. Hospitality and help for the needy are as much a part of the Afrikaner identity as John Calvin and schism.

▬ The Irish bachelor Bob Wright made a good living on a farm near La Rochelle breeding pigs. Every Friday he went to town in his little cart to do his shopping. When that was done he took himself off to one of the two hotels in town and sat drinking and yarning with his cronies until he'd had his fill. By then he couldn't hitch his horses, so his friends did it for him. They helped him into his cart and on the outskirts of town they left him holding the reins, the horse trotting steadily towards home. There were a number of farm gates along the way, but he never had any difficulty — there was always a friendly passer-by to open and shut a gate if he waited long enough. In all the years the de Villiers kids were growing up, old Bob never failed to reach his farm. And in all those years he was never regarded as anything other than a *buurman*, a neighbour, one of us.

▬ Jim de Villiers built a series of dams back of the house, in the catchment area provided by a small rise on the farm. These dams were his life's work. In bad years, which meant drought, he would moodily patrol their banks, contemplating the cracked mud where the sun was evaporating his precious water: the dams were in constant danger of running dry. When the rains finally came they came in torrents, and he would don his ancient oilskins and stand by the dams, gloomily watching the rushing water, convinced they would burst and all he had built be lost.

▬ Jim was a huge man, at one point weighing over 300 pounds. (Maria knew: she made all his clothing herself, and the fabric needs stretched their thin budget.) Like many of the plattelanders of his generation, he was not a sophisticated man. As a boy, Jim had paid little attention to his lessons, despite admonitions from his elder brother; as an adult he had little interest in accounting procedures when he took his produce to market. He got cheated regularly. In the 1930s, when a cinema opened in town, the family took him once or twice and then ceased. He couldn't help himself; he would stand up and warn the good guys when an ambush was in sight, "Pasop! Hy gaan skiet!" (Watch out! He's going to shoot!), until he became as much a part of the performance as the film, to the amusement of the locals and the mortification of his children. In later years, when his son had bought a primitive car, Jim learned to drive. But he was never able to get the hang of going backwards. To reverse, he would carefully station family members along his path, rather like flight traffic controllers, to give early warnings of disaster, and like his sister-in-law Louise, he never grasped the logic of traffic regulations. (Louise once told me that traffic lights were "only for the irresponsible" and that people like herself were entitled to ignore them. It was a view Jim shared.)

■ In the long evenings after a long day, Jim would sit on a chest on the stoop, facing the endless horizons, a huge mug of strong coffee in his hand, contemplating his handiwork and God's, and he would occasionally sigh, and shake his massive grizzled head, saying to anyone who would listen and to no one in particular: "Hêre, tog, die white man's burden, nê?" (Oh God, the white man's burden, hey?) And I, his grandson, would shake my head and sigh and parrot, "The white man's burgen [sic] . . ." My father's first recorded phrase — "waar is neutraal?" — was an abstract of his later life. Mine, lamentably, was a joke phrase from the bad old days of the British raj. The white man's burden! A discredited phrase from an archaic past. Only to Jim de Villiers, as to many of the rural Afrikaners, it was not the archaic past but the anxious present: in the way of his place and his time, he was completely responsible for the care and welfare of the black families who lived on his farm, and the responsibility weighed him down all his life. Like his dams, his obligations towards his black workers were ever-present in his mind. There's no doubt both contributed to his early death.

III

THE BLACK WORKERS OF La Rochelle lived a few miles from the homestead. Their homes were set in a small hollow by a creek. They were primitive structures, not much more than one room with one door and one window, mud floors, thatched or corrugated iron roofs. There were seldom beds for the whole family; the floor was where the youngsters slept. The houses were invariably spotlessly clean, but there was no running water. Light was provided by candles or kerosene; heating came from dried cattle dung burned in braziers in the traditional manner.

The black workers were engaged on a family basis, the adult men working for the owner of the farm and the women helping where needed, inside the home or elsewhere. In many parts of the Free State black workers were allowed to use up to 40 acres of land on which they would cultivate mostly wheat; many of these families created sizeable surpluses, and for a while black peasant agriculture threatened white production.

Early in the century there was an explosive growth of black-owned cattle herds — black expansion severely affected the white farmers there too. The good years simply meant rising tension in the countryside as black tenants agitated against laws transforming them into wage-earning servants. In the O.F.S. blacks were never allowed to own land. In the Transvaal they were permitted to do so until the Land Act of 1913, and there were numerous cases of black tenant farmers banding together to buy farms from absentee white owners. Most farmers tolerated sharecroppers — their black workers would own oxen and would help plough in the extremely short ploughing season, keeping some of the resultant crop. The white farmers defended the practice against the ideologues in the capital. "Very few of us Boers," a farmer named Tylden said in 1908, "can afford to keep more than one span of oxen to plough with . . . it means too much capital locked up in animals which do not increase . . . The farmer therefore gives one or more of these natives, who own perhaps three spans [of oxen] between them, a certain amount of land to plough. The boy [*sic*] finds the labour and often the seed, and gives the owner of the farm half the crop."

The very success of black farmers became a hot issue.

Barney Ngakane, who grew up in a wealthy black sharecropping family near Vereeniging on the Free State border, tells
the story of how Prime Minister Louis Botha addressed a
meeting of farmers in 1912. Ngakane's father was there; his
story was recorded by Tim Keegan in the journal *African
Affairs*.

> At the end of the meeting one farmer stood up and asked a
> question of General Botha, whether it was right that there
> should be black people who were living a life of comparative ease
> when there were hundreds of poor white bywoners. And the
> answer from General Botha was, "No." And then Cronje [the
> Ngakanes' employer] got up and asked, "And, well gentlemen, I
> have seven bywoners on the farm and seven black families and I
> get from one of those black families what I cannot get from the
> seven bywoners together. And so are you going to ask me to take
> food out of my mouth?" This was the way he put it . . . and the
> next thing that happened there was the white farmers all said
> "Donner hom! [Smash him!]"

During the cropping season the women were engaged on a
piece-work basis. Cash wages were minimal, not much more
than 10 or 15 shillings a month. Most were paid in provisions
and rations. Maize meal, skimmed milk, and meat; the children would fetch their rations daily from the kraal or milking
shed. The diet was healthy; there were no deficiency diseases
and infant mortality was low. Each family was provided with
a long roll of evil-smelling tobacco monthly.

White and black lived on the same farm but in different
worlds, which overlapped only at work. There was no social
interaction. Whites never visited blacks except when there
was illness, when white help was needed. At the non-work
level, white and black had little in common. None of the
blacks who sought work had any education. Occasionally it
was possible for black children to go to town for some elemen-
tary schooling; the white farmer was obliged to pay for the
transportation. Those children seldom returned to the farm.
White and black children commonly played with one

another; the traditional craft skills of pottery, weaving, and beadwork persisted among the black community, and the making of small figurines, usually horses and cattle, from clay was always a source of envy among the white children. I remember as a child being instructed in the mysteries of the *kleilat* by a somewhat disdainful black child a year or so older; this involved a ball of clay moulded to the end of a long flexible stick, with which black kids hunted birds, the clay ball serving as projectile. Black and white used to range far afield, spending hours and sometimes days in the veld, hunting wild animals and birds.

Most of the black workers came from Lesotho, then still called Basutoland, or from Thaba 'Nchu, about 50 miles away, where the Rolong people lived. The Rolong mixed freely with the Tswanas, since their languages had much in common. Thaba 'Nchu had been the traditional homeland for the Rolong, and though they had been affected by the *mfecane* like everyone else and had been disrupted by the Sotho wars, stable communities still existed, partly protected by the Wesleyan missionaries who had lived among them from the early part of the 19th century. They had welcomed the missionaries and had become Christianized early and with conviction. Of all the local tribes, the Rolong seemed best attuned to the Afrikaner personality and the Afrikaners to them; in 1944, when Jim de Villiers lay dying in a Bloemfontein hospital bed, he asked Maria to send for Dr. Moroka, a Rolong from Thaba 'Nchu who had qualified as a medical man in Scotland and returned to carry on a flourishing medical practice in the eastern Free State. The hospital held white patients only, but a doctor was a doctor and a friend a friend: no one would have denied him. Moroka went to sit with his old friend in his last days before returning to Thaba 'Nchu. (He later became president of the African National Congress.)

Those were more innocent days; the ideologues in the white legislatures had not yet set about spending the precious store of interracial good will and understanding. Even the

passes, which were to become such a hated symbol of a
regulated and oppressed life, were regarded as more innocent
documents.

The pass in the 1930s was little more than a small sheet of
paper on which the black worker's name and address and,
where appropriate, those of his employer were written. The
pass, which was issued by the central government and had to
be carried in most parts of the country, was used by men
going to visit friends or relatives, by others travelling to sell
sheep or cattle, by men looking for employment, or by
migrants travelling long distances from the Transkei in search
of employment. Later, as the passes became more sophisticated, they were more and more hated, because the more
sophisticated they were, the more they were used as instruments of control. In the early days they were prized documents among blacks, a kind of passport or entitlement to
travel, and were somewhat coveted — they were a symbol of
mobility. The same shift took place in relations with the
police, who later became the state's agents in the control
process. In the rural areas the police played only a minor role
in the regulation of people's movements; blacks commonly
sought out the police to expedite their travels.

The Union of South Africa had incorporated into its
constitution many of the provisions of the old Afrikaner
republics, among them those forbidding blacks to own
freehold property in "white" areas or in the cities. But even
here in the absence of the ideologues there were small victories; a far-sighted local administrator in Bloemfontein
arranged a series of 99-year irrevocable leases, which gave the
black population a measure of stability it desperately needed.

More innocent days: René de Villiers grew up and lived
on a farm at a time when the Sotho wars had become a dim
echo in the ancestral memory; the ear of the Afrikaner had
been tuned to his strident battle with the Briton; the Sotho
and Rolong people had subsided into a gentle murmur, without threat — they were there, but not there, part of life but
not yet of politics. Dingaan was now a memory, a bit of

romance from the heroes of history. And to those in the Free State the Xhosa were of another country; single migrants passed through, but of them one knew nothing. Hertzog's strident rhetoric about the *swart gevaar* found no echo here. African nationalism had not surfaced to any degree.

Blacks, perhaps ironically, lacked the tribal cohesiveness of the Afrikaners, and though they had been defeated in battle they had not yet felt their very culture threatened as the Afrikaners had. It was the Afrikaners' own policies, born of their own hard history and deep insecurities, that created from many separate tribes what black "Africanism" now exists. Like the Afrikaners' own, the blacks' nationalism was a reaction to threat. There was little recognition in Winburg, or, indeed, among whites elsewhere, of the size of the problem. The teeming masses were not seen. Black townships were growing up outside white towns and cities, but there was little awareness of the deep pressures of the massive sea of colour that was causing these small ripples. Blacks, when they were thought of at all, came from "native areas," or from Basutoland. Afrikaners had switched from the age of the generals to that of the politicians; blacks too had lost their generals and their heroes, but were without a political voice, and the seeds of African nationalism were only beginning to germinate in the newly formed black academies at Fort Hare and elsewhere.

René de Villiers spent his boyhood on the farm; the relationships between races were paternalistic and already archaic, but they were seldom harsh; the slow rhythms of farm life allowed black and white to get to know each other — their isolation insisted on it. Even when I was born, in the middle of the Hitlerian savagery, little had changed: the dark dreams of the Afrikaner still remained locked in the heads of the ideologues, and René de Villiers grew up to be that most rare of creatures, the Afrikaner liberal.

IV

"POLITICS," WHICH IN South Africa means ethnic relations, impinged on René only obliquely. As a boy, he remembered being impressed by Hertzog and then by Smuts. His father once took him to an open-air meeting Hertzog addressed near the little Free State town of Reddersburg, where the old general was subjected to a great deal of vociferous barracking by a woman in the audience, a tough old bird who believed Hertzog was selling out to the English. "Boo," she shouted at every opportunity, until the rough-and-ready crowd, Afrikaners all, became heartily sick of the sound of her voice. Finally, an old farmer turned on her. "Vrou, as jy nie nou ophou bulk nie, dan melk ek jou!" he yelled. It loses in the translation to English and sounds crude to an urban audience, but it brought the crowd to its feet and shut the heckler up: "Lady, if you don't stop booing immediately, I'll milk you!"

Later, when Jim had broken with Hertzog and the nationalists over the Nazi question, he took his son to an outdoor political meeting at which the local nationalist MP, Dr. N. J. van der Merwe, was to speak. Jim had a small camp stool and sat on the edge of the crowd. But after a while he got so carried away by the emotions of the meeting that he would shout at the top of his voice: "You're a political bastard!" Why he wasn't assaulted remains a minor mystery.

But life on the farm was in many ways outside politics. The rebellion of 1914 had receded into the past — Hertzog's electoral victory had helped; so had the farmers' resignation to being the creatures of the capitalists. Many people were poor in Winburg, but they were rural poor; the sour moods of the proletariat were foreign to them. As for the English — Donny Mitchell had the next farm, living proof that the English didn't have to be foreigners in their own land; if they acted like Afrikaners, well, maybe they *were* Afrikaners . . . There is a key here, in the easy relations with the ancestral enemy, to a hidden corner of the Afrikaner heart. The ethnic mobilization to the politics of fear has obscured it, but it's still there to be tapped: a fundamental generosity, an inclusiveness that could be used to turn the Afrikaner from the master to the co-host of his own house. No liberal politician has succeeded in making use of this Winburg factor, this other face of the volk. No outside pressure groups seem now to recognize its existence, or, if they do, to see in it a possibility, a chance to make a different future.

It was only when René attended the (all-white) college of the Orange Free State in Bloemfontein that politics impinged directly on him. He fell under the influence there of his uncle, Leo Marquard, a remarkable figure who spent most of his long and fruitful life attempting to make links across the colour barriers. Leo had married his cousin, Nell van der Merwe, and together over the years they helped found NUSAS (the National Union of South African Students), the Joint Councils Movement, which later became the South African Institute of Race Relations and which has had a significant effect in educating the South African public to political realities (its yearbook is still an indispensable guide to race relations), and the Liberal Party, later disbanded because Leo and other leaders refused to obey a government directive to expel non-white members. Nell was a member of the protest group the Black Sash; she also became a friend and confidant of the Pan-Africanist Congress leader the charismatic Robert Sobukwe. Leo was the first president of NUSAS, and René joined when he got to college.

His first eye-opener was a ground-breaking NUSAS conference at the black college of Fort Hare in 1929, where he remembers playing a minor role in the student Parliament debating "Bantu affairs" and an even more minor role in an interracial rugby game on the Fort Hare grounds. The standard of rugby was by all accounts abysmal, but the game's political significance was profound; social interaction between races was not forbidden by law, but neither was it widely practised. It was possibly the very ineptitude of both colours in the game that allowed them to connect; some players, René among them, made friendships that have lasted almost 60 years. This innocent game caused a tremendous fuss, another indicator of the potency of Afrikaner fears — it was just a game of rugby, after all. Free State university delegates were officially reprimanded by the governing body when they returned to Bloemfontein, which to the participants merely proved they must have done something right.

Leo also roped René in as an occasional instructor at a night school he and Nell ran for adult blacks in the Bloemfontein township, where René first became aware of the single-minded hunger for education among the black proletariat; it was not unusual for illiterate black adults from the hinterlands to spend up to 14 years at night school to get their school-leaving certificate. René remembers one man who finally qualified as a teacher at the age of 44. Later, education became a political weapon in the hands of apartheid's ideologues, but at the time it was widely regarded by blacks as a passport to a larger world.

On other evenings, Leo and his sister Louise founded and ran the Joint Councils, a simple idea Leo had picked up among the Fabians in England — the self-help meeting, which in turn had grown out of the Wesleyan revival meetings of the Victorian era. Joint Councils consisted of a dozen or so men and women, black and white, meeting once a month to discuss common problems, such as wages, education, and working conditions. Not much to set against the Calvinist ideologues, perhaps; but their existence, and the existence of the Institute of Race Relations, has kept alive in South Africa a fund of interracial good will long after it should have been used up. As the Irish have discovered, little learning takes place through the smoke of the Molotov cocktails; police terrorism and gruesome black-against-black reprisals in the stinking squatter camps around the white cities generate further violence; it's sometimes hard to remember that there have also been gentler forces at work.

At Leo's urgings, and with £400 borrowed from his aunt,

René went abroad to further his education, spending a year at the London School of Economics, the academic home of the Webbs, Beatrice and Sydney, and of the great socialist theorist Harold Laski. When he returned he had already rejected the primitive Calvinism of his people and a whole grab-bag of other prejudices, but he had retained, as he always would, the Afrikaner's solid attachment to place and spirit. What he cherished most was the easy shifting between Afrikaans and English; the way Winburgers had lived through the bitternesses of the war and the rebellion and had been able to make of each other . . . neighbours. These early memories still drive his beliefs: accommodation, tolerance, Old World courtesies as the basis for a political credo: if old enemies can live together amicably, why not harness this emotion to a political order? It sounds naive in the temper of these times, but in its time and its place it was a radical notion.

Black and brown people played very small roles in the political thinking of the period; the transition from democracy for whites to democracy for all was difficult, and few made the crossing. And it wasn't just the hardliners of the north, the victims of the politics of fear on the Transvaal platteland, that found the change hard. As René says now, "One man, one vote, was not something that came to my generation easily. Many of us were afraid of being overwhelmed by people of colour. We thought it 'safer' to restrict their political power. This shows how undemocratic even relatively enlightened white South Africans were as late as the 1940s. I only later came to realize that nothing less than one man, one vote, would suffice, but even today there are so-called white liberals who are bothered about the implications of a universal franchise." And while René's own notions of accommodation and tolerance between groups and between races do sound other-worldly now, there are hard men on both sides of the colour line in South Africa who see in this "true South Africanism" of his one of the few paths back from the edge of the abyss — an unlikely path, and perilous, but still a path.

René started work in Bloemfontein in 1930, during the depression, on the local newspaper. His father had wanted him to take a law degree, partly because Jim's brother Jaap was then chief justice, but he was unable to get a job that would have enabled him to get a degree at the same time. So when he saw an advertisement for a junior journalist, he applied without delay. The salary offered was £15 a month, and 120 university graduates applied. René got the job mostly because, earlier that year, he had done some small pieces for the paper from that year's NUSAS conference. He started work on Dingaan's Day, as the Day of the Covenant was then commonly if irreverently known. The newspaper was *The Friend*, formerly and redundantly *The Friend of the Free State*. It was a peculiarly Free State institution, in that it was one of the few newspapers anywhere that had a majority readership whose language was not the language the paper was printed in; *The Friend*, written in English, always had more Afrikaans than English readers.

Nevertheless it wasn't until after the Hitler war, when René abandoned secure journalism to work for *The Forum*, a weekly "viewspaper" that espoused an overtly liberal cause, that he finally abandoned the naiveté of La Rochelle, coming into contact with liberal minds broader, tougher, and more cynical than his own. Among them was Alan Paton, whose *Cry the Beloved Country* was published in serial form in *The Forum*; the classics scholar Theo· Haarhoff; and the co-founders (with Paton) of the Liberal Party — Oscar Wolheim, Peter Brown, and Marion Friedman. He fell strongly under the influence of the *Forum's* chairman of the board, J. H. Hofmeyr, Smuts's deputy prime minister and a liberal thinker far ahead of his time.

René had met Hofmeyr in 1927 at a Student Christian Association seaside camp organized by Alan Paton and some of his friends, and although he says his "principal memory of that camp was of a horrible camper [not Hofmeyr] who spent most of his time bullying me — a queer expression of his Christianity, I thought," he had been impressed with the steadiness of Hofmeyr's purpose. "At first his liberalism didn't mean too much to me — I was too naive, I suppose. But when I began to 'practise' liberalism on *The Forum* by regular writing it came to mean much to me."

René worked closely with Hofmeyr, particularly during the three years when he sat in the Parliamentary Press Gallery (1945 to 1947). *The Forum* didn't last long after Hofmeyr's untimely death and René returned to work for the Argus Company, a publishing conglomerate that owned *The Friend* in Bloemfontein, among other newspapers.

V

AFTER THE WAR the tribe began to close ranks: Malan's peculiar vision — under the pressure of the war, the still-recalcitrant English, and the growing realization of the *swart gevaar* — had prevailed. The liberal vision of accommodation and respect between groups that grew out of the heartland at La Rochelle was overwhelmed. But it is there yet, latent perhaps, almost invisible, but there.

Chapter 21

Malan and the theology of separation

I

IN THE EARLY 1940S the National Party leaders paid no attention to the existence among the volk of the small band of
liberals. They were preoccupied with larger matters. The
departure of General Hertzog didn't automatically bring
about party unity; and the party itself wasn't yet completely
identified with the interests of the people. Malan's control of
the Afrikaners' political destiny was diluted on three fronts:
by the Afrikaners still loyally supporting Smuts; by the left-
over Hertzogites, who had formed the Afrikaner Party in
1941 specifically to keep the general's policies alive, and,
finally, by an attenuated strain of the Hitler virus called the
Ossewabrandwag, a paramilitary organization dedicated, in
an ominous phrase from National Socialism, to the purity of
the Afrikaner nation. The name translates poorly: *ossewa* is
ox-wagon and *brandwag* means sentinel, or watch; the name
signifies to Afrikaner emotions a vigilance stemming from the
great heroes of the trek: it is an articulation of the laager.

It's easy to see why the Ossewabrandwag caught on so
swiftly: it came into being in the first furious days of the war,
when Hitler's armies were sweeping everything before them
and his ideas seemed triumphant, even inevitable; it followed
a 1938 symbolic re-enactment of the Great Trek at its centenary, a re-enactment that stirred much anti-English sentiment; it had a paramilitary structure that the Afrikaners fell

into naturally, harking back as it did to the commandos of their history; it spoke directly to the urban proletariat, who remembered the ideas of the commandos but whose lives were governed by uitlanders, and who were confronted directly by the brooding presence of the *swart gevaar*. As always in the past, the commando promised a way to escape the petty squabbles of lesser men. If the politicians are prone to schism — sweep them aside! A history of defeat and retreat breeds romantic notions; the romantic longing for dramatic solutions leading to quick resolution — this the Ossewa-brandwag promised.

The organization was run by a former administrator of the O.F.S., Dr. J. F. J. van Rensburg (a relative, incidentally, of Jim de Villiers), and included in its eager membership such note-worthies as B. J. Vorster, a later prime minister, who was interned by Smuts during the war for his subversive activities. The organization was itself threatened from the right, by Oswald Pirow's New Order, an overtly Fascist group, but at the height of its power it claimed nearly a quarter of a million active members and was causing concern to the strategists of the National Party — it refused to be a nice cultural organiza-tion and play dead politically; it wanted to run things, and that wouldn't do.

In 1942 the Ossewabrandwag caused to be published (in *Die Transvaler*, the newspaper then edited by Hendrik Ver-woerd, the greatest of the apartheid theoreticians) a draft constitution for a republic, a curious document whose authorship remains in doubt — it was never authorized by Malan, and although it was pushed by Verwoerd he never claimed responsibility. In any case, the draft, which among other things reduced English to its "proper place" as a supple-mentary language good only for commercial purposes, aban-doned Parliament (and even the people) in favour of rule by an authoritarian president "directly and only responsible to God over and against the people and altogether independent of any vote in Parliament." While Verwoerd thought this a neat formulation for the governance of a Christian nationalist state, Malan knew the thing wouldn't wash and argued against it at every opportunity — not by directly repudiating it but by casting its authorship in doubt and by portraying the Ossewabrandwag as an organization not acting in the true interests of the volk.

By the 1943 election the power of the Ossewabrandwag had begun to wane, partly because of Malan's superior tactics, partly because a German victory no longer looked inevitable, and partly — there is this — through the good sense of the Afrikaners, who never went holus-bolus for the Ossewabrandwag's brand of poison; it had been a flirtation, not an all-out seduction. In many villages of the platteland, they still believed in their orderly republic.

II

THE LIBERALS IGNORED, the Ossewabrandwag dealt with, Malan turned his attention to the left-over Hertzogites and the Afrikaners who still supported Smuts. The Hertzogites were a push-over. They had never had much power anyway; the Afrikaner Party run by the old general's friend, N. C. Havenga, polled fewer than 15,000 votes in the 1943 election and elected no members. They were easily absorbed in Malan's drive for Afrikaner unity. He promised Havenga a Cabinet seat and a voice in the Herstigte Nasionale Party's inner councils, and the Afrikaner Party gratefully dissolved itself.

Smuts was a more formidable opponent; he was the last of the Boer War heroes, and the attachment of the *oudstryders* — Boer War veterans — to his achievements was emotional and deep. But Smuts, creature of the highveld though he was, played on a wider stage and had no notion of the small emotions now controlling his people. His vision was one of the Afrikaner taking his rightful place on the world stage; the Afrikaner was more concerned with the petty facts of modern life, which were division, penury, threat, and uncertainty. Malan's call to close ranks was potent. He continually pushed his notion that the National Party was not a conventional political party at all but an embodiment of a people's aspirations, occupying a "central position in our national life," the guardian of its ideals, the champion of its rights, the protector of its meagre privileges. Against this, Smuts's vision seemed overly lofty and out of touch.

In the later war years, leading up to the victory in Europe and the National Party's drive for power, the party turned its attentions more and more from the moderate policies of the Cape to the industrial proletariat of the north. Malan's orchestration of the campaign included a new, and more insistent, rhythm. It turned the Dutch Reformed Church's role as the guardian of morality, and the party's role as protector of Christian civilization, into the concept of *baasskap*, bossism, the white man's right to control the labour of others. In the early 1940s the party waged a fierce struggle for control of the trade unions, generally still run by English-speaking organizers whose loyalties were to European ideas. "Civilized labour," the euphemism of the 1930s, was dropped in favour of more overt racism: the Afrikaners had been defeated and impoverished by the English for a hundred years; now Smuts was doing their work for them, he was a creature of the English capitalists, he would allow black labour to sweep the whites aside, he would extend the Coloured vote in the Cape to the rest of the country . . .

In his run-up to the crucial 1948 election, Malan reminded his listeners that Smuts had officially accepted the Fagan Report, a document written by Henry Fagan of the Native Laws Commission. The report had recommended that the government accept the urban blacks as permanent residents in "white" areas; it declared segregation impractical and proposed more, rather than less, immigration from the reserves. Against these heretical notions Malan held up for inspection the Sauer Report, a National Party document put together by Paul Sauer, who was later to be in Malan's Cabinet. Sauer, not surprisingly, argued that "influx to the cities must be subject to every possible restriction" — blacks were in the cities only on sufferance and must be kept to the minimum necessary for economic development.

Throughout the campaign Malan made effective use of a phrase Hofmeyr had used during a speech at Fort Hare, the black university. "Natives," he had told the assembled largely native crowd, "will eventually be represented in parliament by natives, Indians by Indians."

Here was heresy! On the platteland they attacked Hofmeyr — and through him Smuts and his United Party — relentlessly. Where would such a man stop? It was but a short step from there to legislating some sort of *mengsel*, racial mixture, and that would be the end of white civilization. Hans Strijdom, the Transvaal hardliner and future prime minister, and Albert Hertzog, the old general's erratic and fundamentalist son, took up this banal theme with gusto. Strijdom declared that South Africa would be a coffee-coloured nation if Hofmeyr was allowed to have his way; Hertzog was heard declaring that Hofmeyr probably had a Coloured mistress somewhere and that's why he desperately wanted everyone to marry one.

There were more elevated lines of attack — Malan never stooped to this level, and Verwoerd took a loftier tone — but it was widely believed at the time that Hofmeyr cost Smuts the 1948 election that brought Malan to power. This was probably not so: in truth, Smuts's political decline had started much earlier; it had been masked by Fusion and by the world war. The events of 1948 only confirmed his loss of contact with the Afrikaners. They weren't all as eccentric as Albert Hertzog, but Fusion had set off new waves of anxiety. Fusion demanded a collaboration with the English and the world culture that the Afrikaners feared more than the blacks — they feared being submerged in a culture stronger than their own, one that ridiculed and belittled them in their own country, and one to which they had no response except to hurl accusations of disloyalty. None of what followed, the sad history of apartheid, can be understood unless the deep psychological scars and insecurities of the Afrikaner proletariat can be set against the actions of their nationalist politicians: Malan's skilful use of both British and black symbols explains his victory, and nothing Hofmeyr did or stood for changed the result at all. Malan succeeded in persuading the Afrikaners that Smuts would swamp them in English and that the English would allow all whites to be swamped in turn by the inchoate black masses.

III

FOR ALMOST 50 YEARS, ever since the lost war with England's empire, the Afrikaner nationalists had been waiting for a chance to regain their country. In the campaign for the 1948 election, they saw that their chance was finally a real one. In the texts of the sacred history, redemption was now at hand. The election of 1948 was to be the vehicle that delivered it, and apartheid would be its creed. It would demand resolution and clarity of vision to bring about. Those qualities the prophets of apartheid believed they had in plenty.

Apartheid as a coherent theory, or as a subtext of the theology of Afrikanerdom, had been articulated in the seminaries of Stellenbosch and Potchefstroom, in the Broederbond deliberations and in the Koffiehuis in Cape Town, where many seminarians gathered; and it had found an outlet in the writings of many Afrikaner intellectuals, among them Piet Meyer, who was later to head the South African Broadcasting Corporation, the propaganda arm of the nationalist government, and Geoff Cronje, whose book *Tuiste vir de Nageslag* (A Home for Posterity) was an influential precursor of apartheid. Conventional Afrikaner history has it that the 18th- and 19th-century Afrikaners saw themselves as a chosen people; that what drove them was the Calvinism of the Confession of Dort and the ideas of the Dutch neo-Calvinists like Abraham Kuyper. There is a contrary view, that the Dopper theologians at Potchefstroom, with their fundamentalist views and their theories of the Afrikaners as God's executors in Africa, created the mythology for the

apartheid movement and that it was they who gave Afrikaners their "sacred history."

But the sacred history was cobbled together in Stellenbosch as well as Potchefstroom, by Malan as well as the
northerners. Nor did it come from thin air; it was grafted
onto ideas that were already there, produced by 300 years of
turbulent history, by a long search for "proper" governance
between the tribes in the light of what the *eie* demanded.
Apartheid in this sense is an ideology of protest grafted onto
received ideas. It was the First World War and the rebellion of
1914 that provided the final political context in which the
sacred history could be played out.

Apartheid was and is racism, but not all the Afrikaners,
even those who supported apartheid, were or are racists. This
is a crucial distinction, because unless it is understood, none
of the Afrikaners' history makes any sense; unless the distinction is accepted, it's impossible to understand why apartheid
took the form it did. Apartheid is a complex combination of
many emotions, but the first among them is the strict
Calvinist world-view that every aspect of life is God's work
and that every people has its God-given place. There are
many others: the fierce drive for preservation of the *eie*;
insecurity and fear of alien cultures; a class revolt against the
bosses; revenge for too many defeats; and — of course — the
determination to entrench white privilege (racism in action).
The complexities are not easy to see now. So much of it reads
like simple racism, like mere rationalization to justify odious
acts. Which it is and it isn't. It's more complicated than that.

Apartheid is directed, said Cronje, to "racial and cultural
variety as the expression of God's will." Each race (and here
the Afrikaner writers used race in the sense of culture — the
Afrikaners were a race, and so were the English) had its own
role to play and its allotted tasks and its own way of finding its
soul. The Afrikaners have "passed through the fire of imperialist and capitalist domination and exploitation. They still
show the wounds and scars. Their national culture has been
disrupted. As a nation they almost perished because they

served the interests of others. They know what it means to see their own destroyed, but they also know what it means to use their own efforts to promote a national revival and rebirth" (my translation).

And so, he believed, only the Afrikaners could understand the blacks' determination to reject what would alter their essential and ancestral ways. That Cronje hadn't consulted the blacks in question didn't make his statement less sincere — it *had* to be so if the black cultures had any self-respect. (At this point, though, even the theory gets a little fuzzy. Apartheid was to let the blacks develop their own cultures in their own way — at first, naturally, under the tutelage of whites, but later on their own at their own pace. Nevertheless, Dopper logic demanded that these black cultures be Christian nationalist; no Calvinist of the Dutch Reformed persuasion was able to wrench his mind around the idea that their "own way" might preclude Christianity altogether.)

The basic dilemma remained: how to reconcile power with justice? The whites must remain in power as the trustees for the others; and the Afrikaners must remain in charge of the white group because they best understood the need. Trustees must have the power of their convictions — among them the conviction that would allow them to act for the long-term interests of the subject races, not just their short-term wishes. It is, indeed, the Christian duty of the trustees to do so. At the same time, the whites must retain power because only by doing so could they guarantee their survival. It had seemed so simple: one cannot, in Christian charity, deny men freedom. Blacks living in white areas would get, in justice, white freedoms, and that would mean the end of white freedom. The conclusion seemed obvious. Justice demanded separation.

The academics at least had the courage of their convictions. They pushed the theory through to its logical conclusions. Apartheid could not be done half-heartedly. It must be done thoroughly at whatever cost. If it included the Coloureds, so be it. If it cost the Afrikaner the cheap labour to which he had become accustomed, that was a fair price — better poorer and purer. If the Afrikaners themselves had to give up cherished land, it must be done. There was only one way to ensure survival, and that was complete separation. Separation or integration: half measures were not possible. The politicians, being politicians, couldn't afford to be so categoric; yet in 1945 apartheid was adopted as the policy of the Herenigte Nasionale of Volksparty (Reunited National or People's Party), as Malan's renamed group was called until 1951; and the country was put on notice that the Coloured vote was up for grabs. This was an expression that the mystic view, the sacred history, had triumphed: the National Party *was* a *volk in beweging*, a people in movement, after all, fighting not for money or possessions or territory or even privilege, but for the life of its people.

In 1947 Jan Smuts, fresh from the triumph of his war years, invited the British royal family to tour South Africa, confident that the volk would now see they were a part of a great world civilization. The royals were received courteously on the whole (there were exceptions: Verwoerd's *Transvaler* newspaper ignored the visit entirely). I remember as a small boy of seven being taken for miles in a bus to the Cape Town fishing community of Kalk Bay, there to stand for baffling hours, Union Jack in hand, waiting to wave at the king as the motorcade whisked by. But in the rest of the country the urgent call had gone out: this is our last chance. If we fail now, the United Party under Smuts and the English will use the Coloured vote to keep us a permanent minority in our own country. Look at the foreign king in our heartland!

It was, indeed, a potent call. The Afrikaners listened. The dispossessed grasped at repossession. Class interests, ethnic interests, and seductive political ideas that seemed to guarantee their own superiority all coincided. They voted with Malan. The purified National Party came to power: Malan as prime minister and Donges, Strijdom, Swart, the younger Hertzog, and the others as Cabinet members. Smuts, the international hero, the greatest figure his country had yet produced, had lost. I remember our living room, the family huddled in shocked silence around the radio, as the news came in that Smuts had been rejected by his people, his world-view with him.

That was the decisive victory for the new age of the politicians, the real start of the apartheid era. The emotional finale to the old order came two years later, on September 4, 1950, when Smuts died at his highveld farm outside Pretoria; his body was returned to the capital for burial. Veterans of all Smuts's wars lined the railway track to bid him farewell. He was the last great figure of the age of the generals.

The world would now see, Malan declared, what a people with a purpose would achieve.

PART 6

Marq de Villiers: lost in Africa

Chapter 22

The weird edifice: apartheid and its prophets

I

AH, BUT THEY WERE THOROUGH! The white tribe's troubled dreams were invaded and corrupted by a bureaucratic zeal for order. In the years following Malan's victory there was a cascade of laws, all designed to give the vision shape: the Afrikaner was no longer to be threatened. The Afrikaner must be maintained separate and in charge. This was not a final solution, but it was to be a permanent solution; it was designed always to create coherence from the chaos they saw inherent in their African lives. The cascade began just a few months after Malan's triumph:

— The Prohibition of Mixed Marriages Act (1949), which did pretty much what its title expected of it; marriages between blacks and Coloureds, however, were not affected. Only the whites were to be protected.

— The Immorality Amendment Act (1950), which extended the existing prohibition on sexual contact between blacks and whites to contact between whites and all others, including those the whites had created through just such sexual contact, the Coloured community. Sexual contact was defined in gritty and prurient detail.

— The Group Areas Act (1950), the cornerstone of apartheid. Each race group was to be allowed — encouraged — to develop in its own way. Which implied also its own *place*: no part of the country was to be inhabited by more than one race. Blacks were to be "guests" in the "white" cities. This act spelled out the principle; it was left to the bureaucracy to detail the practice. What the practice meant was the whole-sale removal of black (and Indian, and Coloured) communities from newly white areas; in the Cape, it was to mean the shifting of communities from places they had settled more than a century before.

■ The Population Registration Act (1950), to help people tell who was who and what was what — and who was to be prohibited from what. Three hundred years of mixing made this a frequently arbitrary business. The act made provision for a national race register; everyone would be assigned to a racial group: White, "Bantu," Coloured, Asian, "Others." In an oddly cynical exception to all this classification, the Japanese, who bought a good deal of South African coal and iron, were excused and counted as honorary whites. The Chinese were Asians.

■ The Bantu Authorities Act (1951) established primitive political representation for blacks for the first time — but only in the "homelands," which of course were defined by Pretoria.

■ The Abolition of Passes and Co-ordination of Documents Act (1952). Far from abolishing passes, this act made them into womb-to-tomb documents to be carried by all blacks. The passes contained residency permits, job permits, travel permits, marriage permits — even permits about where the new non-citizen was to be allowed to die.

■ The Reservation of Separate Amenities Act (1953). Toilets and cafeterias were defined in minute detail. Where separate amenities existed, employers no longer had any obligation to make them equally good.

■ The Bantu Education Act (1953). In its announced intention, the bill was designed to expel non-whites from white educational institutions, to create new institutions for the blacks, and to tailor an educational system to meet their own special needs. These needs were to be defined by the Afrikaners without consultation with the non-white users of the system. They included instruction in the vernacular and Christian teachings. Afrikaans, too, became mandatory. Hendrik

Verwoerd, then in the Senate and minister of native affairs, rather gave the game away when, introducing the bill, he said it was designed "so the native may be educated to his station."

■ The Resettlement of Natives Act (1954), which cleaned up the areas the earlier act had left ambiguous and added to the "native areas," bringing them up to about 13 per cent of the total land mass of the country. More than 100,000 people were uprooted and moved, many from stinking slums to neat and orderly villages. But they had been *their* stinking slums, in a place of their own choosing, and the hygienic new townships were as sterile as new concentration camps: the razing of Sophiatown outside Johannesburg caused an anguished cry to be heard around the world (through the book *Naught for Your Comfort*, by Trevor Huddleston).

■ The Industrial Conciliation Act (1956). It made multira-cial trade unions illegal and banned blacks from trade union activities. The incorrigible Albert Hertzog, the man who had accused Hofmeyr of arguing for a black franchise only to make the world safe for his "Coloured mistresses," and who by this time was running a militantly racist white mine-workers' union, was the driving force here.

■ The Extension of University Education Act (1959). This act didn't extend university education, of course. It removed the remaining blacks from the white universities and created separate but unequal schools for blacks.

■ The Promotion of Bantu Self-Government Act (1959) and the Urban Councils Act (1961), which set up urban links to the "homelands."

■ The Prohibition of Improper Interference Act (1968), which outlawed multiracial political parties or organizations. Only two parties at the time were multiracial, and they reacted in different ways. The Progressive Party decided to continue the fight in Parliament and hived off its non-white members. The tiny Liberal Party, which to that time had never elected a single member, decided that to disband was the only honourable course.

The National Party was aware that not everyone was

reacting to this legislative deluge with the proper enthusiasm. Beginning in 1950, the government therefore enacted a parallel mini-cascade of laws to ensure compliance, setting in motion a security apparatus as nearly ubiquitous as the party's own *bête noire*, the KGB.

— The Suppression of Communism Act (1950). This allowed the minister of security to ban any organization or person "deemed" to be a Communist; the Afrikaners' own flirtation with the Third International was long forgotten, and the evil forces of international Communism were being blamed for every act of civil disobedience in the country (giving Communism an undeserved liberal reputation among South African blacks). A banned organization was given little choice: disband or go underground. A banned individual became a curious form of non-person. The press was forbidden to quote him or to mention his name; he was to be confined to his "home magisterial district," could attend no gatherings of more than two people, and was forbidden to take part in any political activities. Communism under the act was defined in an all-encompassing way that would be baffling to any true Communists. Among other curiosities, anyone who advocated a universal franchise was by definition a Communist.

— The Criminal Law Amendment Act (1960), the General Law Amendment Act (1964), the Unlawful Organizations Act (1960), and the Criminal Act (1965) all allowed in varying degrees of severity ministerial discretion in banning citizens or imprisoning them for periods of up to 90 or 180 days without charge or trial, usually for activity "deemed" (by the minister) to be "furthering the aims of Communism." The so-called Sobukwe clause, named for the black dissident Robert Sobukwe, allowed these 180-day periods to be serial, meaning in effect imprisonment for life without trial.

Malan's people also launched a furious assault on the Coloureds and the Coloured vote. In their bureaucratic mania for neatness, the Afrikaners' historic association with the "brown cousins" was jettisoned; that the Coloured community spoke Afrikaans, shared the same homeland and the

same origins — facts the Afrikaners had always acknowledged — was simply ignored, discarded. Nothing was to be
allowed to get in the way of the vision. Having decided that
the only way to secure the future was by racial separation,
they could not possibly tolerate more than a million exceptions. They had to put them aside, at whatever cost, in the
name of the larger purpose. So in a series of enactments
through the 1950s the Coloureds were stripped of their rights.
The gates of the mixed marriages and immorality acts were
slammed shut.

The voters' roll presented a special problem. The Coloured franchise was entrenched in the constitution — apart
from the clause ensuring parity of English and Afrikaans, the
only clause to be so protected. A two-thirds majority in a
joint sitting of both houses would be necessary to pry out the
entrenchment. Malan's successor, J. G. Strijdom, who took
over in 1954, at first tried an end run: he simply ignored the
constitution altogether and, in a simple majority in the
House of Assembly, the lower house of Parliament, "abolished" the Coloured vote. A court challenge ensued. The law
was thrown out. The gcvernment responded by ramming a
motion through Parliament denying the court's right to intervene. This, too, was thrown out as unconstitutional. The
government responded by creating enough new Senators to
give itself the two-thirds majority needed. The courts threw
this out too. The government thereupon packed the Supreme
Court, giving itself a huge majority there, and finally had its
way.

Even so, the assault on the Coloureds made some Cape
nationalists uneasy, and several petitioned Verwoerd, who
had come to office in 1958, to allow Coloureds to represent
themselves in Parliament. Verwoerd rejected the notion out
of hand. Whites and Coloureds were parallel streams, he said,
which should never mingle. "Parallel development" was a
refinement of separate development; it was intended to prepare Coloured (as well as Indian) institutions on both the
local and national levels and to develop these bodies "to the

highest level of autonomy." It was this system that P. W. Botha adopted in the early 1980s for his new constitution, when he divided everything into "national affairs," to be largely controlled by whites, and "own affairs," in which each group had relative autonomy. To this end he created two new "Parliaments," one for Indians (their assembly hall was made from a courtyard of a government building, wonderfully well converted) and one for Coloureds (they inherited the old Senate, which was disbanded). No such institution was created for blacks.

II

MALAN HAD RETIRED in 1954 and died a few years later, having led the Afrikaner people through the transition from the age of the generals to the age of the politicians, from an isolated rural people into an even more isolated people discovering the even harsher ways of 20th-century ideas. The former predikant from Graaff-Reinet had lived his life with a clear conscience: God had ordered diversity, mankind had merely to accept his decree and watch over its implementation. Malan's ideas had protected the Afrikaners when they were threatened, as the laagers had in the older days. His particular genius was to have afrikanerized segregation, which had, after all, been practised in the Cape and by Shepstone in Natal in the 1870s; he refined it into a coherent policy that the Afrikaners could believe was their own invention, a policy all-encompassing enough to satisfy not only the white supremacist *verkramptes* (the "narrow ones" — as opposed to the *verligtes*, the "enlightened ones") but also the many idealists who believed apartheid gave non-whites a better opportunity for justice and self-development than they would be given in a brutally open society. Malan had put in place a political system designed to ensure their survival. That his vision was narrow we now know — there were those who knew it then — but his people accepted it gratefully.

Malan was followed by J. G. Strijdom, but he was a transitional figure. Strijdom, the Lion of the North, was a Transvaler; his election to the leadership was a sign that the centres of power in the country and in the party had shifted north of the Vaal — Johannesburg was what mattered now. Under Malan the western Cape had dominated the National Party — seven of 12 Malan Cabinet ministers came from the region. The Malan people, through the university at Stellenbosch and *Die Burger*, created the political strategy that coincided with the national consciousness of the Afrikaners. Strijdom swallowed the ideas without chewing; he contributed to his country nothing but the sour gas of extremism. He was a limited man of no particular vision; his view of race relations was much simpler than Malan's and infinitely more simple than the subtle Verwoerd, who was to follow.

Strijdom believed in *baasskap*, bossism, the white man's right to control the lives of others; he occasionally tried to translate this as trusteeship, but never very successfully: he was too crude, and so was his vision. He believed merely in power. His leadership drove many a white opponent of apartheid to despair of his people and drove many blacks to revolt. He lasted only three years — he died in office in 1958 — and no one missed him when he was gone.

Hendrik Verwoerd took hold of the minds of the Afrikaners in a way no one else had done, not even Kruger, who had been forced into greatness by the wilful blindness of the British. Malan had articulated the dream, but his personality had eluded the Afrikaners, and he remained an aloof, if revered, figure. Verwoerd was a man of a larger cast. His ego filled the country and the imaginations of his countrymen; he believed utterly in his mission as the designer of the future and the saviour of his people.

Early in his rule the country seemed to be slipping into chaos. Black unrest was everywhere to be seen. A mass movement against the carrying of passes in March 1960 led the police, in panic, to fire on an unarmed crowd at Sharpeville, killing 67 and wounding 186, leading to an international outcry. Only a few weeks after that trauma and with the country in a state of emergency, a demented Free State farmer named Pratt shot Verwoerd twice in the head at point-blank range. When Verwoerd survived that, the bonds with his people became more primitive and emotional still. (Pratt, too, survived in a mental institution in Bloemfontein. I remember once, when I was a junior reporter there, finding him crouched under a chair in a dentist's waiting room. He had wandered away from his keepers, and the dentist, who had an eye for notoriety, had called the security police and the press at the same time. Pratt was a pathetic figure, and his assassination attempt had nothing to do with politics and everything to do with his own failures.)

Verwoerd was born a Hollander and had received his academic training there and in the colleges of the Cape; he became a professor of psychology at Stellenbosch. Later, he turned to journalism as an outlet for the urgency of his sense of mission; he was the first editor of *Die Transvaler*, and the paper served as the conduit for his ideas. He took hold of Cronje's sketchy theory of apartheid and, by turning it into the far-reaching theory of separate development, in which "every nation, without any regard to race, colour or stage of development . . . had the right to exist and to protect itself to carry out God's plan," he gave it a structure and a rationale and an intellectual respectability it had lacked before.

In the perorations of his public speeches and later parliamentary statements his voice would grow more sonorous: "We have been set here with a destiny . . . destiny not for the selfishness of a nation but for the sake of the service of a nation to the world of which it is a part and the service of the world to the Deity." Verwoerd was a candidate in the 1948 election but was defeated — the last time anyone rejected him. No matter; the government appointed him to the Senate and made him minister of native affairs. From Parliament he continued his haranguing of the country and his domination of the party. In one of his first speeches he set the tone;

and it was a measure of the awe in which others held him that no one laughed: "In every field of life one has to fix one's eyes on the stars, to see how close one can come to perfection." Everyone understood he was talking of the destiny of South Africa and of his own future as well: in his mind — and in many of theirs — they were one.

He was convinced, he would say over and over, that unity and integration of the races in South Africa would bring ruin to everyone. "I am convinced that integration in a country like South Africa cannot succeed. I want justice for all groups and not justice for one at the expense of the others." And he would declare, in a phrase appealing and therefore deceiving in its simplicity: *Skep u eie toekoms!* Build your own future! By which he meant, talking to the blacks, Seize hold of your destiny, as we have. Move among your own people, build your own place in your own way. We will give you the means. And he meant it. He went much farther than Malan with his more limited horizons ever dared to go: we will give each group that wants it full independence, all the trappings of a national state in which they will be masters of their own destiny. When they are ready, of course. At the same time he declared openly that the urban areas were white man's territory, where blacks would have only the rights of visitors. Verwoerd shifted the ancient emphasis from the Afrikaner to the white; but everyone understood that it was the Afrikaner's duty to lead the whites to the correct path; the English, white as they were, could not be trusted; they would be beguiled by false turnings.

In 1961 Verwoerd engineered and won a referendum making South Africa a republic and doing away, finally, with the trappings of the British monarchy. The same year he took South Africa out of the Commonwealth (though the Commonwealth now seems to have persuaded itself that it righteously pushed South Africa out). On January 23, 1962, the Transkei, the historic "homeland" of the Xhosa, was given "sovereign independence," as promised. The world paid no attention, seeing the Transkei, rightly, as a puppet state. But to the Afrikaner nationalists it seemed another step along the path of their historic destiny. They were on their way to the ultimate triumph of Afrikaner nationalism.

By 1966 Verwoerd had reached the height of his power. What dissident elements remained had apparently been eliminated; he had turned his minister of justice, Balthazar Johannes Vorster, on the opposition, black and white, and Vorster had with uncontrolled fury driven dissent underground or into jail or exile. The economy had rebounded from the shock of Sharpeville, which had caused a flight of foreign capital; intellectually, Verwoerd dominated the country and had shaken off an unexpected attack from the Dutch Reformed Church, experiencing for the first time the trauma of internal dissent. He had called an election and had won without trouble; the Progressive Party had elected precisely one candidate, the irrepressible Helen Suzman, a strong-willed woman from a wealthy Johannesburg constituency who would be virtually alone in Opposition for more than a decade.

On September 6, the rumours spread in Parliament that Verwoerd was to make an important speech. No one knew what it was to be — Verwoerd seldom consulted even his caucus before making major pronouncements — and the rumours covered everything from the release of political prisoners to new relationships with black African states, if any could be found to have relationships with. He had met the previous week with Chief Leabua Jonathan, the latest successor to Moshoeshoe, and maybe this presaged a new direction. The press gallery filled; as a feature writer for the *Cape Times* I drifted into Parliament to watch.

Verwoerd had already taken his seat, his head bent over papers on his desk. He seemed to be scribbling notes, though that was unusual; he was a man who spoke easily in public, sometimes for hours, in logical, well-constructed speeches made without consulting any paper. The rest of the government front-benchers were milling about. Messengers — whites, of course, this being the nature of the place — scurried back and forth. A figure entered from behind the Speaker's chair, a large man of sallow complexion, slightly stooped. Many in the press gallery tried afterwards to remember whether they had noticed him; no one could be sure. I know I didn't. Few reporters were actually peering at the floor below to see the messenger suddenly straighten up, draw from his jacket two silver daggers and plunge them into Verwoerd. There was a hoarse shout, and the minister of sport, a former rugby international named Frankie Waring, brought the messenger down. Too late; one of the daggers had penetrated the heart and the prime minister was dead on the floor.

To say that the nation was shocked is less of a cliché than such colour-commentary chatter usually is. Mostly when the press reports a nation's shock, it's just hyperbole: nations are seldom as shockable as journalistic convention believes. But the abrupt demonstration of Verwoerd's mortality was shocking to the Afrikaners, for he had dominated the intellectual and emotional landscape in a way no one else had; and his casual removal by a lunatic immigrant without any political motivation left the Afrikaners with a sorrow that had no outlet and an anger with no target. And in the years after the shock wore off there was a deeper shock yet — the slow realization that Verwoerd's vision had, after all, been fatally flawed; it could not survive without his mesmerizing presence. The Afrikaner's national aspirations, which had seemed on the point of realization, were to be snatched away once more: grief was compounded by a feeling of betrayal.

III

THE ASSASSINATION OF Hendrik Verwoerd was a turning-point, the beginning of the end of the apartheid era, the start of the modern period. After 1966 the tribe began — but slowly! — to lose faith in the vision; some of them began to see what they had done. It seems unbelievable now that it took so long, that they couldn't have seen earlier that nationalism's triumph was inevitably to become nationalism's defeat, that the weird edifice so carefully crafted was to trap them inside it, that the course they had chosen was self-destructive. The death of Verwoerd forced some members of the tribe to confront the new realities. But it was too late: they were trapped and the trap seemed to have no obvious way out. How to dismantle the edifice without bringing ruin on themselves? How could the *volkseie* be protected in a detribalized South Africa? If Verwoerd's vision wouldn't work, all they had left was the knowledge that if they once lost power it would never be regained — the Afrikaner would never be permitted another chance. The politics of privilege turned again to the politics of survival. They were left with only the sour sound of a policeman's truncheon. They elected B. J. Vorster to lead them.

John Vorster was a cop. He had been, for Verwoerd, a pretty efficient cop. In uncertain times, a good cop is an asset: he will promise you security and can sometimes deliver. And in the aftermath of Verwoerd, security seemed vital. The policies, the precious policies, the *necessary* policies, were coming apart at the seams.

The black presence in the cities grew more ominous rather than less. It was supposed to have shrunk. After all, homelands were being created by the template Verwoerd's vision had provided and were given "independence" — the Transkei, kwaZulu, Bophuthatswana, kwaNdebele, and the rest — but the massive black presence in the "white" areas didn't diminish at all. It kept swelling. Soweto ("SOuth WEst TOwnships") passed a million inhabitants and its growth showed no signs of slowing; outside Cape Town the slums and shanty towns grew despite the bulldozers and the daily trains carrying hapless black families "back" to the Transkei; Langa and Guguletu and Nyanga, the "legal" black townships on the flats outside the city, were swollen with restless black workers; the shanty town of Crossroads farther out on the flats grew even in the winter rains, as families trapped by the Afrikaner dream drifted into the city to look for work, and to build their houses from small scraps of corrugated iron, cardboard, string, sacking, and junk scoured from the white garbage dumps. Verwoerd was supposed to have stopped this growth and here it was, continuing.

There were more blacks than whites in the "white areas" by the time Verwoerd departed. (Under Vorster the inevitable growth continued, and it continues yet — the number of blacks in these "white" areas went up from 8 million in 1970 to 9.5 million in 1980 — more than twice the number of whites.) The segregated society was nowhere being realized as the vision said it would and must. South Africa was in the process of becoming the kind of society it had been prior to apartheid, with all races once again sharing all areas; at the same time it had become the pre-eminent international pariah. None of this was supposed to happen! Disillusionment grew.

Vorster had no new ideas to contribute. Vorster had suppressed dissent, yet here was the young radical Steve Biko and the movement he called Black Consciousness, here was the militantly violent group called Umkonto we Sizwe (the Spear of the Nation), here was the African National Congress renewed and reinvigorated. Even in the shanty town of Crossroads dissent ranged from the sophisticated politics of the United Democratic Front to the mystical opposition of the Black Jerusalem movement, which sacrificed a cock every morning at dawn to hasten the End . . . Vorster was merely a cop.

In international affairs he did have one initiative. He tried to arrange a series of alliances with "compatible" black states, partly to defuse international anger against apartheid, partly to throw a security curtain between South Africa and the rest of the continent. It worked for a while, and he visited Hastings Banda in Malawi and the eccentric leaders of the Ivory Coast; he bullied little Botswana into talks and waged covert war in Angola and Mozambique. But it didn't last. He had a simple mind and a simple-minded view of the world. (The political scientist Hermann Giliomee recounts how Vorster exclaimed, appalled after a visit to Rio in 1968: "There a black man doesn't have a chance!")

Vorster never understood, never grasped why the West was angry with a bulwark against international Communism, nor did he understand the visceral hatred much of black Africa had developed towards the Afrikaners. Even his own army contained more sophisticated notions: Gen. Magnus Malan, the head of the Defence Force, publicly warned Vorster that the solutions to South Africa's problems were "80 per cent socio-political and only 20 per cent military." (South Africa's army has always been to the left of the governing party; it was a sign of the desperation of the liberal white opposition in the late 1970s that they looked forward to an army take-over if things got too bad.)

Vorster's government lurched from crisis to crisis during the 1970s, finally disintegrating in a scandal over misuse of government funds for propaganda purposes, in which many of the militants of the Department of Information were seen to be keeping huge sums of money for their own use. This was a further shock for the Afrikaners: nothing in their body of public myth had prepared them for corrupt leaders. Vorster was forced to resign in 1978.

The debate in Afrikaner circles grew furious. The National Party split, with Albert Hertzog leading the *verkramptes* off to the wild country of the right, where *kragdadigheid*, strength of will in brutal action, was the watchword; Piet Cillie, the urbane editor of *Die Burger*, along with the newly sophisticated academics in Johannesburg and in Stellenbosch, began the intellectual dismantling of apartheid from the party's "left" or *verligte* wing. The former Broederbond member Beyers Naudé broke away from the Dutch Reformed Church, where he had been the Transvaal moderator; the spiritual leaders of the people had no advice to offer. Apartheid became harder and harder to defend. The threat of schism was once more in the air.

With the election of P. W. Botha in 1978, we enter the era of current politics. Botha was an apparatchik, a creature of the National Party machine; it was widely felt he was capable of mastering it and so reducing its influence. Under his leadership the Broederbond's influence began to decline. He moved early to blunt the power of the Verwoerd-appointed bureaucrats, a powerful conservative force in South Africa, by rewriting the constitution to create a strong executive presidency. He forged close and personal links with the armed forces.

From the start, Botha was looking for manoeuvring room. He was searching for the impossible, a way of sharing power without losing control. His political strategy was to attempt the conversion of Afrikaner domination into Afrikaner technocratic leadership — keep the Afrikaner base alive but incorporate into it the former tribal enemies, the English; then attempt to co-opt the Indian, Coloured, and black middle classes.

Although the co-option largely failed, the strategy did threaten Botha's National Party majority, which dropped from 85 per cent of Afrikaners in 1977 to 66 per cent in 1981 to 55 per cent in 1983 — defections to the right-wing Herstigte Nasionale Party of Hertzog on the one hand and to the moderate Progressive Party on the other, as it moved in to mop up the final feeble remnants of the long-deteriorating United Party opposition. There were much-publicized defections from the left, as well as the growth of the lunatic right. The clamour for reform, from internal forces in the country and even from the party, grew. At the same time, the increasing uproar in the outside world was crowding Botha, giving him less room for manoeuvre and less freedom to compromise. The election campaign in the early part of 1987 was unexpectedly fluid. Everyone knew something had to be done and that Botha didn't seem to be doing it. But it seemed that the costs of the political order were not yet so high as to compel Botha to a solution that would threaten Afrikaner national identity, that would put in jeopardy the *eie* itself. He was a more modern man than Verwoerd and a larger man than Vorster, but he was still a part of the white tribe dreaming.

Chapter 23

The "Afrikaner at prayer" and the Christian conscience

WHERE, IN ALL THIS RADICAL remaking of the social order that apartheid represented, were the representatives of the God the Afrikaners had adopted as their own? Where was the Dutch Reformed Church, "the National Party at prayer," the Calvinist voice of the platteland, the church of the governing élite and of the urban proletariat alike? The trekboers who became the Afrikaners had set off into the wilderness without any organized church; there were a few itinerant dominees who accompanied them, but mostly what they took were their well-thumbed Bibles and a chillingly narrow definition of a God of righteous retribution — a God who became identified in their minds with their sorrows, a God driven mostly by anger and the negative virtues of prohibition and control.

The organized church, in the form of good men like the imported Scot Andrew Murray and the Free Staters like Koo Marquard, followed them into the blue horizons, settling into the heartland but never quite catching up with the scarred theology that drove men into the Great Thirstland or left them behind, sullen and angry, on the shabby small-holdings of the highveld platteland or in the dismal houses of the "poor white" suburbs. Nevertheless, the rigorous piety of the church and its small-town preachers had helped keep alive the Afrikaner dream of group destiny during the Century of Wrong; the church was superb as a morale-builder among a defeated people. After the bitter defeats of the Boer War, after the sour failure of the 1914 rebellion, and through the depression and its aftermath, the dominees of the small towns and the new white suburbs helped articulate Afrikanerdom's voice. The trekboers of the 19th century might seldom have seen a dominee, but the idea of the dominee was nevertheless supreme; he was the fibre of the culture, and it is doubtful that the Afrikaners would have held together as well without him. After the trauma of 20th-century urbanization, when the political morale of the Afrikaner nation was at its lowest ebb, it was the Dutch Reformed Church that prevented complete spiritual panic.

The church also shared the preoccupations of its parishioners. It was concerned with knitting together the people, with survival, with helping them overcome defeat. In the dominees' pastoral work on the platteland, therefore, they paid as little attention to blacks as did the national politics of the time. Blacks were not a . . . theological *problem*. It wasn't until Malan came to power that the Dutch Reformed Church (the NG Kerk, the Nederduitse Gereformeerde Kerk), which became the state church by default because it was the church of the new governing élite, came to realize that the politics of its people had shifted ground — what had been survival was now become privilege.

The various synods began to turn their attention from the Church's purely ministering role of moral prop to the weighty problems presented by this new and surprising configuration: what were they now to make of ethnic differentiation and of the awkwardnesses of tribal cohabitation? What of this politics called apartness or, in the Afrikaans, apartheid? What was theologically justified? What was Biblically sanctioned? What was a Christian's duty in this new and perilous world? What should the church's attitude be to the brown and black people its proselytizers were bringing into the fold? If the gospels preached to the different groups were identical, how could separate churches, as demanded by the theory and as practised in many small towns, be reconciled? Was it morally legitimate even to segregate blacks within a church building? If there was no black church available, should blacks be allowed to use whites' buildings?

Throughout the 1940s and 1950s the church leadership wrestled with the problems. The Broederbond and the National Party were both avowedly Dutch Reformed; virtually every Cabinet minister in Malan's government belonged, and the Broederbond made adherence a fundamental requirement for membership. How could the church resist the politicians' pressure? Should it even try to resist the people's pressure? Were there, in sum and in short, theological grounds for race differentiation? Was apartheid to be permitted?

The various synods of the church met frequently, with apartheid always at the forefront of their minds; and while a few influential churchmen resisted to the end, they concluded that the policy of apartheid could be morally justified as a legitimate way of securing the "Christian development" of both black and white. In defence of this slippery idea, they trotted out the readings from the Old and New Testaments so familiar in the American south: the ambiguous Acts 17:26 ("And hath made of one blood all nations of men for to dwell on all the face of the earth, and hath determined the times before appointed, and the bounds of their habitation" — those "bounds" were especially valuable) and the ever-useful Genesis 11:6–9, which concerns the Tower of Babel and God's express wish to scatter the peoples of the earth — can we legitimately gather up those whom God scattered? Independent development, *aparte ontwikkeling* in the Afrikaans, could be accepted if it were done justly and with honour, despite a certain amount of "personal and temporary privation."

There was nevertheless what might charitably be called theological fluidity in the church throughout the 1950s, as the various synods and gatherings took positions all the way across the moral spectrum. And so it came as a considerable shock — and surprise — to the Broederbond, to Verwoerd, and even to many churchmen to find, in 1961, a ringing condemnation of the whole idea of apartheid issued by the delegates of the Church-in-Assembly, a condemnation now simply referred to as Cottesloe, after the Johannesburg suburb in which the meeting was held.

The meeting had been called by the World Council of Churches in 1960, in the high emotion that followed the Sharpeville shootings. It included eight South African churches, among them the largest synods of the most powerful of the Dutch Reformed sects, the Nederduitse Gereformeerde Kerk of the Cape and that of the Transvaal. Its deliberations were lengthy and its conclusions unambiguous. They dealt with the whole structure and purpose of apartheid: no one who lived in the cities could legitimately be declared alien or denied ownership of property or direct participation in government; a church could not legitimately exclude people on the grounds of race or colour; no scriptural grounds existed for banning mixed marriages; migrant labour was inherently un-Christian; job reservation (the reserving of certain jobs for members of specific race groups) should be abolished; Coloureds should be allowed to represent themselves in Parliament; imprisonment without trial was contrary to Christian law and natural justice; Bantu (blacks) domiciled in the urban areas should be given full political rights . . . There was more. The declaration called into question the full range of racially directed legislation dating back even to the Cape colony days.

Verwoerd, enraged, mounted an immediate counter-attack: if the Afrikaner laity was to accept Cottesloe, apartheid would be in ruins.

The main line of his attack was simple. He put his own and his party's constancy on the line against the vacillation and irresolution of the church; the church had been unduly influenced by the liberals in the World Council, who in turn had been undermined by Euro-Marxism; the emotional days following Sharpeville had misled the church into mistaking its way; in the rhetoric of the moment the church had lost sight of apartheid's higher purpose, which was the equitable development of each group in its own way and the eternal preservation of the Afrikaner *volkseie*. The people as a whole would reject the church unless the church found its way back to the straight path and the narrow. He called on the theologians to recant and on the church members to choose between party policy and foreign sentiment.

They chose party policy: a few months after Cottesloe the church hierarchy repudiated the resolutions taken there and, in the person of the Reverend Dr. A. P. Treurnicht, mounted a strong pro-apartheid counter-attack, maintaining that "justice is plurality; and autogenous development is the best exercise of justice." Treurnicht called, in a characteristic phrase, "not for impartial justice but for a holy impartiality for the securing of [each group's] distinctive way." In less oblique language, he meant that separate development best secured justice for all, and with that declaration the church seemed as satisfied as the commanding figure of Verwoerd was.

In spite of this craven recantation, Cottesloe's influence was considerable. In the decades that followed, the secularization of the Afrikaners proceeded apace, paralleling developments elsewhere, as, curiously, black membership in the Dutch Reformed sects grew. The church slowly shifted its emphasis from Biblical justifications of apartheid to support on the practical grounds that apartheid best secured everyone's future; and as its theological underpinnings eroded so did the church's influence. Throughout the rest of the 1960s and 1970s, the church's role was almost wholly negative, as a brake on reform. It wasn't until the early 1980s that the church joined the growing clamour for reform and declared, in a formal document that attracted only small attention — a measure of its diminished influence — that apartheid was a sin. This is still the official policy of the church, though there is considerable dissent among the predikante.

And the repudiation of Cottesloe threw up one major figure, a man of unbending integrity who was to form (and who still forms) one of the powerful centres of domestic dissent: the moderator of the Dutch Reformed Church in the Transvaal, the former Broederbond member and leading theologian the Reverend Beyers Naudé, who in 1961 condemned what he called the whole "false doctrine" of apartheid. He resigned as moderator and set up the Christian Institute to serve as an intellectual centre against oppression and unjust discrimination. His reward was to be stripped of his status as a dominee, to see the miserable Treurnicht lionized in the Afrikaans press, and to find himself castigated as a traitor, a man who had lost touch with his tribe.

Naudé is a man as unbending in his Christian duty as Verwoerd was unyielding in the strength of his vision: he too was shaped by the Century of Wrong, but like other Afrikaner liberals, he drew from it nourishment of a different kind. A gentler vision, but one no less strong.

Chapter 24

The road not taken: the growth and failure of Afrikaner dissent

I

WHILE THE NATIONALISTS were mobilizing the volk through the politics of fear, the small band of Afrikaner liberals wrestled with their apparently insoluble dilemma: how can white politicians controlled by a white electorate that is fearful for its existence reach out to a wider constituency? No South African liberal politician has been able to manage the trick; the closest anyone came was the fatally flawed Jan Hofmeyr.

Hofmeyr is another of the great might-have-beens of South African politics. My father, René, says unequivocally that "he would have been prime minister of South Africa had he not died in his early fifties"; René's oldest friend, Alan Paton, disagrees, and in his biography of Hofmeyr he argued strongly against the possibility. Yet Paton too loved Hofmeyr: he made the first attempt, Paton wrote, to break the chains to the past. "He was a white South African, with a white South African's fears and prejudices and irrationalities, but he knew them for what they were."

René de Villiers had met Hofmeyr at a Student Christian Association summer camp organized by Alan Paton on the south coast of Natal. That was in 1926. He didn't see him again until 1944, when Hofmeyr was Smuts's deputy prime minister and René was in the parliamentary press gallery for *The Forum*, the journal of which Hofmeyr was chairman. They met every week to discuss political events and eventually became friends.

Hofmeyr was brilliant, mother-dominated, controlled in public, diffident, brave, narrow in his Christian intolerance yet driven by those same Christian principles to a more and more radical stance. He never escaped entirely his own fears of the uncivilized masses, but he was insistent on including among the elect the civilized of whatever colour.

Brilliant, certainly, in his academic fashion: a university graduate at 14, a biographer of his famous uncle at 17, a full professor at 22, rector of the new University of the Witwatersrand at 24, administrator of the Transvaal (a Smuts appointment) a few years later. Once in Smuts's Cabinet in the early 1940s, he proved himself arguably the best administrator South Africa's Parliament ever had — at times he ran, with superb efficiency, three Cabinet departments of his own and happily took over the departments of others when they were on holiday or absent, not even excluding the prime ministership while Smuts was in Britain on imperial business.

Mother-dominated, without question: Deborah Hofmeyr ran his life, never allowed him close enough to a woman to contemplate marriage, ran his social life while he was in office (her birthday became one of Pretoria's pre-eminent social functions), chose his friends, coddled and smothered him, stood fiercely over his coffin after he was dead. He lived with his mother all his life — she even accompanied him to Oxford — and even as deputy prime minister would go straight home from Parliament to cry out when entering the front door, Hi ma, I'm home! He made but one close woman friend, and that by correspondence. Fifteen years of letters to the novelist Sarah Gertrude Millin survive; it is only in these letters that the internal Hofmeyr ever emerged from the rigid, overly formal control he imposed on everything he did. (Everything, that is, but his besotted passion for cricket, a game at which he was thoroughly inept.)

Hofmeyr was incapable of small talk, René de Villiers recalls, though he loved political gossip — he would gossip about everyone except General Smuts, whom he revered. "One little sidelight I remember about him was his insistence on using his own car to go to these cricket matches of his. As deputy prime minister he was entitled to government transport, but unless he was going somewhere on strictly government business, he would never use it. His ineptitude at cricket never stopped him playing, of course. It was also typical of him that whenever he wasn't actually on the playing field he liked to keep the scores. That was part of the man I remember: he would shift easily from keeping the national accounts to keeping cricket scores for amateur matches."

Sarah Millin tried for years to persuade Hofmeyr to grasp the greatness she and Leo Marquard sensed was in him. Marquard urged him many times, as did the liberal academic Edgar Brookes, to break with Smuts and the United Party and to form a new party of his own, one that would give a political voice to the liberal conscience, but he could never escape from Smuts's thrall and the chance was missed. After Hofmeyr's death Marquard himself formed a Liberal Party together with Brookes and Winifred Hoernle (a former classmate of Hofmeyr's who married Alfred Hoernle, one of their teachers; she later became a formidable liberal force in her own right). But their Liberal Party never had a leader of real stature and never became a significant force in South African political life. It no longer exists.

In Afrikaner political mythology, Hofmeyr was a militant liberal bent on dragging people of colour into "white" politics, at any cost, and on "handing the country over to blacks" — we have seen how Albert Hertzog and J. G. Strijdom used this canard against Smuts's party in the run-up to the 1948 election. It is not the least merit of Alan Paton's biography of Hofmeyr to show how distorted this picture was. My father reviewed the Paton biography when it appeared and argued then that Hofmeyr was not a "natural" liberal — that it was truer to say of him "that he was a man whose Christianity and honesty and courage drove him steadily forward to a political philosophy of humanism that was in conflict with that of the large majority of his fellow white South Africans at the time."

Hofmeyr attempted to formulate policies in a terrain where no South African politician had yet ventured, trying to find ways of including the politically dispossessed in a system where only whites had the franchise. In the end, it defeated him. With care and delicacy and a long campaign of education such an opposition could possibly have been made to work; but Hofmeyr was facing Malan and Verwoerd, whose ethnic mobilization of the Afrikaners left no room for delicacy and who scrupled not at all to dive into the deep waters of ethnic prejudice. It was a very unequal contest.

At the end of 1948, with Malan as prime minister, Hofmeyr fell ill. He insisted on keeping an engagement he should have cancelled; he was due to play in a cricket game against the Parliamentary Press Gallery. When he showed up at the cricket-ground he was grey and moving with obvious difficulty. René de Villiers tried to dissuade him from playing, but when he wouldn't budge helped him strap on his cricket pads. A few days later he was dead, his mother Deborah dry-eyed and unbending over his coffin.

I was only eight but I remember my father coming home, ashen, exhausted. This was a greater blow than Smuts's defeat: Hofmeyr was the last great hope of the liberal cause. Alan Paton wrote: "So a great light went out in the land, making men more conscious of its darkness . . . Tens of thousands of hearts were filled with unspeakable grief, not only because they had loved him, but because he was the man who had been to them 'as a hiding place from the wind, and a covert from the tempest; as rivers of water in a dry place, as the shadow of a great rock in a weary land'. "

II

WITH HOFMEYR GONE, the United Party Opposition fell into disarray. It managed to maintain its numbers through a couple of elections, but failed to capture the country's imagination. It had a fatal flaw. Every time it seized on an issue with which to attack the nationalist government, some government bencher would taunt: Well, will you or won't you give the vote to blacks and Coloureds? The question haunted the Opposition. They didn't know the answer, and they couldn't search for it without destroying the party. Reject the narrow nationalist vision, yes. But what to put in its place? What are the elements of the new order to come? The lack of an articulated alternative killed the party's effectiveness, prevented a coherent attack and made it even more prone to schism than the Afrikaner mainstream.

With the parliamentary Opposition in disarray, the centre of dissenting energy shifted to extra-parliamentary activity. The nationalists were not the only group to develop a paramilitary wing; the Ossewabrandwag had its opposition equivalent, an anti-nationalist war vets' group that called itself the War Veterans' Torch Commando, which at one point had a membership of a quarter of a million. Its "steel commando" drive on Cape Town unnerved the nationalist government and led it to accuse the commando of plotting armed rebellion.

The Torch Commando came into being to try to prevent the cynical stripping of the franchise from the Cape Coloured community, in a piece of constitutional flimflammery that enraged even the generally compliant South African electorate. But the commando couldn't sustain its momentum; it had a falling-out with the United Party over election tactics in 1953, and the leadership alienated many of its followers by a series of inflammatory speeches which sounded, in truth, as if it were indeed plotting revolution. After the National Party won the election with an increased majority, the commando began to disintegrate; the moral steam went out of it when it became clear that it was the manipulation of the constitution that really concerned its members, a technical constitutional matter, and not protection of the Coloured vote, a moral question. Worse, the commando had only a handful of Coloured members, and, in a tragic denial of its own alleged principles, refused to allow even those to join in the celebration of the victory at El Alamein a decade earlier. Malan effectively finished it off by turning against it the old taunts: naive liberals, Communist stooges, betrayers of white civilization . . .

At about the same time a handful of brave women, among them Ruth Foley, Jean Sinclair, Helen Newton Thompson and Tertia Rybus, formed the Women's Defence of the Constitution League, known almost from the start as the Black Sash from their habit of staging silent protests in public places wearing black sashes, the symbol of the death of rights. The Black Sash lasted longer than the Torch Commando — indeed, it persists still — because it was politically more sophisticated, was smaller in numbers, and had among its members some of the toughest minds in the country. When I was a student at the University of Cape Town we would occasionally join the steely women of the Black Sash in their silent vigils; the hatred that was directed at them was unnerving, but they retained their calm silence in the face of provocation and insult, their presence a reproach to prejudice and a comfort to liberals everywhere.

The Black Sash was a going concern long after the Coloured vote was a fading memory; its vigils continued to protest unjust laws, and as we have seen, these were never in short supply. The group maintained contacts with political prisoners, when these were allowed, visited detainees on Robben Island, when permitted, and set up so-called Advice Offices, where they counselled blacks caught in the ever-widening net of restrictive regulations. Cynical observers, such as the Canadian academic Heribert Adam, have suggested that the existence of the Sash actually served the government's purposes — the nationalists could point to this very visible opposition as proof that South Africa was indeed a functioning democracy. But the women of the Sash had no option. They had to do what they were doing. The alternatives, in any case, were acquiescence and revolt. What else could they do? Meanwhile, the parliamentary Opposition soldiered on, the United Party ineffective and indecisive, the Liberal Party unable to elect a single member, the Progressives with a solitary member for 13 years, the uncrushable Helen Suzman.

III

MUCH OF MY FATHER'S life-work was done through the English-language press. He had, I believe, a healing mission, as so many of the Afrikaner liberals believed they had (though my father would never put it that way). At first, this was to heal the divisions between English and Afrikaner; then, it was to explain to the English (and to the Afrikaner and to the world at large) the great differences between Afrikaner liberal and Afrikaner nationalist: the liberal is a person who puts his loyalty to his country and all its people above loyalty to his race or his party — it is an inclusive nationalism, broadly based, in contrast to the narrow, exclusive nationalism of the Afrikaner nationalist. This view is a linear descendant, of course, of the philosophy of the early Hofmeyr, Onze Jan.

In more recent years, as the nation's focus shifted away from linguistic to racial tensions, René attempted to create bonds between people of different colours — always insisting that the Afrikaners were not all stiff-necked hypocrites, not all nationalists, not all closed to adventures of the spirit. For 20 years he worked on a succession of newspapers, in Bloemfontein, Durban, Cape Town, and Johannesburg. He ended his journalistic career as editor of the *Star*, South Africa's largest English-language daily; for years his carefully reasoned editorials espousing his own brand of gentle liberalism kept the ideals of Leo Marquard and Jan Hofmeyr alive and enraged the ideologues of Afrikaner nationalism, who reviled him in the Afrikaans press as a "verengelste Afrikaner," an anglicized Afrikaner, a mock Afrikaner.

Over the long course of his career, he came into contact with the full spectrum of his people, many of them memorable, some of them tragic, some of them noble, some of them just . . . peculiar.

There was Piet Meyer, for instance, a classmate of René's at the university in Bloemfontein. He was always a brooding, introspective man. After graduation he drifted into journalism of a sort, ending up 30 years after he began as head of the South African Broadcasting Corporation, one of the most influential behind-the-scenes positions in South African life. At some point in his life he joined the Broederbond, and in due course he became its head. Thereafter he operated in the dark, exercising enormous influence in education, culture, economic life, and government. A powerful influence on Meyer's life was Dr. Nic Diederichs, who started in the academic world and ended as state president. René recalls that Diederichs taught political science to him as well as to Meyer, "but without much success, I'm glad to say, since we ended on opposite sides of the political fence." René also got to know J. F. J. van Rensburg, who became head of the Ossewa-brandwag. "He had a brilliant mind," René said in a sardonic note to me, "but little enthusiasm for the democratic process."

In the course of his career, René also met many Afrikaners who made the difficult journey from nationalist to liberal. One he remembers fondly was Kowie Marais, a "bright young man" (everyone said it of him) who started life as a broadcast announcer. His identification with his people drew him into radical Afrikaner politics, and he joined the Broederbond secret society. During the Second World War he was interned, in the company of a motley assortment of nationalists, some of them crypto-Nazis, some of them simply misguided, among them the future prime minister, B. J. Vorster. But at heart Marais was a cultivated man with a soft spot for the underprivileged — it had drawn him to radical politics in the first place — and he began to see the nature of those among whom he found himself. After the war he studied law and rose to become a judge of the Supreme Court. When he retired from the bench he went into politics and joined the liberal Progressives, or Progressive Federal Party, as it came to be called. He died a few years ago believing strongly in the need for an open society — he'd come a long way from the internment camps.

Bram Fischer, who had been a friend of René's in Bloemfontein in his early days, was a more tragic figure. He was brilliant, came from a prominent family — his father had been powerful in the politics of the Orange Free State republic before the Boer War — and could easily have been prime minister or chief justice some day. But he drifted into the camp of the radical left and became a Marxist for whom, as the historian Rodney Davenport put it, "treason, patriotism and humanity were synonymous terms." He was sentenced to life imprisonment and was released on compassionate grounds only a few months before his death from cancer in 1975.

But the man who has made the strongest impact on René, apart from Jan Hofmeyr, and the man he considers the "noblest of the Afrikaners I know," is Beyers Naudé. Naudé's father had a hand in setting up the Broederbond, and Beyers himself became a member for a time. But when he broke from the Broederbond cabals he broke completely and took himself out in uncompromising opposition. For his pains, he is anathema to the nationalists; he was hounded from the church and declared a traitor to the volk. After he set up his Christian Institute as a moral centre in the fight against apartheid, he was "banned" by the government, and for years he was forbidden to see more than one person at a time or to attend meetings of any sort. A letter I keep from René described him this way: "He is, to my way of thinking, a great Afrikaner, a man of courage and total integrity who sacrificed greatly for his principles. He played a great role in helping to bring black and white together. I kept in touch with him throughout the time of his restriction, and my admiration for him grew. It is liberals like him who are the salt of the South African earth. Our history is strewn with their names and I count myself privileged to have known some of them."

Most of the great Afrikaner liberals have been bilingual, my father points out (he himself uses English and Afrikaans interchangeably, as many from Winburg did and do). "This is a potent political factor, I think. Bilingualism as we understand it — that is, an ability to read and write and speak English and Afrikaans with equal facility — is an important ingredient of the kind of South Africanism I believe in. It is all part of the process of producing a South African oneness, which, of course, is the prelude to the greater oneness that will embrace men and women of all creeds and colours."

There are, of course, lesser forces at work. My father recounts how Alan Paton, an English-speaker fluent in Afrikaans, decided to take part in the centenary celebrations of the Great Trek in 1938. He and some members of his staff at Diepkloof Reformatory decided to go to the Voortrekker Monument, where a great rally was to be held. On their wagon, the property of the reformatory, they flew the Transvaal Vierkleur flag. Paton and companions arrived in the great encampment on a hot day and went straight to the showers. "Here," says Paton, "I was greeted by a naked and bearded Afrikaner who said to me, 'Have you seen the great crowds?' 'Yes,' I said (there were a quarter of a million people there). He said to me with the greatest affability, 'Nou gaan ons die Engelse opdonder' [Now we are going to knock hell out of the English]."

IV

IN THE EARLY 1970S, with the Vorster government in some disarray — the *verkrampte–verligte* debate in full swing, *Die Burger* taking after *Die Transvaler*, the more liberal nationalists defecting to the opposition — the Progressive Party seemed to take on a new life. In the election of 1974, it elected 14 members, 13 more than it had had before. One of the new MPs was René de Villiers, retired as editor of the *Star* in Johannesburg and fresh from running *Race Relations News*, the official mouthpiece of the Institute of Race Relations. "I hadn't given the matter serious thought until, to my utter astonishment, I won the Parktown constituency in Johannesburg by a few hundred votes. I often wondered what my father would have said had he been alive: the erstwhile barefoot boy from Winburg sitting in Parliament representing the richest voters in the country! My father, after all, professed to hate Johannesburg and was fond of quoting a sentiment of John X. Merriman [a former Cape premier] who used to refer to it as 'the university of all evil'. "

René spent the next few years in parliamentary Opposition once again being reviled, as Hofmeyr had been and as he himself had been as a journalist, as a mock Afrikaner, as a renegade, a traitor to the volk. "I hadn't really the temperament for Parliament," he will say mildly now, remembering the insults in some pain — no one likes being cast from the tribe. But he will still walk the hallways of Parliament, pointing wistfully at the busts of the few liberals represented there. "Democracy is thinly spread in South Africa and Parliament reflects its thinness. But it was nevertheless exciting being part of a machine [the Progressive Party] that aimed at extending democracy and broadening its base." At the next election he declined to run again and instead became president of the Institute of Race Relations; the honorary degree awarded him by the University of the Witwatersrand some years later cited his work in race relations and in advancing the cause of press freedom — two causes, alas, now casualties of the imprisoned tribal *eie*.

The Progressive Party had its own internal stutterings. It wanted to broaden its base, but like all white parties it was dependent on a white electorate for its existence. Its twistings and turnings on the question of the franchise were troubled: how to give and yet keep? How to attain a just solution and yet reassure whites? It was the same dream that troubled the sleep of all white liberals; they were still South Africans and couldn't quite get their minds around the idea that political rights were not theirs to dispense.

The Progressive solution was to set up a fluid discrimination to replace a rigid one, to discriminate on the basis of education and affluence instead of race, that is, a qualified franchise weighted strongly to bourgeois values. They shared the same optimistic view as many European and American liberals, that education and affluence will bring tolerance and co-operation, that the way to bring the blacks peacefully into the democratic fold was to co-opt them by affluence, by using the flexible instruments of capitalism to give them a stake in maintaining some new and more just status quo. We now know there to be scant evidence for this view: a bourgeois lifestyle is no guarantee of political respectability; higher education sometimes makes only for more articulate intolerance. It was nevertheless a better idea than any put forward previously: at least an individual would be able escape to democracy through his own efforts and not be locked into his racial fate. It was a long way from the rigid prisons of apartheid.

In the early 1980s, with the optimistic forecasts of the Progressives seen to be only optimism, with the Botha government turning once again to the laager, with the black opposition sensing its time was nearing, the leader of the party, Frederik van Zyl Slabbert, abruptly resigned from the leadership and from Parliament. Slabbert had been the last best hope of the Progressive cause. He was a young and charismatic leader; he had travelled a great intellectual distance from his theological studies to the liberal (or liberal-ish) University of Cape Town, from the narrowness of the Afrikaner nationalist vision to the open-endedness of the progressive ideal; he seemed the perfect leader to succeed the decent, dogged, but uninspiring and English-speaking Colin Eglin.

I watched Slabbert speak. He seemed like a man with no sense of public relations but a clear sense of himself; his clarity of spirit and not his rhetoric captured his audiences. I thought he had the chance to become a significant figure; in the early 1980s the world would have embraced an Afrikaner hero. But he resigned instead, abruptly and without warning. For this he was reviled by his supporters. Even my father, who is incapable of reviling anyone, found his resignation disappointing; he attributed it to personal causes. I think, on the contrary, that it was an interesting and possibly far-sighted decision. Slabbert resigned after a private talk with President P. W. Botha. He had concluded at that meeting that the parliamentary Opposition was merely giving legitimacy to an unchangeable system. His resignation, I thought, was pitched to a different constituency: someone has to be there, at the end, to talk to the new black leaders.

Chapter 25
The politics of privilege and the rise of black dissent

AND THOSE BLACK LEADERS? What of them?

Here's a woman and a man and a friendship, and a metaphor for the might-have-been:

The woman: Nell Marquard was born Nellie van der Merwe in the eastern Free State, near Ficksburg, in the heart of the platteland; the van der Merwes, indeed, have become synonymous in South Africa with a certain kind of plodding platteland mentality. Willem Schalk van der Merwe, the first of the Dutch clan in South Africa, arrived on May 5, 1661; the van der Merwes have been farmers ever since.

Nell broke early with the platteland traditions. She was a small person, at the most five feet (in her later years, when her frailness became fragility, she was once blown over on Cape Town's main street by a gust of wind, breaking her hip), but she always had a will as strong as the platteland sun. She married her cousin, Leo Marquard, became an academic, an internationalist, an Afrikaner liberal; with Leo she was a co-founder of the Joint Councils and of the Liberal Party. They had two children, but their real delight was in ideas; their dining room table in Stellenbosch and later in Cape Town was a salon; at their Sunday family dinners, over rice yellow with turmeric, roasted new potatoes, and Karoo mutton, the conversation ranged widely through politics and literature. Always, just before the guavas picked from the garden were placed on the table to signal the end of the meal, it was Nell's summaries that ended things; she had a knack for encapsulating complex discussions. I was just a kid then, and thought little of these meals; now I think that if any ideas deserve to survive the crossing from white South Africa to black South Africa, they are the ideas of Leo and Nell.

The man: Robert Mangaliso Sobukwe entered Fort Hare college in 1947, the year of the death of Anton Lembede, the first of the mystical proponents of black power, whose teachings still resonate in South Africa. Lembede, on his deathbed, issued a final call to arms for African nationalism, "more powerful and devastating in its effects than ... atomic energy." Sobukwe, the labourer's son, heard the call; he joined the African National Congress Youth League and quickly became one of its leaders, along with Nelson Mandela, Oliver Tambo, and Walter Sisulu. In 1949, in a speech to the Fort Hare graduating class, he echoed Lembede's call: "We must be the embodiment of our people's aspirations. All we are required to do is show the light and the people will find the way." The Youth League's aim, he argued, was to give "force, direction and vigour to the struggle for African national freedom."

For the next four years he sat out of politics. He married Veronica Zodwe, a Zulu, and they rapidly had four children: Dini, Miliswa, Dedani, and Dalindyebo. (Sobukwe, a Sotho on his father's side and a Pondo on his mother's, married a Zulu but was usually taken for a Xhosa; so much for tribal exclusivity.) He had been teaching at a high school in the small town of Standerton, but word of his academic brilliance got around and he was offered a teaching post at University of the Witwatersrand in Johannesburg, not yet closed completely to blacks.

He and his family moved to Soweto, and he was plunged back into black politics. He was immediately shocked at the way the ANC had lost touch with Lembede's credo, and he rapidly became the intellectual force in what was to be called the "Africanist movement." In their journal *The Africanist*,

Sobukwe and his followers continually criticized the ANC's public commitment to a policy of multiracialism and formed their own theory, similar to the Black Consciousness movement that Steve Biko developed from American Black Power ideas and articulated two decades later. A major point of division was Sobukwe's continuing belief in the spontaneous uprising of the masses.

What followed is a matter of public record: the break from the ANC in 1958 and the formation of the Pan-Africanist Congress the following year (with the avowed purpose of creating "a black movement without interference from either so-called left wing or right wing groups of the minorities who so arrogantly appropriate to themselves the right to plan or think for Africans"); the announcement of a mass movement against the carrying of passes in March 1960, which precipitated the panic killings at Sharpeville; further shootings at Langa, in Cape Town; the silent march on Parliament from Langa of 30,000 blacks carrying posters bearing Sobukwe's name; the prosecution (for "incitement") of Sobukwe and his chief followers; and, as his three years in jail were about to end, the rushing through Parliament of the "Sobukwe clause," the law that gave the government the power to keep him in prison indefinitely without further charge.

How frightened they were of Robert Sobukwe! They kept him on Robben Island for another eight years, then they released him under house arrest and a strict banning order to a dismal township in Kimberley. They refused him permission to travel to the United States, though he had several offers from universities there. They refused him permission to travel to Johannesburg to seek medical advice for his illness, a recurrence of the tuberculosis that had plagued him as a young man. They kept him in his dreary township until he was safely dead.

The lives that intersect: The 30,000 blacks who marched on Cape Town in 1960 did so in absolute silence. I was standing on a grassy bank near the University of Cape Town as they passed: there was no shouting of slogans, no chanting, only the shuffling of 30,000 pairs of feet and the distant clatter of police helicopters, as nervous as wasps. The authorities in the Verwoerd government watched the events Sobukwe had precipitated in some dismay: suddenly the machine of control seemed more fragile than they would have believed.

To the blacks, this march was the first deep breath of solidarity; they had yet to meet the real fury of the Verwoerd machine and they could believe anything possible. It was in the emotion of this time that Sobukwe was jailed, that Parliament rammed through the clause that would keep him inside. It was in the high emotion of the time that the Afrikaners issued another call to close ranks against the small band of liberals in their midst, another urgent call for solidarity against "uitlanders of the spirit," demanding the immediate establishment of an Afrikaner republic free from British taint. It was in this extraordinary atmosphere that Nell Marquard, the Afrikaner, began to correspond with Robert Sobukwe, the engine that drove black consciousness.

The letters: They were found in her papers after her death, written on blue paper in a firm hand, dated and signed: Robben Island Gaol. They make a stack about an inch thick; I have them on my desk as I write. They span a period of 14 years, from the time of his incarceration until his last illness in the dreary hamlet to which he was forced. They encompass the growing intimacy of two people who had to travel a great intellectual distance to become friends. They cover the minutiae of daily prison existence, the worries about warm clothing, the hopeless attempts to grow tomatoes in the prison yard. They range through the continuing education of Robert Sobukwe and through his gentle educating of his correspondent. Through international politics. Through theatre. Through everything but the central reality at hand, the system that kept Sobukwe in jail.

More than anything the letters show the strength, calmness, and generosity of this man the Afrikaners so feared, imprisoned as they were in their own sour dreams. Sobukwe's opponents in the black movements of dissent counted his generosity towards his opponents and his twin rejections of radical violence and Marxism as his major weaknesses. Posterity will judge: but that this was a fundamental part of his make-up cannot be doubted. More than any political tract, the letters reveal how utterly futile was the Afrikaner insistence on tribal separation; it is a reminder that many in the outside world need, as they draw bogus lessons about African instability from the rest of Africa.

The meeting: They met but once, at the foot of the steps from the boat bringing him back from Robben Island, the prison they had built for him and his kind. He was a big man, gaunt and still dusty from the sand of the prison yard, bent a little from the illness that was to kill him. She was already frail, with limbs like a bird's, grey eyes hidden behind thick lenses. They took this meeting carefully, for they had both travelled a long way for it: he from the townships outside Graaff-Reinet, via black nationalism, to his charismatic leadership that led to the killings at Sharpeville; she from the Afrikaner heartland. Their roads had taken many turns, but they had both eluded the ideological net their training had suspended over their paths, and they had become simple friends through the long years, progressing from "Dear Mrs. Marquard" and "Dear Mr. Sobukwe" to "My dear Nell" and "Dear Robert." He came down the gangplank, stopped to look at her, then bent down in a great hug and held her to him. They held that hug for five minutes or more, then they went together to take tea at Kirstenbosch Gardens on the slopes of the gentle mountain, then he left, to banishment and death. They never saw each other again.

II

IT TOOK A CENTURY OF WRONG and the deaths in the British concentration camps to construct an Afrikaner nationalism that lasted, to bring the clans together as a tribe. Blacks had suffered more than a century of dispossession and war (some of it of their own making, much performed by the

Afrikaners), but there was by the turn of the 20th century no sign of anything that might be called a nationalist movement. As late as 1908 there were clan and tribal uprisings, notably among the Zulu; they were easily put down and were in any case narrowly based. Blacks were far more diverse than the whites had been, by language, custom, and religion; there had been a history of warfare among them; the Zulus, as we have seen, were not notably peaceful. In northern Natal, the Transkei, and Lesotho there were large areas where no whites lived; the inhabitants were peasants with little education and less sophistication — tribal, in the Western pejorative sense. Only in the Cape, where the qualified franchise had been available to blacks (a minuscule number of whom actually managed to acquire the vote), did any kind of Westernized political élite emerge. It wasn't until there emerged in the industrialized Witwatersrand in and around Johannesburg a huge urban conglomerate made up of members of very diverse tribes that any sense of black nationalism could emerge; it was urbanization and industrialization that transcended tribal loyalties — to the extent they *were* transcended, which was, and still is, modest.

There were leaders of stature prior to the apartheid era, but they had only a small constituency. Dr. Moroka, Jim de Villiers's old friend from Thaba 'Nchu, was one. John Dube, who was educated at Oberlin College in Ohio, was another (in the United States he was strongly influenced by Booker T. Washington; in the late 1920s he was the first president of the South African Native National Congress, the precursor to the African National Congress).

But it wasn't until the consolidation of the pass laws in the four provinces and the introduction of Hertzog's first exclusionary legislation that black sentiment moved beyond a tribal horizon. The catalysing components were the white laws forbidding blacks access to land they considered theirs: the peasants reacted by retreat into mysticism, apocalyptic religions, and anger, the intellectuals by retreat into racial consciousness and anger. The Native Land Acts of the 1920s and 1930s were important because they struck at the heart of the tribal system and did the work for black nationalism that the Boer War did for the Afrikaners.

In the 1940s, black leaders of increasing sophistication were evident: Zaccheus Mahabane, Professor Davidson Jabavu, Dr. A. B. Xuma, the young Zulu chieftain Albert Luthuli, who later won a Nobel Peace Prize, and others. In the constitutional tinkering that stripped the blacks from the voters' roll in the Cape, the Hertzog government had set up the Natives Representative Council as a political sop to the opposition. It was never intended to be a body with any real power; its function was to advise, not to instruct. But in 1946, when it contained members such as Moroka, Jabavu, Luthuli, and Professor Z. K. Matthews, the council formally called for an end to all laws of discrimination. It was something of a watershed: before that, black leaders had attempted more to prove they were white at heart than to make demands; after that no black leaders of stature could advocate acceptance of anything less than complete legislative equality.

How to achieve this equality was another matter; in the 1940s the blacks were about as unified as the old Transvaal republicans had been a century earlier. Professor Jabavu, for instance, pushed for a pan-racial alliance, a new movement that transcended and therefore ignored race; for his pains he was derided as a naif, a parlour liberal. At the other extreme was the Zulu chieftain who led the 1905 uprising, Bambata, who advocated regaining the patrimony by armed struggle. For the most part he was dismissed as a Zulu chauvinist lost in some kind of Shakan romance; hardly anyone took a battlefield solution seriously at that time. Bambata might yet come into his own; he is the patron saint of the black township comrades who now sense that their moment is coming.

In the majority in the middle were the ideas that were to coalesce into the Native National Congress (later the ANC), though even here there were divisions, corresponding inexactly to the *verkrampte–verligte* split among the Afrikaners.

Professor Dube was the forerunner of Lembede and the Pan-Africanists; Pixley Ka I. Seme, an Oxford-trained Zulu lawyer, wanted black solidarity mostly for the purpose of winning extended liberty. In the end, Seme's ideas prevailed and formed the basis of the ANC and the Freedom Charter adopted in the late 1940s ("South Africa belongs to all who live in it, Black and White"). The charter was adopted at a 1955 conference at Kliptown, south of Johannesburg, attended by 3,000 delegates, most of them black. This was the so-called Congress Alliance, and it set up a steering committee consisting of the ANC, the South African Indian Congress, the South African Coloured People's Organization, and the white Congress of Democrats. There have been few meetings like it since.

Black tactics differed as much as black intentions did. There had been armed uprisings early in the century — Bambata in Natal, the Israelites in Transkei. There were a few black attempts to emulate Gandhi's South African successes among the Indians; they failed because Smuts showed none of the scruples in putting them down that he demonstrated for the world in his relatively tolerant handling of dissent among Gandhi's people — black uprisings and passive resistance alike were ruthlessly and efficiently suppressed. Through the 1930s there were sporadic attempts at resistance, usually Communist-led; the security police broke them up, often shooting a few of the leaders in the process and locking up the rest.

After 1948, the ANC was more successful in minimizing differences and in creating broad-based campaigns of civil disobedience. There were, however, still problems. Savage fighting broke out between Zulus and Indians in Durban; there were Zulu factional fights at the mines in Johannesburg and in the massive Durban township of Cato Manor; the ancient Xhosa–Fingo splits surfaced again; the Sotho were the targets of hostile demonstrations. The civil disobedience campaign of 1952 fizzled; the pass laws and the Suppression of Communism Act were used to jail its leaders; another attempt in 1955 was simply overwhelmed by the Afrikaners' show of military and police force. The same fate met the series of peasant revolts in the homelands in the early 1960s, which had been kicked off by drought, starvation, increased restriction on movement, and the destruction of tribal politics: all were put down without scruple and without effort.

But they were not without effect: the cumulative grievances strengthened the Pan-Africanist Congress, whose pass boycott provoked the massive over-reaction of Sharpeville and the jailing and banning of Robert Sobukwe. There followed the resort to sabotage by offshoots of both the PAC and the ANC; the creation of the ANC terrorist wing, Umkonto we Sizwe, and its PAC equivalent, Poqo; the "treason trial" at Rivonia for a multiplicity of defendants, black and white, which gave a public forum for the remarkable political credo of Nelson Mandela (the last time his words were published widely and legally in South Africa); and Mandela's own imprisonment, from which he had yet to emerge as the country moved into its 1987 election.

Towards the end of the 1960s Steve Biko began constructing Black Consciousness, a reaction to the severing of racial contacts through apartheid. Biko's South African Students' Organization broke with the white student union, NUSAS; it defined black not as a racial term but as a name for all those suffering oppression, of whatever colour. It stressed black solidarity, pride, and self-reliance; it naturally upset the white liberals, who never understood the need an oppressed class felt to escape the stultifying hand of white helpfulness. In 1972 it launched an adult wing, the Black People's Convention, whose aims were to create unity through black trade unions.

III

THE MAIN BLACK DISSENT is now centred in the ANC and its quasi-legal ally, the United Democratic Front. The UDF is an umbrella group with affiliated white, Coloured, Indian, and black groups. It's not membership-based — individuals can't join; but it acts as a front for independent constituent groups and is therefore hard to suppress.

Differing with the ANC's commitment to radical dissent and to working (violently if necessary) outside the system but in accord with its aims is the Inkatha movement of Gatsha Buthelezi. This is a Zulu organization, ethnically based, with a million paid-up members. It's also controversial. The ANC believes it to be dangerously accommodationist; it has also been accused of pushing for some kind of Zulu hegemony in whatever new South Africa is to be created — something Buthelezi consistently denies. Buthelezi is being pushed by the logic of events farther from his natural moderate stance — he cannot allow himself to be overtaken by newer and more radical Zulu leaders. In the mid-1980s he was beginning to signal to the imprisoned Mandela that he wanted a deal — that he felt he could work with Mandela in a post-apartheid South Africa.

In the political centre, with as large a white constituency as a black one (and as international a following as a South African one) are the church leaders. Among the most prominent are Dr. Allan Boesak, a dominee in the NG Mission Church, elected president of the World Alliance of Reformed Churches in 1982 and put forward as the first figurehead leader of the UDF in 1983; and Desmond Tutu, the Nobel peace laureate who is the Anglican archbishop of Cape Town.

To the right are the homeland leaders, in varying degrees of militant opposition to apartheid. But even the leaders of the Transkei have hinted that they'd like to reintegrate their territory into a unified and reformed South Africa.

To the left are the anti-capitalist and anti-Western groups like the Cape Action League and the Azanian People's Organization (AZAPO). To what degree the ANC is itself Marxist depends on who you listen to. The ANC Mission in Exile, led by Oliver Tambo, has always denied a socialist orientation; about a third of the ANC leadership is Communist, but to what degree they make (or would make) policy is unknown. Tambo himself had been responsible for pushing the ANC's youth wing leftwards in the mid-1950s, which helped Robert Sobukwe decide to break away with the Pan-Africanist Congress. Tambo's "Tambo Constitution," rammed through the ANC in 1957, cast the organization into a more authoritarian model, breaking with the moderate leadership of Albert Luthuli. Tambo has always deferred publicly to Nelson Mandela. Mandela, in fact, is the one black leader to whom everyone defers. He has often said that he's not a Communist but is in favour of social democracy. This has yet to be precisely defined or tested.

There are many conflicts in black politics. Only a few are tribal, and a few racially based (the Zulus have been accused of racial prejudice against Indians). There are splits between radicals and moderates, liberals and socialists, gradualists and revolutionaries . . . in almost all the "homelands," the black leaders now have detentions without trial and jails full of political prisoners, "having learned very well from their masters in Pretoria," as Helen Suzman, the Progressive MP and conscience of white liberals, has put it.

Virtually all black leaders agree on a desire for unity and are united in their abhorrence of apartheid. But unified tactics remain out of reach. There is much evidence that black leaders are scrambling to keep up with the militancy of their followers. It's why Sobukwe's writings and letters and Mandela's writings and speeches bear careful scrutiny: the Afrikaner has locked into his jails the men of moderation and is on a course of creating what he so desperately fears, a faceless black mass in whose future there will be no room for whites. It's in the black townships that the ultimate response to apartheid is being hammered out, only distantly from the political writings of the imprisoned leaders and more directly from the cumulative angers of millions of small indignities. No one yet knows the outcome.

Nothing in the townships is as simple as it seems. It's true that the faceless youngsters who patrol Soweto are disgusted by the system; they pour the liquor of the shebeens, the people's bars, down the gutters and burn with a flame of hatred; the acrid smoke of their favourite assassination device against "accommodationists," the gasoline-soaked car tires called "necklaces," is the purest testimony. The Bantu education system, which was supposed to "educate the native to his station," has been contemptuously rejected.

Worse, it has produced these young "comrades," who now fight side by side with the tsotsis, the young thugs, the most dehumanized victims of apartheid. Black workers returning to the townships are made to give the clenched-fist Black Power salute, and while their arms are raised their watches are stripped from their wrists and the money snaked from their pockets. The jittery police, who will now shoot anything, even a child, if it moves the wrong way, are bad enough; workers also have to reach home through a tight cordon of youths with dead eyes and long spikes cobbled up from bicycle spokes. An old friend, an elderly black woman, weeps because her son is a policeman and she thinks her house will be burned down and she murdered inside it. The townships are hell-holes because everyone is afraid. Transport drivers are afraid. Garbage collectors are afraid. Rent collectors won't go near the townships. Repairmen are afraid. Residents are afraid. God knows, maybe even the tsotsis are afraid. Blacks are killing blacks too, as ancient animosities take hold. But the Afrikaners should take no comfort from this. The black townships are a mass approaching criticality. Everyone searches for a way of defusing them: the Afrikaners, the other whites, the moderate black leaders — even the less moderate black leaders have cause for fear. No one yet knows if a way will be found.

Chapter 26

Lost in Africa: a personal memoir

I
—

I, TOO, GREW UP IN the Boer heartland.

My father was then working in Bloemfontein for that most curious of newspapers, *The Friend*, whose news coverage included the courts, provincial and city governments, and relentlessly local sports (the Under-12 School Soccer League received major play on the sports pages), but whose focus also took in the towns of the platteland — news of droughts, rains, and hailstorms from Winburg, Senekal, Welkom, Tweespruit, Thaba 'Nchu, Maseru, Brandfort, and the rest were big news. Later, after my father had moved on and I was myself working as a junior reporter on *The Friend*, my standard Sunday afternoon assignment would be the platteland weather round-up; I would spend hours on the crackling phone lines talking to dorp officials and rural landdrosts on the state of the crops and the mood on the farms in their areas — this was given decent play in Monday's edition. The assignment was also a deliberate ploy by the news editor, whom I remember only as "Klasie," to force his juniors to understand the nature of the people about whom and for whom we were writing. It worked. It gave us a feel for the heartland we could have got in no other way, and it made me friendships that lasted for years. The company also published the *Farmers' Weekly*, which was always well thumbed in the small dorps and on the farms, before commonly ending up recycled in the outhouses.

My grandfather, Jim de Villiers, died in 1944 when I was

still a child, and I remember him and the farm La Rochelle at Winburg only in a few vivid snapshots: the old man, grizzled and wheezing, drinking coffee on the stoop; the smell of the bluegum trees and the soft noises of the turtle doves; the many snakes — six-foot puff adders, swift water vipers in the irrigation furrows, nests of snakes on the koppies, beautiful and deadly; the sweet barn smells of grain and hay; the uneasy sounds of the flock as the farm workers culled one of them for the Sunday roast.

Of the black farm workers I remember hardly anything. Somewhere in my files I have a Box Brownie snapshot (a real snapshot, not a memory) of a grinning farm-hand draping a dead puff adder over a fence; of the incident I remember nothing except the snake's head pulled back in a snarl, dripping blood. I do recall the black village with its neat swept huts, its three-legged cook-pots, and the singing — there was always singing. My dominant memory is of the singing and of the smiles. Those good-natured smiles I suppose I simply assumed were friendliness; now I would probably take them for secret amusement, a hidden joke at our expense. I don't think there was any anger; in the 1940s we were still in the slow sleepy spring of race relations — the fevered summer was still to come.

Later, as I moved towards the teenage years, I spent time on other Afrikaner farms — with the van Zyls, the Reitzes, the van der Posts. After we learned caution in the bush — how to avoid the wild things of the African veld — we roamed farther afield and came across black children making their own games on the koppies and in the *dongas*, the eroded gullies caused by flash floods the rare times it rained. We would sit on the clay and play games with carved bones, or we would hold elaborate wars in the veld, sometimes lasting days or even weeks. But these were not race wars, never black against white; we looked not for community but for expertise in the weapons of our wars, the *kleilat* and the mudball. We drew no lessons from this. It was just the way things were.

If there were divisions, it was that boys did not permit girls to play these important games. There was nothing special about this. I gather that boys elsewhere behaved the same way, or they did then. At first we ignored girls, then we disliked them, swearing never to have anything to do with them. (The blacks always had more interesting blood oaths than we did, until one of us discovered Rider Haggard and then all of us, black and white, used some blood-curdling formulation from that odd creature's overheated imagination.) Later, of course, our attitudes changed again, and girls became the very focus of our lives and we followed them around, barking and capering like some idiot baboon troop. Black girls or white girls, it didn't much matter then. A girl was a girl.

It was about that time that I stopped going to farms very often, and so never took the logical next step. But I watched it happen in others: adolescent dreams turned to sexuality, and with sexuality came the discovery of power, and with power came the discovery of the larger political worlds of domination and submission, and the awareness that the races in South Africa inhabited different worlds: few white people had much contact with blacks after their adolescent years. South Africa's adult reality intruded.

II

WHEN I WAS AT high school in Bloemfontein, there were no blacks. I don't mean just in the classrooms — though there were none there, of course. I mean they hardly existed in our consciousness and in the consciousness of this most conscientious of schools; as late as the 1940s and even the 1950s, after Daniel Malan was in power and apartheid was taking on its legal trappings, the Orange Free State and its Afrikaner capital were still attempting to heal the wounds caused by *Milner se oorlog*, by Milner's war. Blacks were *there*, of course, but they were taken for granted. The focus of the school and of daily life was on relationships between English-speakers and Afrikaans-speakers.

Grey College had been founded a century earlier by the Cape governor, Sir George Grey, during the brief time of the Orange River Sovereignty. It was the oldest school in the province. It had no blacks, of course, and no girls either. But it was remarkable in another way: alone of the schools in Bloemfontein it was completely bilingual — lessons were interchangeably in English and Afrikaans, and teachers like my great-uncle, Leo Marquard's brother Davie, taught in English or Afrikaans as they pleased. There were also teachers who spoke only Afrikaans, and their pupils took lessons in Afrikaans. Similarly, there were others who taught only in English.

It was, I think, a good school and a brave experiment, and there were many teachers who spent their lives attempting to inculcate in our stubborn English and Afrikaner heads the virtues of tolerance. Their job was not made any easier by the ideologues in Pretoria, who set the official syllabus, or by the hardliners who dragged us off once a year to the Vrouemonument outside town to remember the deaths in the British Boer War camps.

The syllabus was a house crowded with Afrikaner memories and had few built-in closets for tolerance or understanding. It stipulated what legends were to be taught and what facts were allowed to be examined; other races and English settlers got fairly short shrift, and we learned in excruciating detail about the Voortrekker and Afrikaner heroes. The Boer War especially was laid out without care for the sensibilities of the "winners" (now become losers); most of our teachers wound their way through this minefield with what I now think was wonderful balance.

But even in this most tolerant of schools, official attitudes found their outlet. A young boy from England was hounded unmercifully, was pummelled and beaten up and called a *rooinek* (redneck, a contemptuous term for an Englishman, who tended to go bright red under the harsh sun). This young lad stuck it out and beat heads in turn on the rugby field; gradually he made a place for himself, but it left an ugly taste. And no one quite knew what to do with the group of kids from the south end of town, kids from the poor white slums whose fathers worked as menial labourers on the state railway system. They travelled as a gang and were filled with a dangerous rage that occasionally took itself out against the English but came to be turned against the blacks; the white proletariat was threatened first of all whites and moved into the modern age of confrontation sooner than anyone — theirs was never the politics of privilege: they were fighting for their place in the African sun, and they fought with an unnerving ferocity.

Later I came to know some of the people who lived on "the plots," small-holdings on the fluid boundary between town and farm. These were the rural poor, sons and daughters of poor farmers with no farms of their own. The contrast with the generous spirit of the farmers around Winburg was startling. These were people of pinched lives and circumscribed horizons; they clung to their old-fashioned Bibles and kept a picture of Dr. Verwoerd on their parlour walls. They were hospitable to their own and would share what little they had — scrawny chicken and *mieliepap* (corn porridge) for Sunday dinner, the best meal of the week. But their intolerance otherwise filled their lives. Unlike the inhabitants of the white slums, whose rage was undifferentiated, they remembered clearly the great figures of Afrikaner history: they were convinced the English had stolen their land from them and wanted to give what little they had left over to the "kaffirs." Of these kaffirs they knew little. They saw only a looming mass. They knew that if the kaffirs came, they themselves would lose everything. Their lives were spent brooding.

III

APARTHEID HAS EXISTED all my conscious life. We never had to be "taught" apartheid (it was never part of the school curriculum) because it was simply there. Even in my father's household, liberal by South African standards, blacks played no role whatever. We lived our lives in a white world.

And even later, after we became conscious of the larger world and I followed my father away from the teachings of the tribe, I could find no one who "believed" in apartheid. They simply took for granted it was necessary. What other course was there? They wanted to survive, and apartheid seemed to ensure that. *Finish en klaar*, in the bilingual phrase of the platteland. That was that.

IV

AT THE UNIVERSITY OF CAPE TOWN in the late 1950s the National Union of South African Students, entering its second generation, began to wake up to the ugly reality that apartheid had become. I suppose I woke up with it. The university's humanities departments contained a number of extraordinary scholars, among them the historian Leonard Thompson, now at Yale, and the social anthropologist Monica Wilson. Wilson was a tall, gaunt woman of strong character and stronger views; she was one of the few white South Africans who had utterly escaped the thrall of their history; her clear-eyed view of the country's ethnic mosaic and its probable destiny helped shift the thinking of more than two decades of students. NUSAS began to indulge more and more in radical politics.

The events of Sharpeville were a turning-point for many of us. I have described how the silent procession of 30,000 black men protesting against the earlier shootings marched menacingly past the university's ivy-covered walls; like most of my friends I watched as they passed, helpless to join in and equally helpless not to get drawn into the chilling thrill that is the scent of revolution. The marchers were persuaded to disperse peacefully by a police trick, and afterwards the Verwoerdian reaction set in as John Vorster, then minister of justice, turned the full fury of his security apparatus on dissenters. NUSAS was thereafter troubled by the same choices that disturbed the sleep of the women of the Black Sash: acquiescence? or revolt? Or if not those two, what?

After Sharpeville NUSAS split, some of its leaders, some of my friends, indulging in hopelessly amateurish attempts at sabotage and violence, others taking refuge in a kind of apolitical blindness. Many who could see only the white liberals being squeezed between two opposing illiberal forces (the Afrikaner state and an increasing black militancy) instead joined the "chicken run" and left the country for good, to become exiles in countries scattered mostly throughout the British Commonwealth. Most of those who left were not Afrikaners. Some of us were.

I myself took refuge in a British university. As my father had done before me, I spent a couple of years of postgraduate study at the London School of Economics. I learned nothing about Africa there (my major was Soviet government — it was interesting to study another totalitarianism at work); it's banal but true to say most of a South African's learning at the LSE came from the cosmopolitan nature of its population. In one seminar, an anthropology course from the grand old man of comparative ethnic studies, Bronislaw Malinovsky, we were 15 students from 13 countries; the London University hockey team, for which I played, had only one Britisher, a couple of Anglo-Indians, several Pakistanis, an assortment of Africans, a Goan or two, and one Afrikaner. It was suddenly easier to see what Monica Wilson had been trying to drum into our heads: the South African history we had been taught was less "history" than it was the expression of an oppressed people's longing, but that this longing conferred on it no legitimacy whatever — there were other peoples with longings too.

By 1965, after a detour in Canada, I was back in Cape Town, working as a reporter and feature writer on the Cape Town morning newspaper, *The Cape Times*. Dissent was already starting to bubble through the cracks of the weird edifice that had been made of apartheid. But there was no room for doubt in the minds of the ideologues and the bureaucrats. They simply slapped on more mortar. They would bind it in steel if necessary. If they had to.

V

THIS WAS THE PERIOD of the culmination of apartheid, and of the beginning of its end.

VI

DORA WILKERS IS A Xhosa from Cape Town; she was born in the city as her mother was and had never seen her "homeland," as "they" called the Transkei, until "they" forced her there. At the time of Verwoerd's assassination in 1966 she was in her mid-20s, a robust young woman with powerful arms, skin the colour of rich milk chocolate and a round moon face that wanted badly to laugh. She earned her living as a freelance domestic servant, doing laundry in white people's homes for whatever fee she could extract, which was usually pitifully small; even as late as the 1960s most affluent whites never asked themselves how blacks survived on less than a starvation wage. The whites simply assumed they managed somehow, or somehow needed less. Wilkers was Dora's married name. Her husband was not Xhosa, as she was, but Coloured, part of the genetic soup of the Cape.

This presented certain difficulties. By 1966 the Population Registration Act had been in force for six years, but the social engineers were just beginning to wrestle with its implications. Apartheid — the separation of people by ethnic origin — was impossible unless you could tell who was who. The matter was generally simple in the north: in the O.F.S., for example, they knew there were exactly 179 Indians; they knew the number of Coloured persons accurately. The Transvaal was more complicated but not substantially so.

It was in the Cape that the politics of separation clashed rudely with reality; Cape Town, the Tavern of the Seas, had lived with 300 years and more of ethnic slippage as the libido regularly conquered propriety; the population of Cape Town was hopelessly confused — neighbourhoods were confused, streets were confused, even families were confused; the more blurred the line, the less attention was paid it and the easier it was to cross. There were families with a rainbow of colours under one roof — a dark brother with the peppercorn hair of the Hottentot but the sharp Aryan features of the euro-peanized Malay, a pale-skinned blue-eyed sister with the glossy black hair of the Asian, a bronzed brother indistinguishable, truth to tell, from the mahogany tan of John Vorster himself. This was not unusual. There were, of course, clear white neighbourhoods with clear white families, obviously Malay neighbourhoods distinguished more by their religion and their style than by colour, and obviously Coloured neighbourhoods where dusty coffee and curiously bad teeth were the norm. But generally the older parts of the city, clustered around the Castle and the earliest free-burgher farms, were treacherously mixed.

By 1966 the bureaucrats of apartheid were turning their attention to the problem. I was then a reporter on *The Cape Times* and watched the process at work. Every person had to apply for an identity card, on which was to be inscribed that person's racial group — White, Coloured, Bantu, Asian, "Other," by which was meant, presumably, Arabs, Eskimos, American Indians, Uzbeks, or anyone else not specified in the catalogue promulgated by Parliament. Later, the Coloured group was itself subdivided, into Cape Coloured, Cape Malay, Griqua, Indian, Chinese, Other Asiatic, and Other Coloured. There was a clear hierarchy, with white at the top and Bantu at the bottom; the giveaway was in the fine print of the Prohibition of Mixed Marriages Act, where people were allowed to "marry down" without bringing the "down" person "up." The Population Registration Act carried through a similar scheme — a white person could, in theory, have himself classified downwards to Coloured, a Coloured person to Bantu, without bothering to evade any of the rigid restrictions imposed by attempts to go up the ladder. There were also grounds for appeal upwards, though upward mobility was harder to achieve.

The law, recognizing the sad state of the Cape genetic

pool, had hedged its definitions, so a white person under law was to be defined as "a person obviously white in appearance who habitually associates with white people." As you might imagine, this slippery definition allowed considerable scope for reclassification in a city as mixed as Cape Town, and since being white carried with it considerable privilege, families would push their whiter children out to play with other white children if they could. (Nothing changes: the Race Relations Survey of 1984 lists 690 people "reclassified" officially, including 462 Coloureds to Whites, 37 Coloureds to Indians, 31 Indians to Coloureds, 71 Blacks to Coloureds, 9 Whites to Chinese, and a whole permutation of other changes, including one Black to "Other Asian.") The loose racial definitions also meant giving over complete control to the bureaucrats on the classification tribunals who had the power to exercise compassion (and occasionally did) or to rip families apart (which they frequently did), forbidding by their decisions brother to live with brother, parent with child, husband with wife. Of all the many apartheid regulations and laws, this one was the most obscene.

Writing about its effects brought on some of us the unwelcome attentions of John Vorster's Special Branch, as the security police was called. I remember being summoned down to Cape Town's police headquarters one day; in the paranoid atmosphere of the time, I made sure to alert my father and every other influential person I could — people had been known not to return from such interviews. I was left for several hours in a small room furnished with a bed and a naked light bulb, then asked a series of naive but pointed questions ("Would you fight for your country if it was invaded by Communists?" and so on). I forget how I answered — I probably told them what I thought they wanted to hear.

In any case, Dora, who was Xhosa, married Cedric, whose card said he was Coloured. By law, they were not entitled to do this unless he voluntarily classified himself downwards to Bantu, with all the uncertainties and loss of privilege the decision entailed. He did what he had to do and went to live with his wife in the black township of Langa. And at once he entered a world almost as foreign to him as his was to the whites. He acquired a "homeland" whose language he couldn't speak and whose geography was hazy in his mind. He could no longer quit a job at will without losing for himself and his wife the precious permission to live in Cape Town, which had been declared by the Pretoria bureaucrats a "Bantu-free zone" — blacks were there only on sufferance, temporarily, as whites' "guests" and not as residents, a regulation that clashed sharply with the industrial demand for cheap labour and led inexorably to the miserable squatter camps on the grim sand flats outside the city. Cedric now had to carry a passbook that regulated his life and that had to be produced on the demand of any authority, including his employer, his landlord, the police — even a bus driver. He could no longer consider living in the city, on the slopes of Table Mountain, or in any of the traditional neighbourhoods his people had built and cultivated for centuries.

The trouble that followed was inevitable: he could not remember to carry the passbook at all times, as he was now required to do, could not accustom himself to the frequent demands for documents, which he was now required to produce. He was arrested, spent some time in jail, was arrested again, did another stretch. He lost his job, scrambled for another from an unscrupulous factory owner willing to risk employing an illegal at an even more pathetic salary. He was arrested again. In jail the Coloureds were fed scraps of meat; the blacks got thin gruel and porridge; their cells were damp and unheated. Coloureds got to wear shoes, blacks didn't. After a while his system protested, his resistance collapsed. The next time he was arrested he contracted pleurisy, and within a week he died, one more victim of a system that had made love a crime.

Dora was never even given permission to reclaim the body; she lost her husband and her right to live where she lived and her right to earn a living, and with them everything she cared about. She explained all this to us in our kitchen, in a voice tight with control, though her heart was bursting with sorrow; she explained it all before they took her and her two children and sent her away to the home she had never seen, there to be one of many thousands whose lives were destroyed by the neatness and the thoroughness of the bureaucrats of apartheid.

VII

THE "CASE" OF DORA WILKERS — for that's what it had become in the files of the Black Sash's Athlone Advice Office — never made the newspapers and so never impinged on public consciousness. There were hundreds like this, thousands. I remember one at random, a woman named Sybil Dwangu, who could get no legal place to live, though she was born in Cape Town. I have a scrap of a note, a mere flavour: "I was born here at Cape Town. We had a house but after I was divorced I had no house. I went to the office to report that I had no accommodation for my children. So they said I must get married again. But when I was married, the time I separated, I went to the office and asked for a house. He said I must get divorced first before I can get a house. Then I got divorced, and after that he said I must get married because I can't get a house if I'm not married. They said I must write my name on a waiting list. This went on from 1964 to 1982 . . ."

There are others, many thousands of others; some of them we wrote about in *The Cape Times* and other papers, and some of them passed by without any public recognition. But slowly, painfully slowly, the massive heartbreak the law was causing edged its way into the Afrikaner's consciousness. Now, from outside, we can only wonder why it took so long, how they had become so fenced into their chill moonlit landscape that the everyday misery they were causing was invisible. Every now and then the facts would intrude. The story of little Sandra Laing, the schoolgirl at Piet Retief in the Transvaal, was a case in point.

Though she was born of Afrikaner parents, a slumbering

gene had somehow awoken and the Laing child was dark-skinned, with the peppercorn hair of the Khoikhoi. For a few years she was left alone, but when it came time for her to go to school, the entire weight of the apartheid state descended on her and her family and hounded her from school and community, provoking even the Dutch Reformed Church to protest — was *this* the way to justice through separation? With the death of Verwoerd and his ability to focus the Afrikaners' attention on the big picture, the Laing child's case made its way into the uneasy tribal dream: this was surely never intended to be?

Young Sandra later married a black man and "escaped" that way from the tribe that had persecuted her, but her case history, and others, exploded like small grenades against the laager walls, some of them inexpressibly sad, others filled with a pathetic humour — there was a small village in the south-western Cape in which virtually every man was prosecuted under the Immorality Act for carnal knowledge of a person of another colour, in this case a large group of Coloured concubines who were coexisting happily with their Boer menfolk, in a community consequently filled with small children. A zealous officer of the apartheid state attempted to bring the matter to an end by separating women and children from their men, as the regulations demanded, but he was routed by the church and the whole matter was hushed up. But not before this, too, had slipped into the tribal consciousness: how can *this* be squared with the admonition to *skep u eie toekoms*, to build your own future? The apartheid state remained intact, but the stories circulated in public and in private, and even in the dream the legal structure that propped it up began to seem increasingly ugly.

A hard history had made for hard choices, but now a plaintive note began to enter public discourse: the Afrikaner had never intended to transform himself into a bully. Or had he? The uncompromising fierceness that had served him so well in the endless struggle worked when he was the oppressed. Now he was the oppressor. The uneasiness spread beyond the Afrikaner liberals onto the platteland itself. The vision, after all, *was* fatally flawed.

VIII

IF THE WORKINGS of the Population Registration Act caused hardships and heartbreak, the Group Areas Act, a piece of mass social engineering aimed at remaking the ethnic map of the country, caused, in the words of a Dutch Reformed Church report from the 1970s, "suffering too deep to understand." The ethnic engineers in Pretoria wanted to remake 300 years of history; in their rigid vision of an abstract "justice" they tried to undo 300 years of mixing. Everywhere, many thousands of people were suddenly "unqualified" to live where they were living. In Johannesburg, whole communities were uprooted and moved; what had been festering slums on the outskirts of the affluent white city became festering slums dozens of commuting miles away; in Durban the Zulus were shifted from the cities to massive shanty towns on the fringes of what had been Zululand. A few white farmers and a couple of tiny white communities were affected, but the burden was placed on the backs of the powerless and the unprivileged.

In Cape Town there were to be no blacks; the only black residents permitted were those on contract labour or those with a (difficult to prove) "historic right" to be there, plus a work permit, residence permit, and family permit. Black townships in the western Cape near Cape Town were therefore more dismal than most, containing as they did extensive barracks for single men, and when the authorities complained of the high crime rate and hooliganism in the townships, they seemed not to understand that whole communities of womanless young men could be primed for trouble.

Not even the Verwoerdians could assert that the Coloured community didn't belong in the Cape peninsula; but what they could do, and did, was to remake the ethnic configuration there — the Group Areas Act dealt with the big picture, but one of its lenses was a microscope, and no community, no street or row of houses, was too small to escape its scrutiny. Cape Town itself was still an ethnic jumble into the 1960s. There were Coloured families living a stone's throw from Parliament. Under the steep front face of Table Mountain, in the old suburb of Oranjezicht where we lived at this time, there were Coloured streets, blocks, houses mixed in with the white. South-east of the fort and east of city hall was District Six, an old and exotic area of small, intricately wrought-ironed Victorian houses, narrow streets, markets, cafés, spice and curry houses, brothels, gambling dens, jazz clubs, and various low-grade illegal activities like gambling and dagga (hashish) selling, where whites and Malays and Coloured people of all hues lived in a tangle whose language was the Afrikaans of the street and whose culture was peculiarly Cape. Some of us, outsiders who had cultivated a taste for the raffish, spent many evenings there, eating *waterblommetjiebredie*, a spicy stew of curried waterlilies, and drinking cheap Paarl wines. I had an Afrikaner friend who maintained that the Coloured whores of District Six had done more for South African race relations than all the churches put together (though possibly this says more about the conformist nature of the South African churches than it does about anything else).

Further to the south, dotted through the affluent white suburbs of Rondebosch (where the state president lives) and Rosebank and Newlands, there were small streets of white-washed stone houses, usually covered with vines and creepers, where Coloured families had lived for generations. On the lawns outside Kirstenbosch Gardens there was a small stone church that Coloured Christians had used for over a century. Further south yet, in the wide sweep of False Bay, were the communities of Kalk Bay and Fish Hoek, where the fishing fleets that served the Cape had plied their trade since the days of the first free blacks — fishing had always been a Coloured monopoly in the Cape. The next community was Muizenberg, whose beach was a lure for the whole country;

Muizenberg was white, Kalk Bay was Coloured; no one had paid much attention to these matters, since they had always been that way.

In the early 1960s the social engineers of apartheid turned their attention to this mess. From their offices in the Union Buildings in Pretoria they understood none of the sentimental roots of the Cape; instead of a prototype they saw only an aberration. It's doubtful they saw even the poverty and the slums. Although some token attempts were made to justify what they were about to do on the grounds of merciful slum clearance, they hardly bothered; the bureaucrats had eyes only for the master plan. As they had done when they stripped the vote from the Coloureds, they justified their actions on the grounds of a larger vision — in the end, there will be justice for all, you'll see.

Out on the featureless Cape Flats, the sandy plain between Cape Town's downy mountain and the craggy peaks of the Hottentots Holland, new communities were planted. The soil of the flats is beach sand, anchored only with difficulty by Port Jackson willow, once imported from Australia and now become a weed. Even on relatively calm days the Cape winds drive curtains of fine sand into everything; when the "Cape Doctor" south-easter gales are blowing the sand can cut like fine razors. Here they built Bonteheuwel, a product of the planner's mentality — straight streets, small houses, featureless architecture, shops and community centres spaced at maniacally regular intervals, playing-fields too far from anything, churches sprinkled through the whole with a cartographer's neatness. Here they were moving people from the old forests of Newlands tucked deep into the folds of the mountain; here they moved people from the whitewashed mews cottages of Rondebosch; here people were to come from the casbah of District Six, beloved of artists.

I interviewed the chief planner at the time. He was indignant at aspersions cast on his work and his vision. I should bear in mind, he insisted, that Bonteheuwel had (I remember the phrase) "all the socio-cultural amenities of a mature town

built into a new community," and he reeled them off —
schools, churches, meeting halls, a gymnasium; why, there
was even a swimming pool. I found this a chilling vision of
what made a community; for the Coloured people shifted
there from Newlands and District Six it was as if the blood
had been leeched from their public life. More than the
samosa sellers, fruit merchants, tavern-keepers, hookers, and
wideboys (street-smart petty hustlers in wide-shouldered
suits) had disappeared; so had all the life built up by hundreds
of years of settling into a place. The Afrikaner planners could
say of themselves, *Ek is hievandaan*, I am from here, but they
never understood that others could feel the same way.

Within a few years 70,000 people were uprooted from
their homes and the thing was done: the streets of Oranjezicht were cleared and gentrified; the whitewashed cottages of
Newlands were emptied for the white white-painters; the
fishermen of warm-water Kalk Bay had been forced to sail
their boats to the cold waters at the Atlantic side of the
peninsula (they had now to commute to the harbour of Hout
Bay, sometimes from as far as Bonteheuwel, 10 miles or so out
on the flats); the small stone church outside Kirstenbosch was
padlocked shut; and the bulldozers moved in on District Six.
It was then that we, my Canadian wife and I, left the country
again, this time to make a new life in Canada. The end of
District Six was a symbol, a symbol of a failed system and a
dream that went wrong. It has been a symbol for many others
too, a symbol that has lasted. Only Trevor Huddleston's
anguished cry (in *Naught for Your Comfort*) at the clearing of
Sophiatown outside Johannesburg caused as much of a stir as
the razing of District Six, and most of that had come from
outside the country. When District Six fell, Afrikaners and
English, Coloureds and whites lifted their voices in an angry
roar. It had no effect on the bureaucrats of apartheid, of
course, but in the long run it hastened the erosion that the
Sandra Laings and the other manifold injustices of the Population Registration Act had begun. This had surely not been
the plan!

Through the Vorster years, the great scar where District Six had been remained. It was going to be turned over to whites, at first, but that idea was abandoned. Then the government announced its intention to build a community college campus there. Nothing was done. Vorster fell in disgrace, and the scar remained. The rumble of black discontent continued to grow; the brown Afrikaners retreated from their kinfolk into sullenness and rage; the whites grew increasingly defensive as the bony ribs of apartheid became more and more exposed. In 1986, when I was last in Cape Town, the scar that the bulldozers had cut into the city's heart still remained. You could see it for miles across the flats, or from Paarl if you were coming in on the main road from the endless horizons to the north: a great slash across the gentle city, a continuing reminder of an attempt to compress life into a lifeless vision. Still standing in the midst of the desolation that had been District Six were the churches and the mosques, in silent witness to the violence that had been done: they hadn't dared to tear them down. The Afrikaner has called on his God often in his hour of need; that he doesn't dare offend Him now in His house is a sign that in his secret heart he knows what he has done . . .

POSTSCRIPT

Exeunt, under sanction

Postscript
Exeunt, under sanction

I

HARDLY ANYONE BELIEVES in apartheid any more, in the theology of apartheid, in the vision of apartheid as a just social order. No one believes in the grand vision of peaceful relations between independent ethnic states in a "commonwealth" of South Africa. The government doesn't believe in it; even the platteland no longer believes in it. Except in the wilder reaches of the Transvaal and in the fevered minds of Eugene Terre Blanche and the radical right (the bittereinders of their time) the Verwoerdian vision has decayed, and with it the last forlorn vestiges of the Afrikaner dream of communal withdrawal into self-sufficiency.

The Afrikaners are trapped. Out of uncertainty and fear they chose a route that seemed to promise them certainty and security, but which is now seen to have delivered more uncertainty than ever. No one any longer subscribes to the belief that through apartheid they could manage a just transition to a new order, and as the black revolt grows and the apparent inevitability of a transition to black rule approaches, the politics of privilege revert to the politics of survival — how to manage the transition, how to extricate themselves from the dream that soured, how to protect the group, the corporate identity that is the *volkseie*. Outsiders maintain that the insistence on group identity is nothing more than a mask for monopolizing material privilege; that if "white identity" were to mean lower incomes instead of higher, it would be abandoned. I have tried to show that this is an oversimplification. How, then, to find an exit?

Survival may not be a large enough moral posture to sell abroad, but on the other hand Afrikaner survival very likely *is* at stake. South Africa is not like the United States or Britain; political liberalism would destroy the ruling group's political power and therefore power over its own destiny. South Africa does not believe in apartheid any more, but nor do the Afrikaners believe the outside world's cant that the *eie* will somehow be miraculously protected under the new dispensation. They know they are being asked to quietly disappear in the name of a larger justice. What, then, to do?

If you take the long view, what is happening in South Africa is not a dénouement or a culmination at all but part of the continuous, seamless, and restless history of tribal realignment; it will continue long after the Change has taken place and long after the fickle world has lost interest in what happens there. Once black rule is in place, will the world continue to monitor events? Will the indignation level be sustained if things once again go wrong, this time against the Afrikaners? In South Africa's tribal realignment to date, only the Khoikhoi process was halted, and it too has resurfaced in the intractable form of the "brown cousins." The Xhosa process, delayed by the Wars of Dispossession, and the Zulu process, interrupted by the Voortrekker conquests, have resumed at Sharpeville, Soweto, Cato Manor, Langa, and Guguletu. The Afrikaner process, apparently halted by the Peace of Vereeniging but (apparently again) secured by the rise to hegemony of Afrikaner nationalism in 1948, is now again at risk.

What next? From Afrikaner to Zulu hegemony? To some other tribal coalition? To black racism instead of white? Is this what the world wants of the Afrikaners? Should they believe the soothing words of Oliver Tambo and Nelson Mandela? Why? Their own policies have made of Mandela an almost mystical leader. But Afrikaners have seen affairs go awry many times in their own history; should they now trust that

Mandela, who has been locked away by them for more than 20 years, will be able to control the pace and nature of events on his release? Must they now trust to black good will, having done their own worst to pervert it? Will they have any alternative but to call one more time on the bittereinders?

There have been many historic failures in South Africa, failures of nerve and of vision. The Dutch decision to rely on development through the slave trade was the first, a decision with long-delayed and unexpected consequences. The British too have much to answer for. Their decision to sell arms to the white tribe and not to the black tribes allowed the establishment of the Voortrekker republics in the north; their equivocation over the franchise in Natal and the Cape muted the emerging political voice of the Coloureds; their inexcusable abdication over the matter of the franchise at Vereeniging led directly to the present troubles.

None of which frees the Afrikaner, and to a lesser extent the English-speaking whites, from responsibility — they took control of their own destiny and made of it what they could and what their history demanded it should. Here too there were missed opportunities. If they had listened to the Afrikaner liberals they would have co-opted the brown cousins; they could have tried to co-opt the blacks. For a century there has been a large — by African standards — black middle class in South Africa; no attempt was made to give them a stake in the status quo. It's possible such an attempt would have failed — the middle classes have refused co-option elsewhere and have led revolutions rather than frustrating them (the Afrikaner regrouping after the damage of the Boer War was itself led by intellectuals of the middle classes). In any case, no such attempt was made. If the volk had listened to the liberals, they would have adopted the inclusive South Africanism that was implicit in some of Hertzog's writings and explicit in the politics of Jan Hofmeyr and the journalism of men like René de Villiers. They rejected all such views.

The white liberals failed in their turn, for reasons now clear. They were unable to extricate themselves from dependence on a conservative white electorate. For far too long they were obsessed with white unity, with healing the wounds of the Boer War, ignoring "the natives." And they could never quite understand the illegitimacy of creating even a more liberal dispensation for the blacks without consulting the blacks — almost to the end they believed justice was theirs to bestow. Most of them have now been shocked into awareness; but they are, on the face of it, powerless — why should blacks any longer care that some whites once cared?

There may be little in the Afrikaner's future but to control the manner of his going. This is not to say he is unimportant. It may be true, as Buthelezi put it in a conversation in 1978, that "the future is black and we blacks want our future now," and it may be true that the faceless youngsters who control the townships no longer feel it necessary to care how the whites respond, considering them irrelevant, but it is just how far down the Afrikaner will reach into his stern traditions and remembered bitternesses that will determine what kind of future the blacks will inherit.

There are, as we have seen, traditions of accommodation within Afrikanerdom, a small band of liberals who saw the laager for the trap it was. And there are also traditions of despair, of dismay — the hendsoppers of the Boer War. There are historic tendencies to schism — despite the myth of Afrikaner intransigence, Afrikaners are seldom united. But there is also a strong tendency, the outgrowth of a hard history and many bitter defeats, towards the ideas of the bittereinders. There are many Afrikaners who look to the Jewish Masada; for the bittereinders the loss of identity and the erosion of the will to survive as a volk come gradually to seem less terrible than the alternative, which is . . . apocalypse. Those Afrikaners, fuelled by the richness of their anger and the strength of their dismay, could be driven to make the world at least take notice of the manner of their going. Western leaders, in their blind insistence on scoring easy moral points, seem not to notice, nor to care, that they might cause what they claim to want to avoid. No one seems to care that South Africa has developed nuclear weapons. You cannot use the Bomb against internal enemies, they say. I say, look to Masada!

The Western world cannot reach the extreme right; it doesn't need to reach the moderate left. But it must somehow reach the disillusioned and fearful middle. There is a warning bell echoing down from Jewish history, and the world must take notice of its insistent clamour: it *must not* go unheard.

Schism, as we have seen, is fundamental to the tribal nature. It should be exploited. In a modern state, moral legitimacy keeps the population compliant, but it matters more to the rulers than the ruled. The modern state is efficient: we have seen here and elsewhere how it can rule without the consent of the ruled — how legality can substitute for legitimacy. Nevertheless if the rulers lose their sense of their own legitimacy, the will to rule is diminished. That the Afrikaner regime is now morally bankrupt is, ironically, one of South Africa's best hopes — it means that other Afrikaner ideas might emerge, as they have in the past. The ethos of Winburg is not dead: why cannot the outside world devise a policy to revive it, instead of policies that push the Afrikaners to follow their leaders no matter what?

II

I WRITE AT A TIME when some sanctions are in force against South Africa and more substantial economic sanctions are coming. To what end? Sanctions are notoriously tricky to make work — it only needs one evader to negate them, and they can stiffen the resolve instead of weakening it. Sanctions can only work if there is a clear objective in mind. What does the world want them to cause to happen? Does the world have a clear idea?

Will they weaken the Broederbond and the Verwoerdian bureaucrats still entrenched in the ministries? Will they encourage the *verligtes* at the expense of the *verkramptes*? Will they encourage Afrikaner schism, and if so to what end? Will they help reorient Afrikaner legitimacy, separate it from its history of conquests and defeats, and encourage the Afrikaner liberals to reinvent the old inclusiveness? Will they encourage a new political dispensation, and if so, what? Do their proponents understand the tribal process? Do they understand that the Western world is demanding group suicide?

Do the political leaders calling for sanctions even understand the questions, or do they act as if South Africa is just one large violation of civil rights, as if it were nothing more than Selma, Alabama, writ large? Does it matter how the black majority reaches power in South Africa? Is there indeed a black majority, or are there just black tribes, as there are white ones? Does the West want to see a relatively bloodless transformation to a democracy that will stay within the West's orbit? Are the sanctions for real, or just a cynical way for Western countries to ingratiate themselves with those they take to be the inheritors? (If so, they are both cynical and doomed: half-hearted pandering never won over any revolutionaries.) Will sanctions encourage the political ferment within South Africa, or drive the Afrikaners farther into the laager?

The ferment is there. Afrikaners, after all, published 2,500 books in their language in 1986, a huge percentage of them political. There is a lively traffic in new political journals, such as Hermann Giliomee's *Die Suid Afrikaan*, in which Afrikaner heresies are being explored and dissected.

With the collapse of the theology of apartheid, all that the nation's leaders have left is the structure, the ugly reality exposed without its ideological cladding. None like what they see, but they're out of options. There is a dead centre at the heart. All they have left is survival. In an ideological vacuum, they are left with *ad hoc* decision-making, an equal mix of panic and resolution, and an absence of clear direction. They can only react to events, not guide them. Even the Broederbond can do little more than continue to impress on its members the need for ethnic discipline; it has no ideology to put in apartheid's place.

The government is faced with growing right-wing resistance, mislabelled in the West as some queer form of Nazism but more precisely a lower-class revolt against sudden economic insecurity and the narrowing economic gap between black and white; one of the costs of sanctions has been to fan the flames of the ancient tribal fears. But there is some comfort to be taken here: the deadness at the centre means the Afrikaners are freer to think as individuals again. One of the small hopeful signs has been the declared intention of the organized student body at the University of Stellenbosch, the cradle of the tribe, to open talks with the ANC.

Moral bankruptcy and ideological confusion open the door to more pragmatic solutions. But what solutions?

What the outside world misses, and what no one's policy has been designed to let surface, is the common ground—the deep reservoir of interracial good will still existing, incredibly, in South Africa in spite of the manifold injustices stretching over generations. One reason is built into the Afrikaners' fiber: their deep belief in the *volkseie* prevented them from indulging in cultural imperialism; unlike the British, they never attempted to make their way the only way and left black culture largely intact—even if as much through neglect as by deliberate policy. This good will persists despite the escalating violence by whites, and the escalating response by blacks. It persists despite the undeniable brutality of the police and prison system, despite the torture (only rarely punished), despite the locking into prisons of schoolchildren, despite the unexplained deaths in police custody. And it persists despite the retaliatory violence, despite the revenge bombings, despite the now discredited "necklacings," many of them by those same schoolchildren.

Frederik van Zyl Slabbert's ringing call, in his book *The Last White Parliament*, for a national convention of all races to discuss a constitution was not an idle one. The Afrikaners and the Zulus and the Xhosa and the Sotho could talk, secure in the knowledge of their Tribal Own. They all understand that they all belong. They all accept that there are no colonialists in South Africa, to be packed back to the mother country when their time is up. (In any case, emigration could not be an option. Where would they go, these 5 million whites? This intractable 15 per cent?) All the blacks have accepted and still accept that whites are natives too. But will they talk? Where is the desire? Where is the policy from outside that would encourage it?

There is a perilous edge between Masada and the accommodationists: the old debates are open again. Yet the West is saying there is no middle ground between an all-out assault on the Afrikaners and complete moral betrayal.

In the midst of the rioting towards the end of 1985, in the Johannesburg offices of Nelson Mandela's lawyer, I spent much of an afternoon listening to anecdotes that showed how unembittered Mandela remains — how he remains as adamantly against black domination now as he has been steadfast against white domination for 20 years; Winnie Mandela, the same afternoon, called South Africa a sick and racist society but insisted she held no animus against anyone, even the Afrikaners — there is no reason why we cannot share the country, she said.

South Africa is full of mixed messages. As his township went up in flames, I had a grave conversation with a young man about chess. In Cape Town, John Kani and Winston Ntshona put on a play called "The Island" before a largely white audience; it's a play about the prison of Robben Island, dedicated as an endorsement "of the local and international call for the immediate release of Mr. Nelson Mandela." The audience approves the play and its dedication both. In the townships, factional fighting goes on; but in November the cricket season was beginning, and 15,000 white and Coloured people spent a lazy summer afternoon at Newlands cricket-ground, watching a match in which black players and white buffeted each other good-naturedly. Beyond the picket fence the state of emergency clamps down, the police open fire at a funeral, and in the townships a black mob impales a small black boy because his father is a policeman. A very strange society, indeed.

The government announces the end of the Mixed Marriages Act and then solemnly, with due bureaucratic zeal, publishes a catalogue of expected permutations: the government wants people to know where the children of such marriages can be slotted in. The government in Pretoria announces the end of "petty apartheid" — Cape Town's beaches are now open to all races. The conservative provincial council denounces the action and says the segregation signs will remain. Cape Town city council declares that the police will simply ignore those signs; a week or so later it formally declares that the city will no longer pay any attention to any apartheid regulations. The government is silent; it doesn't know how to respond. The pass laws are abolished, a belated admission that influx control has failed; job reservation slowly falls to economic necessity.

There is change everywhere. Nowhere is it seen to be enough.

The world is in a hurry, having failed to notice for centuries. All over the Western world apartheid has become the fashionable cause. Musicians, men and women of great good will and small political insight, generously raise money for the fight. On campuses everywhere it is the one issue that stirs an apathetic student body. Some good reporting is being done, but most media coverage is stunningly ignorant. In the national media of the country I long ago adopted there is an almost pornographic eagerness for the cataclysm to happen — almost as if they want to whip the Afrikaners. A morally bankrupt prime minister tries to salvage his credibility by making easy common cause with the frontline states, as South Africa's neighbours are called. And so on and so on and so on. South Africa is an international pariah, and its people have brought it on themselves. It is also a scapegoat: the Western world's moral indignation can legitimately be viewed with the deepest cynicism.

In the absence of a controlling ideology, the South African government no longer knows what to do. There are nationalist MPs in Parliament who remember the Afrikaner poet Van Wyk Louw's promise that the Afrikaner would be "a bridge between the heroic west and the magical Africa," and they are ready for change; I was at school with one, and he confides in the parliamentary dining room that he is ready for the "dramatic gesture," but he doesn't know what this gesture may be. There are other MPs, likely the majority, who still believe it is the Afrikaner's special task to bring about change; they don't yet understand the contradiction. Very likely the present government will prove incapable of any such gesture anyway; its political base is too narrow. It is caught without manoeuvring room in a world context that will demand nothing less than a complete transformation. Its own policies have trapped it; the outside world makes the trap more secure.

The opposition is demanding "social democracy," whatever that is. In the West it's a code-word for socialism, but in South Africa it seems to mean anything anyone wants it to, as long as it means demolishing white domination. Does the imposition of sanctions give to the imposers the right to demand definitions?

The Buthelezi entourage is floating the rumour of the "Natal option" — maybe the government will make a real power-sharing deal with the Zulus, turn over to them the province of Natal, giving blacks for the first time a major port and real power . . . The cynical say that if it did happen it would only be because Natal has few Afrikaners and many English. Would the Natal option be a sufficiently dramatic gesture to impress the townships? No one thinks so; nothing less than the release of Mandela and the calling of a genuine national convention will do any longer. (On the other hand, it would give the Afrikaners 6 million formidable allies.)

Soweto has become a metaphor for change, for the transition to come. There are now Sowetos everywhere. Everyone speaks of the Change. Some speak of it with foreboding. But — and this is new — there are those, whites among them, who look to it with eagerness.

There are even queerer rumours among the Afrikaner élite. The extraordinary option of calling on the Soviet Union for help has been considered — offer the Soviets the naval base at Simonstown in return for their help against the guerrillas, reject the West utterly . . . It has the satisfaction of drama (that would show them!) but not of politics — why would the Russians care? They have only to wait, and South Africa will be theirs. Or so they believe. Will the West prevent it?

On the other end of the scale a book written by two conservative white South African libertarians, Leon Louw and Frances Kendall, unexpectedly hit the bestseller lists and stayed there, attracting a bizarre set of approving readers: Hendrik Verwoerd's son liked it. So did a number of nationalist Cabinet ministers, the Anglo American Corporation (which helped fund it), Buthelezi, and Winnie Mandela herself. The Solution, as the authors call their Utopian vision, involves the by now shop-worn libertarian thesis that big government is the problem; the authors propose that the solution lies in radical decentralization, creating from the country's 306 magisterial districts 306 quasi-autonomous mini-states — Stellaland and Goshen revisited. What enfeebled central government existed would have strictly circumscribed powers; it would almost certainly be black dominated, since the authors argue it should be composed of all political parties through proportional representation. Well, and why not? Is there some way the proposal could salvage the savaged *eie*? Could the Afrikaner accept a retreat to the platteland, there to brood in his tiny homelands, small laagers as breastworks against the restless black sea? A very strange society . . .

The election of 1987 was more fluid than any since 1948,

mostly because of these unknowns, because of this uncertainty, because of this emptiness at the core. Afrikaners everywhere were pushing for reform. Nowhere was the nature of this reform spelled out in detail. No one knew how it would go.

It went, of course, to the right. Botha's National Party maintained its stranglehold on Parliament, with 123 seats in the new House, but the right-wing Conservatives pulled ahead of the PFP (the Progressives), 22 seats to 19. It was the purest expression of the politics of survival: fear drove the Afrikaners to the right — fear of the ANC, fear of the UDF, fear of the future, fear of dangers known and unknown, but mostly fear of the disintegration implied by loss of control.

This is what the election of 1987 meant: fear drove the Afrikaners deeper into the laager; van Zyl Slabbert had been right to resign — there was no future for a whites-only opposition; the outside world, "in the mistaken belief that a ruined economy would lead to political paradise" (Alan Paton's phrase), would impose further sanctions and make things worse; Botha and Buthelezi and Mandela remained the three men on whom everything hinged. But in the end, it all came back to the Afrikaner and his melancholy history: he had "won" his struggles with the British and the blacks. Would he now lose the struggle with himself?

How to extricate themselves? "Unweave themselves," in the poet Breyten Breytenbach's phrase, "from the unending self-created plaitwork of a bureaucratic totalitarianism"? The black demand and the world demand is clear: the survival of the Afrikaners is less important than justice, because there are more blacks than whites. True, but this is mathematics, not politics, and it solves nothing: that way lies Masada.

The export to South Africa of British-style politics — the so-called Westminster model — failed because nowhere in its parliamentary theory did it take account of ethnic divisions. The centrifugal forces, it turned out, were more powerful than the cohesive ones — tribal communal loyalties proved stronger than any national ones that emerged, and as such local loyalties did in other parts of Africa, the *eie* proved stronger than attempts to transcend it. The idea of survival was more persuasive than the willingness to risk a leap into the Great Unknown. Who is to say other tribes would have done better?

So what's left? A degenerative collapse of all authority? A continuing state of siege? A racial federation? A return to the Verwoerdian dream of a mini-commonwealth of ethnically based mini-states, only this time more fairly managed? A central Parliament in which the tribes have an absolute veto over matters that affect their own affairs? P. W. Botha was reaching for this when he revised the constitution to set up racially based assemblies whose powers were divided into National Affairs and Own Affairs, but he remained a creature of the apartheid bureaucracy and a prisoner of his electorate and was unable to bring himself to genuinely share power.

Could business help? The Afrikaner business community represents a power centre increasingly at odds with the government. Unrest is bad for the bottom line: businessmen supported apartheid until it began to damage the economy. The South African economy is modern enough to need a work-force that at least marginally shares its values — the more sophisticated the economy, the easier it is to sabotage. Business could be persuaded to act in its long-term interests and to opt for pacification rather than repression; this is already happening to some degree. The widening split between economic and political power-holders increases the possibility of change: another small comfort here.

Political power-sharing solutions are being argued in the South African academies and among people of good will of all races. The academic version is called "consociation"; though it varies in its details, it is generally taken to mean communal rather than geographic representation. It involves a formal recognition of South Africa's tribal nature. Central power would be distributed proportionally; each tribe would have complete internal autonomy; there would be no geographic separation and no territorial "homelands" — apartheid of the mind, not the body.

The plan involves almost insuperable difficulties — where to find leaders who could claim legitimacy from the tribe and yet govern with the moderation the system would demand? Even to contemplate such a solution would demand an eerie moderation on the part of the Great Disaffected in the townships and a self-abnegating rejection of the politics of survival on the part of the Afrikaners — these would be dramatic gestures on a grand scale. But the sanctions-driven alternative would be a continuing deterioration, a continual escalation of urban violence, until the beloved country were governed by a killing frenzy. If this happens the West will have to take some of the blame.

The grandest gesture of all would be reconciliation through a national convention, as Slabbert has demanded. There are after all interesting precedents for this in Afrikaner history — the spirit of conciliation that prevailed at the convention that led to union in 1910, for instance, when defeated Boer sat down with victorious English in amicable discussion. There was also the multiracial Congress Alliance of 1955; although this did not include the Afrikaners it set a precedent for the way such gatherings might work. If the South African government were to pass enabling legislation for a constitutional assembly on the basis of one person, one vote, this single act would restore political legitimacy lost through decades of apartheid's fraudulent promises.

Heribert Adam, the Canadian academic, has suggested such an assembly in his book South Africa Without Apartheid. Delegates, he says, could be elected through proportional representation, which would guarantee that all interests would be represented, the strength of each competing claim fairly recognized. Working coalitions would emerge around constitutional agreements. The new constitution would be put to the test of a referendum. Pretoria would still be in control until the new constitution had passed its major tests. After all, the government would have set the terms by initiating the process. What at present may seem like voluntary suicide might yet appear the most rational way in light of worse alternatives.

Soothsaying is an occupation full of perils. There have been many attempts made in South Africa. One of the best known was by Arthur Keppel Jones, whose book *When Smuts Goes* forecast dire consequences for South Africa, some of which have come to pass and some of which have not. (The book prompted a sardonic response from Alan Paton: "Keppel Jones, Keppel Jones/Let me ask you in sepulchral tones/ The night was so stark/The dark was so dark/How could you see when you threw the bones?")

In a pamphlet he wrote for Potchefstroom University's Institute of South African Politics, my father threw a few bones of his own:

> I believe . . . group identity [will become] recognized only in the proportion that it's useful, profitable and desirable, but without race classification, without job reservation, without mandated separate facilities. Why not? Just as English and Afrikaans literature complement and enrich each other, so can population groups, without one having to oppress any of the others. No reasonable person can deny the complicated pluralism of our society; what we need is a formula that will assist the components of that pluralism to work together to produce a new form of citizenship.

Has the outside world the stomach to follow policies that would help achieve such a transition? Any change that comes would mean a dramatic lowering of white living standards. The West has been obsessed with punishment. Why not offer rewards? Instead of the stick, why not the carrot? Why should the West not mobilize massive resources, promise huge amounts of aid to keep the post-Change economy healthy and its social relations honest, to make South Africa into a example of the best of Western thinking instead of the worst? In a world where Ireland and Lebanon and Kampuchea exist, could we not use such an example, the focus for a moral crusade? Would the world not feel better having created something rather than merely having prevented something worse? South Africa could yet become the crucible for social change the dreamers have dreamed of. The raw material of malleable raw emotion is there to be worked with. This is a naive vision and unlikely. But the West will damage its own economies through sanctions — why not through creative giving, massive aid with substantial strings attached? And in any case, where are the alternatives?

There are Afrikaners whose hearts are large enough to make the dramatic leap, Afrikaners who can see in the Great Trek an adventure of the spirit and not a retreat from reality; when they think of the trek they are reminded not of grievances left behind but only of the restless search for new horizons, for the endless blue horizons of the African interior. For them, the Afrikaner *volkseie* is a large enough space to contain fresh spiritual horizons of its own, a place for the tribe to go, the safe haven ultimately found, finally a place for dreaming. Of course, Afrikaner history is against them. There have been many sour defeats and there is great fear. The growling of the black masses and the clamour of the outside world intimidate smaller spirits. The horizons are closed off, the Thirstland no refuge, Beulah only a wistful memory, a dream never claimed. For the moment, the laager stands.

SOURCES

The libraries are full of general histories of South Africa. Their points of view vary from right-wing polemics through the magisterially dull centre to lively but empty exercises in Marxist rhetoric. I have been dipping into this sea of words since I was at school, and for the last year or so have been virtually submerged. The waters were not always very clear: there was much silt, of various hues and textures, and currents going in all directions at once . . . A lifeline, then:

The Oxford History of South Africa. General editors: Monica Wilson and Leonard Thompson. 2 vols. (London: Oxford University Press, 1971). An indispensable general history, the first to attempt a genuine history of all the people of South Africa. Contains some excellent chapters, especially by David Welsh, Leo Kuper, René de Villiers, and others. Kuper's chapter on African nationalism was censored from the South African edition.

Davenport, T. R. H. *South Africa: A Modern History.* First published in 1977 by Macmillan in London. The third edition, issued in 1987, was published in the U.S. and Canada by the University of Toronto Press. Davenport shares the virtues of Wilson and Thompson, and therefore their point of view. His presentation is structurally more orthodox. For the non-initiate, this is likely the only general history needed.

A few others I have used as checking material for the present volume:

de Kiewiet, Cornelius. *A History of South Africa* (London: Oxford University Press, 1957). Solid and old-fashioned.

de Klerk, W. A. *The Puritans in Africa: A Story of Afrikanerdom* (Harmondsworth, Eng.: Penguin, 1976). An odd book, mystical and solid in turns. Hermann Giliomee, among others, has strongly criticized de Klerk's reliance on the Afrikaner's Puritan heritage as an explanation of virtually everything, but the book is still worth reading. Solidly rooted in the Afrikaner psyche.

Elphick, Richard, and Giliomee, Hermann, eds. *The Shaping of South African Society 1652–1820* (Cape Town: Longman Penguin, 1979). A history, but also a strongly argued point of view. Aimed at the specialist (and contains several chapters of specialists arguing with other specialists), but for the most part plainly and clearly written.

Marquard, Leo. *The Story of South Africa* (London: Faber and Faber, 1968) and *The Peoples and Policies of South Africa* (London: Oxford University Press, 1969). Two popular histories by one of the founders of South Africa's Liberal Party, with a strong small-l liberal point of view.

Theal, George McCall. *History of South Africa from 1503 to the Conquest of the Cape by the British in 1795* (London: Swan Sonnenschein, Lowery & Co., 1887). Magisterial, exhaustive, and underestimated.

van Jaarsveld, J. A. *The Afrikaner's Interpretation of South African History* (Cape Town: Simondium, 1964). For the non-Afrikaner, something of a curiosity.

PART 1
Jacques and Abraham de Villiers: the establishment of the Way

The material on the de Villiers family in France was derived from personal research in the hinterlands of La Rochelle, from family documents and letters, from Boucher (see below), and to a lesser extent from Dan de Villiers's *History* (see below).

The story of the family's arrival at the Cape and the early Huguenot settlement came from family documents in the possession of the author, from the archives at Cape Town, from the many publications of the Van Riebeeck Society in Cape Town, from correspondence between Delft and the Dutch governor at the Cape (on file in Cape Town), from Graham Botha (see below), from the genealogical tables compiled by Christoffel Coetzee de Villiers (see below), and of course from numerous general histories.

Among the books I have drawn on:

Arbousset, T., and Daumas, F. *Narrative of an Exploratory Tour to the Cape of Good Hope* (Cape Town: Struik, 1968; facsimile reprint of the 1846 edition). Pious and cynical at the same time. Good observations of native life.

Botha, Graham. *The French Refugees at the Cape* (Cape Town: Struik, 1970; first published in 1919). Probably interesting only to the descendants of said refugees. Contains ships' manifests and other useful data.

Boucher, M. *French Speakers at the Cape: the European Background* (Pretoria: University of South Africa, 1981). Dense with information.

de Villiers, Dan. *A History of the de Villiers Family* (Cape Town: Nasionale Boekhandel, 1960). Eccentric, but there are nuggets for those of us who are written about. Dan discovered some useful documents in the Cape archives, many of which I subsequently consulted.

de Villiers, Christoffel Coetzee. *Genealogies of Old S.A. Families.* Revised and updated by C. Pama. 3 vols. (Cape Town: Balkema, 1966). Exhaustive — a life's work. I reviewed Pama's revised edition in *The Cape Times* when it was reissued in 1966. Unfortunately for me, he had misplaced my father by one generation and effectively written me out of history. *Tant pis*. The book is otherwise (I believe) solid.

Elphick, Richard. *Khoikhoi and the Founding of White South Africa* (Braamfontein: Ravan Press, 1985). First published as a

Yale PhD thesis in New Haven and London in 1975. Elphick has helped to rescue the Khoikhoi, or Hottentots, from historical oblivion: most South African historians paid them no attention. He has helped give background to what is, after all, one of South Africa's largest ethnic groups.

Fagan, Gwen and Gabriel. *Boschendal Renascent*. Undated pamphlet published by the current owners of the Boschendal estate, Rhodes Fruit Farms, on the occasion of the restoration of the manor house.

The Van Riebeeck Society has issued dozens of fascinating historical documents, reprinting many lost to the general public. Recommended titles include:

- *The Diary of Adam Tas 1705-6*. Fouche and Smuts, eds. (Cape Town: VRS, 1970).
- Heinrich (Henry) Lichtenstein. *Travels in South Africa*. 2 vols. (Cape Town: VRS, 1928).
- *The Journal of Hendrik Wikar 1779 & The Journals of Jacobus Coetse Janz 1706 & Willem van Reenen 1791*. E. E. Mossop, ed. (Cape Town: VRS, 1935).
- Carel Brink. *The Journey of Capt. Hendrik Hop into Namaqualand 1761 and Ensign Tobias Rhenius 1724* (Cape Town: VRS, 1947).
- Thompson, George. *Travels and Adventures in Southern Africa, parts 2 and 3*. V. S. Forbes, ed. (Cape Town: VRS, 1968).
- Sparrman, Anders. *A Voyage to the Cape of Good Hope, Towards the Antarctic Polar Circle Round the World and to the Country of the Hottentots and the Caffres, from the Year 1772–1776*. 2 vols. V. S. Forbes, ed. (Cape Town: VRS, 1975 and 1977).

PART 2
Pieter Jacob de Villiers and the Century of Wrong I: the search for Beulah

Few family documents survive from this period: the frontier

farmers were too busy to keep notes. What small scraps exist I have mentioned in the text. The local tax assessors kept some farm notes; there are slave registers on file in local archives. Henry Lichtenstein, the indefatigable German tourist, proved useful too, since he ran into family members here and there. The missionaries left, as missionaries are wont to do, copious propaganda for their cause. Beyond that, it was a matter of sifting prejudices. Afrikaner historiography is angriest on this period, and its rhetoric most strident. Apart from these sources and the general histories, these books proved useful:

Guy, Jeff. *The Destruction of the Zulu Kingdom* (Johannesburg: Ravan Press, 1982). Places the blame where it should lie, on the British.

Heese, J. A. *Slagtersnek en Sy Mense* [Slagtersnek and its people] (Cape Town: Tafelberg, 1973). Claims to be a "re-investigation," and does contain some new material. I used it to check family connections. Published in Afrikaans only. Heese has also published a book tracking the ethnic origins of the Afrikaners: *Die Herkoms van die Afrikaner 1657–1867* (Cape Town: Balkema, 1971).

Legassick, Martin. "The Northern Frontier to 1820: The Emergence of the Griqua People," in Elphick and Giliomee, *The Shaping of South African Society* (see above).

Philip, John. *Researches in South Africa*. 2 vols. (New York: Negro Universities Press, 1969; reprint of the Christian Mission edition of 1828). This is the infamous Philip of Ordinance 50 at his polemical best: propaganda of a very high order. Like many of the missionaries of the time, Philip was more intent on politics than theology, and it shows.

Ritter, E. A. *Shaka Zulu* (Harmondsworth, Eng.: Penguin, 1978). Romanticization of the Zulu tyrant.

Theal, George McCall. *History of the Boers in South Africa 1887* (Cape Town: Struik, 1983; reprint). Like his general history: meticulous but a touch ponderous.

Thompson, Leonard. *Survival in Two Worlds: Moshoeshoe*

of Lesotho 1786–1870 (London: Oxford University Press, 1975). Excellent biography of a fascinating character.

van der Merwe, P. J. *Die noordwaartse beweging van die boere voor die Groot Trek* [The northwards movement of the Boers before the Great Trek] (The Hague: undated).

PART 3
Jacobus Johannes Luttig de Villiers and the Century of Wrong II: Blood River and the consolidation of the tribe

The material on the family's penetration into the interior came once again from family documents and also from information supplied by the Huguenot Museum in Fransch Hoek, with an assist from the Genealogical Project files of the Church of the Latter-Day Saints (Mormons), who preserve in their Salt Lake City archive many useful marriage, birth, and death notices from obscure South African villages.

Some more general sources I have drawn on:

de Kiewiet, Cornelius. *British Colonial Policy in the S.A. Republic 1848–1872* (London: Longmans Green, 1929). Respectable, academic, and dry.

de Kiewiet, Cornelius. *The Imperial Factor in South Africa* (New York: Russell & Russell, 1966). Respectable, academic, slightly less dry.

Grobbelaar, Pieter. *Die Vrystaat en Sy Mense* [The Free State and its people] (Cape Town: Tafelberg, 1980). In Afrikaans only. Glimpses of daily life in the Boer heartland.

Haggard, H. Rider. *Cetywayo and His White Neighbours, Recent Events in Zululand, Natal and Transvaal* (London: Kegan Paul Trench Trubner, 1906). Disreputable history, but lively reminiscences.

Hofmeyr, J. H. *The Life of Jan Hendrik Hofmeyr (Onze Jan)* (Cape Town: Van de Sandt de Villiers Printing, 1913). An oddity, written when the younger Hofmeyr was 17. Useful documents. Contains many of Hofmeyr's speeches that would otherwise have been lost, and is good on Afrikaner Bond politics.

Muller, C. F. J. *Die Oorsprong van die Groot Trek* [The origins of the Great Trek] (Cape Town: Tafelberg, 1974). Not available in English. Solid, respectable, and orthodox.

Muller, C. F. J. *A Pictorial History of the Great Trek* (Cape Town: Tafelberg, 1978). Good collection of Trek memorabilia, with apposite commentary.

Schoeman, Karel. *In Liefde en in Trou: die lewe van pres en mev M.T. Steyn* [In love and in faith: the life of president and Mrs. M. T. Steyn] (Cape Town: Human and Rousseau, 1983). Schoeman has also published an excellent history of the town of Bloemfontein: *Bloemfontein: die ontstaan van 'n stad 1846–1946* (Cape Town: Human and Rousseau, 1980). Wonderfully well written, using his novelist's eye. Not yet available in English.

Selected Articles from the Cape Monthly magazine 1870–76 (Cape Town: VRS, 1978).

Sillery, Anthony. *John Mackenzie of Bechuanaland* (Cape Town: Balkema, 1971). Sillery, who has an engagingly novelistic style, is particularly good on the turbulent politics of the western Transvaal.

van der Merwe, P. J. *Trek* (Cape Town: Nasionale Pers, 1945). Some good detail, especially on the origins of the Trek.

PART 4
Jacobus Johannes de Villiers and the Century of Wrong III: the bitter defeats

Most of the material in this section was drawn from family letters. Some of those written by Margaret Marquard were later edited and published by her son Leo (see below). My grandmother, Maria Marquard (de Villiers), wrote her diaries of the Boer War when she was in her early teens; her journal of the 1914 rebellion, more than a decade later, she wrote as a young married woman. None of Maria's material has been published before. Much of the rest of the information in this section came from personal interviews and from the reminiscences of participants. I have also used as background a number of books:

Churchill, Winston Spencer. *From London to Ladysmith via Pretoria* (Durban: T. W. Griggs, 1982; originally published London: Longmans Green, 1906). Self-aggrandizement of the worst sort, but very readable.

Grunlingh, A. M. *Die Hendsoppers en Joiners* [The hands-uppers and joiners] (Cape Town: HAUM, 1979). A polemic, but contains useful insights.

Kruger, D. W. *The Age of the Generals* (Johannesburg: Dagbreek Pers, 1961).

Marquard, Margaret. *Letters from a Boer Parsonage*. Edited and with an introduction by her son, Leo Marquard (Cape Town: Purnell, 1967). I have generally followed Leo's editing of the letters, and have annotated his description of the village of Winburg.

Pakenham, Thomas. *The Boer War* (London: Weidenfeld & Nicolson, 1979). Much criticized, but very thorough: you'll never need to read another book on the war.

Reitz, Deneys. *Commando: A Boer Journal of the Boer War*, preface by J. C. Smuts (London: Faber & Faber, 1929). Skilfully written, gives a good feeling of what it was like on commando.

Van Reenen, Rykie. *Emily Hobhouse: Boer War Letters* (Cape Town: Human and Rousseau, 1984). The Boer War heroine wrote as well as she ministered to the sick in the concentration camps. Van Reenen has contributed useful background material.

PART 5
René de Villiers and the creation of the sacred history

Most of the material in the section on Fusion and its aftermath, and in the sections on life in the Afrikaner heartland,
came from interviews with the participants and from the
notes and journals of my father, René de Villiers.

Other useful sources:

Adam, Heribert, and Giliomee, Hermann. *The Rise and
Crisis of Afrikaner Power* (Cape Town: David Philip, 1979).
Intelligent and influential. Highly recommended.

Cronje, G. *Tuiste vir die Nageslag* [A home for pos-
terity](Johannesburg: Publicité, 1945). The classic early argument for apartheid.

de Klerk, Willem. *(R)evolution: Afrikanerdom and the Crisis
of Identity* (Johannesburg: Jonathan Ball, 1984).

Keegan, Timothy. "The Sharecropping Economy: Afri-
can Class Formation and the 1913 Native Land Act in the
Highveld Maize Belt," in Marks, Shula, and Rathbone,
Richard, eds. *Industrialization and Social Change in South
Africa: African Class Formation, Culture and Consciousness
1870-1930* (London: Longmans, 1982).

Kruger, D. W. *The Making of a Nation* (Johannesburg:
Macmillan, 1969).

Munger, Edwin. *Afrikaner and African Nationalism* (London: Oxford University Press, 1967).

O'Meara, Dan. *Volkskapitalisme: Class, Capital and Ideology in the Development of Afrikaner Nationalism* (Cambridge:
Cambridge University Press, 1983). Aimed at the academic
reader.

Paton, Alan. *Hofmeyr* (Cape Town: Oxford University
Press, 1965). Possibly the best book on Afrikaner liberalism.

Pelzer, A. N. *Die Afrikaner Broederbond: eerste 50 jaar*
[The Afrikaner Broederbond: first 50 years] (Cape Town:
Tafelberg, 1979).

Thompson, Leonard. *The Unification of South Africa*
(London: Oxford University Press, 1960).

van Jaarsveld, F. A. *Van van Riebeeck tot P. W. Botha* [From van Riebeeck to P. W. Botha] (Johannesburg: Perskor, 1982). A layman's political overview; the point of view is orthodox Afrikaner, done for the general reader.

PART 6
Marq de Villiers: lost in Africa

Most of the material from 1966 on, including the account of the assassination of Hendrik Verwoerd, is drawn from personal notes and files of the author, from interviews with contemporaries, and from newspaper and magazine files.

For the rest, there is an ever-proliferating deluge of books on various aspects of South Africa and its politics. Among those I have found illuminating:

Adam, Heribert, and Moodley, Kogila. *South Africa Without Apartheid* (Los Angeles: University of California Press, 1986). Speculations on the post-apartheid dispensation. Manages to be both cynical and optimistic. Worth reading.

Biko, Steve. *The Testimony of Steve Biko* (London: Panther, 1979).

Carter, Gwendolen. *The Politics of Inequality* (New York: Praeger, 1958) and *Which Way is South Africa Going?* (Bloomington and London: Indiana State University, 1985). Carter is widely respected by South African historians.

Giliomee, Hermann. *The Parting of the Ways: South African Politics 1976 to 1982* (Cape Town: David Philip, 1982). Tough-minded and readable, as Giliomee always is. Admirably clear.

Huddleston, Trevor. *Naught for Your Comfort* (London: Collins, 1956). An influential book that alerted the outside world to the forced movement of populations under apartheid. An unashamed Christian polemic.

Lelyveld, Joseph. *Move Your Shadow: South Africa, Black and White* (New York: Times Books, 1985). The best written of the outsider views. Lelyveld was the *New York Times* correspondent in South Africa. A terrific reporter. Essential reading.

Louw, Leon, and Kendall, Frances. *South Africa: The Solution* (Bisho, Ciskei: Amagi, 1986). Libertarian view of what might be. Good-hearted, readable, odd. Bestseller during 1987 election campaign.

Marquard, Leo. *Liberalism in South Africa* (Cape Town: South African Institute of Race Relations, 1965).

Ries, Alf, and Dommisse, Ebbe. *Broedertwis* (Cape Town: Tafelberg, 1982). Deals with the schisms within Afrikanerdom in the early 1980s. Informative and delightfully gossipy.

Sampson, H. F. *The Principle of Apartheid* (Johannesburg: Voortrekkerpers, 1966). The case for the "humanist justification" of apartheid.

Slabbert, Frederik van Zyl. *The Last White Parliament* (Johannesburg: Jonathan Ball, 1985). His political credo, written just before he abruptly resigned.

Various publications of the South African Bureau of Racial Affairs (SABRA), including *Integration or Separate Development* (1959) and *The Philosophical·Underpinnings of the Policy of Separate Development* (1971). SABRA is the pro-apartheid counterpart of the anti-apartheid Institute of Race Relations.

South African Institute of Race Relations, *Handbook*, annual. Indispensable facts and statistics on current events.

Thompson, Leonard, and Butler, Jeffrey, eds. *Change in Contemporary South Africa* (Berkeley: University of California Press, 1975). Some good thinking.

van der Merwe, Hendrik, ed. *Identiteit en verandering: Sewe opstelle oor die Afrikaner vandag* [Identity and change: seven essays on the contemporary Afrikaner] (Cape Town: Tafelberg, 1975). Uneven but valuable.

Index

FOR THE BEST IN PAPERBACKS, LOOK FOR THE

In every corner of the world, on every subject under the sun, Penguin represents quality and variety—the very best in publishing today.

For complete information about books available from Penguin—including Pelicans, Puffins, Peregrines, and Penguin Classics—and how to order them, write to us at the appropriate address below. Please note that for copyright reasons the selection of books varies from country to country.

In the United Kingdom: For a complete list of books available from Penguin in the U.K., please write to *Dept E.P., Penguin Books Ltd, Harmondsworth, Middlesex, UB7 0DA.*

In the United States: For a complete list of books available from Penguin in the U.S., please write to *Dept BA, Penguin,* Box 999, Bergenfield, New Jersey 07621-0999.

In Canada: For a complete list of books available from Penguin in Canada, please write to *Penguin Books Canada Ltd, 2801 John Street, Markham, Ontario L3R 1B4.*

In Australia: For a complete list of books available from Penguin in Australia, please write to the *Marketing Department, Penguin Books Australia Ltd, P.O. Box 257, Ringwood, Victoria 3134.*

In New Zealand: For a complete list of books available from Penguin in New Zealand, please write to the *Marketing Department, Penguin Books (NZ) Ltd, Private Bag, Takapuna, Auckland 9.*

In India: For a complete list of books available from Penguin, please write to *Penguin Overseas Ltd, 706 Eros Apartments, 56 Nehru Place, New Delhi, 110019.*

In Holland: For a complete list of books available from Penguin in Holland, please write to *Penguin Books Nederland B.V., Postbus 195, NL–1380AD Weesp, Netherlands.*

In Germany: For a complete list of books available from Penguin, please write to *Penguin Books Ltd, Friedrichstrasse 10–12, D–6000 Frankfurt Main 1, Federal Republic of Germany.*

In Spain: For a complete list of books available from Penguin in Spain, please write to *Longman Penguin España, Calle San Nicolas 15, E–28013 Madrid, Spain.*

In Japan: For a complete list of books available from Penguin in Japan, please write to *Longman Penguin Japan Co Ltd, Yamaguchi Building, 2-12-9 Kanda Jimbocho, Chiyuoda-Ku, Tokyo 101, Japan.*

FOR THE BEST IN HISTORY, LOOK FOR THE

☐ **ON WAR**
Carl Von Clausewitz
Edited by Anatol Rapoport

In his famous treatise of 1832, Clausewitz examines the nature and theory of war, military strategy, and the combat itself.

462 pages   *ISBN: 0-14-044427-0*   **$5.95**

☐ **TOTAL WAR**
Causes and Courses of the Second World War
Peter Calvocoressi and Guy Wint

This bold and comprehensive account places as much emphasis on the political, social, and moral forces behind the War as on the ensuing clashes of arms. *Total War* is the definitive history of "the war to end all wars."

966 pages   *ISBN: 0-14-021422-4*   **$10.95**

☐ **SIX ARMIES IN NORMANDY**
From D-Day to the Liberation of Paris
John Keegan

Keegan's account of the summer of 1944's momentous events on the battlefields of Normandy is superb; he "writes about war better than almost anyone in our century."—*Washington Post Book World*

366 pages   *ISBN: 0-14-005293-3*   **$7.95**

☐ **WOMEN IN WAR**
Shelley Saywell

Shelley Saywell tells the previously untold stories of the forgotten veterans of our time—the millions of women who faced combat in some of the most important military struggles of this century.

324 pages   *ISBN: 0-14-007623-9*   **$6.95**

You can find all these books at your local bookstore, or use this handy coupon for ordering:

Penguin Books By Mail
Dept. BA Box 999
Bergenfield, NJ 07621-0999

Please send me the above title(s). I am enclosing _____
(please add sales tax if appropriate and $3.00 to cover postage and handling). Send check or money order—no CODs. Please allow four weeks for shipping. We cannot ship to post office boxes or addresses outside the USA. *Prices subject to change without notice.*

Ms./Mrs./Mr. _____

Address _____

City/State _____ Zip _____

Sales tax: CA: 6.5%   NY: 8.25%   NJ: 6%   PA: 6%   TN: 5.5%